LESSONS IN LIVING
RECIPES FOR A GOOD LIFE

by L. Charles Burlage

Author of *How to Think Yourself to Happiness*
and *Let the River Flow*

LESSONS IN LIVING
RECIPES FOR A GOOD LIFE

by L. Charles Burlage

The L. Charles Burlage Foundation for Drug and Alcohol Abuse
Virginia Beach, Virginia

THIS BOOK IS DEDICATED TO MY FAMILY.

The Burlage Corporation
800 Atlantic Avenue
Virginia Beach, Virginia 23451

Library of Congress Cataloging in Publication Data
        Burlage, L. Charles, 1923–
        Let the river flow
        1. Conduct of life. 2. Life I. Title

ISBN 0-9616208-0-3
Portions of this book was previously published in *Let The River Flow* and in *How To Think Yourself To Happiness.*

Printed in the United States of America

TABLE OF CONTENTS

FOREWORD

The purpose of this book is to suggest a code or a system of values, ethics, and morals which has helped this author live a happy and contented life for his first 72 years. Let's start this book by trying to put every life that has ever been lived into a perspective that crystallizes living down to its raw essentials. What is the bottom line concerning this entire business of a human being's existence on this planet? What should a person do to try to understand the forces that ultimately govern all our lives? Is it possible to obtain a meaningful understanding of the day-to-day principles that will enhance the chances for happiness? Is happiness an obtainable goal for anyone? Finally, is it possible to teach America's students a doctrine or way of life centered solely on human interests and values that will make life better for everyone in America? The author believes the answers to all these questions is an emphatic YES.

ACKNOWLEDGMENTS

This book is an attempt to deal with a problem that has many thoughtful people perplexed and groping for answers that are not readily available. The principal question being asked can be stated as follows: How can America legally teach morality, values, and ethics to students in a pluralistic society? Since the ancient source of these teaching—religion in all its forms—cannot be taught, how do you find an agreeable communality that can legally be taught in our public educational institutions on the subject of values, ethics, and morals? Is it possible to formulate material on these subjects that can legally be taught? Since American society is pluralistic, does this mean that we have to abandon all ideas of inculcating in our students thoughts that will teach them how to "live the good life," in addition to our present efforts which are aimed at teaching them "how to make a living?"

In writing this book I have made use, first and foremost, of a lifetime of incredibly varied and exciting experiences. The historical material came from many sources. These sources include, but are not limited to, *Webster's Encyclopedic Dictionary of the English Language,* one of the greatest dictionaries of its type ever written and a rich source of historical material. The *Story of Civilization,* the *Story of Philosophy,* the *Pleasures of Philosophy*, and the *Adventures in Genius* by Will and Ariel Durant. Will Durant's writings, with the able assistance of his student-wife Ariel, constitute some of the most insightful writings of the last 200 years. Another helpful book has been *Familiar Quotations* by John Bartlett which helped the author verify the exact wording of certain quotations from famous people in history. *A History of the Modern World* by R. R. Palmer aided the author in understanding some of the broad historical movements since the disintegration of the Roman Empire. The work of Paul Johnson entitled, 'Intellectuals' is incredibly penetrating in its analysis of intellectuals and their contribution to the modern moral malaise.

The contents of the Bible dominated the teachings of the clerics for 1,400 years. The teachings of the Bible were invaluable to the author in his understanding of the current ills of modern society. In the education of Western European conciousness, the Greeks showed man his mind, the Christians showed man his soul. Christianity was revolutionary in that it taught that there was only one god for all of humanity and in one fell swoop it swept away all lesser pagan deities.

The *Great Books by Encyclopedia Britannica* contain a wealth of information on the intellects that fostered the intellectual and the anti-Biblical revolution beginning around 1800. This source was most helpful to the author. *The Statistical Abstract of the United States*, 1994, published by the U.S. Government Printing Office, was used as a source of data relative to modern society and to establish the sociological consequences of the behavior and habits of America's younger generation. Lastly, the newspapers, such as the *Washington Post*, the *New York Times*, and the *Norfolk Virginian Pilot*, and television all contributed significantly to the material found in this book. To all of the above I am most thankful and especially to my wife Carol who, as an English major, was able to find and correct many grammatical errors.

An Introduction
by Charles E. Parker, D.O.

As Ernest Becker has so well illustrated in his book *Denial of Death,* we are indeed unique animals—capable of imagining our own ends. Yet in that capacity lies a tragic paradoxical flaw, in that just as we can imagine our own death, so can we deny it. As we are able to deny that frightening future separation, we can also deny the effects of fate, the interposition of external reality, and indeed any aspect of what our own ignorance, faults, or conflicts have led us to. We can, essentially, deny the reality of what has happened, whatever the source, and enter into a living dream state—a fantasy of existence—a separate relative reality conjured up by our own fear of grasping the truth, and touching the concomitant pain.

Indeed, we have evolved as a nation plagued by suffusion and insulation. Permissiveness and entitlement are trained into children as they are hurried prematurely into adult roles. Verbiage and stasis abound, grey leaders talk around important issues, responsibility shifts with the company, and plain talk flashes only occasionally a welcome beam through the collective fog. Adults and adolescents alike have taken it upon themselves to avoid either giving or receiving painful criticism as most everyone seems to be floating adrift in some psychological angst, frozen, while scanning for the "correct" remark approved by everyone from Freud and Jung to the most current tome on how to raise children. We are duly protected, development subsequently is postponed, and all return to their living dreams.

Nowhere is denial more obviously alive than in the epidemic drive for personal gratification through external sources. The specific gratifications often take on a special life of their own—as alcohol, drugs, sex, gambling, wealth, power, food, violence, and even "love" serves as a means of avoiding the reality of our own mistakes, our own problems, and our own lives.

In a refreshing effort to codify lessons that take us away from ourselves, Charlie Burlage has drawn together from his full life aphorisms of plain talk that ring true in a practical, yet contemporary way. His emphasis on man's relationship with himself and his fellows, presented in specific, readable examples, becomes in fact, a modern code of ethics. Not unlike the Samurai in Hagakure (Tsunetomo, 1700) or Hereclitus' advice to his son from ancient Greece, this compendium unravels man from himself and offers constructive alternatives to the short view of life. To be viewed in its entirety, or measured slowly, painting by painting, his collection is comprehensive and clear. It is, in fact, a revealing personal autobiography of one man's struggles with himself and his own tour with fate. Herein, an uncommon common man lays out observations that are at once timeless and timely, with a spiritual thread that chuckles at our mortality.

Dr. Parker is Medical Director of Eastern Virginia Psychiatric Associates and a Diplomat of The American Board of Psychiatry and Neurology.

Author's Introduction

A PHILOSOPHICAL OVERVIEW OF EVERYONE'S LIFE

In examining our lives, we should picture ourselves sitting on a riverbank and the stream which flows endlessly before us contains "all" that comprises each of our lives. Each of us is absolutely "alone" on the bank of our own "river." Our loved ones are a part of our "river"—they do not sit on the bank with us but flow by us each second of our life. Each of them in turn sit "alone" on the bank of their personal "river" and we are a part of the flow of the "river" of their life. We all sit alone on the bank of our own "river." All of the individual rivers of mankind flow inevitably to the "ocean," which "ocean's" composition in turn makes up the overall quality of life on this planet. The "ocean" is the ultimate depository of all the "rivers" of life. Its power to control favorably or unfavorably all life on this planet, is totally affected by the quality of the outflow of each individual "river."

In each of our "rivers" downstream is yesterday and upstream is tomorrow. That portion of the "river's" flow which is directly in front of us constitutes the "now" or the "present" moment, which is where we exist throughout our lifetime. If we cannot enjoy the "now" or the "present" moment, then we cannot have a joyful or rich life.

In this "river of life" flowing before us without interruption, there is everything, every experience, and every individual who is a part of our life. Birth deposits us on the bank of our "river of life" and death removes us. Only death stops the flow of our "river of life," or to phrase it another way, only death ends the experiences of life on this planet or in this plane. As long as we live we must deal with the ever changing character of our lives. We have no option since our "river" flows as long as we are alive. This "river" contains all our hopes, mistakes, strengths, weaknesses, sins, good deeds, courage, fears, successes, failures, loves, hatreds, phobias, friends, enemies, wisdom, ignorance, compassion, prejudices and/ or sadness. Everyone who has ever lived or who lives now, has had to deal with this uninterrupted flow of people and events. Yesterday is gone forever and tomorrow hasn't arrived. That leaves the present moment, the "now" which constitutes the totality of our lives. Everything anyone will ever be is directly related to how intelligently the present moment, the "now" was handled.

Philosophers down through the ages have attempted to deal with this moment—the "now moment" with varying degrees of success and failure. It matters little whether you read Voltaire, Socrates, Plato, Spinoza, Hegel, Kant, Descartes or anyone of a myriad of philosophical thinkers of the last 30 centuries the underlying theme seems to be the same. They all seem to teach that we should let the natural flow of the "river" of our life continue free of and unimpeded by mental aberrations. Mental aberrations result in unwise conduct or thoughts, which prevent us from experiencing the great happiness and moments of a truly fulfilling existence.

Never before has a greater need existed for books that have the objective of helping people lead happier lives. Mankind has been described by modern thinkers as feeling "threatened" by the sweep of modern events. Life in the closing moments of the 20th century is neither as secure nor as tranquil as in prior days. Writers belabor the fact that society is changing at an ever increasing tempo. What was accepted without question yesterday is being routinely discarded today. It becomes more difficult, especially for young people, to find something of lasting value in which they can believe. We are living at both a faster pace and at a more superficial level than ever before. Communicators from the media are becoming increasingly competitive in their attempts to attract our attention. While we attempt to relax and watch our favorite movie, the media attempts to sell us every type of product, service, or lifestyle available through the ingenuity of man. As many as ten back-to-back commercials will be shown at a particularly inopportune portion of a story, thus disturbing or lessening our ability to relax. The media reports, twenty-four hours a day, on every tragedy that has occurred and every frightening possibility that exists, anywhere in the world. We cannot escape the tragedy and the turmoil of our time regardless of where or when it occurs. We can see it unfold as it is revealed by television. The news that sells concerns tragedies since good or pleasant occurrences have little news value.

The atomic age, ushered in during the mid-1940s, causes us perpetual consternation and insecurity. Computers predict catastrophe based on the levels of pollution, world food supply versus world population, the adequacy of fossil fuel reserves, atomic proliferation, creating the possibility of a renegade government possessing the capability to deliver such a weapon to the target of its choice, moral degeneracy, drug usage, loss of the ozone blanket that surrounds the earth, unethical conduct by public officials, and in many other areas of human activity and concern.

In this tumultuous environment we have turned to many activities, substances, practices, and philosophies in order to cope with modern stresses. We have become increasingly introspective in our search for inner peace and happiness. Astrology has attracted many believers. Conversations between strangers often begin with an inquiry concerning the other's astrological sign. Transcendental meditation comprises another popular attempt to find happiness. Far Eastern philosophies of all kinds are becoming popular in the West in the hope that they will assist in our search for the full and rewarding life. Physical exercise is pursued in the belief that a healthy body, exhausted by exercise, is a big part of the great secret of a rewarding life. We turn to religion in the belief that it will magically steer us on the right path towards our goal. Drugs of all forms have been enlisted in this effort with predictable tragic results. We are desperately trying to find happiness in the world as it exists today, fraught with uncertainties and dangers.

Happiness is all internal. It cannot come from outside one's own body and mind. We all possess the tools for the attainment of a good, enjoyable and useful life. It simply remains for us to be schooled or guided in their use. This guidance or training could and should begin to be made available to America's children at the elementary grade level. It should continue to be taught through high school and through the four years of a college or university education. It is sad when one realizes the sorrow and suffering which could be avoided by the most basic exposure, in an academic environment, to the basic realities of life. We must teach young people as early as possible how to arrive at a reasonable and healthy compromise with our fellow humans and our environment. No one can live happily in ignorance in this crowded modern world. Knowledge alone can give us the power to play "the game of life successfully," to the betterment of everyone with whom we have contact. Useful, harmonious existence is the great goal we should all strive to attain. When we begin this search we will have entered upon the path that will lead to the greatest possible fulfillment in life on this earth.

We must begin to teach our young people how to live in addition to teaching them how to make a living. We can teach them how to search for the truth in all their relations and in their undertakings. After all, truth alone contains the most beauty, because false perceptions lead to nothing but disillusionment and personal tragedy. We must recognize that false perceptions of the truth constitute reality to the perceiver. Such a perceiver bases his or her life's actions on false premises. Such a course is a prescription for disaster. We must give our young people the tools and judgmental skills to search for elements of value in all their activities. Only by knowing what has value and knowing what the probable consequences of our acts will be, can we determine our proper course of conduct. The solutions we decide upon will determine whether we become contented, useful, contributing, and happy members of society.

No thought in this book is original with the author. Philosophers and teachers have all expressed them before in the accumulated writings of the ages. They have all wrestled with this "bear," called life. Unfortunately these intellectuals have all too frequently expressed their thoughts and writings in archaic or difficult to read and comprehend writings or speeches. Thus the full impact of their meanings has been lost or lessened on ensuing generations. For example, 2,500 years earlier in the Peloponnesian War, in an address given at the opening of a military cemetery, Pericles expressed every thought that Abraham Lincoln later used in his immortalized Gettysburg address. The difference being the utter simplicity of Lincoln's words and expressions.

The style of this book is to suggest a topic which students can discuss on situations that they will encounter in their daily lives. These are all situations or subjects that typically must be dealt with in the process of living. Students will no doubt suggest other

AIDS

Wages of Slots: Death to Md. Rac

of Maryland's ailing horse-racing
concerned about the economic
Laurel and Pimlico racetracks.
ks, wagering on live racing has
ore than 50 percent since 1989.
s, president of the tracks, has
e solution—following Dela-
allowing slot machines at
rack betting parlors around
t year's General Assembly
a bill to implement this idea
ted. both because of the

lion's share of the revenue; live racing is
withering away.

This contrasts with the situation elsewhere. Without the introduction of slot machines, Churchill Downs and Penn National in
Pennsylvania registered mutuel play increases of 193 percent and 146 percent, respectively, during the same time. And in Maryland, Timonium racing at the Maryland State
Fair nearly tripled its take from 1993 to
1995.

Long before Delaware turned to slots, Lau-
having problems for
in the racing commu-
xpenditures have de-
1989 to an unbeliev-
nnually. The recent
rack's summer meet
ss fanfare than the
ival (which also had

vements have lagged
capital available for
a result, few casual
the tracks "for the
track betting parlors
fail to meet appropri-
gators some

Marijuana Users'
Air of Defiance

*Some Area Teens Say Drug
Is Widespread, Not Harmful*

By Robert O'Harrow Jr. and Eric L. Wee
Washington Post Staff Writers

The heaviest marijuana smokers gather near
their high school after class, plannin
party, arranging a buy, som
on the spot. The meeting pl
names—"The Wall" near B
High School, "The Woods"
High, "The Hill" beside Langl

Other suburban teenagers
stoned on school days but rout
on weekends in their homes wi
sent. Still others haven't tried
it is a constant temptation, a c
turns up at almost every party
to any one high school clique.

"Frankly, I know more people

2.8 percent of American
adults in prison system

About 5.3 million people were in
prison, on probation or on parole
in 1995, according to a Justice
Department study released
Sunday. Since 1980, the total
number under correctional
supervision had almost tripled

**Moral values
urriculum
an stirs up
tle protest**

IN TROUBLE

THE ISSUE

d character traits
be emphasized in
rooms, possibly as
as January

Most violent cr
number of c
increasing. Contrib

As some Virginia Beach teenagers see troubled tee

I am an eighth-grader at Great Neck
Middle School. I read the report "Troubled Teens" (news, Oct. 13). I agree
with the article's contents 100 percent.
Being a teen, I know what goes on. The
only way to understand what happens is
to actually be with the kids and know
what they are talking about.

About one-third of my friends in my

that each day I step out of my house
may be my last.

I've seen what drugs, guns, gangs and
alcohol can do, but what hurts me the
most is seeing kids killing kids.

FANTASY J. CRAVEN
Virginia Beach, Oct. 16, 1995

time they are rejected
closest and best friends.

The solution starts w
Parents need to make
have a close relationship
and must always be th
when they need to talk.

Maybe if politicians w
tening to teenagers wh

k at cleaning up the sewer of TV's talk shows

DOWD

ward the toilet. It's
not good."

Bennett would like
society to resume
what he calls "con-
structive hypocrisy."
"People should act
better than they are.
You say, 'Good morn-
ing, Miss Jones, how
you?' rather than
Miss

timhood over personal responsibility, confrontation over civility, psy-
chology over morality.

Confession began in a small
dark box, with a screen separating
priest and penitent. It is still in a
small dark box, and there's still a
screen, but this one is in everybody's living room. In the new medium of confession, people violate
their own privacy, spilling their
guts not for absolution but for
ndication.

hing to see people al-
used like

tattooed man. The abnormal is
normal, and deviancy will be back
right after the commercial.

On Gordon Elliott's show, a
blonde screams at her ex-husband,
"William, you won't let me pick
my son up on my Harley." On Jenny Jones, a fat woman waves
handcuffs to entice a slender man:
"I chose the handcuffs because if
you're going to be my bad boy, I
want to keep you under control."

On "The Marilyn Kagan Show"
a man is getting his privates
pierced, and on "The Gabrielle
Show," a woman gets impregnated
bank.

that each

She says she makes sure that
guests who seem troubled get
counseling after shows. "I pay for
it," she said. "I stick it in the bud-
get under curtains for the new set,
or transportation."

Springer says Bennett should
"get a grip" because kids will not
want to be transvestites just because they watch them on TV.
"My parents came to this country
fleeing the Holocaust," he says,
"and I still believe people can express their views and lifestyles
here without being censored."

When Ms. Lake attracted a lot of
younger viewers, shows began focusing on teen anguish with panels
such as "Oversexed Teens" and "I
To Kill My Mom."

in New York,
of

more socially conscious. "Kids are
fascinated by these shows," she
says. "And if you want to transmit
values, you have to take every opportunity to do it where young
people are looking."

Ms. Raphael is not interested.
"The more intellectual you make
it, the more they yawn and go
away," she says.

Lieberman raises the specter of
the V-chip if talk shows don't listen up. "First we want to try to
shame them to stop appealing to
our lesser natures to get a bigger
audience," he says.

Good luck. In this society,
shame is fame and sin is an instrument of upward mobility. And upward mobility is the American
way.

*Dowd writes for The New
42nd St., New*

RACH
irginia Beac

year-old girl
alcohol, te
tc. I think t
out of hand.
re are some
doing this st
c, with lyrics
K, is respons
teens. Peopl
is, however,
tions. A coup
re 88.5 FM W

sure is some
that if eve
then it is OK
ugs or having
l life, a good
I would sug
ving sex befor
can't find
et involved w
hborhood, I
olved with a
lub at school

Weather

Today: Partly sunny, hot, humid,
ternoon thundershowers
igh 94. Low 76. Wind 8-16 mph.
onday: Partly sunny, breezy, hot.
ow 66. Wind 10-18 mph.
aterday: Temp. range: 71-81.
: 62. Details on Page B2.

The Washington Post

N YEAR   No. 208

SUNDAY, JUNE 30, 1996

Price May Vary in Areas Outside
Metropolitan Washington

n the Internet, a Worldwide Information Explosion Beyond Wor

By Elizabeth Corcoran
Washington Post Staff Writer

4, Samuel! Morse unleashed the
nstant communications by
four words from
to Baltimore: "What hath God

t question every time a new
eeps across our culture.
mple is the World Wide

ago at a lab in
puter scientist Tim
sed a novel way for
e informa

make expressions of slan
they're hit. A com
Want a
Nationa
which ha
maps and
knowledge
and scholar
Or go to the
Resource, wh
the area's salt w
and weather re
the Internet Rem
that sends out e-
birthday that's for
In one sense, the
communications tool
with the proper ne
a telet

1844
The telegraph

1876

1991
The World
Wide Web

Survey: Drug arre
on campuses for 3

WASHINGTON — Fo
straight year, drug arr
1994 on American coll
es, according to a new.
Results being releas
The Chronicle of High
revealed 6,138 drug vio
percent more than in
lows increases of 34
and 46 percent in '92.

Alcohol contribution
arrests. There were
ated violations am

lues: Norfolk schools to teach character traits

tinued from Page B1

ar school curriculum begin-
as early as next January, said
l member Robert F. Williams,
has pushed the plan.

ard member Anna Dodson,
served as co-chair with Wil-
, said the committee repre-
d a "cross section of our entire
unity," and included students,
ts, educators, and religious,
unity and business leaders.

didn't want to turn anyone

good, but education without values is useless."

Superintendent Roy D. Nichols
Jr. said public schools once routinely taught children about moral values, citing an example from his
days as a sixth-grader when his
teacher emphasized cleanliness by
checking students' fingernails to
make sure they weren't dirty.

Nichols said schools stopped
teaching such values in the 1960s
and '70s because of threats of law-
suits, but that now it was "time to

those things that are wholesome."

Williams said the low turnout at
Monday's hearing indicates that
Norfolk's plan "is not a profoundly
controversial issue."

"We know there will be citizens
who disagree, but I think they represent a distinct minority view," he
said.

Omar Hawk, a junior at Booker
T. Washington High School and
committee member, said after the
hearing: "Finally somebody's going
to do something about all the bad

wondering: How on earth did they think of
that? And sometimes, *why?*
Visit a site called Brad-style game
find a whimsical arcade-style game
created by office workers at the
University of Missouri—you
photographic cutout
(the cro

examples of daily experiences that need to be discussed. The point of this entire book is to get young people thinking about the serious business of living a productive and happy life. Each chapter begins with a statement that the author believes to be truc. The body of the chapter explains why the author believes the statement to be the truth. The entire discussions can be held within the constitutional framework of the separation of church and state.

The author has long believed that far too little is taught in our schools, colleges, and universities about a subject that is far more important than any other study—the ability to be relaxed, secure, and contented in our modern world. In short, the ability to lead useful and happy lives. Hopefully this book can become a textbook or a starting point for students to learn some of the truths about a sensible approach to life, values, and human relationships. This is one author's recommended approach to teaching American's youth values, ethics, morals, and cause and effect principles in a pluralistic society, within the constraints of the First Amendment to the United States Constitution.

PART I
Life In General

Learning

"Learning never ends."

The more inquisitiveness anyone has, the more such a person will be driven to learn. All one really has to do to understand just how little knowledge he or she has, is to walk slowly through any public library. Observe the multitude of books stacked on every shelf and realize how little of man's accumulated knowledge any one person can possibly possess. For example, there are in excess of 800,000 new books written every year. Even though Denis Diderot (1713–1784) together with Jean le Rond d'Alembert (1717–1783) edited and for the most part wrote the French Encyclopédie which, supposedly, represented the accumulated wisdom of mankind to that date, there is little doubt that those volumes were inaccurate and incomplete. This would have been true then and would be especially true today, since accumulated knowledge has progressed geometrically since the 18th century. No one living in 1996 would be in danger of acquiring anything close to the totality of human knowledge which exists on the shelves of libraries around the world. Actually Messrs. Diderot's and D'Alembert's works constituted little more than an exercise in egomania.

To the wise person knowledge is power, knowledge increases one's chances for success, knowledge helps one have successful relations with fellow human beings, knowledge increases security in one's life, knowledge tends to cause humility, knowledge helps eradicate fear, knowledge helps one increase his or her personal health, knowledge helps one better understand the many paradoxes and inconsistencies in human nature and life in general, knowledge helps one make better judgments about people and events, knowledge increases the desire for more knowledge, the greater one's knowledge the more one realizes just how little he or she knows, lastly and probably most importantly, knowledge increases one's awareness of the severe limitations of knowledge.

Yes, knowledge increases one's chances for personal fulfillment and happiness simply because it increases understanding. Philosophers down through the ages have said that great wisdom and understanding tend to eliminate all anger and resentment.

If knowledge is all that valuable it goes without saying that one should try to accumulate additional knowledge every day of his or her life. To stop learning is equivalent of being dead. Politicians who pride themselves in saying that they hold the same views on political issues at age 70 and that they held ate 21 are saying that they either had total wisdom or stopped learning at age 21. Either interpretation is ridiculous on its face. What they are trying to say, is that they have the virtue of consistency. Even that interpretation tends to question their wisdom. Wisdom dictates that new days bring newly acquired knowledge which requires a change in one's views. To hold the same viewpoint from age 21 to age 70 and to thereby claim the virtue of consistency points to ignorance and not virtue.

To ensure that learning never ends one needs to develop, early in life, an insatiable thirst for knowledge and nourish it throughout his or her lifetime.

FAIRNESS
"There is no evidence that life is fair."

One has very little difficulty encountering all sorts of observations and opinions about the general subject of life. They range from "life is tough," " life is what you make it," "life is great," to "live is to have problems," and a thousand other reflections about this serious business of living. In some ways and on some days all these opinions are true for all of us. An awful lot depends on our predisposition towards the diversities which all humans experience. Almost nothing goes as planned and the living experience abounds with inequities and undeserved tragedies. The question might well be asked, "What rules govern our lives and is there any rule that guarantees just treatment for the innocent or punishment for the wicked." The answer from the author's experience is a resounding, "No!"

There simply are too many tragedies that befall innocent people to conclude that there is an essential justice at work in the affairs of humanity—innocent children racked with pain from all sorts of killer maladies, good parents being literally tortured to death by wayward and evil offspring, millions of people being killed and starved to death in wartime environments, innocent children being gassed in Hitler's Germany, children being born with crack addition or irreparably damaged by a mother's alcoholism during pregnancy. With these, and in thousands of other instances, it becomes quite clear that there is no basic justice system that applies to the affairs of humankind.

The first principle that should be learned from the foregoing paragraphs is that no one deserves anything either good or bad. No one merits any special luck or punishment. Things happen to people on a hit or miss basis and there seems to be no special principle of fairness or merit at work. If this observation is true then one might ask, "What can any of us do to achieve a desired outcome or goal?" The answer is that there will be no guarantees no matter what you do. However, one can increase the odds in a certain direction, while understanding that there can be no certainty. This increase in the likelihood of a certain outcome can be accomplished by hard work and perseverance. Always bear in mind that the person who puts forth absolutely no effort might attain the same or a superior goal than does the hard working individual.

The following statement might well explain what seems to work with the highest degree of certainty in the affairs of humankind. First let it be understood that no one is blessed with a recognition that he or she deserves this or that treatment. One gets what happens to them regardless of the justification. It's somewhat predictable that a focused person through hard work, struggle, and perseverance will get what they desire through this method. Again it might be said of such an individual that they merited nothing but having accomplished their goal, they deserved what they got. Sometimes in life one gets what one works for, but there is no assurance that it will happen.

PERSPECTIVE
"There is rarely anything new under the sun."

The earth is anywhere from 5 thousand to 15 billion years old depending on whose version one is willing to accept. The Book of Matthew in the Bible places the age of this planet at about 5,000 years more or less based on the Generations of Man as outlined therein. Geologists, aided by the science of atomic aging, place the age at 15 billion years, more or less. Either version makes this a very old planet. The facts are that it's rarely possible for anyone to come up with something that can be described as truly new or novel.

Albert Einstein (1879–1955), a mathematical physicist, said that the only idea that was new or novel that he ever contributed to accumulated human knowledge was the formula $E=MC^2$. Ancient computer-like devices have been found in the scrap heaps of history. Long before penicillin, sulfur drugs and other "miracle" cures were discovered, pioneers dressed wounds with a poultice made from fresh cow manure which was later discovered to contain important elements typical of the "wonder drugs." Indian medicine men for centuries discovered medicinal cures for many illnesses that modern medicine is just discovering. For example, an Indian medicine man can make an inhalant from natural herbs and spices that excels in its curative effect, any similar product that can be found in the most modern medical facilities. The engineering complexities of the ancient pyramids, their true north-south alignment, the finely matched meshing of huge rock boulders, cannot be exceeded by modern methods. Man has been around a long time and has encountered countless times in the past, the core elements of every problem facing the modern world. Modern man gets in serious trouble when he decides that he is going to discard the accumulated wisdom of mankind and start with entirely new solutions. The likelihood is overwhelming that modern solutions have been tried before and have been discontinued because they were found to be unworkable, ineffective or harmful.

Does the above paragraph suggest that modern man should not continue his search for knowledge? Of course not, it suggests nothing of the sort. What it does mean is that as we grope for solutions to modern problems we need to first consider carefully what we might learn from our ancestors practices. We shouldn't believe that somewhere there lies a "silver bullet" solution that will be a cure-all, because our problem has had no historical roots in the past. We should never fail to take into account past solutions because we believe our ancestors were ignorant or unenlightened.

The best solution to the problems facing the modern world necessarily lies in an artful blend of past practices or solutions adjusted to allow for different conditions. The point is not being made that we must accept all that our ancestors did *carte blanche*. No, it's obvious that many of the errors of the past should be beneficial to the extent that they are not repeated. Modern people should learn from our ancestors both through their errors as well as their truths. In the search for solutions, previously unknown problems will rarely be discovered; since there are very few problems that our ancestors didn't face.

CAUSE AND EFFECT
"The end depends upon the beginning."

The above words are inscribed on the walls of one of the most prestigious prep schools in the Northeast. George Bush and Jack Lemon are some of the illustrious graduates of Phillips Academy. No truer words have ever been written or spoken. This same principle is inherently recognized in such saying as: "An apple does not fall far from the tree," "As the twig is bent, so shall the tree grow," and "Spare the rod and spoil the child." Most people die with the philosophy or religion learned in their childhood. There are literally hundreds of sayings that have as their fundamental premise, that which was learned well in childhood remains throughout one's lifetime. It is really hard to argue with the logic.

Parents who try to teach their children about the pitfalls awaiting everyone "just around the corner" often despair in the belief that their children are even listening to their preachments. Practically everything they say seems to be going "right over their heads" without having the slightest beneficial effect. These same parents are often astonished to witness these same children, in later years, "imparting" to their children some of those same tidbits of parental wisdom. The same insight that they believed fell on deaf years. Make no mistake about it, early training goes a long way towards the ultimate development of a useful, successful, and contributing member of society. It seems that the very nature of childhood involves placing knowledge and training in storage for later use as the maturation process evolves. Youth seems to be saying, "I appreciate the validity of your training, however, since it's impeding my youthful style, I'll store it for a while. As soon as I finish sowing my wild seeds, and start raising my own family I'll start using your pearls of wisdom."

The principle of the benefits of early training are very well established and are irrefutable. It therefore behooves every parent to start beneficial training early in the lives of their children. This same process necessarily involves the caliber of school that is selected for the child's education. Training in a value system which includes the principles of cause and effect. Values, ethics, and morals are also essential to a well-rounded person. Remember always that the values learned in youth are the ones that will have the most beneficial and lasting effect.

One of the great advantages of a thorough and excellent early training program is to get some sense in a young person's head before they ruin their chances in life by youthful aberrations. Foolish actions while young can ruin an adult's chances or hopelessly brand them as a criminal for the rest of their life. An adult is going to have to pick his actions and pathways by wisdom. The whole idea behind parents giving early training in the art of successful living is to deliver an unblemished product at adulthood. Yes, the end does indeed depend upon the beginning.

COMPROMISE

"No person, venture, undertaking, or piece of property has everything desirable thus necessarily making every choice a compromise."

A man was going with two women. One was beautiful but could not cook, while the other was a gourmet cook but seriously lacking in the "beauty" department. He decided to marry the good cook. When he awakened the morning after his wedding night, he turned to his "ugly" bride and said, "Darling, you had better get up quickly and prepare the best breakfast you ever made." This person weighed the various attributes possessed by the two women and opted for the more practical side of life. This choice becomes necessary in everything we do. Nothing possesses all desirable features. There are no perfect choices. Everything is a "trade-off" or a compromise.

In deciding between two or more people, for any purpose, it is wise to list the desirable attributes possessed by each individual. Having done this, it is also wise to list the negative qualities of each person. Having completed this, one should then decide which person is the most desirable. The ultimate decision necessarily will be based on a compromise. No one person will possess all the good qualities. The final decision will be based on a "trade-off." This process is at work throughout all human endeavors.

Frequently, careers conflict with one's personal or family life. Careers are usually pursued for reasons of economic necessity. Careers, among other factors, are the method most of us use to pay our bills. Sometimes the most lucrative or satisfying choices we can make in our careers involve the greatest sacrifices to our personal lives. Military men often pay the "price" of frequent lengthy absences from their families. Entertainers sometimes make a great deal of money, but pay a price of constant turmoil in their personal lives. Professional politicians may reach the height of adoration and praise, yet it is often done at the expense of an unhappy family life. Usually the greater and higher one becomes in his chosen career, the more sacrifices he must make in his personal life. Consequently, every career decision we make necessarily involves a choice between alternatives that have both desirable and undesirable characteristics.

Since all choices involve a weighing of the various positives and negatives, some people find it very difficult to make a decision. They endlessly weigh all choices and the more they study a situation the more they become incapable of making a choice. They endlessly torture themselves over characteristics that are usually inconsequential. Since no choice will result in perfection, we should learn to settle for that choice which promises to carry with it the highest number of desirable traits. Having settled on a course of action, we should avoid "second guessing" or constantly reappraising our decision. This practice is totally negative and productive of no worthwhile results.

All of our lives we will be compelled to make decisions which involve alternative choices. Each alternative has both negative and positive qualities. Remember that no alternative possesses everything we are seeking, so learn to settle for imperfection. Life is nothing more than a movement "ever-forward" which involves a constant need for choice. Once a decision is made, do not look backward, but learn to proceed and be content with the realities you confront in the pathway that you have selected. After all, nothing is perfect and no choice possesses "everything."

IGNORANCE

"When we are subjected to or become aware of the many unjust,
improper, illegal, and cruel actions by human beings,
remember that what we are seeing is not evil, but ignorance."

When Adlai Stevenson visited Dallas, Texas, a woman spat in his face. The police asked Stevenson if he wanted them to arrest her. His answer was: "No, just educate her."

As we look around the world in which we live, we see innumerable human actions of such a nature that upon superficial glance, we could easily categorize them as being evil. What we are really looking at is man's ignorance. The Nazi torture chambers were an example of evil emanating from man's ignorance. War is another example of man's ignorance. People really tend to do the best they know how based on their understanding of readily available facts.

Jails are filled with ignorant people. Criminals always have mental deficiencies that result in their behavioral aberrations. It would be very depressing indeed to look at the human deficiencies in the world as being representative of evil. Such a viewpoint would cause the observer to be bitter and unforgiving. However, when we consider that we are looking at human ignorance, then the world, with all its obvious defects, becomes much more palatable and bearable. One can then look at human frailty with much more love and compassion.

Lest we become too haughty in our understanding of human

nature and its massive ignorance, always keep in mind that when we look in a mirror, we are witnessing the same percentage of ignorance in ourselves that generally exists throughout mankind. This ignorance that we possess can just as readily be judged to be evil by our acquaintances as we would be prone to judge it in our fellow man. Wisdom will command, however, that we call it ignorance and not evil.

With this enlightened view of human behavior, we will soon learn to divide the world between wisdom and ignorance and not between good and evil. Wise people are filled with love, compassion, and understanding and become incapable of violence for any one of a thousand acts of impropriety.

The world makes the tragic mistake of interpreting intelligence as wisdom. Intelligence really has nothing to do with wisdom. When a person is educated, he does not thereby acquire wisdom. This is unfortunate but true. What he acquires is knowledge. Wisdom comes from the very process of life itself, and many people live their lives entirely without acquiring it. It cannot be taught to someone. It is what "Uncle Remus" possessed in that classic Walt Disney film entitled *Song of the South*. When a person has wisdom, they avoid so much of the pain of life. Unfortunately, man as a group has never demonstrated sufficient wisdom to avoid the tragedies of this world—hence, my characterization of the massive ignorance that exists everywhere in this world.

The next time you witness some excessively brutal or cruel act, perpetrated by one human against another, examine it from the premise that it was caused by ignorance and not evil. When you use this approach, you will come closer to finding the truth concerning such an occurrence. This same premise will enable you to investigate the entire affair with less emotion and with more wisdom. Any "cure" that it may be in your power to direct will tend to be more appropriate it you approach the situation from a proper premise. Whenever you become excessively convinced of your own superiority, remember that you too are filled with ignorance. With this thought always before you, you will become a much happier and wiser human being.

AVOIDING TENSION

"Avoid people or situations that make you unhappy or that make you needlessly tense or nervous."

We cannot avoid every unpleasant situation in life. We may have to get our tooth pulled or go to our parent's funeral or help excavate the dead and dying from a wreck. However, short of these types of things, there are many unpleasant situations surrounding our life which can be avoided. In those instances, where we have the option to circumvent or avoid unpleasantness of any form, we should do so every time. Why get involved in an awkward situation when, with the slightest amount of wisdom, we can avoid it entirely? The premise in this discussion is that you don't have to become involved in the unpleasantness. Nothing concerning your attendance is mandatory. Neither you nor anyone else will gain from your presence. In those situations you are wise to absent yourself from the experience.

If you don't like to be around people who are intoxicated, for example, why go to bars or cocktail parties? That is where you'll find most of them. If you don't like to be around crowds, don't go to the theater or to sporting events. If you can't stand the tension of a courtroom, then try your best to settle the case before it comes to trial. If you don't like gambling, then avoid Las Vegas or Atlantic City. If you don't like politicians, then don't go to political meetings. If you don't like sunburns, then don't go to the beach. If you have an acquaintance who is argumentative, then avoid his or her company as much as possible.

In addition to avoiding tension filled situations, one should visit people and places where one's joy is at an optimum. Uncle

Remus, in a famous Walt Disney classic, referred to a "laughing place." That phrase puts it best. Everyone should have a "laughing place" and should frequent it as often as possible. Certainly it is wiser to go to the "laughing place" than to the "crying place" or to that situation where we know in advance we will be unhappy and tense. Search your list of likes and dislikes and frequent those people, places, and activities which make you the happiest. Frequently they are the simplest situations in life. Maybe it is the mere company of a little child, or simply a walk; watching the sun rise, going to a zoo, or watching a sporting event or a soap opera on television; reading a good book, or enjoying literally any one of thousands of people, places, and things that the infinite variety of life offers to each of us as a diversion. If we are wise, we should have many different people, places, and activities that constitute our "laughing place." The more the merrier. The most vibrant, alert and happy people have many "laughing places."

It becomes a matter of survival. A morose, sanguine, and tense person cannot eventually be a healthy person. We know already that he can't be happy, but we are now discussing survival. A negative outlook will eventually convert itself into ill health and early death. Involved in this same proposition is the quality of our life while we are alive. A year of happiness and contentment certainly has a higher quality to it than does a year of tension and unhappiness. The only difference frequently involves nothing more than our outlook. The option lies in our wisdom and therefore in our mind. Just think about it for a second; your mind can decide whether you'll be sad or happy, tense or relaxed, successful or unsuccessful, fulfilled, or unfulfilled. It is literally that simple and the results are that far-reaching. So start today by spending all your available time at, of what I hope for your sake, is one of many "laughing places." Perform the necessary labors but take care of yourself and in so doing make life more enjoyable and successful for all your loved ones.

An Economic Plan

"It is important for young people to adopt a plan for their economic life as early as possible."

It is not enough for a young person to simply say that he wants to be rich. Just making this statement will not make it come true. You have to decide in what field of endeavor you wish to spend your life's work. Once this decision is made, the next step involves making the plans to decide what preparatory steps are necessary to realize the goal. These steps necessarily include an educational and training period. Most people who are successful in a field almost always started by going through a proper period of education and training. There are no magic formulas. The game of success is played by hard work. There are very few short cuts. What you have to do is develop of master plan for entry into your desired field.

Just sitting around and thinking with no "follow-through" will never get you started up the ladder of economic success. At some point in your analysis you have to leave the arena of thought and enter the arena of action. Thought alone will not make things happen. One can never learn mathematics, for example, by simply studying or thinking about it. At some point in the process you have to pick up a pencil and start working math problems. You cannot learn the game of golf without picking up a club and starting to hit a ball. Once you start acting or working, things begin to happen that eventually lead to success. If all you do is think and study, they will not start. Excessive analysis will result in paralysis of action. It is important to think but it is equally important not to "over-think." Ernest Hemingway put it best when he was asked how to write a book. His reply was, "You have to pick up a pencil and apply the seat of your pants to the seat of a chair and start writing." He was saying that to merely think about writing a book will never get the book written; eventually you must start writing.

It is a fortunate young person who knows early in life what he wants to do. If you want to go into the professions for example, you can start including in your educational curriculum subjects aimed at increasing proficiency in your chosen field. A lawyer for example, would be better in his profession if he were well-versed in grammar, English literature, Latin, political science, and report writing. All these subjects can be taken during the high school years and can also form the subject of private selective readings. A person who wants to be a doctor would be well advised to emphasize scientific subjects, including mathematics, chemistry, and biology, in his high school years. This type of early preparation can only come when the career decision is made early in life.

Never forget that those of greatest service to others are not necessarily in the highest paying fields. Frequently, the most important serviceman in the neighborhood is the mechanic who keeps everyone's car running. The only truly satisfying work in life is that work which makes us of service to our fellowman. When you view life in this perspective, there is a world of desirable careers aside from the high paying professions.

Bear in mind at all the times that life involves some very simple obligations. You have to find work that is remunerative so you can p*ay bills and meet obligations.* We can "wax" philosophically all we want to but there remains the bottom line; we must meet our obligations. With this uppermost in our minds we should train our children to start searching early for the field which will ultimately constitute their life's work. *Work is actually fun.* It is almost impossible to be fulfilled and happy in life unless we are gainfully employed in meaningful work that aids our fellowman.

Mind-Set

"Your mind-set is the most important part of your life. Within your mind lies the power to affect dramatically your enjoyment of life and your success in life."

As a test of the power of your mind, try standing in a cold shower. Start the water running lukewarm if you must, but tell yourself that by the sheer power of your "mind-set" you will be able comfortably to withstand a cold water shower. You will be pleasantly surprised at your ability to withstand cold water if you have obtained a powerful "mind-set."

Absolutely everything becomes tolerable if not enjoyable by the simple process of altering favorably your attitude towards a given incident. By your mind alone, you have the power to alter your reaction to any situation. With the proper mental outlook, life can become a far more enjoyable process. Wisdom cries out for the advisability of acquiring the most favorable "mind-set" concerning all of life's encounters with reality. Reality becomes whatever you make it in your mind. If you can literally alter reality by the simple process of exercising mental powers, it becomes the incredibly wise thing to do. There can be no valid argument against such a practice.

To comprehend more fully the power of your mind, perform a simple test. For example, *tell yourself on a Sunday night that you will enjoy everything you encounter on Monday.* Develop a powerful "mind-set" that no matter what you encounter you will react pleasantly and gracefully. This "mind-set" should include the powerful determination on your part that you will perform all your duties cheerfully and with no negative mental reaction. Fill your mind with such powerful positive attitudes that a negative thought will have no chance to enter your mind, much less to assume a dominating position. With such a powerful "mind-set" you will successfully reject all negativism long before it acquires a dominant hold on your thoughts and emotions. With this "mind-set" in force, you will be surprised how much you will enjoy Monday. You will find that tasks you normally dislike become highly endurable if not enjoyable. With a minimum drain on your emotional forces, you will find that the entire day was far less taxing on your physical well-being than normal; consequently you will feel more vigorous and refreshed.

This book outlines positive "mind-sets" on many of the problems and/or incidents we encounter in our lives. To a serious student, it will convey many thoughts that will make for a long and happy life. Why destroy your life with your mind? If your mind can make the difference between happiness and unhappiness, why not choose the happiness highway? All it takes is wisdom and practice. The power of your mind will amaze you. Experimentation will reveal it all to you. You are what you think. What you think can be altered by mental practice or mental calisthenics. The entire process is not that difficult. The more you practice, the easier it becomes. If your "mind-set" has placed you in a mental prison filled with failure and unhappiness, escape now by the simple process of changing your "mind-set."

VARIABILITY

"All things in life are variable except measurements or fixed units of capacity or extent."

If I tell you I worked hard, I have given you an opinion based on my assessment of what constitutes hard work. The truth is that what seems like hard work to me may not constitute hard work to you. In other words what constitutes hard work is variable; it varies with different people. If I tell you that a certain woman is beautiful, I am in effect saying that based on my subjective opinion a given woman is beautiful. However, what constitutes a beautiful woman to me may not be the same with you. You may have a different standard of beauty. Again, we are dealing with subjective matters that vary greatly from one individual to another.

This same variability permeates almost all of life. A beautiful sunrise, a fast race horse, a good athlete, a good dancer, a wealthy person, a kind person, a good child, a good spouse, a good golfer, a good politician, a good doctor, a good preacher, a just cause, fine food, a pretty animal, a kind human, a religious person, a terrible event, are but a few examples of subjective matters that really represent nothing more than the speaker's opinion. The listener may hold quite a different opinion; therefore, you are confronted with yet another of life's variables.

Measurements, on the contrary, are fixed and constant. A pound of weight is the same everywhere. A distance of a kilometer or a mile is the same everywhere. A second of time is precise and constant. So in a world of limitless variables, we must remember some measurements are fixed and constant.

The above principles are outlined in order to make the following assertion with reference to life in general. Always remember that what you hear stated as fact, unless it is a measurement in reality, represents nothing more than opinion. Do not accept as absolute fact a statement concerning a variable. Always bear in mind that the speaker necessarily and obviously is just giving his opinion. Though he may have concluded to his own satisfaction that "apples taste good," do not accept this positive assertion about a variable because upon investigation you may have a different opinion. When you understand that you are only getting someone's opinion, then you will be inclined to take another's conclusions as being his opinion and nothing more. You may place more emphasis on one individual's opinion based on a long life association and respect, while you may dismiss another person's opinion on the basis of previous unsatisfactory experiences.

Just remember that what you are hearing is opinion and not fact. When you bear this uppermost in your mind, you will not be inclined to leap head first into wild or ill-advised ventures just because someone told you to do so based on his favorable evaluation.

People arrive at evaluations for many different reasons. For example, they favor their friends and loved ones even at the expense of being factual and objective. They may give greater value to a person who shares their religious faith or belongs to the same civic or fraternal organization or who comes from the same "hometown" or who went to the same school or who belongs to the same political party, etc. The list of reasons for biased and consequently inaccurate evaluations is endless. Therefore, you can't be too careful in reaching a decision about the value or worth of a given situation.

Learn to decide your own matters after initiating your own inquiry. Remember that all subjective situations have many variables. The only constants in life are some measurements such as distance, time, weights, etc. Withhold your decision until you have obtained as many facts as possible. By doing this you will increase your chances of success and happiness.

THE FUTURE
"Man's outlook for the future."

If I could pick any date from the beginning of time to the present moment to be born, I would without hesitation pick the present moment. The advances that are yet to occur in the area of living on this planet are beyond comprehension. During the years 1900 to 1950 man doubled his knowledge. He then doubled it again in the following 25 years. Breakthroughs in the field of knowledge that are presently undreamed of are just around the corner. These advances will ultimately work towards an improvement in the living conditions on this earth.

Do not fear the atomic age. All it has done is to render unthinkable the ancient practice of "all-out" war. There is no doubt in the author's mind that Russia would have marched successfully into Western Europe were it not for the atomic deterrent possessed by the West. With global war at best a suicidal undertaking, would-be conquerors will have to turn their energies to other pursuits.

This new direction, in the author's opinion, will be toward the laboratories to improve the overall human condition. Advances of inestimable value are being made in the field of energy, through research in nuclear fusion. Scientists have known for 30 years how to unleash incredible amounts of energy in the same way as the sun. What is being perfected is the technique of controlling this energy in manageable ways. Research is being carried on extensively in this field and is reaching a critical juncture. When the breakthrough occurs, as it will, man will be in possession of unlimited, pollution-free energy being produced out of matter through nuclear fusion. Research has also found a way to split water molecules through vibration of the hydrogen and oxygen atoms. Once the atoms are separated the hydrogen becomes another source of pollution-free energy in unlimited amounts.

Humanity literally has the capability of offering every living person a higher standard of living than any single individual has ever heretofore known or experienced.

Arthur C. Clark, one of the greatest futurists of all time and the author of 54 books dealing with the future, foresees the following advances in the twenty-first century:

— The end of gasoline-powered cars.
— A reversal of the population explosion resulting in only a few million inhabitants on earth.
— Farming replaced by petroleum-produced proteins, using a process similar to fermentation.
— Super intelligent animal servants produced by genetic engineering.
— First moon landing by 1978 (predicted in the early 1950s).
— Computer-controlled mating of sperm and egg on a space craft, 20 years before reaching its destination.
— Child rearing by robot nurses.
— Rendezvous with intelligent life during our voyages into deep space.
— The contraceptive pill.

- Undersea farming.
- The geosynchronous communications satellite as the precursor of a revolution in world communications.
- The three-man moonship making round-trip voyages.
- Whales trained to work as undersea sheepdogs.
- Transcontinental communications centers in most offices, making business travel unnecessary for almost all of our transactions.
- Satellite television broadcasts to improve education in underdeveloped countries.
- The creation of one global language, thus putting an end to political strife.
- The Russians would beat us into space if we delayed long-range rockets (as we did).
- Colonization of other planets by the year 2000. Being alive at this time, Clark stresses, means acknowledging a reality beyond our own and being prepared to cope with it.

The future belongs to the brave who work hard and optimistically make things happen. While this generality has always been true, it has never been truer than it is today.

THE WORKER

"The worker is the most deserving of all humans."

The person who makes the world function as well as it does, the one who deserves the honor and love of his fellowman is the worker, the one who works or labors; toils or performs. He is the giver, the one who by his work assists others; the one who pays for the space he occupies on this planet. To such a person should go the highest honors. There is no valid reason that free enterprise capitalism should not emulate the one who toils.

The type of work one performs is not important. Whether it

involves high or low responsibility should not affect the respect and honor given. Whether the compensation is high or low is equally irrelevant. Whether the person is chairman of the Board of General Motors or a worker on the production line is of no consequence. The fact of work is sufficient to warrant the recognition that such an individual is contributing to the complex business of life on this planet. The person who accumulates vast wealth and thereafter lives from such accumulation solely for his own pleasure is a taker and does not deserve as much respect as the lowest of workers. Such a person has ended his usefulness and is of very little value to his contemporaries. Interestingly, according to Jewish law, when a person suffers irreversible brain damage and can no longer perform a "mitzvah" (an act of helping his fellowman), he is considered a vegetable. Work is not given a position of honor high enough in our society. We respect wealth too much and we do not respect work enough. Our value system is reversed. This lack of respect afforded the worker has caused him to lose respect for himself. As a consequence, productivity is lower than it has ever been in this country. The worker seems to be saying, "If there is no honor involved, nothing uplifting, then I may as well get everything I can and give as little as possible."

This type of thinking bodes ill for the future of our nation. Our declining productivity is an outgrowth of our value system. Work is glorious and fulfilling. The true hero of our country is the unrecognized worker who plods along every week for forty or more hours and does this week after week until he retires. He does this without recognition or honor. The housewife who puts everything together for her family without adequate recognition is but another example of the unrecognized hero of the world. Work of any kind is helpful to others. It is a contribution of vital importance. The world cannot move forward without it. The truly ugly human being is the perpetual loafer. He contributes nothing and the world is better off without him.

The next time you go to a garage, for example, and see a greasy, smelly workman, visualize the enormity of his contribution to life. Once you study his importance carefully, you will no longer see nor smell the grease and dirt on his clothes. Instead you will visualize the beauty of his life and value of his work. When you do this you will pay the worker the honor and recognition long overdue.

Throughout this work I refer to mankind and the worker in the masculine gender for simplicity's sake—certainly without intending to eliminate the good woman whose work is never done.

BOREDOM

"Boredom seems to be man's greatest enemy."

Lord Byron, the great English poet wrote: "The great object of life is sensation—to feel we exist, even in pain."

The basic thrust towards excitement and away from the number one enemy of life—boredom—causes more misery to mankind than all other drives possessed by man. Collectively for nations this drive has been used by world leaders to take their citizens' minds off their otherwise drab existence through the means of starting a war. Mankind seems to periodically get bored with its lot and is easily led into disastrous wars for ridiculous reasons.

One of the greatest historical examples of this characteristic is The Crusades, continuing more or less for 183 years—from 1095 to 1272. There was great misery in Europe, and the prospect of going to the Holy Land to rid Jerusalem of the Muslims was both exciting and spiritually fulfilling. Wave after wave of Christian Crusaders came to fight and mostly to die with no success in the Holy Land. Nevertheless, the Muslim Turks retained control of the Holy Land until driven out by the English in 1918 during the Great War.

The American War Between the States is yet another example

of a great conflict that could have been easily avoided by peaceful (possibly less exciting) means. This war, which no doubt was more exciting, caused citizens of Washington, D.C., to dress up in their Sunday finery, complete with picnic baskets, to observe some early battles. They must have regarded these early battles as having entertainment value, taking their minds away from an otherwise drab existence. For the balance of the Civil War and thereafter, true to the observation of Lord Byron, the nation, with 620,000 casualties, did indeed "exist even in pain."

In 1925, in Macedonia, a Greek soldier's dog ran across the border into Bulgaria. The soldier chased after his dog and was shot and killed by a Bulgarian sentry. In retaliation, Greek troops invaded Bulgaria and killed and wounded 48 Bulgarians. The conflict escalated and only an emergency session of the League of Nations secured a peace.

In addition to this war over a stray dog, other wars have been started for ridiculous reasons. A sixteen-year-old Hindu girl who began a war by running off with her Muslim schoolteacher (The 1936 Waziristan War), is another example. Others include: a wife who deserted her Zulu chieftain husband (The War of the Fleeing Wife, 1879—Great Britain vs. the Zulu nations); the Spanish cutting off the ear of the captain of a British ship (The war of Jenkins' Ear, 1739). The British Fleet desired to watch a cricket match in which the British participated. The fleet sailed into Zanzibar's harbor so the officers and sailors could disembark to watch the match. This concentration of warships so irked the Sultan of Zanzibar that he immediately declared war, sending his lone battleship, the *Glasgow*, into action. The war lasted 37 minutes and 23 seconds— the shortest in world history, but ended only after 500 of the Sultan's soldiers and sailors were killed (The War of the Cricket Match, 1896—Zanzibar vs. England).

Down through history, war more than any other human activity, will take a nation's collective mind off whatever previously occupied it and fill it with a new anticipation and sensation. If two peoples hate each other enough, they will find a good reason to start a war. History is filled with examples of wars starting over a lot less than, for example, the deposed Shah of Iran visiting the United States for cancer treatment.

THE WARRIOR

"Man the Warrior."

Man has proven himself to be, above all the other characteristics which he possesses, a warrior. A disinterested observer from outer space, looking at the planet earth periodically for the last five thousand years, would observe one constant activity—warfare. Man is comparable to a couple in a residential neighborhood, known for their constant fighting. When noises of combat come from such a house, the neighbors will merely say, "Well, the Browns are at it again." And so it would no doubt be concluded by our outer space observer that, "The earthlings are at it again."

Some interesting conclusions can be reached about wars. Most wars have an economic basis. In Cypress, the Greeks had the wealth and the Turks wanted it. In Ireland, the Protestants have the wealth, and the Catholics want it. In Lebanon, the Christians have the wealth, and the Moslems want it. In Portugal, the farmers have the wealth, and the city folks want it. In Africa, the Caucasians have the wealth and the black people want it. The pre-Civil War plantation owners in the United States had, as an important part of their financial statements, the slaves they owned. When they borrowed money from the bank, they listed slaves as assets. The abolition of slavery rendered this asset worthless. The preservation of this financial asset was a big part of the reason for the Civil War. The great resistance to integration was due to a fear that assets would be reduced in value. Houses would drop in value when a neighborhood was integrated; or a restaurant would lose its business if a black person was allowed to eat there. Man has not proven to be a very noble creature. He has shown that greed will cause him to fight faster than anything else.

Historically, political power has frequently followed religion as the force that originally created a presence in a foreign country. The Hawaiians have a sad but humorous explanation of the American domination of their beautiful islands. "Two hundred years ago your missionaries came over here. At that time, we owned all the land, went around naked or partially clothed, made love under the trees, and the missionaries owned all the Bibles. Now, two hundred years later, we have all the Bibles; you own all the land; we wear clothes; and you have set up nude beaches where your people run around naked." The result is that descendants of missionaries control the islands (Dole Pineapple for example); and America totally controls the economic and political life of the natives.

Political control, over a region or country, places the economic assets and the commerce of that country under the control of man, the warrior, fighting not for ideals but for wealth because of his insatiable greed.

PERSPECTIVE

"If you can visualize that all of humanity glides along on the wings of time and that nothing we do of a material nature has any lasting effect then you will begin to get this business of living it is proper perspective."

The statement that "this too shall pass" is eminently true when it comes to any material achievement made possible by the efforts of man. Astronomers tell us that in the very distant future (maybe as much as 50 billion years from now) the sun will expand and destroy or melt, with indescribable heat, everything on this earth. This will necessarily include obliterating every achievement of mankind of a material nature. Scientists therefore confirm that all of man's achievements of a material nature will ultimately become nothing. This being true man should not place too much emphasis on material possessions. These become nothing quicker than most people realize.

If we pin all our hopes and aspirations on the acquisition of material goods, our peace and tranquillity will rest on a very tenuous and weak foundation. Material possessions create additional reasons to worry and be concerned, lest they be destroyed, or somehow taken from us. There is nothing wrong with setting aside material gains for future use. But when this scenario of acquisition becomes foremost in our lives, we have little chance of being truly happy. The wisest course is to always remember that anything material can be quickly taken and therefore not to nurture an unreasonable reliance on possessions.

What we should do is to remember that the one irreplaceable asset we have is "time." Time is a thing, that once expended, can never be replaced. All one has to do to realize how fast time passes is to watch the second hand on a clock. It moves quite rapidly and without interruption. Remember that in a lifetime of 70 years we have 2,207,520,000 seconds to expend. Once a second passes it can never be replaced or relived. This, of course, is contrary to material possessions; almost all of which can be replaced. Time, that precious gift, therefore becomes our most valuable possession. In our youth, we take it for granted and almost never think of its expenditure. Once we reach middle age, we begin to realize quite vividly how unique time really always has been. It is then that we realize we have been, and will continue to be, carried relentlessly along on the wings of time.

If this be true, and I submit it is manifestly so, then we should concern ourselves with the need to spend this precious asset as wisely as possible.

TIME

"Ultimately we all realize that 'Time' is the most valuable and irreplaceable possession we are given."

When we are young we live with no thought of the severe limitations that time places on all our lives. The concept of running out of time never occurs to us. Usually, the only time periods we are concerned with are the days until school starts or recesses, the number of days until Christmas, or until some other major event will occur in our lives. This total disregard for the "time factor" in our lives usually continues at least until we are 40. As we cross the 40-year mark in age, we go through a slight shock that is "time" related. We start to think in terms of getting old. This shock is increased by geometric proportions when we pass 50. This is especially true when parts of our body begin to show signs of aging. We notice that we can't start walking smoothly as soon as we get out of bed in the morning. We start to notice aches and pains in muscles and joints that we never experienced before. Finally, the awesome prospect of death looms continuously on the horizon. We may not realize it or we may not fear it, but we must respect it. It becomes a paramount consideration in our planning. There it is; we can't ignore it. Suddenly we realize that we can't plan too far ahead. We are running out of this precious commodity called "time." We can no longer accomplish many of the things we have in mind. The awesome apocalyptic, precious, character of time becomes obvious to us as never before in our lives. We have arrived at a new and deeper understanding of the temporary nature of our life.

If we live the "traditional three score and ten" or seventy years we will have 613,200 hours of life; 36,792,000 minutes of life; 2,207,520,000 seconds of life, or 25,550 days. These measurements are precise and from the moment of birth the clock starts ticking away. When you consider that everything you hope to accomplish or everything you want your life to represent must be compressed into this time frame the whole process assumes a slightly different perspective. We now start thinking in terms of using the time left to us in meaningful pursuits. We arrange for many things, such as our final will and testament; we pick out our burial place or make other arrangements in the event of our death. We start dropping little suggestions about family heirlooms. In short, we start thinking slowly of our demise.

Once we become acutely aware of the short amount of time in our life spans, we need to set about accomplishing those things that we have been postponing until a later date. It may be a trip to Europe; or some type of charity work; joining a church; or it may be nothing more than slowing down and enjoying some of the details of living. Whatever it is, it will be done with the idea that it might soon be our last experience of this nature. We learn to savor the beauty of life and take the time to enjoy it longer. Things that we wouldn't notice in our youth suddenly become quite enjoyable and beautiful. Many of us mellow and start treating others with a little more consideration. We have arrived at that period of life once described by Elizabeth Barrett Browning in part as follows: "The best is yet to be, the last of life for which the first was made."

PROGRESS

"Mankind is poised for a tremendous surge of growth and progress."

The entire world is headed for changes which are unprecedented in their social, economic, and political impact. Long accepted social, economic, and political structures will be inexorably swept away and will be replaced with something different and better. This has been the history of man.

Many of man's current practices result in terminable chart graphics. Some typical examples are the automobile, fossil fuels, atomic proliferation, population explosion, pollution, racist practices, military-industrial complexes, food supplies, and capitalistic-communistic struggle, energy sources of all types, fraud and other criminal practices by world leaders, refugee problems, taxation, destruction of the family unit, pollution by television and news media of all types, pollution of our minds and bodies by pornography and drugs, the greed of dominant economic forces around the world, the growth of terrorist groups prepared to die for their respective causes, and many others too numerous to mention.

From this maelstrom of chaos there has emerged a frightened and insecure humanity. World history suggests that from this condition there will result a war of apocalyptic proportions. The track record of mankind suggest that the human animal lacks the intelligence to avoid suffering, but once encountered, possesses a remarkable ability to endure it. All the elements for a worldwide "shoot-out" are present, hate being the principal ingredient. The capitalists have a reciprocal hatred with the communists; the Muslims have a reciprocal hatred with the Jews; the blacks with the whites; the Chinese with the Russians; the world has a hatred of America (probably based on jealously) even though almost every world citizen heads for America the minute "the local sheriff gets on his tail"; and so forth. Compromise is no longer practiced since the positions of the antagonists have hardened, leaving no room for peaceful solutions.

As has happened before in perilous times, religious groups have retrenched to the most conservative forms of their respective beliefs. We now see the Shiite Muslims emerging as the most powerful force in their religion. This same principal now finds a tremendous growth in the so-called "born-again" movement in the Christian countries. Witness the fact that 1,400 radio stations, 30 television stations and 66 cable systems now specialize in religious broadcasts, with religious radio stations starting up at the rate of one a week and television stations at the rate of one a month. All this now represents a 500-million-dollar industry annually in the United States. The Jewish people of the world are concerned as never before with securing their national boundaries in the Holy Land. Meanwhile, the Shiite Muslims are equally concerned as never before with preventing this occurrence. Most of the religious friction comes from believers of the Bible and the Koran—the latter discussing biblical characters in great detail.

Meanwhile, a better world can be glimpsed around the corner—unlimited, pollution-free energy from sea water through hydrogen fusion; exciting medical discoveries, and most importantly a growing awareness that hatred must somehow be replaced by love. Before this happens, however, I predict man will first suffer terribly.

THE NEW GENERATION

"Each new generation that comes along brings a new supply of love, adventure, and tolerance to humanity. Without this phenomena, viewpoints would become less flexible and tolerance and adventure would tend to completely vanish."

Most people solidify their viewpoints as they grow older. Their mental postures on most issues becomes fixed and immobile. To attempt to change their minds is a futile undertaking. Their opinions on a thousand or more different subjects have been arrived at through a process of trial and error affected mostly by their own living experiences. As their viewpoints harden, any attempt to alter a viewpoint or even to suggest that a given incident should be considered as an exception is doomed to certain failure. People tend to "close" their minds to any new ideas after they get older. They have stopped learning and oftentimes do not really want to learn because they are relatively happy with the views they already have. They simply do not want to disturb their tranquillity with controversial new ideas.

These same "fixed" views transposed on an international level often lead to wars. The older portion of the population of each country around the world provides the leadership for each of these countries. Consequently, when their leaders sit down in an international conference to seek peace, they all adopt uncompromising positions that result in no new ideas coming from such a meeting. These meetings usually end with a "diplomatically" worded statement and with all the underlying causes of friction still intact. From these unresolved differences, wars start and humanity continues the same vicious cycle that has been the practice of mankind for all of recorded history.

The great hope seems to reside with each succeeding younger generation that comes along. They don't seem to be handicapped by all the fear, hatred, prejudice, bigotry, ignorance, and cruelty possessed by older people. They may never solve the serious problems facing mankind but at least while they are in their "questioning" years, they will add to the totality of love, adventure, and tolerance that exists among men. They may grow up and adopt the same ignorance possessed by their elders, but at least for a while, they will explore new areas of human relationships, seeking love where it was not known to exist, giving tolerance where it had long since been withdrawn, and being adventuresome where such activity was no longer considered worthwhile. It is just possible that this new approach on the part of each new generation of youngsters may improve infinitesimally the overall condition of human relations. The important part is that each new "wave" of young people somehow seems to try an approach that has been abandoned by their elders. This constant effort raises hope in the hearts of everyone that improvement is possible.

If you observe real close, you see little areas of improvement brought about by the efforts of young people whose efforts we had previously consigned to the trash heap of failure. The so-called hippie movement had many negative aspects. But something of value came out of it. There emerged a "tell it like it is" theme that added to the body of truthfulness in the world. With truth and justice on the rise, hypocrisy had to decline. Now this "movement" certainly did not eradicate the evils of the world but it definitely increased the amount of truth that existed in human relations. To some extent the younger people have aided, however slightly, the problems in dealing with race relations. Somehow the young black people and the young white people seem to have constructed a bridge of understanding that exceeds the tolerance existing between older people. Man's hopes and dreams may not be fulfilled tomorrow but they will be aided by those never-ending generations of young people yet to come along.

JUDGMENT

"We always have an audience making important judgments about us."

Everything we do every new day becomes part of our ever changing "image" on which our contemporaries judge us. Regardless of what our "image" is on Monday we can start creating a new one when the sun rises on Tuesday morning. As long as we are alive we have the opportunity to change the whole pattern of our life. We are literally never stuck with the past. Nothing is final about anyone as long as he is alive. With each new day we can start anew. Judgments can never be final until we are dead. We all make mistakes. The important thing to remember about mistakes is that they are not final unless we die from them. To err is human. All we have to do is rededicate ourselves to any goal we desire. The main ingredient is not to despair or surrender. As long as we don't quit trying, the future is unlimited. In any event it is limited only by our imagination and creativity. It is very encouraging to know that tomorrow can bring any change we may desire in our lives.

As we plod through life we may erroneously believe that no one is watching us. We may feel terribly isolated and believe that the entire world has ignored us and that it really makes no difference what we do. We think that we won't get our just reward— why bother to do good? Actually nothing could be farther from the truth. Everyone who ever lived has something called an "image." Now this "view" that others have of us may differ remarkable from one person to another. This is readily explained by the fact that different people have had different experiences with us. Consequently their mental image of our character and personality may vary greatly. The principal point is that we all have a so-called "image." Everything we have ever done goes to make up the totality of this picture in our acquaintances' eyes. It is also a picture that changes constantly so long as we live. Through acts we think go unnoticed, our acquaintances develop a deeper insight into our character. Each such new development will change our "image" either for the better or the worse, depending upon the character of the act. Never believe that you go unnoticed or that your activities are unappraised. There are eyes that watch even though they may be unseen.

What is really the most important thing is that we should lead our life along the proper lines. When we live the good life we don't have to worry about our "image." The truth will come out eventually. We can exhibit our personality and behavior before all mankind since it is exemplary and we have nothing to hide. It is only when we do those things that are unsavory or improper that we should realize that we are being watched. There really are no "freebies." Everything negative costs us in some way and everything positive assists us. Paraphrasing Abraham Lincoln; we may fool all of the people sometime and some people all the time but we can't fool all the people all the time. For every improper action you can be assured that a penalty will be exacted subsequently. If nothing else our "image" will be diminished in brilliance in the eyes of those people who are aware of our actions.

This thing called character or reputation or image is something that eventually quite accurately follows the conduct of our life. The two match quite evenly. Ultimately very few secrets are ever left. It is not in the nature of people to keep secrets. If they see you do something that is either good or evil they may honestly promise to keep it a secret. Eventually most people will "tell all." New books are being published, frequently representing some ex-servant, employee, or acquaintance of a famous or powerful person, who for monetary gains tells all the world about the deep, dark, and dirty secrets of their famous acquaintance. Lead the good life and this chapter will not apply to you.

SUCCESS

"Silver slippers coming down the ladder of success
are met by wooden shoes climbing that same ladder."

A young man whose father is rich and powerful is confronted with problems that are seldom appreciated. When such a person looks beyond the security of his family or looks out his front door, every pathway leads downhill. In his finest hour, he would be hard pressed to equal or excel his father. Nothing he could hope to achieve in the world of commerce could equal the level of his own childhood and circumstances at home. Such a young person feels quite intimidated by this condition and finds it difficult to work really hard for his own personal advancement. The problem is that he feels inferior to his father and loses all desire to even try to equal or surpass him. A lethargy based on despondency soon descends and you have another pair of "silver slippers" all set to descend the ladder of success.

Contrariwise, when a young man born of a father who is an economic failure, or at the least of exceedingly moderate success, surveys the world outside this home, he sees many ways to equal or surpass his father. Such a young man charges out into the world filled with dreams and ambitions. His energy seems boundless and he communicates excitedly with his proud parents, informing them of his every success. When this happens you have "wooden shoes" climbing the ladder of success.

It appears that a generation of achievers is often followed by a generation of nonachievers, that in turn is followed by a generation of achievers. Success seems to come with every other generation. The children of achievers clearly take prosperity as a natural thing and fail to appreciate their parents' station in life, nor do they seem willing to exert their efforts to duplicate it in their own life. Since success comes only with great efforts, this generation soon "falls by the wayside" once their parents die. By then, it is too late for them to do anything about their missed opportunities. Many of these types live out lives of bitterness, frustration, and unhappiness. They learned too late that you cannot keep prosperity, without expending wise and intelligent efforts.

The usual scenario of the achievers is that they want their children to have what they didn't have. Tragically, achievers do not realize until it is too late that *they* had the greatest opportunity that a young person can have in life. Every road from their home led up the ladder of success. They were naturally endowed with the necessary motivation to be successful. They could see a thousand ways that they could surpass their parents. Since every possible pathway led upward to success, they never considered any alternative but the use of maximum effort. They had the greatest asset a child or young person can have—a life filled with challenges. Now the achiever usually wants to give his children all material things (both necessities and luxuries) without the children earning them. He in effect robs or denies the children the opportunity to meet their own challenges. To climb their own mountains, so to speak. What the achiever should do, and this requires the wise cooperation of both parents, is make their children work for everything they get from the time they are old enough to understand. They have to have indelibly imprinted upon them that they will get nothing unless they work for it. It is said that the Rockefellers were so well-trained as children that they would walk ten blocks to save five cents on a hair cut. This is the sort of training to keep in mind. This approach for achievers in dealing with their children is so terribly necessary to their children's happiness that it cannot be over emphasized. A deprived child is really a child who is not allowed to meet his own challenges. If everything is given to him, his sense of values becomes destroyed. He will become a non achiever and meet those "wooden shoes" going up the ladder of success while he climbs down unhappily.

INDEPENDENCE

"One of life's most valuable lessons involves learning to be happy, contented, and secure when a person is without human companionship."

Numerous mistakes are made because of the fear that a person will be alone or without friends and companions in his private life, business life, and/or social life. Everyone wants to belong; wants to be a member of the group; wants to be a meaningful participant in business and social activities. Everyone wants to share his life in a meaningful way with someone else. In the process of achieving these ends, costly errors, both financially and emotionally, are made by many people.

The fear of being alone and without friends causes many persons to make foolish decisions. Many people feel insecure and inadequate starting a business enterprise on their own, so they actively seek and invite the participation of a partner. They don't need the partner so much for his technical know-how or his capital contribution; what they seek is whatever emotional stability that can be obtained by having a partner to share the venture with them. Foolishly, their insecurity drives them into acquiring a whole new set of problems, i.e., their relationship with a partner. Frequently, the trials, tribulations, and tensions associated with their partner are more disruptive of their emotional stability and well-being than any problems related to business. They begin to find out the habits and idiosyncrasies of the partner, making their business life unpleasant, which inevitably carries over into their home life. Their basic fear of being alone in business, with the consequent necessity of making all decisions and shouldering the responsibility for them, drove them into precipitously acquiring a partner. Instead of solving problems, such a situation creates problems. Instead of contributing to emotional stability, it contributes to emotional instability. Had such a person been content to be alone in business, his problems in the long run would be far less.

In the realm of finding a mate, man often makes his most profound errors, both of a financial and emotional nature. Marriage is often literally grasped at the first opportunity because of a deep fear of being alone. Both men and women fall victim to this irrational practice. A young girl, of 23 or so, suddenly realizes all of her friends are married, or getting married. She immediately panics at the thought of being an old maid. She sets out on a desperate search for anyone to whom she can be married, thus avoiding the terrible curse of being alone. Little does she realize that there are far worse situations than to be alone. She gets married, not because she has found a man with whom she is in love, but primarily because she is afraid to pass up almost any opportunity to avoid a life without a mate. Such a precipitous marriage usually generates nothing but unhappiness for both parties. Frequently, such a union results in a divorce several years later with a child to support and raise. Then she is alone with the child and with far less of a chance to marry in the future. Her fear of being alone drove her into getting married for the wrong reasons. Her ultimate problems are more severe than any that existed before her marriage.

This same fear drives men into precipitous marriages with the same disastrous results, and in addition—divorce laws being what they are—a considerable financial outlay. If a child is born of the union, continuing future expenses are incurred which last for a long time. Often, such a child can seldom be seen or visited by the father, since the chances of life can take either the mother or father away to a distant place. All because the man had a deep seated fear of being alone.

People are driven into many other foolish acts because they have never learned how to be alone successfully. It becomes important to develop activities that can be carried on without the presence of another human being. In order to do this, you have to understand and like yourself.

What kind of person are you? Do you look in a mirror with rose-colored glasses or do you take a realistic look at yourself? How do other people see you? Do you have a lot of unresolved fears? If you do, then your true personality will never get a chance to come to the forefront. It will be marred and distorted by fears that no doubt are illogical and stress-provoking. Are you greedy, or selfish, excessively jealous, or excessively proud? Any one or all of these qualities will keep the true "you" from coming to the forefront. If you keep all these evil tendencies in check, then you will have no trouble liking yourself nor will your peers have difficulty liking you. If you are unable to control any one or more of these sins, then it may be necessary to seek outside professional help.

Having mastered yourself, the next step is to learn to enjoy activities which can be carried on alone. These are too numerous to mention; however, a minimum of thought will suggest such activities as reading, listening to music, walking, writing, watching television, praying, painting, home-crafts, and many other pursuits that can be followed alone.

Rejection

Sooner or later we all experience rejection in one form or another. Some people may be rejected more often than others, but eventually we all encounter it. While it is a part of everyone's life, the incident leaves us all a little sadder and with feelings of hurt and even anger. The extent of the reactions depends largely on our own feelings of self-worth. Those of us who have an adequate self-image are able to bear the damage to our sensitivities with a minimum of pain. Others may suffer endlessly and needlessly in a self-imposed prison. This article is addressed especially to those people who for many conceivable reasons do not know how to handle rejection and the natural feelings that flow from this situation.

First and foremost we must realize that we are not alone in being rejected. It is a part of everyone's life. No matter how great or compctent or wealthy or athletic or religious or scholarly one may be, there is always some group in which we do not qualify for membership or inclusion. A capitalist, for example, would not qualify for membership in a communist organization. A Republican does not qualify for a membership in an exclusively Democratic organization, nor does a Catholic in an exclusively Protestant group, nor a Gentile in an exclusively Jewish group, nor a white person in an exclusively black group, nor a man in an exclusively woman's group and the list could continue endlessly.

If we are rejected on the basis of being Italian, or Catholic, or Jewish, or black, or Chinese and that rejection is based on prejudice, it is again important to realize that we are not being singled out as an individual but that we are the victim of "age-old" prejudices over which we have no control. When we realize this, our sensitivities are more endurable since the incident is not based on personal deficiencies. In rejection that is based on prejudice against a whole class of people, we are merely encountering a defect in humanity. The real loser in such a situation is not ourselves but the entire human race. If we let ourselves become unduly distributed by such a rejection, we are taking a problem that is not ours and by ignorance we are assuming its burden.

Rejection oftentimes allows a wise person to improve himself or, to place it in the vernacular, to "clean up his act." We all develop undesirable traits which offend people and which make us less desirable companions. This is especially true of those people whose entire life is based on a secular or worldly foundation as opposed to one whose life is based at least in part on a religious footing. When we are totally secular in our thinking, our habits have a tendency to envelop and dominate our life. We somehow lack the incentive and the willpower to successfully combat the unending pressure to let our vices and negative habits control our lives.

When we are rejected for any reason from any group, we should examine ourselves to make sure that the defect is not in our behavior and/or our lifestyle. If a prudent examination reveals this to be the case, we should be optimistically thankful for the remainder and then proceed forthwith to correct the defect. Sometimes it takes a shock to make us realize that we are less than perfect. If we conclude that the fault lies with us then the entire incident is nothing more than an opportunity for self-improvement. If you are wise, you will be thankful for such an opportunity to increase the quality of your life and your consequent happiness.

REPETITION

At a very fundamental level, life involves constant repetition for everyone. For example, on the most important level, our heartbeat and breathing are necessarily repetitive. Beyond these basics, almost every important aspect of all our lives involves constant repetition. Before life can become meaningful, one has to train himself to appreciate the little things of a non-repetitive nature that occur daily in all our lives. After all, the big movement of our lives on a daily basis is almost totally repetitious.

We all awaken after sleep. If we are sanitary and have the facilities, we brush our teeth; we either shave or make up our face; we bathe, go to the bathroom; we dress and then we begin our daily routine. If we work, we arrive at our work place, greet our associates with the time of day, and prepare to work. Our daily work schedule involves essentially the same type of thing. We eat three meals a day, if we're lucky; and our evenings tend to follow similar daily patterns. At the end of our day, we prepare to sleep again. On our days off, our schedule again assumes a similar repetitive routine. Our vacations are usually spent in some activity we enjoy, which tends to be similar from vacation to vacation. This repetitive process occurs in all our lives whether we are a nation's leader, an entertainer, a student, a playboy, a labor leader, a worker, a businessman, a religious leader, a mother and housewife, or any one of thousands of different human activities. The point is that everyone's life soon adopts a repetitive process which tends to be evidenced in a fashion that is unique to any given life-style.

If we are to be happy and lead a fulfilling life, we must learn to cope with life's routine. We cannot let ourselves become bored or depressed simply because our life involves constant repetition of the same routine. The successful ones learn early that repetition is the characteristic of all life and deal with it wisely. The most important aspect is to "hang in there" on a daily basis. The large number of people who do not live successfully tend to "give up" once their lives assume a repetitive theme. What they fail to realize is that everyone's life involves essentially similar repetitive processes. The cycle of repetition will be different from life to life, but the repetitive characteristic occupies every life. The repetition of modern life tends to be more burdensome since it is further removed from nature than in a previously agrarian society. Under an agrarian lifestyle, the surprises and delights of nature add excitement and beauty not found in a modern metropolitan lifestyle. For example, a hen parading proudly from a wheat field with newly hatched chicks, or a mare with a newly born foal provide excitement that cannot be found in an "asphalt jungle."

Happiness can be experienced by appreciating fully the little out-of-the-ordinary happenings that occur in all our lives, such as an unexpected visit, a surprise party, the achievement of a goal, a raise in pay, the completion of a successful economic venture, meeting a new sexual partner, graduation from a school or college, the successful loss of weight or any one of a million occurrences slightly out of the ordinary. Even while we are following the daily repetitive routine of our life, a wise person searches for opportunities to make the routine seem more enjoyable or fruitful. All other approaches to life are less desirable.

REALITY

It may be surprising, but reality is quite different to different people observing the same occurrence at the same time. Ten people can simultaneously observe a car accident, for example, and be immediately asked (separately) to describe what they saw: answering as truthfully as they can, the probability is that they will give, in varying degrees, ten different versions of what happened. The conclusion is that reality is that which exists in the mind of the observer.

This fact presents a great opportunity for a wise person to enjoy life. It is possible to almost manufacture your own reality by the sheer power of your own mind. Reality can be changed by the simple process of altering the way we see and observe something. The interesting aspect of this entire subject is that the ten people observing the car accident mentioned above can all be correct even though their individual accounts may vary. People see with their heart and their mind. In the process they also happen to use their eyes. But the heart and the mind govern.

A bright, sunny morning can be greeted with a morose concern for catching skin cancer from too much exposure to the rays of the sun or with a thankful prayer to a beneficent Almighty who made the life-giving qualities of the sun available. A rainy day can be condemned for ruining plans associated with outdoor activity or one may be thankful for the rain's ability to sustain and renew plants and all other forms of life on this planet. Ignorant people can be cursed for their ignorance or one may be thankful for their plentiful existence, thus making it possible to compete successfully in a world filled with ignorance. Personal problems or tragedies can be condemned for the suffering they inflict, or one can be thankful for the experience because it represents an opportunity to grow.

To one who experiences all the occurrences and/or situations in the preceding paragraph, the world in reality could become either a terrible place or a beautiful place depending on which aspect of reality we seek to stress. Both people could be correct even though their descriptions appear to be exactly opposite. It, therefore, seems apparent that reality becomes what you seek to make it. Every human experience has many characteristics and our appraisal depends on which quality we seek to stress.

Some people are naturally optimistic in everything they do, feel, and say. They strive mightily to find something good or enjoyable in everything and/or everybody. This trait seems to start in childhood and continues throughout life. Happy child—happy adult—happy old person seems to be the scenario. The contrary also seems to be true—unhappy child, etc. Wisdom can change all of this. We can learn to develop and manufacture our own pleasant reality far short of hallucinatory practices. It would certainly seem to be a wise objective since it will make our trip from the cradle to the grave far more enjoyable.

If it is not your habit already, then start tomorrow morning with the thought that nothing is going to prevent you from enjoying the day. Start to develop a positive philosophy aimed at increasing the happiness level in your life. Actually, the entire process is not difficult and the rewards are enormous. The person who is happy all the time faces the same type of problems that the sad and/or pessimistic type person does. It therefore becomes important to change your way of looking at life's problems. Look for the brightness and ignore where possible the darkness.

WISDOM AND IGNORANCE

The theater, the movies, the news media, world politics, and humanity in general, divide the world between the "good guys" and the "bad guys." The dividing lines are always drawn between good and evil. When a couple divorces, there always has to be one "good" person and one "bad" person. When a friendship ends, one is depicted as the "bad" guy and the other as the "good" guy. It seems that the "good" end of a situation or incident is depicted as being wholly blameless and the "bad" end is wholly at fault. This fallacious method of judgment leaves many questions unanswered and does violence to truth and logic.

As a starter, let us recognize that no one is without some merit and conversely, no one is without some fault. Therefore, it must be concluded that the consideration of pure justice demands that merit and fault be assigned in some ratio to both ends of a controversy. Everyone has reasons for their actions, which to them are valid. This opinion, as to validity, is only arrived at after the computer, which we all possess (the human brain), decides on a given course of action. This decision is arrived at after the input of value systems, childhood experiences, emotional reactions, intellectual levels, mental health, religious training, ethnic background, and the myriad of other senses that all of humanity possesses. We are all a product of our genes and environment, both past and present. Instead of the "good guy" or "bad guy" method of judgment, the far wiser course would be to divide humanity between wisdom and ignorance. Robert Browning, in an 1864 poem entitled "Apparent Failure," states that "It's wiser being good than bad . . ."

People are either "wise" or "ignorant." No one is all wise, nor is anyone all ignorant. What the world calls "good" and "evil" is actually "wisdom" and "ignorance." The young man who robs a gas station for money is actually more "ignorant" than he is "evil." The risk to his future happiness does not warrant this venture. If it's money he needs, he can work and produce the same results without running the risk of destroying his life. The young girl who becomes a prostitute is more "ignorant" than she is "evil." The person who takes drugs is, again, more "ignorant" than he is "evil." The possible examples of ignorance being called "evil" and "wisdom" being called "good" are endless.

The far more intelligent way to look at the world is through the dividing lines of "wisdom" and "ignorance." Presumably, if we all knew the ultimate truth about life, we would all act in much the same way. The objective of all of us should be to obtain as much wisdom as possible. We should all strive to become the best person of which we are capable. In this fashion, our actions will be based on increased wisdom and our chances for happiness will be greatly enhanced.

INEVITABILITY

To a large extent much of life is governed by an inexorable, inevitable, unchangeable, evolutionary sweep of events over which we have little control. As to any matter that falls in that category, we should relax and enjoy life to the fullest possible extent since we really have no control over these types of developments or conditions. Wisdom will tell us when we are confronted with developments or conditions over which we have no control. That same wisdom will also enable us to enjoy our life to the fullest notwithstanding such inevitabilities.

Nothing in this discussion is intended to imply that our life should not be a constant exercise in self-improvement. Once an analysis reveals that there is something that we can do about conditions, we should immediately set out to improve the situation to the extent that it lies within our power to accomplish. Having done our utmost, we should then sit back, relax, and let the river of our life flow freely and unimpeded by needless mental upheavals.

Atomic warfare is a possibility; yet, its ultimate occurrence does not lie within our power to prevent. This is a condition of life with which we have to live. It is indeed a frighteningly awesome prospect; however, nothing we can do will add or subtract significantly from its possible occurrence. If it is out of your control, minimize the entire spectra in your mind.

Halley's Comet may or may not one day collide with the earth. If it does, we can do nothing to prevent it. It is due to visit our area of the universe in the 21st century. Whenever it occurs, it is beyond our power to prevent.

Devastating earthquakes are always a possibility on the planet earth. The more one studies geology, the more evident it becomes that the surface of the earth is anything but stable. Oil prospectors, for example, have discovered fossilized clam shells 2,500 feet beneath the surface of the land in Oklahoma. The Blue Ridge Mountains are 500 million years old and were once far higher than the Rocky Mountains. Notwithstanding these facts, wisdom should allow us to live happily with this knowledge since the entire situation is utterly beyond our control.

Cancer looms as a more frequently encountered prospect as people live longer. We should concern ourselves with cancer-causing agents and eliminate them to the extent possible from our diet and lives. Beyond these precautions, we should enjoy life to the fullest possible extent.

With the advent of the drug culture and poverty living side

by side with affluence, we find that society is confronted with a serious crime problem. It is only natural to do all those things necessary to minimize our chances of becoming a victim of crime. Once we have done everything possible to maximize the safety in our lives, we should then learn to enjoy our life to the fullest.

HAPPINESS

"It is not normal or necessary to be happy at all times."

People get in trouble when they try to be happy "on schedule." Entertainers go on stage and predetermine that at "curtain time" they have to be experiencing a "high." Since human personality and behavior does not work this way, these types of people find it necessary to rely on some form of artificial stimulant to make their personality effervescent and bubbly at a prearranged hour. However, the more often this artificial stimulus is applied, the more artificial and chemically controlled becomes our emotional life. This often results in a spiraling descent into a "hell" that results from the excessive use of drugs or alcohol or both.

Who says we have to be happy and carefree all of the time? Anyone who believes this is living in a fool's paradise. Anyone who smiles all the time is either crazy or vastly deceptive. It is not normal to be always happy. Emotional life in it's normal pattern goes through "high's" and "low's." Everything is cyclical in nature; and for every "up" cycle there soon follows a "down" cycle. When you have your "good" and "bad" days, you are experiencing normal human personality fluctuations.

Ordinary people who go to a party somehow believe that they need to be in exalted spirits when they arrive. To ensure this occurrence they take a few drinks before they get there. When they arrive, they are all aglow and full of smiles. This condition pleases them and their hosts even though the entire scene is artificially based on mind-altering substances.

Strangely enough, when a person totally abstains from drugs of any form, a type of happy tranquillity descends upon him that is almost childlike in its refreshing characteristics. Aside from the normal "ups" and "downs" we all naturally experience, a person who totally abstains, from the use of drugs (including alcohol), experiences a pervasive tranquillity and happiness that is most noticeable. They seem to be bright-eyed and cheerful in a manner more natural and convincing than anyone who uses drugs to obtain this effect. The naturalness of the "drug-free" individual's well-being is readily detected and enjoyed by all of his acquaintances. Anyone who has been using drugs to alter his state of emotional well-being must realize that this "natural euphoria" will not occur for several months after the use of drugs in discontinued. It will take some time for the accumulated levels of drugs to leave his system to the extent that they no longer influence his emotional well-being. He who discontinues artificial stimulants will first go through a period of nervousness, followed eventually by a feeling of well-being not experienced since childhood.

Even with this natural euphoria, expect periods of depressed emotional levels that you must realize are normal for all humanity. When this occurs, have little tricks to use which enable you to go through these "rough" periods with a minimum of discomfort. Take a walk, or go for a swim; play golf, or tennis, or watch a sporting event; or play cards. Do anything that is mind and thought diverting, that at the same time isn't harmful or constitutes the acquisition of a new negative habit. These "down" periods are as much a part of living as are the "up" periods. Have faith in the overall pleasure of life. Observe your "drug-free" acquaintances and note that their lives are predominately happy. Believe that your "down" mood shall soon pass. Don't insist on feeling good all the time. The only way this can be done is to use artificial stimulants, and this only works for a little while. When drugs no longer make you feel good, you are in trouble. So be content with a normal emotional life of "ups" and "downs." This is the best possible way to live.

TRUTH

"The most difficult part of any controversy is for a neutral party to establish the truth."

A learned trial lawyer once observed that the truth never "walks" willingly into a courtroom. He further observed that it is usually dragged into a court of law against its will, kicking and screaming. While this may be an exaggeration, it describes vividly the difficulty of ascertaining the truth in any controversy.

Some people are better equipped than others by reason of intelligence, training, or dedication to more accurately describe a situation or event. For example, if four people witness an exciting event such as a bank robbery or a car accident or a natural disaster or any one of a million different things that can happen, it is very interesting to record each one's version of what happened. In reading the description given by each of the four people, one sometimes has difficulty realizing the same event is being described by all four. In an actual "hold-up" situation, one eye witness has been known to describe the bandit as being 5'2" with black hair, while another eye witness describes the bandit as being 6'2" tall with blond curly hair. Both of these people are honestly relating what they believe they saw.

Facts really get confusing when it comes to a marital squabble. The wife has one version; her husband another; the wife's friends have a version; and the husband's friends have yet another version. The children of this couple usually have their version which differs from all the others. The actual truth is frequently different than anyone's version. In a divorce situation, it frequently becomes necessary to decide on the relative propriety of the parties' situation. Who was right and who was wrong? Usually both parties were partially right and partially wrong.

One principle we should learn very early in any search for the truth is to make up our minds only after we have investigated as thoroughly as possible. This is especially true, if the answer is important. Don't make up your mind to quickly. You may talk to the first person and be given the most logical, cohesive story imaginable. Yet this seemingly accurate account may be totally wrong, either through ignorance or intentional distortion. Don't make up your mind until the last minute. The longer you delay your decision the more accurate will probably be your final conclusion. Once you've made up your mind, don't hesitate to reconsider if newly discovered facts warrant this course of action.

History, biographies, and autobiographies contain an amazing amount of untruths. For example, Thomas Jefferson constantly wrote letters extensively outlining his position on every facet of his life. When he did this, he knew he was controlling what history would ultimately have to say about him. Historians, in writing about the life and times of Thomas Jefferson, read some 18,000 letters that he conveniently left for their perusal. He, of course, conveniently destroyed those letters that would cast him in a light he deemed undesirable. Biographers usually write about people they adore; people for whom they have great affection. These human emotions significantly effect the clarity and accuracy of their writings. Autobiographers usually do their writing through "rose-colored glasses." This practice again distorts the accuracy of their writings. History, of all types, is probably only 50 percent accurate in many significant ways.

Magazines, newspapers, television, and radio probably lead the parade of inaccurate disseminators of the events of the day. Do not believe too much of what you hear or read from either source. The tendency is to editorialize, which practice requires coming to all sorts of conclusions. It is while engaged in this undertaking that important inaccuracies creep into all accounts of current events. Just remember the "truth" is difficult to find and once found, it is the last thing many people want to hear. The best practice is to form your conclusions very slowly and train yourself to recognize inaccuracies and untruths. Your life will be much happier because you took the time to be careful.

WAITING

"Since waiting is a big part of life learn to enjoy it."

Almost everyone first remembers waiting for Christmas to arrive. Impatiently and with considerable tension, children the world over wait for this event. As we grow older, we find that there are thousands, maybe even millions of occurrences for which we must wait. If we pace up and down neurotically, waiting for every one of these, our life has to be quite unpleasant.

Impatience can ruin a life. Since almost everything we want or anticipate has a "built-in" waiting time, we will be happier if we learn how to wait as pleasantly as possible. Patience, like every other desirable quality, has to be practiced to be improved. Impatience is a trait that will stay with us if we do not work against it. If we simply adopt the attitude that we are impatient, then this undesirable trait will stay with us and dominate our personality. Everything from work to pleasure involves waiting. We wait for a traffic signal to change; we wait for the sun to go down or to come up; we wait for special events to occur; we wait while engaged in leisure-time activities such as golf or tennis, cards or handball, or any other type of activity. Waiting is forever a part of our lives, so we should learn to deal with it successfully.

The best way to wait for something is to direct your mind to other thoughts. Don't dwell on the event for which you are waiting. Once your mind turns to other subjects, the waiting time will shrink and the whole experience will be more pleasant. If it is a question of just sitting and waiting, as in a doctor's office for example, then you should anticipate the wait and bring reading material or something else with you to make the time pass faster. If it is a wait that occurs at your work or your home, then you should be able to fill up the waiting period with something useful.

Always bear in mind that while we are waiting for important events to occur, life goes on as usual. In fact waiting is life. Any average person should have any number of events that they are waiting for at all times. This is what the "game of life" is all about. Let your joys continue as you wait for the events of your life to unfold.

Remember that the present or the "now" is the only moment it is possible for you to enjoy. Tomorrow hasn't arrived and yesterday is gone, so that leaves only the "now." If you are going to be happy then learn to enjoy the present. Even though the present includes tremendous anticipation of pleasant future events to occur, learn to put these desires in the background. Subordinate them to present pleasures. If you properly take care of the present, the future will take care of itself. Overeagerness for the future to arrive can rob a person of any opportunity to enjoy the present. Once you have done everything you can with respect to future events, then let the passing of time do the rest. If the present is well-spent, the future will arrive soon enough.

People don't like to associate with impatient people. Excessive impatience ruins everyone's opportunity to enjoy themselves. Patience is absolutely necessary in the world of commerce. Impatience will ruin one's opportunity for commercial success. Impatience tends to cause nervousness and ulcers. Patience is very relaxing and tranquilizing. It aids sleep and the digestive processes. It makes you a more enjoyable person to be with and thereby increases your opportunity for material success and happiness.

FORTUNE

"Good fortune is never as pleasant as it first appears nor is misfortune as unpleasant as it first appears."

When Napoleon Bonaparte was crowned emperor of the world, he was experiencing the fruition of a struggle that had occupied his brilliant mind his entire adult life. This memorable event could be expected to please the heart and soul of Napoleon beyond any other experience of his life. Yet on the day of his coronation, he expressed the thought that he was a sad, lonely, and disillusioned man. He couldn't believe his feelings. Anwar Sadat stated that the years he spent in an Egyptian prison were in retrospect the happiest years of his life. This would hardly seem likely when one considers the austerity of prison, especially that of an Egyptian prison. Somehow good fortune is never as good as one would believe it to be nor is misfortune as unpleasant as one would expect it to be. Realization somehow never equals anticipation. There is always a gap between imagination and reality.

When good fortune proves to be less exhilarating than anticipated, there is a feeling of being "let down" or of disillusionment that follows this realization. Usually good fortune takes the form of attaining some long sought after goal. As an individual thinks about the attainment of a treasured goal, all sorts of happy feelings overcome his being in anticipation of this joyous event. When after what is often a long struggle, the goal is reached, there is a depressive reaction. The whole experience really wasn't as great as we believed it would be. We are like a child on Christmas day, sitting in the middle of all his toys, with wrappings and boxes lying all over, "crying his eyes out." For months he dreamed of receiving all of "Santa's" gifts and the joys of discovering and using them. Yet, in the exhilaration of the moment, when the slightest thing goes wrong, we find him crying. So it is with all good fortune—it is simply never as great as we anticipate it will be for us.

The opposite occurs when it comes to misfortune. Whenever anything happens to us that we fear or dread, we visualize all sorts of unpleasant experiences occurring. Our anticipation builds a mental picture of unpleasantness and disaster. Death is no doubt in this category with many people. Yet when it occurs, a surprising number of people leave this life with smiles on their faces. Many seemingly unpleasant occurrences short of death often prove ultimately to be blessings. If nothing else, they may prove to have been a great learning experience from which an individual can derive great benefits. Most advances are forged in the crucible of pain or disaster or misfortune or parts of all three. Whenever anything happens that would appear to be unfortunate, wait awhile before making a final decision. First of all, you will realize that the experience wasn't really as bad or unpleasant as you thought it would be; and secondly, if you keep your eyes and mind open, the probability is you will learn a lot from it. This knowledge will help you become a better person in the future. Additionally, when you realize that the realization was not as unpleasant as you assumed it would be, you will experience a happy feeling.

Consequently, it can be said that the final impression or feeling on good news, events or occurrences ultimately becomes a "downer" and the final impression on bad news, events or occurrences ultimately becomes an "upper."

CONTROL

*"The great occurrences of our life are to a large
extent beyond our control."*

The greatest occurrence of one's life has to be the fact that he was born. Now, the mere fact of birth is manifestly an event over which we have no control. None of us asked to be born. We have no choice over what ethnic background we have. There are literally hundreds of different ethnic or cultural parents that we could of had. Yet, we had no choice whatsoever in this matter. We could have been born red, white, black, or yellow; and this fact, while having enormous consequences, was not in the least under our control. Whether we were born of rich or poor parents will affect our lives enormously and yet the simple accident of birth determined the whole economic status of our birth. The time of our birth, again, was totally out of our control; as consequently would be our astrological sign, which supposedly determines a whole lot about our personality. Our nationality depends entirely on the laws of the nation of which we were declared a citizen; again this was determined entirely by the accident of birth.

The type of religious, intellectual, and philosophical thinking we were exposed to in our formative years is also a matter of supreme importance; and yet, it is something over which *we* have no control. It has to be said that the thinking of our youth profoundly affects us throughout our lifetime. The type of training we received was determined by our guardians; and again, we have no control over who they were. Though our early teachers are normally our parents this is not always true. We are now exposed to other influences at a much earlier age due to such modern inventions as television. Dictators have always believed that it they could get control of a young mind early enough and train it to their standards the adult person would follow them. "As the twig is bent so shall the tree grow." It is a very rare and difficult exercise to successfully reject and overcome the religious, philosophical, and intelligent thinking of our youth. For example, most people die with the religion of their birth.

Most of the system of values by which we live is taught to us in little bits and pieces while we are young. Our reaction to drugs and other vices is often determined by our early training. The type of woman we marry is often determined by the image we have of our own mother as formulated by our relations with her. Contrariwise, this is also true of a woman based on the type of image she has formulated of her father. Our reaction to intellectual pursuits is again determined by the importance attached to education by our guardians. Our economic values are determined by the training we received early in life. Our attitude towards work falls in this same category. Every one of our actions based on our value systems will therefore be determined by the training we received early in life. Again, we had no control over the caliber of this training.

Lastly, the fact that one day we must die is again a matter over which we have no control. We may control where we die and to some extent when we die and how we die; but the fact of death is inevitable. All of these great occurrences affecting our lives are determined by factors other than ourselves; and they leave us somewhat helpless in the inevitable, inexorable sweep of events that control all our lives. The wise approach is to relax and enjoy it all.

EFFECTUALITY
"One person has a certain effect; yet, in the broad spectrum of life and nature even the greatest of us does not control our life nor the lives of others to any great degree."

The hardest thing to do is to get anyone to really listen to what you are saying. People, while they may give you polite lip service, are really not interested in what you are saying or doing. This has to be qualified. If what you are saying or doing affects others' lives as a supervisor for example, then they would be interested. However, if your works or actions exercise no control over their lives, then others are not interested. You are very lucky for another example, if you can even get a waitress or waiter in a restaurant to accurately record your order.

Mahatma Gandhi was a great man, yet his legacy or teachings were almost completely forgotten soon after his death. So, when you can't get anyone to listen to your ideas or thoughts, don't be discouraged because far greater people than yourself have tried without success.

We sometimes think the advertisements we read or see are outrageous. People will affect ridiculous dialects, appearances, or situations in their struggle to be unique and thereby noticed. You

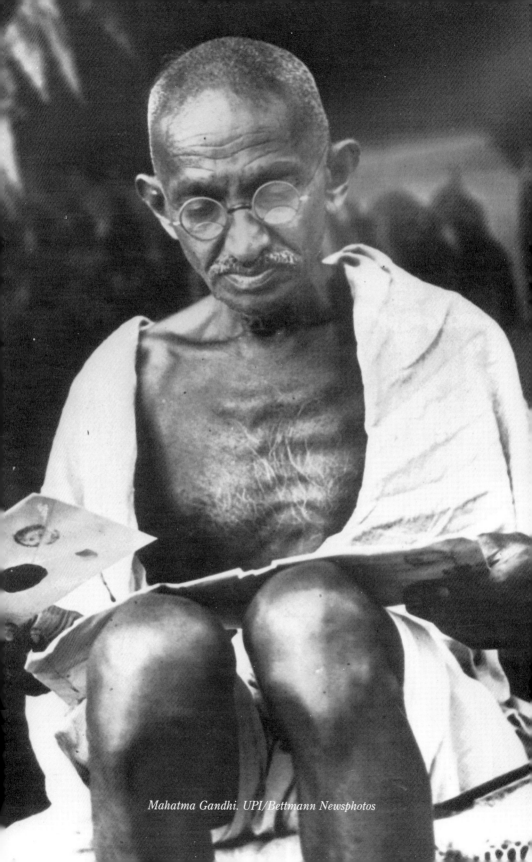

Mahatma Gandhi. UPI/Bettmann Newsphotos

have the entire entertainment world, the commercial world, the communications world, the political world, and every other kind of world imaginable struggling for your attention. If a situation is presented in an ordinary manner, you will not notice it. To attract, your attention, there has to be something different—hence, all the unique attempts to gain your attention.

Even after someone has attained a position of great importance and is able not only to gain your attention but is also able to have his ideas infiltrate your thinking, that person's effect will not be lasting. In the swirl of ideas and events that continue uninterrupted after his removal from the scene, his principles will soon be replaced by newer and fresher approaches to old problems. The point being that hardly anyone, regardless of his greatness, will dominate thinking for any great period of time after his death.

If these observations are true, and I submit they are, one should simply try to keep that little area of the world over which he exerts control in as fine a condition as possible. Do not worry unduly about the rest of humanity since they really are only worried about their own problems. Keep your home, your family, and your circle of acquaintances as happy as you possibly can and let your worries stop there. Remember also that as soon as your children grow up (and often before then) their interest turns to their own problems. You will certainly come second to their problems after they get married. If you don't, you at least should. So, to a great extent, whatever control you have is over your own life and you really control very little of that. Therefore, in order to be happy and not lead a life of disillusionment, be acutely aware of the severe limitations that beset you at every turn. This is all part of the master plan of living. Recognize it and live life on a realistic basis.

MONEY

"Money does not bring happiness nor does the lack of money bring unhappiness."

Just because you have great wealth and maturity and can have almost any sex partner you may want won't ensure your happiness. The lives of Freddie Prinz, Jean Harlow, Jimi Hendrix, James Dean, Montgomery Clift, Janis Joplin, Lenny Bruce, Marilyn Monroe, Rudolph Valentino, Elvis Presley, and many, many others will attest to this fact. Conversely, just because you lack great wealth does not mean you lack happiness. The lives of Dr. Albert Schweitzer, St. Thomas Acquinas, and Mahatma Gandhi attest to this fact.

Sheer money as a guarantee of happiness has proven to be quite unsatisfactory. Howard Hughes, who ruthlessly acquired wealth and power throughout his lifetime, found this to be brutally true. He believed, in his maddening dash for incredible wealth, that every man could be "bought" for a price. The only task was to find out what that price was and meet it. He relied only on wealth. Before he died he was surrounded by a group of larcenous souls whom he had "purchased"; and they made him a virtual prisoner of his own wealth. No one really cared for him in a loving, tender sense. He in turn cared for no one else. His only power and influence over others lay exclusively in his wealth. In a literal sense, he lived and died by the same sword, i.e., money as a weapon. J. Paul Getty, who deemed it necessary to install a pay telephone in his palatial mansion in England, is another example of the same mentality. He too died alone and friendless. It seems to be a rule without exception that excessive love of wealth and power always leads to tragedy and consequent unhappiness.

As a minimum, it is necessary to have the basic needs to life in order to be happy. One has to have clothes to cover his body; food to eat and shelter from the elements. Anything much beyond this is really not necessary for a happy meaningful life. The secret of the whole scenario seems to be that contentment with one's station is a prerequisite to happiness. This contentment, or lack of it, grows out of philosophical wisdom on the part of each of us. If you do not limit your desire for wealth, there is virtually no way for you to be happy. Thomas Gray (1716–1771) in his "Elegy Written in a Country Courtyard" (1750) states: "The boast of heraldry, the pomp of pow'r, and all that beauty, all that wealth e'er gave, avoids alike the inevitable hour: The paths of glory lead but to the grave."

So, if you want to be happy, look around and determine where you are positioned in life. If you are contributing by your work to the betterment of mankind in general, you will never have to worry about getting the minimum needs for satisfactory survival. This contribution can be in a million or more different ways. Basically it involves doing whatever you do to the best of your ability. This then becomes your contribution to humankind. Learn to be contented with your station in life. Want what you get. Don't ruin your disposition with envy of your peers. If you could swap their total life environment for yours and if you knew all the facts concerning their life, the likelihood is that you would keep what you have. So work hard, relax, and be contented with what you have; and let yourself and your loved ones be happy. That's what life is all about.

OPPORTUNITY
"Every problem that comes your way contains the seeds of your next opportunity."

A smooth sea never made a good mariner. A clear sky never made a good pilot. Steel can only be made by holding it in a hot forge. It is through our problems that we grow, mature, and become more proficient. A perfect life without trouble would be utterly boring. So be thankful for all your problems because each one of them presents an opportunity to grow and to become a better person.

You can look back over your own life and realize that occurrences, which at the time presented themselves as unwanted problems, were viewed later on as blessings in disguise. The alcoholic arrested for drunk driving who was intelligent enough to quit his drinking solved a grave problem in his life because he was arrested. The boy arrested for breaking into an automatic drink dispensing machine as a result of his erroneous ways can look back on the experience as benefiting his life. The gambler who lost all his money while he was young enough to recover and thereafter gave up gambling can look back at the whole experience as being beneficial. The hardworking businessman who developed health problems associated with tensions at age 35 and who changed his emotional reactions to business problems and thereafter lived a full healthy life can be said to have benefited from the whole experience.

Remember that every problem you will ever have contains, hidden inside it, the seeds of your next opportunity. Instead of becoming discouraged by problems, we should be thankful for them. We must simply be wise enough to benefit from the experience. Our character is strengthened through experiences which often include suffering. A little bit of suffering never hurt anyone. These incidents present invaluable opportunities to grow and become a better person. The wisest and most serene person among us is no doubt the person who has weathered the most storms on the sea of life. If you ever want to be truly wise you should welcome problems. They have the same beneficial effect on a man's character as does a file in the sharpening process of a saw. It results in a better product.

When a problem comes your way, don't panic. Smile and tell yourself that you will emerge from this experience as a wiser and better person. Don't let fear overwhelm you or impatience discourage you or greed depress you or pride anger you. Simply look at the problem in a calm detached manner and start peeling off the layers. If you peel long enough and search hard enough, you will find a "pearl" inside. To the intelligent person, this "pearl" makes the whole experience beneficial. If we know ahead of time that this is the case, we should welcome problems, not abhor them.

After all, the most successful people on this earth are usually the ones with the greatest number of problems to solve. Learn to be a problem solver rather than a problem hater.

HAPPINESS

"Remember that happiness is a primary goal of life."

When we seek happiness as our primary goal, we must realize that no one can be happy unless his entire life is based on ethical precepts. Happiness cannot be constructed on a foundation of another's unhappiness.

With the above qualifications in mind, you should seek happiness as your primary goal: a happiness that can only come from a life of integrity and ethics. Seek every opportunity you can find to help other people in their struggle along life's pathway. All of us have opportunities. Animals also need help on an almost daily basis. Who hasn't seen a wounded bird or a hungry dog in need of treatment or food or shelter?

Old and young have numerous needs which casual acquaintances can fill. It may be nothing more than opening a door or helping them across an intersection, carrying a bag of groceries or any one of a thousand little needs people have. Train yourselves to be on the lookout for these opportunities to be of service.

If you want to be unhappy, then remain totally preoccupied with your own selfish needs to the exclusion of everyone else. This method is the surest way to be friendless and unhappy. Such unfortunate people are concerned solely with their own needs and never consider others. These types are unfortunate because their lives will be increasingly filled with unhappiness.

The best way to stay happy is to stay and live as close to the truth as possible. Train yourself to recognize as much of the truth as quickly as possible in any situation. The more you practice this the more expert you will become. Don't live a fool's world of lies and false pride.

Figure yourself out as early as possible. Start with the assumption that you're imperfect and then list your imperfections. Beware of insincere compliments and false friends. As soon as you spot them, recognize immediately that those relationships will be severely limited. Any relationship based on lies and deception can never become very important. When the occasion demands a statement, tell people the truth as you see it or understand it. The truth is always most beautiful in the long run and the most productive of happiness for everyone concerned. *Remember, most of the people you know are not your friends; they are merely acquaintances.*

When your actions and words follow this broad outline, the will produce as much happiness in your life as possible. When you act in this manner you are striving to attain one of life's most intelligent goals.

DISCIPLINE
"Discipline is happiness."

The constant and unswerving adherence to a life of discipline increases our happiness and sense of well-being. To lead a contented life we must resist the temptations we all face, such as to eat too much, or eat the wrong kinds of food, to drink too much, to smoke, gamble, or take drugs, to be unfaithful to our mate, or any one of hundreds of desires that we all have, which if unchecked, will harm us in some way.

Let us consider a person who drinks too much alcohol, who gambles too much, who eats too much, and who smokes too much. These four vices are fairly common to many people. First, we must realize that it would be very difficult for such a person, unused to personal discipline, to "kick" all these negative habits or vices at the same time. The shock would be too great and the probability of success would consequently be greatly reduced. We must remember that someone with four habits, all of which are carried to any excess, is obviously an undisciplined person. Such a person first has to learn discipline. *It is also very important to believe that it is possible to kick any one of these negative habits.*

Let us assume the plan of attack involves giving up the drinking habit first. By just tackling one habit (drinking) while keeping the other three (smoking, gambling, and excessive eating) the chances of succeeding in this limited objective are increased. After a sufficient period of time has passed (maybe as much as a year) without any alcohol to drink, a person can obtain much satisfaction from the fact that the drinking habit has been conquered. This knowledge will fortify the belief that it is possible to kick a negative habit. A sense of personal discipline will develop that should encourage a further step to abolish (or kick) yet another negative habit.

Perhaps the best habit next selected for abolishment is gambling. Enough confidence is bound to exist since the drinking habit has been kicked to make it easier to abolish the gambling habit. With every successful exercise of personal discipline, will come a further enhancement in the personal power one possesses over negative desires and habits.

With the abolishment of both the drinking and gambling habits, a successful attack on the smoking and excessive eating habits becomes much easier. Once all four negative habits have been successfully abolished a sense of contentment and well-being will exist that far outweighs any pleasures that were derived from the practice of the vices or negative habits. This victory will greatly enhance the personal happiness that all disciplined people experience.

In order to preserve the victories, it may be necessary to occasionally list the pleasures derived from the continued abstinence from these habits versus the pleasures derived while they were being practiced. Since the pleasures of abstaining far exceed the pleasures derived from the practice of negative habits, such a comparison can only strengthen the resolve to continue the exercise of personal discipline.

RETICENCE

"The less you speak, the better off you tend to be in all of your activities."

People who talk excessively tend to be listened to the least. Their verbiage is so voluminous that the listener tends to "turn them completely off" in all their contacts. The law of supply and demand seems to be at work. The more words a person makes available to his listener, the less the demand seems to exist for his words. Conversely, the less words a person makes available to his listeners the more demand there seems to be for his conversation.

Most people, when they reach the end of their life, could have gotten along a lot better by speaking 50 percent less than they actually did. Most verbiage is redundant. Some people talk because they like the sound of their voice. When Lincoln uttered his immortal words at Gettysburg, he spoke less than five minutes while the principal speaker spoke for several hours. The only thing remembered by man of what was spoken at the dedicatory ceremonies at Gettysburg is Lincoln's speech. It is possible to observe, at a small conference or meeting, the value of a paucity of words. It can be noted that usually one or two people will be doing most of the talking. Usually there will be one or two people who speak perhaps only once during the whole meeting. When the meeting is over, the few words uttered by the silent ones will be remembered to the exclusion of the excessive verbiage of those who did most of the talking. Additionally, greater wisdom will frequently be attributed to those few words and to the person who uttered them than their inherent quality actually deserves. The verbose speaker may have uttered the greater wisdom, but this will be lost in the avalanche of his conversation. Winston Churchill was asked to give the commencement address at a University in England when he was in his middle eighties. People came from all over by the thousands to hear this great man deliver his address— many thinking that it could be his last public speech. After his introduction, Churchill simply said, "Never quit; never, never quit; never, never, never quit"; and sat down. Those nine words were his entire speech. He dealt with but one subject. How memorable and powerful must have been the impression of those words on the minds of his young listeners. When it was over, there could be no doubt that they remembered the advice of Churchill. That advice will probably be remembered by the listeners for the remainder of their lives. Churchill dealt with one subject, concisely and dramatically. Needless to say, he got his message across in a memorable manner.

When we speak briefly and to the point, we have the same impact on our listeners. If we speak too long or cover too many subjects, the whole meaning and purpose of our conversation tends to become lost in a haze of excess words. This is true whether we are giving a speech, engaging in a conversation, or attempting to instruct a subordinate or a child in some aspect of work or life. People are only capable of absorbing so much in any given conversation. Any attempt to teach too much will result in nothing being learned. It will all have become an exercise in futility. Likewise, if in a conversation too many subjects are discussed, the listener will remember nothing except the fact that the speaker was awfully wordy and tended to skip from subject to subject. If you are wise, you will realize that all of life's activities and social intercourse ultimately come down to what is possible—not to what is desirable, but to what is possible. If you want to inform your listener of one thing, do so and change the subject. It is not possible for the average listener to remember ten points concerning any subject. Unless the subject is technical, the probability exists that the ten points could have effectively been reduced to one point.

People who talk excessively have difficulty analyzing a person or situation effectively. Any subject usually has a controlling characteristic from which all other characteristics emanate. In analyzing a situation or a person, go beyond the question of what happened or what was said. Go instead to the far more important question of why it happened or why it was said. The "whys" in life produce far more meaningful answers that the "whats." Having asked "why" and obtained a truthful answer, any explanation becomes far briefer and more meaningful to the listener. The American people elected Nixon over Humphrey and Carter over Ford. These results have many "whats" to them. The "whys" will produce a much more brief and meaningful answer. Nixon was no doubt elected over Humphrey because the American people felt Nixon had more answers to inflation and the Vietnam War than did Humphrey. Carter was probably elected over Ford because Ford pardoned Nixon who was believed by the American people to be the architect of Watergate; and because after the excesses of Watergate, the apparent ethics and religious character of Carter came along at a time the American voters wanted ethics and integrity in government. They also probably felt that Ford, a mighty fine and honorable gentleman, was too close to the Nixon administration to represent any great change. It can be seen by this analysis that the question "why" always enables the speaker to give more concise and meaningful answers to an occurrence, situation or person. Always ask: "What is the highest force or the apocalyptic event which triggered the situation?" If an accurate analysis is made, then the explanation becomes simple and brief.

People tend to talk excessively when they don't understand what they are talking about or their information is not based on a complete set of facts. The more one engages his mind before he "turns on his mouth" the briefer will be his utterance. Wisdom tends to be brief while analyzing and ignorance tend to be lengthy.

Many times people are too lazy to get the facts and make up for a lack of knowledge by an excess of words. This fact is almost always discerned by the listener to the detriment of the speaker. The wisest course is to say nothing when the facts are unknown or only partially known. It becomes important for a person to learn what he does not know. A wise person does not have difficulty knowing the difference. Conversations can be greatly diminished in length when the speaker is thoroughly acquainted with his subject.

Public speakers will tell you that a long speech is not difficult to write and requires less knowledge of the subject than a short speech. When you give a short speech that is meaningful, you have to know what the most important aspect of your subject is and how to arrange each element in its proper place in order to have the maximum impact. The same is true of all the daily contacts human beings have with each other. The man who speaks the most tends to know the least; and the man who speaks the least tends to know the most. So, if you want to be respected, subject to the observations outlined in this chapter, keep your conversations short and to the point. Let your deeds do most of the speaking for you. The result will be that you will end up in far less trouble by your conversations; and your life will tend to be more tranquil and happy.

TRUTH

"Always speak and seek the truth; it is better than an untruth."

The greatest light in the world is the truth. It shines brighter and is more beautiful than any other version of a belief, condition, or past occurrence. Truth has a special ring to it that is recognizable and which carries with it its own special beauty. When one hears the full truth, it is somehow apparent as such and places the speaker in a credible light. People who have a habit of speaking the truth are soon recognized for this and acquire in the process an enviable reputation. The aura surrounding a truthful person is a great benefit in the furtherance of any goals he may have.

The truth is best spoken when it does not needlessly or brutally offend someone. Many times a speaker of the truth is best advised to stand mute and say nothing. To speak the truth does not necessitate that it be done at the embarrassment of someone else, when to do so does not contribute to the furtherance of a conversation or a situation. One should not thoughtlessly pronounce a truth with the insensitivity of a non-caring person. The truth should always be spoken with a high regard for the feelings of others.

When an individual speaks only the truth as he knows it, his heart will be gladdened and his spirit will be lifted. Speaking the truth brings a very special blessing to the practitioner. His heart is lightened and his nervous system tranquilized. When the truth is always spoken, an individual can, on every occasion, speak without trying to remember if he spoke the same way on the same subject in a previous situation. He can speak without fear of contradiction or embarrassment. He need not have a good memory concerning his prior utterances. He need not try to remember whether he spoke to the same individual previously and whether or not he said the same thing before. He can be relaxed and tranquil. He need not ever worry about "loss of face" or reputation by his spoken word.

A dedication to the truth will not permit an individual to repeat a story, the details of which may or may not be true. A "speaker of the truth" is not a gossip-monger. Practically everything one hears in the form of "gossip" is usually 10 percent truth and 90 percent fiction. People who spread gossip are almost never respected by their peers. If an individual will spread a malicious rumor about someone else, the listener realizes this same individual will do the same thing about him.

When one forms a habit of speaking the truth, he will find a happiness that is solely attributable to this practice. Additionally, this same individual will develop his powers to recognize the truth far more accurately than ever before. If he trains himself to look for the truth in any situation, he will soon find that his powers of perception are amazingly increased. When one is able to see the truth in any situation, his judgments are far more accurate, and his progress in life toward his goals will be much more rapid and pronounced. The ability to judge people accurately can be immeasurably increased by following the habit of seeking and speaking the truth. This ability, once well developed, is an enormous asset for anyone to possess.

Once an individual speaks only the truth, be becomes free to accomplish higher goals which he may have set for himself in life. He does not become mired in the muck of deception and intrigue that is the natural accompaniment of lies and falsehoods. No longer does he have to expend energy and time needlessly on the facts of life. All problems can only be solved if the facts are known. If one is trained to seek the facts, once they are known the solution generally becomes easy. The hard part is to get the facts. Distorted facts result in inadequate solutions which tend to solve nothing. The truth over a period of time tends to keep an individual out of serious trouble and unhindered by needless complications. Once an individual is traveling down a road paved with the truth, he becomes free to concentrate all his talent and energy on his life's goal. The feeling from this source alone adds immeasurably to an individual's happiness.

Truths spoken may not be appreciated at the time of their utterance but will always be recognized ultimately for their worth. If a drunk is told he has had too much to drink in order to drive safely, he will ultimately appreciate this advice. If a young person is told they have to apply themselves more to their studies, they will ultimately realize the wisdom of the utterance. Had some of the Nixon administration insiders spoken out earlier during

Watergate, they would have ultimately been appreciated for their truthfulness. Truth is always the most beautiful comment one can make; and it gets better with age. Lies depreciate with the passing of time whereas truth appreciates. Liars decrease in stature with the passing of time; and truthful people increase in stature with the passing of time. The final or ultimate impression of a truthful statement is always good while the final or ultimate impression of a lie is always bad. Ultimately the truth will be recognized and appreciated. Contrariwise, a lie will be recognized; and when it is, it will be detested.

A person who lies creates a lot of needless tension and unhappiness both for himself and others who may be the target of his untruths. He has to live in fear of being caught in a falsehood which, when it occurs, will cast him in a bad light. Lies are negative forces and always come from the mouths of people who are frightened and insecure. Their motives and causes are as varied as mankind himself; but the result is always to bring dishonor on the liar. Lies tend to make the mind of the liar restless and turbulent. Practiced enough, it can affect his sleeping ability and ultimately the general condition of his health. It will surely affect his success in life. Once an individual is branded or regarded as a liar, he will lose the respect of his peers; and his chances of success in his life's endeavors will be greatly diminished. His mouth will have become his worst enemy.

On the basis of wisdom alone, and if you please, purely on a selfish basis if nothing else, it is far better to always tell the truth. When this is done, your spirit is free to pursue higher goals. Your business or job or career opportunities become increased in number as well as their ease of attainment. Ultimately, we are all looking for a simple, happy life. Why place artificial stumbling blocks in our path to impede our progress? Why become one's own worst enemy? Why not let the golden light of the truth be reflected in all our utterances? It will be far more conducive to happiness.

The greatest falsehood in life is the half-truth. Nazi Germany was, and Communist dictators were the masters of the half-truth. The end result of a half-truth is to completely distort the real significance of an incident or occurrence. The distortion mixed with a little bit of credibility makes a falsehood more believable and the sinister nature of the practice even more diabolical. A person who persistently twists the truth to serve his own purpose, will soon be recognized accurately for his techniques and be judged in an unfavorable light by his peers. The truth includes giving a totally accurate picture and impression of a situation. A half-truth or a distorted version of the truth is the greatest lie of all.

If you want to be happy and lead a simple and contented life, learn to deal only with the truth.

CONCERN

"Any matter of direct interest or one that creates anxiety
or worry in a person can be said to concern that person."

The extent of such concern that one feels goes a long way towards defining such a persons intellect, character and compassion. Expanding concerns to an international level has resulted in the creation of the United Nations. It can be said that any gross injustice that exists anywhere in the world is the legitimate concern of the United Nations. Philosophers and thinkers throughout the ages have held that if one having the power to correct evils or injustices refrains from so doing then such inaction is tantamount to saying that injustice can be permitted to prevail everywhere. The British Empire and other empires historically have concerned themselves with the happenings throughout their respective spheres of influence. The United States in 1996 is without an equal among the nations of the world in concerning itself with events and injustices that occur and policies that exist everywhere in the world. In the realm of international politics, concern is nothing more than enlightened self-interest.

Concern, from the standpoint of an individual person is quite another matter. This type of concern goes a long way towards making this planet and the United States a more pleasant and enjoyable place to live and work. Existence would be governed by the law of the jungle were it not for human concerns for one another. Admittedly we do not live in a perfect world, but to the extent that reasonable people have genuine concerns for the less fortunate, the joys of living and working are greatly enhanced.

Concern that is motivated primarily by a personal selfish self-interest is not the caliber of concern contemplated by this discussion. A concern that is created by a genuine compassion for a fellow human's plight and unrelated to such a caring person's personal affairs is the type of magnanimous concern that benefits the world.

Concern and nothing more is ineffectual and meaningless. Once an injustice, a hardship, or a tragedy has been spotted, the next logical and proper step is to take meaningful action. Shedding tears and nothing else will benefit no one. Effective action must be taken on a timely basis, to alleviate, treat or assuage the pain and suffering that may be taking place. To be a mere spectator in the balcony of life while profusely expressing sympathy for the suffering taking place in the main "arena" is wholly inadequate.

The greatest example of concern that was not followed by effective action was the world's response to Adolph Hitler's monstrous treatment of the Jews. The world knew, the world watched, the world expressed concern, but the world did nothing while Hitler and his criminal thugs executed millions of Jews in Germany's death camps. This is the type of so-called concern that this discussion seeks to condemn. Admittedly it can be very difficult to speak out about grievous wrongs that are taking place in a community, because it usually means opposing the enemy that's in your own backyard. It's not the one in the state house or the

White House but the one who can get right in your face. But these are the most important injustices to eliminate, since they exist where people live and work. If this can be done in every little community throughout our great country, the quality of our national life will be greatly enhanced.

FEAR

"I have rarely met with two-o'clock-in-the-morning courage."
—Napoleon Bonaparte
"The only thing I am afraid of is fear."
—Arthur Wellesley, the Duke of Wellington
"Courage is resistance to fear, mastery of fear—not absence of fear."—Mark Twain said, "The only thing we have to fear is fear itself."
—President Franklin Delano Roosevelt
"The thing I fear most is fear."
—Montaigne, 16th century

It would be a very simple matter to find hundreds of great intellects from history who expressed similar views regarding fear. Fear is something we all must confront and learn how to deal with it. Everyone who ever lived has experienced it many times in his or her life. All the great thinkers of the past have relegated fear to the level of a totally negative emotion. Fear is instinctive in most human beings and can be utterly destructive of happiness, success and general well-being. It keeps people from being what they otherwise could be if they could only learn how to discard fear along with its utterly destructive powers.

Teach yourself not to entertain or to dwell on your fears. If you let fear roam freely through your mind you will become paralyzed by its powerful presence. The longer you let fear exist in your mind and capture your thinking processes, the greater will be your incapacity and the consequent injury to your life's goals.

It has reduced many human beings to ineffective, unhappy, frustrated, noncontributing, unsuccessful creatures. Fear and all its consequences and excesses is nothing but a habit that many people allow to dominate and control their destinies.

When fear comes "knocking" at your mind and heart you have to let yourself know immediately that it is not welcome in your life. Make it go away by replacing it with pleasant thoughts. Convince yourself that you have the option through your will power and intellect, to establish zero tolerance for its presence in your life. Practice this unfriendly attitude towards fear as a continuing habit. You will be pleasantly surprised how this approach will add quality to your existence and give you a peace of mind, success and render you popular amongst your family and acquaintances. All you must do is simply make fear unwelcome in your existence. Eventually it will get the message and seek more receptive victims.

Nothing is this section is intended to convey the idea that fear can be totally eliminated from your or anyone else's life. A certain amount of fear is healthy and could keep a person out of harms way. Its only when it becomes a dominating, a constant, an illogical, a disabling and a destructive presence that fear needs to be seriously classified as an aberration. If you can't get it to subside by your own mental processes then by all means seek professional help. Excessive and uncontrolled fear can make a person's life miserable and on most occasions it can be corrected by the slightest use of logic and common sense.

PART II
Your Health

Relaxation

*"Try to live a relaxed existence. Tension reduces the quality
of our lives. Most tension is artificially and needlessly created."*

When we are relaxed, everything we do and say is more enjoyable and better accomplished. Most tension is based on fear,
selfishness, pride, and/or insecurity. In order to be relaxed, we
have to learn to overcome our fears, reduce our pride, become
less selfish and increase our security. Relaxation is a way of life
with wise people. It is the sort of thing we can develop if we work
at it. If you find yourself half-running to an appointment, catch
yourself, slow down, and start ambling towards your destination.
You will be fresher when you get there and more effective in accomplishing whatever your objectives were in going to the meeting. We like to be around relaxed people. Tense people make others nervous. They are not enjoyable company. Being relaxed reduces itself to being wise.

Fear is the greatest producer of tension in mankind. Fear is a
way of life with some people. They literally fear everything. Again,
one's wisdom can go a long way towards overcoming whatever we
fear. We may fear the loss of the love of a woman, or we may have
the fear of going bankrupt; fear of failing in an undertaking, of
being humiliated or of any one of a thousand different things. If
we sit down and rationally assume that the worst possible result
has occurred, we will soon realize that its occurrence is not as
catastrophic as we feared. We will soon seen that we can live quite
comfortably with the result. Most fears are based on nebulous, ill-
considered occurrences which in fact do not have the tragic results that we first imagined.

Pride produces a lot of tension. It is difficult to relax when we
have too much pride. Pride makes us very vulnerable to criticism
and fear of failure. Humility, which wisdom can give us, will go a
long way towards reducing any tension emanating from pride.

Selfishness creates tension because such a person is always unduly concerned lest he not receive his disproportionate share of all good things. This is uppermost in his mind, and results in his being constantly upset at the possibility of not receiving his expected share of life's blessings. Since a selfish person is a "taker," his concern is always about keeping or receiving something he values. True giving never occurs to him as being a particularly worthwhile occupation. Because of these problems, a selfish person is seldom a relaxed person.

Insecure people have a difficult time trying to relax. They never feel assured of their place or of their basic self worth. This constant questioning of their basic position leaves them little time to deal intelligently with a problem or a situation. Their mind is constantly turned inward towards themselves instead of outward toward the world and its problems. Under these circumstances, an insecure person has great difficulty relaxing.

Yet, life can be enjoyed mostly if you are relaxed both mentally and physically. Relaxation starts with a tranquil mind. In order to have a tranquil mind, we have to think pleasant, peaceful thoughts. All disturbing thoughts have to be driven from our mind. Wisdom can do this, coupled with practice and determination. We have to learn to understand ourselves and how to improve ourselves. The battle for relaxation can only be won in the mind. It resolves into a question of wisdom. So get wise and learn to relax.

Food

"We are what we eat."

Modern experience indicates clearly that our health is directly related to our diet. We are learning more each day about the effect foods have on our health. The result is that eating habits have changed drastically during the last generation. People are being more particular about what they put in their bodies in general.

Our well-being is linked to the water we drink, the alcohol we consume, and the food we eat. If this be the truth, then an intelligent person should watch what he puts in his body.

A lot of people overeat and gain a lot of weight; then they go on a "crash" diet and lose weight. Once they get their weight at a level that is agreeable, they go back to their old eating habits and start gaining weight again. The newly gained weight is followed by another crash diet and thus the cycle endlessly continues. Some people, by this "roller-coaster" habit of eating, have literally lost many hundred of pounds over the period of their adult life. They are really never content with themselves because they are either on some ridiculous diet or are overeating. They have difficulty keeping clothes that fit the ever changing size of their body. The single business or practice of eating thus becomes a very unsettling factor in such a person's life. This is true because this type of person has never established sane habits for eating.

What is needed in everyone's life is a system of eating that permanently maintains weight at a desirable level. Once the proper formulas or combinations of food have been determined, we should adopt permanently a diet that meets our weight and energy requirements. The search for the right quantity and types of foods to eat is not very difficult. It should start with a book on calories. These books are not very lengthy and they give the reader a clear insight into which foods contain what number of calories. Once these charts become reasonably familiar, you will find yourself eating on the basis of the caloric content of food. It will be easy for you to decide upon the ideal number of calories you should consume on a daily basis. Having aimed at an ideal total, it then becomes simple to watch your caloric intake. The idea is to start thinking in terms of a permanent diet; of caloric intake; ideal weights; and above all else on the types of food you should eat.

I personally believe that the best diet for everyone should be limited to vegetables, fruits, and nuts. We should not smoke or consume drugs and/or alcohol of any form, and once this regimentation has been established I think we should then be on the proper course. We should eat to survive and not for pleasure. If however, the above diet does not suit you, then I would additionally recommend fish and poultry. Under no circumstances should you eat red meat. Drink a lot of water that does not contain chemicals, especially chlorine. Mountain mineral waters are available for this purpose.

Once you get your weight at your desired level, it becomes a simple matter of personal discipline to keep it there. Think of the pleasures of being healthy with your body in the desired condition. Your entire welfare depends on it. Your life will have a great quality to it. Your happiness and self respect will exceed that of your friends, who do not pursue such a wise dietary course.

ENDURANCE

Life can be a terribly exciting and fun-filled experience. It has dark days and bright days, wet days and dry days, warm days and cold days. Life has days that are difficult and days that are easy; days that are sad and days that are happy; days when we receive good news and days when we receive bad news; days when we feel well and days when we feel sick; days when we are victorious and days when we fail. That variety is what lends color and depth to our existence. The totality of it all represents the human experience.

Before we can be in a position to get the most from each of life's undulations, we must learn to endure. Isometrics teaches us that we must hold a muscular position of strain for a period of time with our breath inhaled in order to gain the maximum benefits for our body's conditioning. And so it is with the business of living a full life; we must learn to endure while undergoing strain or tension. This ability, fully developed, gives us an enormous feeling of well-being and accomplishment.

Toys are made that march across a room and the instant they run into a wall, they immediately turn and go in another direction. The first obstacle changes the course of the toy. And so it is with a lot of us in life, when we are going great towards a given goal and change our direction because we run into the slightest obstacle. Overcoming hurdles adds a great feeling of self-achievement to our personality. It builds character. In order to achieve difficult objectives, we have to learn the pleasure of endurance. Unlike the toy which changes direction the instant it runs into a wall, we, in life, must test the strength of that wall for a reasonable time. We must not continuously run into an impenetrable or insurmountable wall; to do so, would be foolish and self-defeating. But we must endure long enough to either conclude that an obstacle is insurmountable or that its conquest is not worth the effort. Before we can truthfully ascertain these facts, a reasonable amount of endurance must be exercised.

Nothing worth achieving can be done without varying degrees of difficulty. Learning to play golf or the piano; getting an education or developing friendships all require the need for "staying power" or endurance. Overcoming hardships is the only way worthwhile goals can be achieved. The history of great achievers is often the story of people who endured beyond the normal. Franklin Roosevelt with his polio; Helen Keller who was deaf, dumb, and blind; Beethoven who wrote some of his greatest works while almost totally deaf; and Thomas Edison, with his severe hearing problem, are but a few of the many examples available.

Life is so rich and full when we meet all challenges with endurance. The sooner we realize this, the more meaningful will be our existence. It is fun to endure. It is as necessary a part of successful living as eating and breathing. The underprivileged person is really the one who has never had to endure; the one whose obstacles were overcome for him by someone else. Conversely, the privileged individual is the one who has successfully endured long enough to have surmounted many obstacles. This endurability must continue as long as we live.

RELAXATIONAL VARIETY

"Living is like climbing a mountain, difficult and strenuous. Therefore, it is necessary to occasionally 'get off the mountain' and rest and relax. To stay on the mountain continuously is to never be refreshed, to dull your thinking and to ruin your creativity and efficiency."

Hard work is a necessary part of a happy life. Only hard work can result in "soul-enriching" or worthwhile achievement. Anything easily obtained is not too highly regarded. That which comes after strenuous effort is prized and productive of a sense of well being.

Though hard work is necessary for a meaningful existence, the human body and mind are comparable to a machine. Constant uninterrupted stress will tear it down. Periodic periods of spiritual and physical rebuilding are necessary to keep the "human machine" functioning for its maximum duration at its ultimate efficiency. As Uncle Remus did, we must find a "laughing place" where we can "recharge" our human battery. One's ability to occasionally "get off the mountain" and retreat to the "proper cave" goes a long way to determining just how happy and successful a person will become.

These necessary periods of relaxation must be found and enjoyed. Destructive vices such as alcohol, drugs, gambling, etc., do not relax an individual, but only in the final analysis make him more tense. His body will often endure greater stress during these misspent periods of "relaxation" than if such a person continued to work without interruption.

The more types of wholesome recreation one can develop, the greater the benefits. Learn to enjoy many and varied activities.

Don't go overboard on just one method of relaxation for example. To do so is to run the danger of over-dependence. For example, to rely solely on the game of golf for relaxation could result in a severe emotional crisis if for some reason one became physically unable to play the game. The more wholesome ways one has to spend his periods of relaxation the more secure will be his emotional well-being.

Anyone who, when questioned about his continuous and uninterrupted work habits replies, "my work is my hobby," is telling you that he has not been wise enough to develop interests outside of his work. A person who only works usually does not live long once he retires. These recreational habits have to be developed early in life. You cannot sit back smugly and say that "my work is my whole life and when I retire I'll find something else to keep me happy." By the time such a person retires, he simply does not know how to enjoy anything but work and soon becomes a very sad spectacle.

Just remember that hard work and happy hours spent in wholesome recreational activity are both necessary to a happy and creative mind and a healthy body. The more recreational activities we enjoy the broader will be our base of enjoyment and the greater will be our physical and emotional well-being and happiness.

RELAXATION TRICKS

"You should learn all the little tricks it takes to relax.
It is difficult to be happy and successful if you are tense."

Tenseness is a quality that prevents many people from enjoying life. It is not difficult in the modern world to become "uptight." Usually this is founded on ignorance, greed, jealousy, unresolved anger, unresolved fears, selfishness, or foolish pride. Sometimes people adopt a tense life-style as a matter of habit. It is not difficult to learn how to relax. The first thing a person should learn to do is to overcome his fears. The average person comes into this world with unresolved fears. As he gains in wisdom and maturity, he starts to overcome his fears. Actually, all he has done is arrive at an understanding of what caused those fears in the first place. We should all approach the subject of fears with the conviction that they can be overcome. Most successful people learn how to do it with their own mental processes. However, some perfectly wise people may need the help of outside professional counseling. The important thing to know is that your fears can be overcome and once this happens, your ability to relax will be greatly increased. Foolish pride can cause a person to have continuing tenseness. All it takes to eliminate this hindrance to relaxation is to know that pride is counterproductive and creates tension and unhappiness. Learn to replace this harmful characteristic with dignity, humility, and thankfulness. When this occurs, your ability to relax will be further increased. An extremely selfish person is usually a tense person. Selfishness in your dealings with other people produces much friction. This friction wreaks havoc in relationships and consequently produces much tension for everyone concerned. Learn to deal with it if you can't eliminate your selfishness. Think of the other person; when your mind deals with his problems, it will not be thinking of your own self-interest. When you no longer dwell on your own self interest, you have eliminated the principal trait leading to selfishness. Once this becomes a habit, you have surmounted another obstacle to your ability to relax.

Usually a relaxed person is a happy person. A relaxed person tends to be an effective and respected person. A relaxed person often has many friends. People like to be around relaxed or easygoing people. Tense people make others ill-at-ease and they shy away from them. People who are congenial and relaxed are usually liked by their co-workers and are often promoted before someone who is tense and introspective.

Thus, it becomes a wise objective to learn to be relaxed. Believe that you too can be relaxed. It is very important that you believe this. Once you have embarked on a course towards relaxation, try and isolate those factors in your life which make you tense. Is it your uncontrollable temper? Your greed? Your lust? Covetousness? Jealousy? Fear? Are there certain people who make you nervous when you are in their company? Is it an addiction of some sort? Whatever the answer, immediately start to work on eliminating the problem from your life, or if it can't be eliminated, then change the way you let it affect you. If you don't know what the problem is then it would be wise to seek professional counseling. Briefly, you should do those things that relax you as often as possible and reduce to an utter minimum those things that make you tense. Physical exercise is the most healthful and effective means of reducing your tensions. But this will vary for different people. As Uncle Remus said in the great Walt Disney movie, *The Song of the South*, "You've got to find your 'Laughing Place.'" Just be sure it's healthy and doesn't lead to more serious problems as is the case with drugs and alcohol. You don't need these to relax if you're wise and want to be happy.

EXERCISE

"Physical exercise accomplished when your mind is tranquil and relaxed is necessary for a healthy and happy life."

Relaxed exercise carried out routinely keeps your muscles toned and improves your overall well-being. Your body becomes sedentary and your circulation diminishes if you don't routinely undergo vigorous exercise. A very important part of your body that needs exercise is your backbone. It houses the electrical system that runs from your brain to the various working parts of your body. If you don't manipulate your spine through regular exercise the entire system of electrical impulses will be slowed down affecting your whole body. This will produce sluggishness of both a physical and mental nature. Another important thing to do is to get blood into the upper part of your body by standing on your head. When you do this you reverse the pull of gravity on your organs. Instead of pulling them down as gravity does throughout your lifetime, you stand on your head and pull them upward.

The type of exercise one takes is very important. Aside from the obvious beneficial effects, jogging can be very damaging to the pelvis connection at your hips. When your feet strike the ground while jogging, your body weight is multiplied two or three times, having a damaging effect on the ball of your hip where it joins the pelvic region. "Sit-ups" are harmful to your back. "Push-ups" hurt the sockets of your arms where they join your shoulder. The best exercise is where you put pressure on your muscles, inhale, and hold both your breath and the muscle tension for 20 seconds. Then when you release the tension, exhale. This is essentially the same exercise a feline takes to keep muscle tone, even under conditions of captivity. The lung exercise which goes with the muscle exercise is of extreme importance. These isometric or possibly yoga-type exercises can be accomplished in 15 minutes in the morning. Thirty minutes a day is not too much time to invest in keeping that mechanical gadget, your body, in the best possible working condition.

The unexpected bonus one receives from faithfully following this exercise program is that somehow you will learn more about yourself than you ever knew before. Gradually, you will build up a discipline that you never ever knew you possessed. This discipline will extend to areas totally removed from exercise. It will extend to your negative habits such as alcohol, tobacco, or drug consumption. In some strange fashion your whole life will be much more disciplined. It won't happen suddenly, but will occur after you become addicted to this exercise program.

Great advantages result in the way you will feel physically and mentally. You cannot start an exercise program of the type described herein without your mind eventually turning to your dietary practices. When this happens your health will improve noticeably. With this improvement will come a marked increase in your competency at work. In short, your life will be improved in numerous ways. Primarily, you will feel better all the time.

MORE NOTES ON EXERCISE

"Physical and mental health can be attained by the right type of exercise."

This chapter discusses probably the most important thing a person can do to be physically and emotionally healthy. A person who is not prevented from taking exercise by a physical handicap greatly increases his chance for happiness if he will follow this chapter and the one on dieting or some similar type program.

The following isometric and breathing exercises can be done in 30 minutes in your bedroom either in the morning or evening. After you have followed this program for six months, your entire life will change for the better. You will be amazed at what it does for your physical and mental well being.

Do as many of the following exercises as your physical condition permits:

1. Stand on your head in the following manner and count to 500.

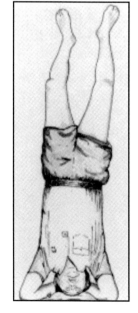

2. While standing, tense your arms and upper body muscles in the illustrated manner 10 times. Breathe deeply while tensing your muscles and exhale while relaxing the muscles. Hold your tense muscular position and your deep breath while you count to 20.

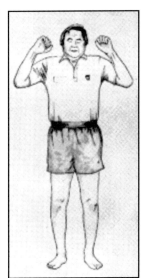

3. Squat in the position noted while counting to 50.

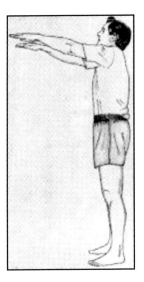

4. Circle your head to the right and to the left 135 times each way.

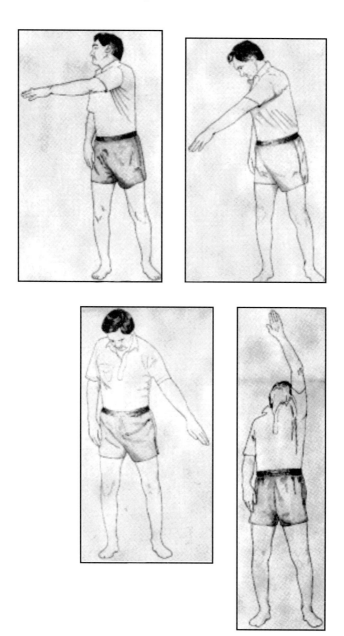

5. Do the bend exercise 20 times, breathing in when you straighten up and exhaling when you bend over and touch the floor.

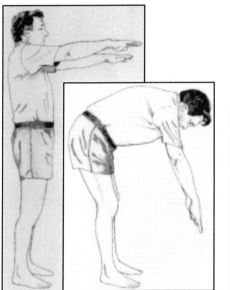
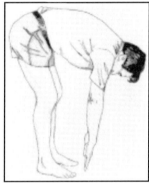

6. Do 15 sit-ups in the manner indicated, inhaling when you sit up and exhaling when your back is straight.

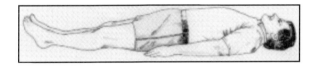
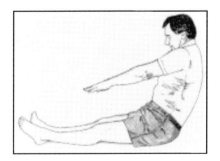

7. Do this 20 times: inhale and hold your breath while counting to 20 each time your back is arched and release your breath as your back is straightened.

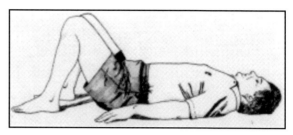

8. Tense your arms and fists and take a deep breath and hold this position while you count to 20. Exhale and release your muscle tension. Repeat this process 10 times while holding your legs straight and off the floor continuously throughout the exercise.

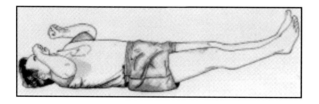

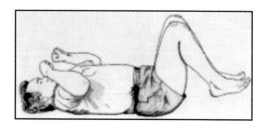

9. While lying on your left side, grab your right foot with your right hand and hold this position while counting to 50. Then, move to your right side and reverse the process with your left hand, grabbing your left foot.

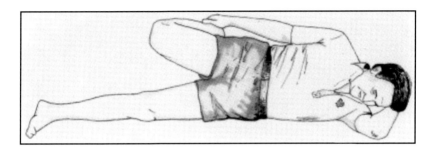

10. Move your stomach muscles in and out 150 times while breathing deeply with each movement of your stomach.

 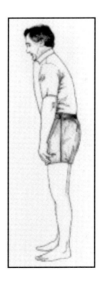

You can alternate the order of these exercises as you see fit. Once you start following this program you will soon become addicted to it. The best time to do these exercises is in the morning. Before you do it in the morning, you should eat a good fibrous cereal with skim milk and fruit. When you finish your morning exercise, your body will release all the waste material it has accumulated in the previous 24 hours. Getting rid of these poisons promptly on a daily basis is extremely important. This exercise will make constipation a "thing of the past" in your life.

After you are thoroughly addicted to this exercise program you will find that you have no trouble staying relaxed. It will relieve your tensions without the use of harmful agents such as drugs or alcohol. The program will help you sleep. It will reshape your body. It will cause you to concentrate more effectively and continuously on the overall condition of your health. You will eventually be less inclined to harm your body with drugs, alcohol, and cigarettes when you see so many benefits coming from your exercise program. Being more healthy and relaxed, you will be more successful in your work. These exercises will reduce your blood pressure and your pulse rate.

In short, you will become a happier and healthier person by investing 30 minutes a day in this exercise.

EXERCISE AND HAPPINESS

"Energy expended is energy received. A physically active life tends to be a happy life."

The great tendency of all mankind is to "take it easy" from a physical standpoint. Lethargy is the age-old enemy of good health. We all prefer lying in a hammock, lounging on the beach, lying in bed watching television, or any one of an innumerable array of sedentary habits which tend to be the easy way to pass the time.

Television more than any other single factor, has caused us

to become lazy not only physically but also mentally. The first thing most people do when they get up in the morning is turn on the TV and watch the morning news. The last thing most of us do at night is turn off the TV before we go to sleep. The hours spent watching television are hours in which we are completely inert, with the additional probability that we are munching on some foodstuff which does little else other than make us fat. We also tend to go to movies, where we sit and eat popcorn and/or confections while we watch a production, the quality of which is continually on the decline. Everywhere we go and everything we are exposed to invites us to sit back and relax while someone or something entertains us and probably does our thinking for us. This tendency of modern life to relax, relax, relax has gotten man to the point where widespread hypertension permeates the population as never before. Good old-fashioned exercise has literally become a habit of the past. If we have two or three blocks to go, we get in the car and drive. The idea of walking is a prospect seldom seriously considered. Modern technology has taken most of the physical exertion out of industry and reduced the whole need to that of pushing a button. The opportunity to get physical exercise in the normal course of our life is almost nonexistent, so that many people tend to be overweight. Mankind suffers from many ailments emanating from a simple lack of physical exertion. People constantly complain of nervousness, feeling badly, an inability to sleep, improper bowel movements, and many other ailments that tend to develop in a person who leads a lethargic life. In order to escape from this syndrome of inactivity, it is necessary to do those thing which will cause one to escape from the modern life cycle and return to the physical activities of the past.

In order to lead a happy life, you have to be physically active. It is one of the ironies of life that in order to have physical energy, one has to expend physical energy. It is the same old story—the more you give the more you will receive. In order to keep yourself physically fit, some daily physical activity should be engaged in that will result in perspiration forming on the body and the heart beating rapidly for several minutes. This is with the understanding that your physical condition has not deteriorated to the point where physical exercise of a strenuous nature will present a danger. This can only be determined by a licensed physician who, along with other techniques, is able to administer a stress test which will predict one's capability to undergo physical exercise. When the heart begins pumping rapidly, a person's entire system is re-energizing. Blood is vigorously pumped into every part of the body and especially to the brain, which controls all body functions. This rapid pumping of blood, as a result of physical exercise, renews more effectively all working or functioning parts of the body. If you submit your body to the above process, when it is all over and you have taken a shower to refresh yourself, a good feeling will come over you. Your mind feels fresh and alert, and your body feels vigorous and refreshed. In short, you have more energy than you would have had by not taking exercise. You also feel more relaxed and tranquil. A quiet confidence in yourself seems to come to the forefront of your being. Your personality brightens and your work does not seem as tedious and unpleasant. Everything and everyone takes on a more favorable hue. Also, you feel alive and more capable of handling life's problems.

You should seriously consider which type of exercise is best for you. Our Western culture advocates the very physical type such as jogging, swimming, bicycling, handball, volleyball, tennis, golf, touch football, and myriad activities the result of which is to place your entire circulatory system under physical stress while the activities continue. The Far Eastern cultures advocate yoga, meditation, and other activities which are less strenuous, but if carefully followed (especially yoga), tend to put an individual in excellent physical condition. Remarkable results have been obtained by the studious practice of the ancient art of yoga for as little as 15 minutes a day. Generally, it explains why a lion or tiger enclosed in a small cage never has muscular atrophy at a time and under conditions in which it has no room for physical exercise. In fact, the very concept of yoga was first suggested to the Far Eastern culture by observing a tiger or a lion stretching extensively in a small cage.

The author will not recommend his preference for Western exercise versus yoga. Yoga would seem to be more appropriate for those persons who have more fragile health. Most large cities have yoga centers which, for a fee, will teach the student the ancient practice of yoga. Additionally, many books are available explaining in detail the intricacies of the art. Yoga teachers and literature stress the beneficial effect of yoga on the tranquillity of the mind. Generally, physical exercise of all forms has this additional important effect.

Health spas have sprung up all over the United States where Western-type physical conditioning is taught under supervised conditions. Charts are maintained on the members so progress can be graphically measured. These exercises include sit-ups, push-ups, leg-lifts, swimming, jogging, and many other activities designed to put one's body and mind in better condition. Usually, if the only incentive a person has in taking any of these exercises is to put his body in shape so he looks better, the probability is that such a person will not long continue in a health program. What should be sought after is an actual love of doing physical exercise for the sheer enjoyment of it. Once this attitude is attained, then the probability exists that the student or practitioner will continue physical exercise in varying degrees all his life. The need, therefore, exists to enjoy the activity required in physical conditioning. Joggers believe that to engage fully in the sport over a lengthy period of time, one has to love to run. If you jog simply to be with your friends or if you jog simply to attain certain desirable physical measurements, then the probability is that the practice will not continue. Whether your activity is swimming or bicycling or jogging or tennis, try to develop a love for the activity. To do so will tend to ensure its continuance. If you look at the activity as some horrible sacrifice or ordeal that you must endure daily, then the entire undertaking will be short-lived.

Once a physical activity has been incorporated permanently in your lifestyle, you will become more conscious of all your health habits. (This includes such undesirable habits as excessive drinking, smoking, drugs or other poisons which tend to deteriorate your health.) After a period of time, new vistas will open to you. No longer will you feel too tired to do things. Activities of all kinds will be enjoyed more. Your life will take on new meaning. Your professional, business, or occupational careers will become more successful. All your goals will become easier to attain. You will be pleased with the way you look and feel. Simply, you will have added a new dimension to your life.

PART III
Yourself

ACCOUNTABILITY AND MATURITY
"Blame yourself for your problems and you will improve as a human being."

The easiest short-term solution to failures in life is to blame the next person for one's problems. It is a very easy way to explain failures of any description. For example, the author once knew a lawyer who promised potential clients remarkable results if they would let him handle the case—results that he must have known were impossible to attain. He would promise anything just to get the case and the fee. When the results turned out far less favorably to his client, he used a very glib excuse, "I'm sorry," he would say, "the judge was crooked," or "the cop was crooked," or "a crooked witness altered his testimony, and this caused the unfavorable result." He would never admit that he lied initially or that he was the only crook in the case.

If one who habitually blames others for his failures does not get the advancement that he wanted, for example, he will immediately look around for someone to blame for his misfortune. The fact that his job performance may have been sub-standard, will not be mentioned. No, he will blame everything on someone else who "knew the boss," or "spread lies about him," or "dated the boss's secretary," or any one of a hundred excuses that pinpoints someone else as the responsible party. Such a person never goes through a period of introspection which can only lead to self-improvement.

Zoroaster (660–583 BC) a prophet in ancient Persia suggested the following eight standards for self-improvement and successful living:

— 1. One should learn to speak clearly and not critically of any one, and

— 2. One should develop an informed vision relative to people and events, and

— 3. One should learn to take appropriate action as warranted by conditions, and

— 4. One should use sufficient energy to accomplish necessary tasks, and

— 5. One should develop a wholesome attitude concerning one's environment and acquaintances, and

— 6. One should develop a practice of concentrating adequately on all matters affecting one's life, and

— 7. One should make one's livelihood in a legal and honorable manner, and

— 8. One should develop wholesome and honorable intentions in everything one does.

The promise to anyone who followed this strict Code of Ethics 100 percent of the time was a successful life or a good destiny. The key word is 100 percent. This philosophy did not allow you to "run with the foxes" and "sleep with the hounds," simultaneously. It did promise a good life for an individual who ethically performed all his volitional actions.

It's obvious from this brief discussion that self-improvement begins with a complete assumption of total responsibility for one's actions and words.

A POSITIVE RESOLVE

"Resolve that you will make a difference for the betterment of life."

A life that is spent without a beneficial or uplifting purpose or one that is not filled with goals that are designed to be helpful to others is of little value to such a person's fellow human beings. To live and merely exist with little purpose or plan, is a sad way to

O. J. Simpson. UPI/Bettmann

spend one's existence on this planet. It is a way of living that presents few opportunities to be happy and truly alive. It is the elixir of living to attain a noble goal after failure and frustrations that affects all humans. It is one thing to suffer failure and defeat while striving for a worthwhile objective but it is incredibly sad and demeaning to experience these "slings and arrows of outrageous fortune," while striving to attain worthless goals. Defeat, if suffered while striving mightily to help others, carries little sadness in its wake. The victory lay in the direction and the efforts put forth for a noble purpose. The victory that cannot be stolen was obtained by virtue of the fact that an intelligent human deliberately set out on a course of action which was designed to help others. A failure to achieve such a lofty goal cannot remove the eternal beauty of the effort. One has to fight to achieve victories that are important and that "make a difference" in peoples lives. The principal question is simply, "what side of the battle were you on?" While the eventual outcome is important, the highest honor goes to the person who fought on the correct moral side of the conflict. This is true even though the battle was lost.

No later than December 13th, 1995, the headline in the *National Enquirer* reads, "O. J. (Simpson) tries to kill himself with drug overdose." One might ask the question; if victory is all that matters and since he was acquitted of his ex-wife's murder, why would he take a drug overdose? The answer lies in the fact that he killed his ex-wife and by all sorts of gamesmanship and connivance, he was able to "win" the verdict. The jury, by its verdict, however, was unable to absolve his fundamental guilt. Meanwhile, the prosecuting attorneys who tried but failed to convict O. J. Simpson, have gone on to great success and happiness.

One becomes valuable to all his acquaintances when his efforts are aimed at favorably affecting their lives. People soon learn the "direction one is coming from," by their judgment of his methods and intentions. If their opinion is favorable, happiness and prosperity will be the probable reward. A feeling of joy and euphoria will keep such a lucky person's spirits on a constant "high." "Lucky is used because the individual was "lucky" enough to have the intelligence to see that "making a beneficial difference" in people's lives was the "way to go." Life will then have its highest and most beautiful meaning. Friends will forever come to his aid and comfort, since this "giving" person "made a beneficial difference" in their lives. This feeling, this experience, this joy is as good and meaningful as life gets, it doesn't get any better.

GIVING UP

"Don't 'fold your tent' just because you failed."

No stock on the New York stock exchange goes straight up nor does any person succeed in everything that is tried. Failure is but a part of the natural uncertainties of life. It's these very uncertainties that keep life interesting. If everything was known in advance or if one never experienced failure, consider how boring and unchallenging life would become. A golfer, for example, who pars every hole will often be heard to remark, "This is getting to be boring." It's those ups and downs, those successes and failures that adds sizzle and excitement.

Everyone learns a lot more by failure than by success. People tend to give themselves too much credit for success. Life abounds with examples of these tendencies. A child who is a model in deportment and scholastic achievement is often considered by its parents to be proof of their superiority in the art of parenting. A successful investment, that was probably more luck than skill, is often considered by such a fortunate person as an example of his or her superior expertise in the field of money management. Successful candidates for electoral office frequently take too much credit for their victory. The truth behind their victory frequently can be explained by broad social and political movements over which the victor had no control or cognizance. "He or she just might have caught the tide right." Failure on the other hand results in soul searching, for the wise person. "What did I do wrong?" "What could I have done differently?" "Should I try to do it differently the next time?" These are but a few of the questions that should be asked about every failure.

Thomas Alva Edison. The Bettmann Archive

Joe Louis. UPI/Bettmann

The tendency is to overreact to failure, to give up. To denigrate oneself. These are only normal reactions but they should be discarded immediately upon reflection. Positive ideas should soon result from creative thinking once the initial shock of failure has subsided. The thought of having failed shouldn't prevent you from succeeding. Take inventory and start over. Remember you are the principal asset you have in your arsenal. Marshal all your reserves and get up off the floor. You are not beat until you stop trying to get up. It matters little how many times you have been "knocked down"—the principal question is—did you get up one more time than you were "knocked down." As long as you are on your feet with a positive mind set you are not defeated. Never, never, never feel sorry for yourself. Banish self-pity from your mind, it's totally self-defeating and unproductive. The world cares little about your problems, it's really not interested in your "sob story." Don't let the thought of failure paralyze you into inaction. Put a great smile on your face, reinvent yourself and your approach and tackle the problem all over again.

All great lives have been sprinkled with a healthy dose of failures. Failures keep everyone humble and in the process help to build compassion and humility. In short, it makes everyone a better person.

WINNING

"Winning is not a sometime thing; it's an all time thing.
You don't win once in a while; you don't do things right
once in a while; you do them right all the time.
Winning is a habit. Unfortunately, so is losing."
— Vince Lombardi, Coach, Green Bay Packers

What a beautiful thought! What a significant thought! What an incontestable thought! What a great rule to guide your life! What a great explanation for Mr. Lombardi's incredibly successful record as a football coach!

Let's leave the football field and the sports arena in general and let's take this thought and apply it to the daily routine of our lives. Let's take the word "winning" and replace it with the word "success." Once these slight changes are made, Mr. Lombardi's statement becomes inspirational and highly relevant to our lives. Success can indeed become a habit—especially if one refuses to become unsuccessful. It's true that one should not look at life as a game of winning or losing but as a series of uninterrupted experiences lasting throughout a lifetime. Once this philosophy is adopted a person, by habit and training, can start to turn his "scars" into "stars" or putting it another way—he can turn his mistakes into the seeds for his next successful endeavor. He can learn to maximize the benefits each of his experiences can bring to his life, in the form of training and preparation for his next venture. A wise and mature person is nothing more than one who has benefited from his past mistakes.

The idea that you have to do things right all the time is an important part of Mr. Lombardi's concept. If you don't do something correctly it becomes difficult, if not impossible, to isolate the reason for the failure. If you don't know what caused the failure then there is little that you can learn from it. Failures are very important as a learning tool. It's by this very process that man has learned every skill he has acquired down through the ages. Failure means only as much as one is willing to attach to it in the way of importance. Actually failure becomes a wonderful thing when it is considered as a step towards success. No one who has tried to accomplish great things, has ever done so without failures along the way. For every dig that "struck oil" there has to be a bunch of "dry holes." That's the way life is.

You must learn to do things right all the time. Consistency is another attribute of achievers. The quality of your work has to represent your best efforts. You can't say to yourself, "Well I won't try today. I don't feel good, so if I fail today, it really doesn't matter." Let me ask you this question: how would you feel if the crew of a Boeing 747 leaving for Europe or any other place, adopted this hit or miss attitude? Or the doctor who is about to operate on

Roy Campanella. UPI/Bettmann

you? Or the conductor on Amtrak? Or a hundred different servants in whom you had to place your trust? No, it becomes clear
that anything worth doing is worth doing to the best of your ability or don't do it at all.

Blaming

"If you slip and fall, you are not defeated unless you blame someone else for pushing you."

A truly competent and intelligent person assumes control of his own life and blames himself for his own failures. By the same sort of reasoning, successes are ultimately due to the efforts that one expends towards well formulated goals. It is true indeed that everyone is helped along the pathways of life by friends, acquaintances, luck, and a myriad of extrinsic factors. But opportunities have to be exploited to be meaningful. This usually means that everyone has to train and prepare himself to exploit good fortune when it comes his way. We have to anticipate that opportunities will come our way. Without advance planning, these golden chances will usually pass us by without benefit to ourselves.

The classic "loser" will think of hundreds of excuses to explain his failure. He will point to any person, event or circumstance that will exonerate him for his responsibility for "missing the boat." Throughout his lifetime he will look to outside events as an explanation of his inability to succeed. Denial, denial, and more denial will suffice this type of ignorant person as a satisfactory explanation for all his woes. A denial that he himself is the reason for his low status or financial ruin. He can never improve himself or his chances of succeeding in life because he simply hasn't identified the problem. How can a person solve a problem that he doesn't understand? He will be looking for solutions in all the wrong places. Even his parents will adopt his spin or version relative to the events of his life.

He divorced his wife because of her improper actions; he failed in business because his associate did something wrong; he didn't get promoted because someone spread falsehoods around the workplace. These are but a few of the classic excuses that failures use to satisfy their minds and the minds of their loved ones. It's always the other person. They never accept the responsibility for events in their own life.

The facts are that a person can begin to change his life and his future every time a new day begins. Every time the "sun comes up," through introspection and truthful realistic self-criticism, one can start to change the entire course of one's life. For example, the divorce might truthfully be attributed to his own imperfections; likewise the business breakup or the failure to be promoted can be attributed to the same cause. The question should be asked, "What did I do wrong to cause this to happen." In looking for causes and in trying to prevent a reccurrence, make yourself the first suspect. A lot more good can come from self-criticism than from blaming others. Remember you can do little about what others do, but you can change what you do.

VICTORIES
"Fill your daily life with victories."

It is a very simple and successful way of life to learn how to have meaningful victories every day of your life, throughout your lifetime. This doesn't mean that every day one has to experience or achieve some overwhelming, colossal, or apocalyptic success over some adversary. In fact most of the important victories one can ever achieve involves no other human beings. The only adversary in the most important victories available to all of us is oneself. Yes, we all need to achieve a victory over those habits, character traits, or fears that everyone has in experiences of his or her life. The final appraisal that is made of a life often depends on the types of battles a person fought during his lifetime, the persistency displayed during those encounters and of course the ultimate outcome of those skirmishes.

Generally speaking, the battles we fight with ourselves should involve self-improvement. Everyone who has ever lived has had to overcome his or her own unique personal "devils" in order to achieve the full richness that this business of living has to offer. Let's first examine the habit of overeating or of eating the wrong types of food—for example, food containing too many fat grams. This problem presents the average person with the most opportunities to have significant victories every day of their lives. You are at lunch and you are asked, "Do you want butter with your bread?" You reject the butter and eat the bread without it. This is a clear victory against fat intake. You can have this same victory every time you confront food. If you have a habit of being supercritical of your acquaintances, and you refrain from commenting critically about some person, you thereby achieve another victory over a negative habit. You decide to stop smoking cigarettes; you decide to stop drinking; you express your love for someone close to you; you apply yourself more seriously to your work, or your studies or in a hundred different possible areas of potential self-improvement. All these areas of possible self-improvement present exciting opportunities to have satisfying victories over the darkness that lies within all of us. Happiness results from overcoming habits that tend to impair our health or our relations with others.

The problem everyone has in his or her relations with other people or with issue oriented matters represents yet another opportunity for victories. The fact that one disagrees with other people relative to issues or has difficulty associating with them for reasons associated with personality clashes or a myriad of other causes, doesn't have to result in such people being enemies. One simply needs to learn how to disagree in an agreeable or amicable manner. The late Senator Everett Dirkson of Illinois was a classic example of how to disagree and still maintain a friendship with his adversaries. It can be done; one simply has to lower the level of rhetoric and temperament while understanding that the adversary has his or her valid reasons for a different viewpoint. Always argue with at least the suggestion of a smile on your face.

Jackie Robinson. UPI/Bettmann Newsphotos

POSITIVE VS. NEGATIVE
"Accentuate the positive—eliminate the negative."

The above statement was the title of a very popular song in the 1940s. It was not only a nice song to listen to, it was also very good advice. People do not want to be around "negative" people. The difference between optimism and pessimism is well illustrated by the people who say, for instance, that the glass is half empty instead of the ones who say the glass is half full. Pessimistic outlooks tend to be self-fulfilling. This can be illustrated by the following inscription found on the tombstone of a well-known hypochondriac, "I told you I was sick."

People who are optimistic tend to forge ahead in spite of difficulties. Witness the following example: A psychiatrist was instructing a class of students of the differing characteristics between a pessimist and an optimist. He placed the pessimistic youth in a brightly colored room filled with toys designed to gladden any child's heart. He placed the optimistic youth in a room filled with horse manure. He left both of them in their respective rooms for one hour. When he opened the door to the pessimist he found the child sitting in the center of the room crying uncontrollably. He then opened the door to the optimistic child and found him singing and digging with all his might. When asked, "Why he was so happy?" the optimistic child responded, "With all this horse manure there is bound to be a pony around here somewhere." This illustration explains why optimistic people are much more successful than pessimistic people. Put simply, pessimists tend to quit trying while optimist never, never quit. How can a person be defeated who never surrenders? Just because a person is frequently "knocked down" doesn't mean he or she is defeated. Defeat occurs when he or she fails to get up or doesn't even try to get on his or her feet.

Life is tough for everyone. Shakespeare's "slings and arrows

George Washington Carver. The Bettmann Archive

of outrageous fortune" occur in everyone's experience. When misfortune visits one on the way to an objective, "bad luck" has to be taken in stride. That doesn't mean that the direction needs to be changed. What is does mean is that a greater dedication and effort is required. It means that nothing worthwhile is easy to accomplish. Remember that if every victory was automatic, without occasional pitfalls or dedicated effort, everyone would be doing it and a victory under such circumstances would be valueless. The "Modus operandi" should be to dig in and keep smiling.

The game of life is best played as a team sport. It's difficult to succeed as well by one's own efforts. Even Albert Einstein (1879–1955), not withstanding his genius, had assistants. People don't like to be around negative people. A cheerful upbeat and optimistic person attracts others who will be helpful and provide a meaningful uplift to his or her life's efforts. If you notice, politicians seem to be forever smiling. People who have their picture taken are always asked to smile. Professional photographers are masters at getting people to smile or look pleasant while having their picture taken. Accentuating the positive soon becomes a habit and beneficially permeates all of one's life and relationships.

SOLVING PROBLEMS

"Always strive to apply the intelligence, expertise, and experience you have acquired to the solution of problems over which you have partial or total control."

Unapplied intelligence is equivalent to ignorance. Conversely, applied intelligence constitutes wisdom. If you know, for example, that it is harmful to smoke cigarettes, and you continue to smoke, then your actions on this particular subject are tantamount to ignorance. The resulting actions become the same as if you did not know that cigarette smoking is harmful. We should apply our intelligence to the solution of every problem we confront in our daily lives. When you follow this practice, it is not very long before you will notice that your life is proceeding quite smoothly. It is only when we stack one unresolved problem on top of the other that our life becomes very complicated, unbearable, and consequently unenjoyable.

Let's examine briefly the practical application of the rule that applies our intelligence, expertise, and experience to the solution of all problems that we confront daily. Let's assume that there is a hole in the screen that allows flies to enter to the discomfort of anyone using the porch. We may know how to solve this problem, that is to fix the hole in the screen, but if we do nothing about the situation, then the result is the same as if we were ignorant of the solution. Wisdom requires that we do what is necessary to repair the screen as soon as possible. Or let us assume that the wheel alignment on our car is improper and as a result the wheels shimmy as we drive it. Intelligence and experience tell us that unless we promptly correct the wheel alignment our tires will soon be destroyed. We should also know that improper alignment will result in a "rough riding" automobile. Even though we recognize the problem and know how to eliminate it, it matters nothing unless we do those things necessary to correct the situation. If we do nothing and let the tires be prematurely destroyed, our failure to act constitutes ignorance. Wisdom would require that we correct the alignment immediately.

Intelligence, expertise, and experience alone are not enough. "Jaw-boning" alone will never solve a problem. Some of the greatest failures on earth can instantly verbalize a solution to any problem that exists. The difficulty seems to be in their inability to convert their intelligence into effective action which results in a solution. *Therefore, a great part of wisdom is the ability to convert intelligence into timely and effective action.* All the knowledge in the world will amount to nothing and be meaningless unless it is appropriately applied to the solutions of life's problems. Therefore,

Whether Nat Turner's slave uprising was effective action is a question for the historians. The Bettmann Archive

we must all practice converting our thoughts into effective action. Wisdom requires no less.

Another aspect of solving problems is in finding the best possible solution. Many problems are solvable in many different ways. The wisest amongst us solve problems with the greatest of ease. If a window pane is broken, there are a number of ways to replace it. The simplest method would be to take the broken window out completely and clean out the old putty down to the frame. Then measure the window and get a hardware store to cut a glass to the size needed. Having done this, replace it with putty. The alternative would be to buy a glass and attempt to break it in the proper size. The probability of chipping would suggest this to be an unwise approach. A truly wise person finds the simplest and easiest solutions to their problems.

Once you develop the habit of applying your intelligence to the problems over which you have partial or total control, the happiness level of your life will increase significantly. Become a problem solver rather than one who simply discovers problems and who may or may not discuss them but, in any event, does nothing to solve them. Your actions will also increase the happiness of all the lives with which you make contact. In addition, you will also set a shining example for others to emulate.

POSITIVE EXPERIENCES

"To lead a disciplined, exemplary, and successful life, many, many personal struggles have to end in victory."

To lead a disciplined life, personal weaknesses have to be constantly overcome. There is no end of these struggles. They continue throughout life. *The battle to keep your weight at a desirable level, for example, must be waged daily throughout your lifetime.* Since there is no end to this battle, thousands of victories must occur as you successfully fight off or repress the urge to eat fattening foods. The struggle to overcome an addiction to alcohol, cigarettes, or other drugs is also endless. Throughout a lifetime, millions of little victories have to be won as an addict successfully suppresses the urge to submit to his addiction. Many of life's battles are a one-time struggle; and with victory, the fight is over. For example, one may win a foot race, sports contest, or graduate from college. In the latter example, the "degree" is permanent testimony to the successful struggle. One is better equipped to fight the "one-time" struggle and enjoy the subsequent final victory. Unfortunately, many of the most important struggles do not have a "final victory" feature. The struggle is over only at death. These types of struggles are the most difficult to wage, since there is no final

Bill Cosby. UPI/Bettmann

victory so long as life continues.

In order to wage successfully the endless struggles that are a necessary part of a disciplined life, one has to acquire a deeper understanding of the real issues involved. First of all, to live is to have to struggle. Secondly, many struggles are never finished. Final victory is not possible in many important areas of our personal life. We must prepare ourselves to do battle endlessly throughout our lifetime. Personal addictions or negative habits are more easily overcome the more successfully we struggle to overcome the negative aspects of our personality and character. We build up the strength of our resolve by victories. We must clearly understand that the battle is endless. Just as our heart has to keep pumping throughout our lifetime to sustain our life, so must our willpower and resolve continue endlessly if we are going to lead a disciplined life. Once we acquire the positive habits of overcoming our negative traits, the temptations will become less severe and farther apart. In short, the battle will become easier.

Most people get discouraged when they see no end in sight and no prospect of a victory. Actually there is a great fallacy in their thinking. The fight to overcome a negative addition, a negative habit or personality trait, provides each of us with the opportunity to experience many victories daily. Each time we successfully resist the urge to smoke a cigarette, eat fattening foods, take drugs or alcohol, or gossip about someone, we have won a tremendous victory. These victories over ourselves give us a tremendous feeling of self-satisfaction and accomplishment. The cumulative result will be an enhancement of our self-image, and others will soon emulate our life style. From your example, your friends and family will draw strength and encouragement needed in their own personal struggles.

Remember, it is not easy to lead a disciplined life. Good things only start to happen after one endures hard work and sacrifice. Much knowledge will come your way as you experience victory after victory in your own personal struggle. The final product of such a life will be the great meaning that has been added to your existence and to the existence of those who emulate you.

REALITY IS TRUTH
"One should learn to accept the most important reality
of life as early in his life as possible—that reality is truth."

All the truths of nature are inescapable and never ending. The law of gravity, motion, cause and effect, to name but a few, confront us every day in our lives. There is simply no way to escape the operation of these natural forces that exercise a powerful influence on each of our lives. You may not choose to recognize the great body of truths comprising all the natural forces that govern life on this planet, but if you ignore them you will be brutally reminded of their existence. The person under the influence of drugs, who imagines himself to be a bird and attempts to "fly" off a building, will soon be reminded of the law of gravity. Thus it is with all the truths embodied in nature. They are a part of reality that you must recognize and deal with every day of your life.

There are other truths that affect our lives daily which also embody an indispensable part of the reality of our existence. If we choose to ignore, manipulate, or falsify these truths, the effect on our personal welfare and happiness is as devastating, cumulatively, over the long run, as it is instantaneously for the person who attempted to "fly" off the building. I refer to these multiplicity of truths which comprise such an important part of our existence, partially represented by the following: Did you get drunk yesterday? Did you put gas in the car? Did you take the ten dollars off the dresser? Did your son do his homework last evening? Did you have lunch and cocktails with a handsome or beautiful member of the opposite sex? Are you going to fulfill the terms of a warranty you gave for work performed? Did you nudge your golf ball towards a better "lie" in the "rough" before you hit it? Are you going to do what you say you are going to do? Did you do what you said you did? Did you try to get your friend a job? Do you really think another person is as accomplished as you say he is, or are you just saying this for your personal gain?

Everyone of these questions can be answered truthfully or by a half-truth or by an outright falsehood. It is your policy towards these sort of truths that will have an overwhelming affect on the success and happiness of your life. A great part of the justification for this book is represented by a discussion of this subject.

It is so very important for everyone to formulate a policy towards truth and/or reality as early in his life as possible. Are you going to live in a world of illusions created by your own distortions, half-truths and falsehoods? Or are you going to confront reality, as forthrightly as possible? If you decide to accept reality, or the truth, then you are wise to accept it all the time. You have to be one or the other. You will find that the more you deal with the truth as an important part of reality, the happier will be your existence. Your mind and/or soul will become tranquil. You will find that this policy will never get you in serious trouble. You will have the additional benefit of structuring your life on a solid foundation. You will not find it necessary to fear constantly a collapse of everything you hold sacred. For if you deal in truths, you will have constantly discarded meaningless values and relationships as they were encountered.

This book is all about the truth as I see it. It is an attempt to get you thinking along the lines of solid and substantive values. Everything mentioned here is an attempt to explain the reality of many situations that we all encounter daily in our lives. Once you train your mind to search for and accept the truth as the only reality of your life, then you will experience a totally beneficial transformation of your existence. You will replace an illusion filled with confusion and uncertainty with a reality that is comprised of clarity and dependable truths.

MOVING ON
"Life involves many endings and beginnings.
Learn not to dwell on endings and learn

to look with anticipation and excitement to all beginnings."

The great hope of life is that for every ending there has to be a beginning. Something cannot end unless it is followed by something else that is beginning. Frequently, the endings are a cause for much sadness; and people dwell excessively on such occurrences. Endings represent the past or that which has transpired. Nothing can be done to change the past. In truth, history cannot be changed. Once an occurrence is past, it will be fixed for all time. Nothing can be done about it; therefore, it is unwise to dwell excessively on such matters. Let your mind turn to the future and new beginnings. This type of thinking or "mind-set" produces much happiness.

The past should not be ignored. Experiences are the greatest method of acquiring wisdom. The past should be the crucible where our policies and beliefs are forged. Neither dwell on the past, nor ignore the truths the past has brought to you. Use these insights to guide your future course.

Most excessively torturous endings involve the termination of a relationship with another human being. This ending may result from death or divorce, a broken friendship or love affair, or the termination of a close relationship between parent and child. For every one of these endings, realize that life continues. Whether we like it or not, we have 24 hours of every new day to expend. We can accomplish nothing through needless fixation on a past relationship that has ended, but we can look to the future and concern ourselves with new beginnings. As long as we live, something will always follow every termination. That which begins or follows has had to be studied and considered. Something can be done about events and situations that have not yet occurred. All pending matters can usually be altered by those individuals directly concerned. A new love affair can always replace an old one that has ended. The world is full of lonely people looking for love in a meaningful

Lyndon Johnson. UPI/Bettmann Newsphotos

relationship. If you fix your mind and heart on events of the past, you do not give new relationships a chance to blossom fully. If you are trapped in fear and cynicism by events of the past, you prevent the development of a beautiful new and exciting life.

Likewise, failures in our careers do not represent a finality unless we choose to make them final. If we decide to stop and deal morosely with past failures, then we will not give potentially exciting new opportunities a chance to develop. We are never defeated until we decide to stop trying. Every new day presents an opportunity for new challenges and it remains simply for us to search for new horizons which hold promise for our future. As long as life continues, new situations will develop that can beneficially affect that life.

But opportunity must be discovered and then exploited. Optimism and good cheer are the best tools with which to explore new vistas. *Everyone has his share of failures. They are a necessary companion to living.* Failures keep life exciting. It would be very boring if you succeeded at everything you tried. Meet the future with a smile while learning from past mistakes. Dwell on beginnings and let the endings be forgotten.

CONFRONTING REALITY

"Learn to confront reality in a confident manner using the degree of seriousness that the situation requires."

Many people are so filled with fear and insecurity that they react to situations improperly. Instead of confronting a situation quietly and confidently with the degree of seriousness the situation requires, they may give a totally false impression of their feelings towards a given problem. They make jokes and act frivolously when they should be serious, or they may avoid an expression of their beliefs rather than confronting the problem squarely and forthrightly. They may fear that their listener will be provoked if they say something with which he disagrees. Rather than risk his displeasure they will hide their true feelings by ignoring the subject. In this manner, many people avoid confronting most of reality throughout their lifetime. The tragedy of this practice is that through fear and insecurity, such people fail to achieve many goals simply because they never forthrightly expressed their desires and beliefs to the right person at the proper time. As a consequence, they lead lives of emptiness, failure and frustration.

Always remember it is not what you say but how you say it that matters very much. When you deal with a controversial subject, attempt to explain your position in a calm and pleasant manner. It will help immeasurably if you can do this with the faintest suggestion of a smile on your face. It you speak in a tense or argumentative or strained voice, you will enhance the controversial aspects of your subject. This approach will invite a similar response from your listener. If you are calm and pleasant, your listener may disagree with you, but he will tend to do this in a pleasant manner. You may not get what you want, but you will have expressed your views on a controversial subject without incurring the listener's wrath.

By properly dealing with subjects that the fearful and insecure avoid, you will become more interesting to your acquaintances and new vistas will open in your career and life. We must deal with all the necessary subjects that confront us. It staggers the imagination to consider those whose lives were stunted and rendered far less enjoyable and successful simply because they were afraid to face reality. Often the reason was that they really did not know how to handle the situation so they avoided it completely by remaining silent. Feelings of despair and frustration are often the results of this approach.

Train yourself to deal completely with all the facets of your life. Do not avoid or ignore that which should be confronted. If it is necessary to confront life realistically, then no correctly thinking person can resent a discussion of your problems, if you do so in a pleasant manner. If something is necessary, do not ignore it, but learn how to deal properly with the subject. If you consider life as being filled with unavoidable tasks, then there is really no such thing as a problem which cannot be openly discussed with those individuals who are concerned. Do not let fear and insecurity prevent you from reaching your maximum potential. Work on your style and manner of presenting the problems that life brings your way. The results in happiness and achievement are more than worth the effort.

Unapplied Knowledge is Ignorance

"Unapplied knowledge is but another example of man's ignorance."

You may be a very intelligent person, but if you lack the wisdom to apply your intelligence, then you are ignorant. To know something, and not apply it wisely to your life, is equivalent to not possessing the knowledge. You may know that smoking or excessive alcohol consumption, gambling, gossiping, using mind-altering drugs, excessive eating, lack of exercising, or any one of thousands of negative habits are injurious to your health. Notwithstanding, if you do not take the positive steps necessary to apply this knowledge to your life, then you are ignorant. Unapplied knowledge on important matters constitutes a very serious lack of wisdom.

The only knowledge that is significant is that which is put to use. You may be the most knowledgeable person in your community, but this does not constitute a measure of your wisdom. Wisdom and knowledge are quite different. Wisdom would demand that you apply all knowledge you possess to your life. Frequently, people with relatively little knowledge seem to be very successful. Usually this type of person applies a very high percentage of his knowledge to the betterment of his life. Some people seem incapable of acting effectively on the knowledge within their grasp. They seem to possess knowledge but totally lack the wherewithal to successfully apply it. The world describes this as lacking in "common sense." Colleges are filled with educated people who are not wise. This tendency is so widespread that the world is distrustful of the so-called "egghead" type. "Hell's Kitchen" in the Bowery of New York has more than one inhabitant lying on the sidewalk who was awarded a Phi Beta Kappa key for exceptional intelligence while in a college or university.

The world ultimately judges people not by their potential but by their results. Results, of course, constitute proof of someone having exercised the wisdom of applying knowledge to the practical solution of life's problems. The world is quite justified by this approach. Results cannot be denied. Anyone can readily solve all problems by glib conversational techniques. However, what can readily be solved "on paper" or in "conversation" will prove quite difficult in the world of reality. In practice, nothing ever evolves along theoretical outlines. Human factors enter into every solution and produce practical results quite different from theoretical prognostications, hence the importance of results.

It is very important to acquire as much knowledge as possible. Certainly, if the truth is not known, then nothing can be attempted. We should constantly search for the truth in all endeavors toward the objective of acquiring knowledge. We should learn to listen. There is not a person on this earth from whom we cannot learn something. We may regard the knowledge as worthless, but listening shows we never know when we will learn something really worthwhile. Always remember that you can learn more with your mouth closed than with your mouth open.

Once knowledge has come to us, we should examine ways in which to put this knowledge to practical use. Desirable results are harder to obtain than one would at first glance surmise. Practical implementation of knowledge is an art unto itself. Some people naturally accomplish this with little apparent difficulty. Others seemingly find the entire process quite perplexing. We should always bear in mind that unapplied knowledge is ignorance. We should also believe that almost all knowledge can easily be applied to practical usage in our daily lives. The rest is up to your dedication and common sense or, to use a better word—*wisdom*. Do you have the wisdom to convert your knowledge to a practical application? We all have this wisdom in varying degrees. Start working on it as it applies to your life.

LET IT HAPPEN
"Do not try to force events or desirable results."

Through our anxiety to achieve our desired goals, we tend to lose patience and attempt to force or pressure participants into performing that which will accomplish our goals. We, of course, will do our part of what is necessary in our anxiety, but we do not stop there. We try to force actions or events that we do not control. When this occurs, we create great tension within ourselves and usually create forces that operate against us in a counter-productive manner.

Though our desires are great and our motives noble, the world will make little note of this. Generally, everyone is too concerned about their own problems to spend sufficient time evaluating the merits of our cause. Their actions in our behalf will be unhurried, and any attempt on our part to force or hurry their responses usually operates against our best interest. We should do our share, and then wait peaceful for events to evolve. While this "waiting process" is going on, we should remain peaceful and relaxed. This should only occur after we have done everything within our own realm of responsibility which would be wisely designed to accomplish our goals.

It is important that we formulate goals and objectives for our life. It is rather difficult to be successful or happy without them. We should always know how much of the control is within our power and how much will depend on the efforts of theirs or on the occurrence of events over which we have no control. Those matters beyond our power need to be identified, and a philosophical attitude towards these factors needs to be adopted. If things happen as we hope they will, then we should consider ourselves lucky. If these external factors evolve in a direction contrary to our hopes, then we need be prepared to accept these results. We should know that we cannot "force" extrinsic matters in the direction our goals may require.

What I am really saying is that we should not be selfishly preoccupied with our own limited objectives to the exclusion of all the problems of the rest of mankind. This "selfish preoccupation" is so unfavorably regarded by most that it casts one in a most undesirable light. People who adopt this position are really very uninteresting. They can talk about nothing but their own objectives. If another subject is broached to them, they immediately display a total lack of interest. They will either be quiet, or they will insist on talking about their own problems or objectives. We must remember that everyone has goals, objectives, and problems. Most people are not really interested in the next person's affairs. They may display a surface concern in order to be polite, but you can be assured that they are not really concerned. Therefore, learn to keep your affairs to yourself. If the next person insists on talking about his, there is nothing you can do about this; but at least you can be dignified and private about yourself.

Once you have done everything possible in your behalf, the rest is in the hands of fate. While events evolve, learn to pursue your life happily in a relaxed fashion. Always have two or three alternative goals or even more in the event that your primary objective is not achieved. Life does not have to proceed according to only one plan. Other alternatives can be equally satisfying. Learn not to be uncompromising, since to act in this fashion will lead to great unhappiness. Compromise each time it is necessary to continue the progress of your life. Do not consider that by compromising you have suffered a defeat or displayed a weakness. Have great faith in the proposition that everything that happens seems eventually to have happened for the best. Many times the very thing that we want is not really in our best interest. Consequently, the art of compromise becomes a valuable tool for happiness in our lives.

STRIVING FOR EXCELLENCE

"People who constantly strive to become the best possible people they are capable of being tend to feel secure in life."

Underdeveloped talent never helped anyone. Frequently we hear it said that someone has so much natural ability that it is pitiful he never uses it. *Or we see people with severe limitations, be they physical or mental, reach unbelievable heights of success.* These types of people utilize their assets to the maximum. Whenever someone constantly strives to improve himself he tends to overcome the feelings of insecurity which all of us experience in life. There is nothing that adds to our sense of well-being and security more than knowing we have become the best person we are capable of being.

Everyone at one time or another is hounded by feelings of insecurity. This insecurity may relate to the ability to perform an assigned task, or it may deal with relationships with other human beings. When this feeling occurs, it usually means that the person involved is functioning at a level far below his capability. This feeling of insecurity which permeates a personality is probably due to a guilt complex caused by not utilizing one's talents. A person who has worked hard at maximizing his abilities knows quite certainly what his limits are relative to his abilities. The mere fact that he has fully developed them will give him a feeling of satisfaction. The person who has only developed 50 percent of his talents doesn't really know himself. With this ignorance of "self" comes a deep-seated insecurity caused by being unsure of yourself as a contributing human being. With this waste of talent comes insecurity, depression, and consequent unhappiness.

If you want to be secure, successful, and happy, work on self-improvement. Strive to the last day of your life to upgrade yourself. You will find that you are a far more capable person than you first thought possible. As you constantly strive to better yourself, you will be thrilled and excited by the results. Just consider, for example, how far Helen Keller (who was deaf, dumb, and blind) was able to progress. The human brain is an endlessly fascinating mechanism. Startling results will follow dedicated efforts. Never

Helen Keller. The Bettmann Archive

believe that you can't improve yourself. You can do anything you can convince yourself in your mind that you can do. So why not get started on your personal self-improvement program? It will bring a new dimension to your life.

Security is also important in the economic aspects of our lives. We all want enough food to eat, a place to sleep, and a roof over our heads. In short, we need the basics. People who sit around worrying instead of working begin to feel terribly insecure about their finances. Those who are busy working do not have time to feel insecure. The truth is that busy, hardworking types usually meet with success, and lazy, worrying types usually meet with failure. These results only tend to increase the insecurity of the underachievers.

People, both family and others, respect those who develop their skills to a maximum. With this respect comes confidence and a feeling of security. The world respects functionaries at all social and economic levels. The question is simply, "What kind of a human being are you?" This question applies regardless of your station. You can be president of the United States, and if you are an unpleasant or unfair or detestable human being, people will condemn you for it. You will never attain such heights that you will be excused for not being a decent human being.

Therefore, the simple principle becomes one of improving yourself to the maximum level of your talents. The objectives should be to become the very best person of which you are capable.

ACCEPTING REALITY

"Learn to look reality in the face and act according to the dictates of wisdom."

Many people spend all their lives avoiding a confrontation with reality. They are frightened by the prospect of facing the truth. They believe the truth can be avoided if they simply refuse to deal with it. One of the saddest examples of this that life has to offer is the mother who gives birth to a severely retarded child. The first reality she must face is the fact that the child is hopelessly retarded. Usually the scenario is that she is the last person to abandon hope of normality and accept the fact of retardation. Eventually that same mother has another confrontation with reality. This problem deals with the fact that it is better for the severely retarded child to be placed in an institution so that it will have established a "routine of living" by the time its parents die. Again, the mother is usually the last to accept the truth of this reality, i.e., the child is "better off" in an institution.

We all have less profound confrontations with reality almost daily in our lives. They may involve a letter we believe contains unpleasant news so we leave it unopened on our desk for several days; or a necessary dismissal of a subordinate; visiting a bank for a loan; going to a doctor to discover what may be wrong with our health; recognizing behavioral problems that we or our loved ones may possess; That we are drinking or smoking too much; that we are losing control of our temper; that our marriage is in trouble; or that we are getting too fat; or any one of a million different types of things that we must face in life.

The point is that a refusal to realistically face the truth of a situation will not make it disappear nor will it tend to lessen the gravity of the problem. While it is true that the mere passage of time solves many problems, the fact remains that many problems worsen with inattention. Reality is a fact that governs all our lives. The pattern of our lives is not set by dreams and castles in the sky. No, I'm afraid our lives follow a path of truth and reality; and unless we recognize the truth, we are ignoring the motivating forces which control the direction of our lives.

As strange as it may seem, truth or reality is always more beautiful, more meaningful than is ignorance or a plain refusal to recognize the truth surrounding our existence. Once you force the habit of grabbing truth and reality by the "throat" and dealing with it wisely and promptly, your life will assume a deeper meaning. You will start living closer to the deeper truths of life on this planet. After all, man's advances have always been painful and have come about

179

by the trial and error method. While we all want life to be a "bowl of cherries" it's really quite different. Life necessarily involves living, working, suffering, and dying. While this story is being "played out" you should find as many things to enjoy as possible.

The true realist is usually the most well-adjusted of our acquaintances. His "ups" and "downs" are less severe. He is the person whose peers come to him for advice. They do so because they realize he is factual and realistic. They believe he will give them an answer that is closest to the truth. A "dreamer" is never sought for advice. He floats along on a cloud of his own imagination and sooner or later crash lands on the sea of reality.

You can never get far away from reality regardless of how you dream or ignore the truth. Life has a nasty habit of brutally returning us to the reality of the situation. If you allow yourself to float through the sky on the wings of a dream, the inevitable crash landing will be all the more painful. The solution is to always stay close to the truth and reality. Your life will be enriched by the practice.

ACCOUNTABILITY

"Remember that if you do not say or do something, you will not have to defend or argue about your words and/or actions."

Many people keep themselves embroiled in controversy by words that should never have been uttered, or by actions that wisdom would suggest should never have been taken. Why keep the "pot boiling" when it is wiser and easier to remain silent and refrain from taking needless controversial actions. There is no moral requirement that you speak out on every controversial issue that comes along. Actually, people are usually not interested in an opinion that differs from the opinion of the listener. Nothing can be gained by expounding at length on your views. The only predictable result will be a whirlpool of conflict and anger.

There are really very few occasions in life when your opinion is really needed. Most of the time the world does not need to know nor does it little care what you think. Most people are contented with their own views and will not change them just because you come along and state something which is opposite to their convictions. They will summarily dismiss your views without giving them careful consideration. A politician is frequently called upon to state his views on controversial matters. The successful ones try mightily to equivocate and not adopt strong opinions that may run counter to the views held by their constituents. A judge in a courtroom has to render his opinion in a controversy. He is paid to do this; it is his job. A teacher has to state his views to his students. A preacher has to state his beliefs to his parishioners in order to project the tenets of a religion. But always remember that for the overwhelming body of humanity there is little need to express our views.

When we constantly render our opinions on controversial subjects, we agitate and irritate our friends. The practice of constantly and openly flaunting our views wreaks havoc on relationships. People do not like to have their statements questioned or their views denigrated. Wisdom dictates that for the most part we should keep our views to ourselves. It is wisdom that says it is better to lead a tranquil and happy life than a turbulent and quarrelsome one.

It is also true that the less frequently we express our opinions the more our opinion is respected and sought after by our peers. As we have said one who is forever giving his views on a thousand subjects is soon dismissed as "blabbermouth" and tends to be ignored. By his excessive discussion of many different subjects people soon turn a deaf ear to him. Generally, one might say his opinions have been devalued by their plentiful supply. The law of supply and demand has somehow entered the picture. The demand for his opinions having decreased because their quantity is excessive.

To get back in this discussion to the basic premise of this topic; you don't have to defend what you don't say. Controversy does not exist, nor is it created when you keep your views to yourself. You are surrounded by tranquillity and friendship. Your opinion will not change another's mind anyway, so why get involved in a controversy which was unsolicited and unnecessary in the first instance? It's different when you are paid to give your opinion or when a moral or ethical duty exists to openly express it. In the preponderance of situations an opinion is neither sought after nor appreciated, so why get involved?

It is far wiser to sit quietly by and absorb the opinions of others without comment. All opinions, except those dealing with measurements of weight, time, or distances, are variable anyway so that the speaker could well be correct based on his value system. This would not exclude you from also being correct even though you may hold a contrary opinion. Since on many occasions differing opinions on the same subject could both be right, why not keep your views to yourself? It will add to your wisdom and happiness.

POSITIVE ATTITUDE
"With wisdom it is possible to make all the incidents and duties of our life more enjoyable by a simple determination to accept the necessary and inevitable cheerfully."

A person may hate to get out of bed in the morning. Some people torture themselves unbelievably by this daily occurrence. If you are healthy and have no handicaps, it is absolutely necessary that you arise each morning. Since this is a necessary daily ritual, start examining ways to make this more enjoyable. First of all, thank your God that you are healthy and able to get out of bed. Secondly, it may be wise to get a radio that turns on automatically at a pre-determined hour. With the sound of music you start to associate with daily activities. Probably you are a "night owl" and don't get to bed early enough. You should know from experience that your body needs eight hours rest, for example. If you need to get up at 6 a.m. then you should retire by 10 p.m. At first you may not be able to go to sleep at this hour; but due to the body's remarkable ability to adapt to almost anything you will soon be able to go to sleep or at a minimum start resting by 10 p.m.

Be sure that you arise early enough so it won't be necessary to go through a "mad rush" each morning to arrive at work on time. Once wisdom determines those things which make this "unpleasant" experience enjoyable, you will find that you will start enjoying the process of awakening each day.

This ability to turn unpleasant or feared experiences into enjoyable events permeates every facet of life. It applies to everything at work, all of your domestic affairs, and to the entire spectrum of your relationships with other human beings. Your attitude and wisdom can turn an unpleasant experience into an occasion of fun and enjoyment. The entire battle is in the mind. It depends entirely on how you choose to view something. If your mind says a given duty is unpleasant you can be assured that it will be unpleasant. The only reality in your life is that which exists in your mind. If your mind tells you that something is red, then to you such an object is red even though it may be orange in color to the rest of the world. You don't have to look far for happiness because it's no further away than your own mind.

In order to change your life in the direction of happiness, you must start with the deep conviction that the mind can change everything. You have to believe this to a moral certainty. Once this hurdle is negotiated, the next step is to adopt a positive mental attitude. It is so easy to sit around and complain, and make each and every duty of our lives unpleasant. While it's easy to do this, it's also very ignorant to adopt these negative positions. Just think about what is involved. By the simple act of adopting a proper mental attitude you can be happy and contented. Your life can illuminate the entire area around you and bring cheer and happiness to everyone with whom you come in contact. Contrariwise, by the simple act of adopting an unwise mental attitude, everything you do can be made more difficult, everyone you meet can be rendered less happy and tranquil because of their contact with you. Think about the profound difference your mental attitude makes in your life. The ultimate result is a great enjoyable life that is a model for everyone to behold, an inspiration for all whom you encounter, while the other result is the envy of no one.

Why not decide to be happy? It is really not very difficult. Enjoy your work, your play, and every facet of your life. All you have to do is put forth an effort in the right direction. The rewards will be overwhelmingly favorable. You will regret that you didn't think of it earlier. You can be assured that your family and friends will also regret that you didn't take the "happiness road" earlier.

POSITIVE ATTITUDE THROUGH ORDER

"We should strive to keep order in everything we do and guard against a 'what's the use?' attitude."

The methods we use to handle the details affecting our lives will add richness and meaning to our existence and to everyone with whom we come in contact. Picture this: We get up in the morning and take off our pajamas; we can either hang up our pajamas neatly in the closet or throw them in a pile on the floor. We can either throw our underwear on the floor or place it in the clothes hamper. When we take a shower and dry ourselves with a bath towel, again we can either throw the towel on the floor or place it in the clothes hamper. We can either leave the sink and the bathtub wet and dirty or clean and neat. We can keep our closet and dresser drawers neatly arranged or carelessly disarranged. If we have clothes to take to the cleaners or tailors or a list of groceries to purchase or any one of a thousand details that emerge daily in our lives, we should strive to handle as many of these matters as possible. The more we do and the less disorder we create, the less there is to do by those with whom we share our life. This attention to details removes burdens from our loved ones and heightens their love and appreciation of us.

There is a tremendous tendency to adopt an attitude bordering on "I don't give a damn" or "What's the use?" All we do when we live by such credos is pass the burden onto someone who does care. It means we are not upholding our share of the burden. When we shirk our responsibilities, we increase the work and responsibility of our loved ones. Just remember that someone has to care. Someone has to take care of the details of life. *It would be a terrible world if no one cared.* So why not strive to be the one who cares; the one who takes care of his share of life's little tasks; the one who by adding order and neatness to all that he touches makes existence more pleasant for everyone.

What we're really talking about is that we should always try to be the best person we are capable of being. We should get "our act" in as good a shape as possible. We should develop all our talents to the maximum extent possible. When we maximize our natural gifts, we become more contented with ourselves as human beings. People appreciate our efforts and tend to enjoy our association and comradeship. The world, in a very subtle way, will start beating a path to our door. This reaction will reveal itself in ways that are difficult to pinpoint. People will want to be around us. This feedback can't help but enhance the way we feel about ourselves. Some of the greatest tragedies imaginable concern people who, though they are the recipients of incredible talents, seem to squander all their natural abilities. On the other hand, we see people with an absolute minimum of natural talents maximize every ounce or bit of them. These people are the bright spots on the face of mankind.

Let your actions make life more enjoyable for everyone. Carry more than your share of life's burdens. Do it all with a smile. Minimize your complaints and spread cheer and confidence wherever you go. When you do this, you will be the greatest beneficiary in the entire process. The world will love you for your attitude.

LEADERSHIP

"Learn to recognize your leadership qualities, and exercise them for the benefit of those people whose lives you touch."

One of the great problems with the fast-moving, dangerous world in which we live is an appalling lack of leadership, especially in the Western democracies. Leaders no doubt exist; it just seems their voices are never heard above the din of the radicals. *In this world of enormous distractions, it seems only the most outrageous people capture center stage.* The quietly logical ones are, if not ignored, at least not listened to, if heard at all.

Most of us can do very little on a national or international level about the incredible paucity of leadership. What we can do concerning this subject is learn to recognize whatever qualities of leadership we personally possess and exercise and develop them for the benefit of our acquaintances. Everyone has the capacity for exercising leadership in some areas over some people; we can't be heard to say that we have no leadership qualities. What is important in the beginning is to learn something about that intangible called leadership and see which of these qualities we possess.

Democratic as opposed to dictatorial leadership involves, but is not limited to, some of the following characteristics:
— (a) A leader listens.
— (b) A leader admits his mistakes and shortcomings.
— (c) A leader is truthful.
— (d) A leader is humble.
— (e) A leader is slow to criticize.
— (f) A leader keeps confidences.
— (g) A leader does one or more things very well.
— (h) A leader has great control over his negative habits, such

as drinking alcoholic beverages, drug consumption etc.
— (i) A leader is not gossipy.
— (j) A leader does not hesitate to give praise when due.
— (k) A leader will chastise when it is warranted.
— (l) A leader loves people.
— (m) A leader minimizes his contribution and overstates another's.
— (n) A leader, while he may not be loved, will at least be respected.
— (o) A leader concerns himself with matters that are important to people's lives.
— (p) A leader is wise, compassionate, honest, just, and understanding.
— (q) A leader is secure in himself as a human being.
— (r) A leader is hardworking and conscientious.

No person normally has all the above qualities in significant amounts. But any human possesses one or more of these attributes. An intelligent person will recognize whatever leadership qualities he possesses and enlarge upon them at every opportunity. Careful self-analysis will reveal traits that are undesirable and that should be eliminated. Wisdom suggest that we strive to improve ourselves constantly by eliminating the negatives and accenting the positives. This process of self-improvement should continue to the day or second of our last conscious thought.

As we go through life, opportunities to provide leadership will occur to all of us at different times in unpredictable ways. When these events occur, we should not squirm away but should commit ourselves to the best of our abilities to complete any task assigned to us. This is the contribution we owe to our fellowman. We should not refuse cowardly to lead under the false guise that we are humble and seek no honor for ourselves. Whether we obtain honor from a given mission or not is irrelevant; what is relevant is to expend our energies for the alleviation of problems associated with the human condition. This can be thought of as the rental we must pay to occupy space on this planet.

Leadership usually means order, sanity, progress, optimism, and happiness for all concerned. Once you try it, to paraphrase an old saying, "you'll like it." It will also give you self-respect and make you happy. It will lend meaning to your life since *it will make you a giver instead of solely a taker.*

PAY ATTENTION
"Learn to study more closely all of life's observable features."

If they walked through a one-acre lot with no obstructions to their view, many people would not notice a giraffe within this one-acre site. This exaggeration is given merely to make a point. None of us notice 100 percent of all the features available for any given incident, place, event, or person. We all notice and observe a varying degree or percentage of those things which are available to be noticed. The powers of observation depend entirely upon how thoroughly you train yourself to notice important features of whatever it is that you are studying.

If a person looks at his arm, he will notice skin with hairs growing therefrom and a brownish tint or color to the arm. Upon a cursory examination, this is about all we see and probably this is all most of us will ever see. If such a person is asked to describe a male person's arm in detail, he would no doubt describe an extremity in terms essentially as I have stated in the opening line of this paragraph.

Now, look at this same person's arm a little more carefully and thoroughly. Take a powerful magnifying glass and hold it to the arm and determine what you then see. You will no doubt see something quite different than was described earlier. Do you see huge tree-like protrusions that seem to have a pit or indentation at the point where they grow out of the arm? These tree-like objects are, of course, magnified human hairs. The pit or indentation at the base of each hair is a magnified version of the point where the hair exits the arm. A close examination of the arm will reveal bumps and pits that approximate pictures you have seen of the surface of the moon. This again is a magnified version of the surface of the arm.

Your position while observing a particular event or thing or human is of paramount importance in determining exactly what we see. If you take an equal amount of salt and an equal amount of pepper and thoroughly mix it, you have a substance that looks gray. Neither the features of the salt nor the pepper predominate. You see nothing white or black but only something gray. Now if you put a very tiny insect in this quantity of equally mixed salt and pepper, and asked it what it saw what do you think it would answer? The answer, of course, would be a large number of huge white pieces (salt) and an equally large number of huge black pieces (pepper). This insect would see nothing gray. To it everything would be black or white. Both descriptions are accurate depending on the position of the observer at the time of the viewing.

Learn to observe everyone objectively from afar and also closely. Both views are necessary in order to have a careful, well-developed opinion about a given person, thing or incident. From an airplane at 20,000 feet on a clear day, New York City looks one way, but to limit your description of New York to only this vantage point would limit severely the accuracy of your appraisal. To understand New York City more completely, you have to walk its streets, meet its people, and visit and observe its buildings from the ground. The latter observations coupled with your previous aerial view will give you a more accurate picture of New York. Therefore, learn to withhold your final judgments until your observation has been as thorough as possible under the circumstances. Don't judge too early because it will lead to many errors.

DEPENDABILITY

"Learn to be dependable in all your obligations. Once you promise to do something, be sure that you either do it or have an intelligent explanation for your failure to perform."

People like to be around those upon whom they can rely in situations that we all must face. *Leaders usually come from the ranks of the dependable.* Man places a high premium on dependability and elevates those humans who possess it to high positions. In wartime situations dependable leadership is imperative. Soldiers speak of the ideal comrade with whom he fights in combat. He is, above all else, a dependable person. Employers promote those people who perform their daily tasks in a dependable manner. Voters elect representatives whom they believe are dependable. Women and men in their logical moments hope to fall in love and marry a dependable person. Children literally crave dependability in their parents. They ignore their parents' spoken instructions but instead look to their actions. The demand is unending for people who have good character and who are dependable.

Dependability is not necessarily a trait we possess at birth. It involves a learning process that continues throughout our life. Wise parents give young children minor tasks to perform and praise or chastise them according to the manner in which they accomplish their duties. Traits of dependability have to be taught. They involve morality, attitude, love of and respect for your acquaintances, a sense of duty, and a willingness to help others. The traits listed in the preceding sentence are not intended to be a complete listing but rather highlight the type of background from which a dependable character is formed. Usually the traits developed in childhood, while being trained under the loving eye of a parent or guardian, are the ones that predominate and continue throughout a lifetime. Even though you may not have learned the value of dependability in your childhood, be assured that it's never too late.

Many people make ill-advised commitments or "over-promise" just because it was the correct thing to say at the time. Be very conservative in your verbal commitments. If anything, learn to "under-promise" or to "overproduce." This characteristic will make all the difference in your success and consequent happiness.

When you really consider the subject carefully, what value does an inherently undependable person possess? The answer is obvious. You cannot be associated with them in any of life's serious matters since you cannot rely on their performance. You will, if you're wise, avoid them in all important situations which require that you put your trust in someone else. Consider how far-reaching this trait of dependability becomes. Most of the worthwhile activities of living are serious matters. Since to live means to depend on others, a person recognized for his lack of dependability will soon be isolated. Your entire future will be adversely affected by this one flaw.

Yet the entire matter can begin to be "turned around" with the rising of tomorrow's sun. One day won't erase a lifetime of irresponsibility. But one day traveling in the right direction will make a difference and it will represent a start. Two days will be further progress and as each day passes a new "image" will soon emerge. Don't hesitate to admit your previous irresponsibility. It will tend to cause those who were already aware of it to further believe the veracity of your expressed intentions. Mere words won't get the job done. *You can only erase the past with positive actions.* This involves quietly going about your life meeting all your obligations without fanfare. You will slowly gain a new respect from your acquaintances and success and happiness will come your way.

DISAPPOINTMENT

"One must learn how to handle graciously the unpleasant experiences of life."

Life is a combination of pleasant and unpleasant duties and experiences. Everyone can handle the pleasant aspects; it is the unpleasant duties and experiences that, if not properly handled, can ruin a life. One has to learn how to face the unpleasant experience and to handle the unpleasant duty. For the lack of a better phrase, one has to learn how to "bite the bullet" in order to lead a happy life.

Pleasant duties and experiences can be handled and absorbed by most people in a fairly acceptable manner. Some examples are to get a promotion; to marry the person you love; to win the Irish Sweepstakes; to pay-off the mortgage on your home; to be told that a suspicious growth is benign; to get an "A" on an examination; to win an election; to accomplish a long-sought goal; to acquire an important new client; to achieve any goal or acquire an object that is considered desirable. Everyone has no difficulty reacting to such occurrences.

Unfortunately, the pleasant aspects of life are only part of the story. Everyone's life also contains many unpleasant incidents. The ability to deal with the unpleasant side of life will determine whether an individual can be said to be happy. Knowing how to cope with difficulties is one of the most valuable tools in building a full and happy life.

One must first approach any problem with the belief that there is a logical and intelligent way to deal with it. Many people, when confronted with a problem, deal with it by ignoring its existence. This type of person tends to accumulate a "mountain" of unsolved problems which ultimately tends to overwhelm him. Others attempt improper solutions based on an inability to understand the correct nature of a problem. Others, while understanding a problem, attempt the solution which involves the least amount of unpleasantness or requires the least amount of courage.

Picture a man-woman relationship which has soured as far as one of the participants is concerned. Let us assume for purposes of discussion that the woman sees a need to end the relationship and the man desires the continuation. Her first concern is to keep from hurting the man's feelings by hiding her convictions from him. So the woman procrastinates out of fear or compassion or both. She is certain in her mind that the relationship is over, but she hesitates to "bite the bullet" and reveal her feelings. She fails to do what must be done and that is to frankly and openly discuss her viewpoint with her mate.

She begins to live a lie. One thing is certain and that is it won't get any easier. When the break finally occurs, it won't hurt any less. The man will undoubtedly begin to sense a change in her feelings. But since "love is blind" he will probably ignore it and continue as if nothing has happened. Both parties will continue to invest irreplaceable parts of their lives in a situation which is hopeless. The more the investment, the greater the ultimate loss.

Once the truth is revealed by a frank and open discussion, a certain relief will be experienced by both parties. The woman will feel it because she has finally exposed her feelings and the man, though disappointed, will be grateful for hearing the truth about something he has already sensed. His doubts will be resolved once he knows the truth. The longer the delay, the harder it will be for both parties.

We must all learn to "bite the bullet" sooner or later. It can be delayed, but it cannot be successfully escaped. It is part of life. This need arises in thousands of different ways. An employee needs to be fired or promoted instead of another, or his work habits must be corrected. A close companion needs to be told to bathe more frequently, do something about mouth odor, or excessive profanity, drinking, or drug usage, negative personality traits, or dress habits, excessive bragging, or personal hygiene. Someone needs to be informed of the death or serious injury of a loved one, the adverse health of a loved one, the defection or betrayal by a loved one; or any type of unpleasant information concerning a loved one.

A beloved pet must be disposed of by a mercy killing, A son or daughter must be placed in a home for retarded or handicapped children. A parent or other loved one must be placed in a nursing home for the aged or infirm. Failure must be recognized concerning a long-cherished goal and another course pursued; a personal need to stop drinking, or smoking, or taking drugs, or to discontinue a habit which has brought much happiness and contentment in the past; an admission that one is not as young as formerly, requiring a change in life habits; the need to start dieting or to commence strenuous physical activities. For some, the need simply to work and earn a living is a very difficult and unpleasant undertaking. The necessity of being alone is very difficult for most people; or to stop gambling, or chasing women, or chasing men, or to stop any activity which has become harmful to the individual concerned.

In the above illustrations, all of which are a part of life's experiences (and many more too numerous to mention) one has to learn how to do what must be done, In short, you have to learn to "bite the bullet" gracefully and effectively.

ACTIONS, NOT WORDS

"The way to speak and be heard is to let your actions and your deeds speak for you. In so doing, your message gets across much more vividly and with a more lasting result."

Many people find it necessary, probably on a psychological basis, to verbalize about their abilities and accomplishments. Consider that even if what they say is true, it is very unwise to proceed through life in this fashion. If the ability or accomplishment is sufficiently rare, then the only effect the speaker will have in the mind of the listener will be to create envy or hatred. At the least, the listener will feel outdone or intimidated by the speaker and any relationship that has developed between the two will be either destroyed, or at best, greatly reduced in value. The old saying, "If you've got it, flaunt it" couldn't be further from the truth. "If you've got it, don't flaunt it" because your possession of some unique ability or accomplishment will be recognized soon enough and when this occurs, it won't be necessary to recount it to anyone else.

If an individual possesses a rare ability or accomplishment, he will not have to say a thing about it. As soon as it is discovered or recognized, his friends and acquaintances will do all the talking for him. When this type of talking occurs, it usually is done in an admiring, affectionate manner which creates an enormous amount of goodwill for such an exceptional individual. Whereas, if the exceptional individual immediately points out his ability or accomplishment, the listener will speak of it in a derisive manner, such as: "So-and-so can shoot a 70 on the golf course, but he lets you know that within five minutes of meeting him." The ability or accomplishment is stated for what it is, but the individual possessor is spoken of in a derisive manner.

Actions always speak louder than words. Their impact is greater and lasts far longer than any verbal recounting ever can. If you can paint a beautiful picture, don't discuss it. On the proper occasion, just show the picture. One picture speaks a thousand words. In the final analysis, you are going to be judged by your deeds and not by your words. If you are able to prepare a gourmet meal, don't tell someone, "One night I am going to invite you to my apartment and cook you a meal. I'm a gourmet cook." Rather, without advance fanfare, invite the individual for dinner and let your cooking ability speak for itself. By stating in advance that you are a gourmet cook, you have raised the guest's level of expectations to unreasonable heights, and even a great meal would be only mildly appreciated as such, since your advance verbalizing has already caused him to expect too much.

The above principle applies throughout every activity of life. If a person tells a friend, "My girl friend is positively the best looking girl in the world" that friend, upon meeting the girl, will immediately start looking for attributes which make her less than the "best looking girl in the world." When one verbalizes or even brags about some ability, the very act of bragging puts one under tremendous pressure to perform up to a standard of excellence.

Is it far wiser and far more productive of tranquillity to give no advance billing, make no such statement in advance, and unobtrusively and quietly simply go out and do the job? When this happens, the observer won't be able to get away from the performer quickly enough to tell his friends in a friendly, admiring manner of the ability of such a person.

Bragging about your abilities creates needless tensions and jealousies, whereas quiet, humble performance results in friendly admiration by your peers. Happiness is certainly easier to attain when your peers have a friendly admiration for you than when they are jealous, resulting in derogatory statements.

In the long sweep of life, you will be judged by your deeds. Why not let them speak at the outset for themselves? They always have the last say and make the final impression anyway.

DIGNITY VS. PRIDE

"Do not confuse pride, which is ignorance, with dignity, which produces happiness."

All the great thinkers of all times condemn pride. Pride is a trait that causes you to imprison yourself within your mind. You construct invisible barriers between yourself and the world, and won't take them down because of your pride. How many times have people permitted enmity to continue for years simply because pride wouldn't let them say they were wrong or that they were sorry.

When needless ill feelings continue because pride will not permit someone to say or do what is necessary to end it, then such a person is extremely unhappy. But pride will not let you admit even to yourself that you are unhappy or that such unhappiness is foolish. Pride is probably the cause of more needless human misery than any other characteristic possessed by mankind. Learn to recognize and understand foolish pride. It is not that difficult to admit a mistake. After all, most humans know in advance that we all make mistakes. It won't hurt you in the eyes of your friends if you admit a mistake. Actually your image will probably be enhanced since by admitting your error you will simply reveal a very human quality which everyone appreciates. Likewise, it is not very difficult to tell someone you're sorry. It is far wiser and better to openly admit you're sorry for a mistake than to extend ill feelings needlessly for years. It is absolutely amazing to discover "grudge" relationships between people that have continued for years over some ridiculously simple incident that should have been instantaneously forgotten. For years, such people won't speak to each other and experience awkward social situations rather than simply forgetting their foolish pride and renewing their previously warm relationship.

What you need in your life is dignity and thankfulness. If my child makes straight A's in school while yours fails, I should not flaunt my child's grades. Rather, I should be thankful that I have an intelligent child. With this attitude of thankfulness and humility, you will be more understanding of my feelings for my child's good grades and actually rejoice in them even though your own child is failing. All the good things that happen to us should not cause us to be proud, but they should cause us to be thankful. If we are considered to be handsome, we shouldn't be proud of this fact but rather we should be thankful we had parents who, by their features, enabled us to be handsome. If we emerge financially successful from a business venture, we should not be proud of our wisdom, but we should be thankful for our good fortune.

Instead of pride, which we should all do without, we should learn to develop dignity and thankfulness in our daily lives. This comes from never boasting; always expressing intelligent opinions in a quiet, logical manner; working hard in our chosen field of endeavor; never gossiping or speaking scandalously about anyone; rendering genuine praise whenever circumstances and conditions warrant; dutifully fulfilling all the obligations that life places upon us; carrying out our duties without a complaint; and generally making everyone we meet a little happier because they met us.

We hear it said that, "He has no pride," or "I have my pride." This implies that pride is a desirous thing to have. Incredibly, many people believe this to be true. Actually, pride is damaging and produces much unhappiness. I believe what these people are trying to say is that they have dignity. Dignity is not divisive, whereas pride creates much hatred and tension. If you want to be happy, forget your pride and replace it with thankfulness and dignity.

PERSONAL DIGNITY

"When you project yourself and your personality in a dignified manner, the world's impression of you will be favorable and your chances for happiness will be increased."

Personal dignity is very hard to define; but when you have it, your acquaintances know it. It's that quality which helps you to remain humble in victory; to accept defeat with grace; to never repeat or initiate critical comment about an acquaintance; to handle pressure with grace; to be helpful to your fellowman; to resolve differences smoothly; always to be well-groomed; to be soft-spoken, yet followed; to be a leader of others; not to be guided or governed by your ego; to be quick to give deserved praise without limiting it by criticism; to be relaxed; to be trusted by your friends; to be sought after socially; to be respected; to be asked for your opinion; to be able to keep a confidence; to have your motives unquestioned; to have a presold image of tranquillity and reasonableness; to be assigned leadership roles without asking for them; to have the help and assistance of your peers in your endeavors; to have the total effect of your personality on your fellowman always favorable; to have your word trusted and your promise believed; to be moderate in all your vices; to never lose your temper; to not attempt to force your opinion on others; to be quietly efficient; to cause your acquaintances to feel relaxed and happy in your presence.

Dignity is always appreciated, even though the observer doesn't really know why he respects a person. The lack of dignity is always negative in its effect, even though the observer may not know why he has a lower opinion of one person rather than another. Great world leaders who have had dignity include Mahatma Gandhi, Dwight Eisenhower, Winston Churchill, Abraham Lincoln, and Dr. Albert Schweitzer.

A person of "low" station in life can possess a great deal of dignity, for its presence or absence bears no relation to wealth or social trappings. Dignity is inherent in one's personality and cannot be purchased. It cannot exist in the same personality with braggadocio, vindictiveness, drunkenness, dishonesty, promiscuity, or immorality. It necessarily involves honor, patience, and sobriety. It has nothing to do with wealth or station; it has everything to do with one's inner soul.

Dignified people are able to retain this characteristic in times of stress as well as in times of peace and tranquillity. The very self-assurance which seems to be the essence of dignity is present at all times and under all conditions. Its shining example is visible and envied at all times by all ages and both sexes. The world gravitates to people who possess this quality, both in their social life as well as in their business and recreational activities. Such a person is never at a loss for friends and loved ones. A truly dignified person, as opposed to a superficially dignified person, embodies the finest qualities to be found in mankind.

If by your actions, you are thought of in a dignified manner by acquaintances, your acceptability by all people for all purposes is enormously multiplied. Such a favorable position has to be earned, and in the long run, cannot be fraudulently acquired, or if acquired through artifice, cannot then be retained with any degree of permanency or certainty. When such a favorable position is reached, many doors are automatically opened and many opportunities are automatically presented. To be important, these doors and opportunities must necessarily involve service to one's fellowman. From these advantages can come much happiness that will make life more meaningful and interesting.

Dignity brings happiness to its possessor. His ready social acceptance; his being sought out for his opinions; his knowledge that people like and respect him results in much happiness to such a person. When a person has that undefinable quality known as dignity, it goes without saying that he has developed in his personal life such character traits that are valued and respected by his fellowman. He is envied for his qualities, but his fellowman is not jealous of them. He is appreciated and respected for what he is, and other people tend to be drawn towards him.

If you seek to acquire personal dignity, start out by watching your dress habits very carefully. Your personal hygiene and appearance is a significant step down the road towards achieving dignity. Then continue "down the road" by not making derogatory remarks about your fellowman. Never "run around" nervous and anxious, but always appear calm and serene. Learn to do whatever you do as efficiently and effectively as possible. Take pride in yourself and your work, but do not go too far in the direction of egomania. Learn to criticize yourself even in public. Learn to laugh at yourself. Learn to accept criticism from others gracefully and try to discern whether there is merit in what they say. If there is merit, then apologize to them for any transgressions or mistakes. No man is ever bigger or stands taller as when he is sincerely and gracefully admitting his own mistakes. Don't become paranoid concerning your station in life or your relations with any aspect of your environment. Just remember that everyone who lives has problems quite similar to yours and that the real test of a man is not whether he has problems, but in how he reacts to and meets his problems. Consider very carefully what you are doing wrong with yourself and correct it tomorrow. Why perpetuate a mistake? If you are doing something wrong or injurious to yourself, don't do it again. It's illogical. If you have a tendency to brag, stop it. If you are good at anything you don't have to brag about it, people will know it and recognize it without your telling them. When they find it out by observing your deeds and not by listening to your words, they will do the bragging for you. You won't have to say a thing.

Dignity can be best described as that calm, relaxed, efficient, humble self-assurance that is very helpful to its possessor in obtaining an unusual amount of happiness for his life or in achieving almost any other objective such a person may desire. Anyone can possess dignity. So why not start right now on this goal for yourself? It can bring you unimagined peace of mind and consequent happiness. It is not hard to obtain and doesn't cost money. Rich or poor can have it or not, as they desire. It is a very wise goal.

SELF

One of the hardest lessons to learn in life is the practice of not putting our own private interest ahead of every other consideration. The habit of constantly asserting our own rights or claims ahead of all other matters is difficult to overcome. We see this played out every day in international affairs, in our own politics in America, and in our relationships and the relationships of our fellowman. The net effect of personal interests being given top priority around the world has had a devastating result on the quality of life on this planet.

One might say that human nature has always been self-centered and will continue to be, so long as man exists. Though this is probably true, a wise man can easily see that true happiness can only be attained by taking our thoughts away from our own problems and letting them travel to the problems of our fellowman. If we constantly think only of our own problems, they become magnified out of proportion to their true character. After all, it is impossible for most people to even remember what they worried about a year ago. Even a newspaper headline that may have startled you a week ago is no longer remembered. Therefore, if our own worries and problems are so easily forgotten, why worry about them at all? Look beyond yourself and think outward to your fellowman and his problems. It is a wonderful habit to start; and once you find yourself successfully on this course, your level of well-being will be greatly enhanced.

Remember that all difficulty starts in the mind—to the extent you successfully put it out of your mind, it doesn't exist. If you think outward instead of inward, you will not get upset about a difficult period through which you may be passing. Your mind will be on other things removed from your own person or world. This fact alone will do more to improve your own health and well being than you can imagine.

Nothing said herein is intended to indicate that you shouldn't have legitimate concern for important matters affecting your life. But don't dwell on them to the exclusion of the outside world and its problems. One cannot experience the great joys of life unless he goes beyond his own person. The vast world out there is meant to be enjoyed. In order to do that, you must escape the prison of "self." "Self" is a mountain we all have to climb before we can see the great beauty of what lies beyond. Do not let the concept of self block-out your entire view of the world. To do so, is to miss much.

Self-centered people tend to be unhappy and depressed. Outward thinking people tend to be happy and have many friends. Self-centered people are always complaining and never stop discussing their own problems. Outward thinking people joke about their problems, if they bother to mention them at all. Self-centered people usually greet you with a frown, while outward thinking people always seem to have something to smile and joke about. Wise people are outward thinking while ignorant people are self-centered. It's more enjoyable to associate with an outward thinking person, so why not become one today?

HAPPINESS AND ATTITUDE
"Attitude: Happy children tend to grow into happy adults."

Man has been probing the depths and mysteries of the human mind for ages with only limited success. Although our knowledge of the human mind is limited, it is obvious that the mind is analogous to the control panel on a computer. Everything seems to begin in the mind. Nothing exists except that it originates in the mind. This least understood part of the human body makes everything a reality. Until the mind tunes in, all is tuned out.

Happiness rests entirely with the mind. The way the mind looks at something or views some experience is the way that "something" is to each individual. A flower, a girl is beautiful or ugly; an experience is useless or worthwhile; someone or something is loved or hated; life or work is good or bad, depending upon how the mind perceives it. This mental receptivity is called, for lack of a better word, one's attitude. We have heard it said that everything depends on our attitude. We are happy or sad, depending on our attitude. The single most overpowering force in all our lives is our attitude.

Scholars increasingly agree that much of our health depends on our mental responses to the stresses of life. Arthritis has been diagnosed as having its origin in the mind. Hypertension has long been blamed on mental attitude. Heart trouble is frequently caused by the mind. Cancer has been noted as frequently afflicting people with a sour or sanguine personality. Asthmatic attacks are often nothing more than anxiety brought about by mental pressures. Hypochondriacs can develop the very diseases they at first imagine. Heart palpitations, sweaty palms, muscle spasm, stomach ulcers, shortness of breath, are but a few of the body's illnesses overwhelmingly attributed to mental attitude.

We all face difficult pressures in life. Some people remain happy notwithstanding, and others are totally conquered and subdued by them. It's not the difficulties we face which create the problem. The problem comes through our mental reaction to life's difficulties. Do we minimize the hardships or do we maximize them? Do we underreact, or do we overreact? We are far better off to minimize our pain and sufferings and to maximize our good fortune. Why stress the negative? Laugh heartily every time you get a chance.

Happy children tend to grow into happy adults. Sad children tend to be sad adults. People tend to be happy or sad all their lives. If they're happy at eight years of age, they tend to remain happy at eighty years of age and conversely. Very few incidents in life have lasting consequences. Most hardships represent an opportunity to learn and to grow. We should be thankful for these opportunities, for they only tend to make us a better person.

We should know that everything of importance in life depends on our attitude. With this knowledge, seek early in life to develop a happy, optimistic outlook that takes the difficulties we all encounter in stride. After all, everyone has essentially the same battles to fight. Work on developing a healthy mental attitude.

HARD WORK AND SACRIFICE

When a young person enters the world, he has before him two enormous tasks. The first and most pressing is to find his opportunity for a career and in so doing, to become a useful member of society. The second, and ultimately the more important, is to remain happy and useful throughout his lifetime and thereby enjoy life to its fullest.

Young people are happiest when they are affectionately disciplined and have their own work schedules and sacrifices to perform. In the truest sense of the word, an underprivileged young person is one who has all his work done for him, all his sacrifices made for him, and is showered with unearned luxury and compensation. Such a youth has no opportunity to gain self-confidence or self-respect. Such a youth becomes an unhappy nonachiever, ill prepared to meet the inevitable future tests of life.

After man matures and establishes himself in the world, he then has the continuing problem of remaining happy and contented throughout his adult life. Ultimately, deep reflection tells us that man's basic condition is that we live on a huge ball with an equatorial diameter of 7,900 miles. Its surface rotates at the speed of 1,000 miles per hour, thus completing a rotation every 23 hours, 56 minutes, and four seconds. Earth's average distance from the life-giving sun is 93 million miles, which it orbits every 365 days, six hours, and eight minutes. Earth's age, together with its planets, is generally believed to be 4.6 billion years old. Additionally, our solar system orbits within the Milky Way Galaxy, which in turn, orbits with billions of other galaxies. We came from an unclear starting point or beginning, and we are constantly speeding towards an unknown or uncertain destination. So far as has been proven, we are traveling endlessly through a hostile space at incredibly high speeds—all alone. I say all this to make the point that basically, we are all on a "space ship" orbiting constantly in at least four different patterns. In order to avoid a pervasive feeling of being alone, we are all well advised to limit our thoughts and activities to tangible, attainable goals arrived at through hard work and sacrifice.

One should never stop working so long as he has the health to do so. The need to work and to be of service to others bears no logical relationship to one's wealth. People constantly dream of the day on which they plan to retire. Retirement is frequently the most disheartening experience of man. Retire to what? When one retires normally such a person deteriorates both mentally and physically. Everything atrophies—the mind and the body. If you don't use it, you lose it. Why not stay active and useful to your fellowman? Why sit around and wait to die? After total retirement, the next significant event in such a life is death. Why sit around and wait for death? Live to the last possible moment. Let death grab you while you are busily engaged in the pursuit of life. Since death is certain to come to everyone, stay busy with the objectives of living and let death come unheralded by excessive foreboding.

Work and sacrifice are the blessed gifts of a productive life. They give life a special dimension. The achievement of goals through hard work and sacrifice gives one the feeling of accomplishment that nothing else does. Work and sacrifice necessarily involve assistance to others, and it is this latter result that gives the worker's life a special significance. Lazy people are uninteresting and unhappy and really do not pay "rent" for the space they occupy on this planet. Working people cause good things to happen. They create forces which reverberate throughout society whereas lazy, nonproductive people have a totally negative impact.

Work is positive; it creates happiness; it fights boredom. As a result, we should never stop working and being useful.

GOALS

A life without goals is a life adrift, a life without purpose. Without a goal there is nothing to obtain—there is no objective. There is nothing by which to measure success.

By the word *goal* I don't mean to suggest some "once in a lifetime" objective that one strives to obtain for many years. I do not mean to approve of the working man who has but one goal and that is to retire and "go fishing" for example. Such a singular objective is too long-term in character. It involves too much of a wait. Another goal is often to wait until "the children are grown" or until the "house is paid for." These goals are honorable and proper but they are long-term in nature and if they are not mixed with hundreds of interim goals, life becomes very suspenseful and wrought with tension and anxiety. These latter results occur because such goals are so infrequently obtained and provide few opportunities for the relaxation and satisfaction that comes from attaining a goal.

One should have no less than at least five attainable goals every day. Examples of these kinds of goals are too numerous to mention. The following are representative of what I have in mind; to wash the car; to stop by the health club for a workout; to go for a swim; to visit a sick friend; to perform a kind and thoughtful service for another person; to donate to a charity; to play sports with the children; to visit your parents; or to call them on the telephone; to go for a walk; to go for a bicycle ride; to get a haircut; to visit the doctor's or dentist's office; to go to church; to accomplish something at the office; to accomplish a task at home such as repair work or cutting the grass.

The above are but a few examples of the type of goals that should be on our agenda on a daily basis. Having accomplished five such goals in a day, an individual has the opportunity to experience the joys of achievement on a daily basis throughout a lifetime. These goals are achievable daily and provide joy and satisfaction to an individual. Some of the goals may involve unpleasant or arduous work. These tasks become quite pleasant if one can learn to tell himself during the work phase of achieving the goal that he is accomplishing a worthwhile goal—doing what he wants to do. This thought makes the unpleasant all the more endurable.

Longer term goals can be added to these daily goals—goals that may take a week, a month, six months, a year, or even five years to achieve. In short, the most enjoyable life involves many goals of differing time periods. Just remember that the achievement of a goal is an immensely satisfying experience. This pleasure is available to all of us. All we have to do is to establish goals. Let your long-term goals also remain but keep many shorter term goals.

My belief is that our primary goals in life should be to be useful to others and to be as happy as possible. In short, our primary or number one goal should be to simply enjoy life.

When selecting your many goals, always keep this Number 1 goal in mind. If you do, you will have a balanced and worthwhile life.

STRENGTHS AND WEAKNESSES

The most important knowledge that you can have is as complete a knowledge of yourself as possible. You should learn your own strengths and weaknesses.

To the extent you are perceptive and wise, you will penetrate the halo with which we all tend to surround ourselves and get to the core of your personality. To go through life and not really know and understand yourself is a tremendous handicap. We all have to train ourselves to be perceptive and observant because we are not born with this ability. Many of us are so sensitive to criticism that we never get to know the real person we truly represent. One way to begin to learn yourself is to sit down with pencil and paper and list, for your own private knowledge, all your positive and negative points. Do it again a year later and repeat the process annually with the objective of eliminating your negatives.

Once you have established your strengths, do not discuss them openly or in a bragging manner. Keep the knowledge of your strong points to yourself. If you talk about them, others will criticize you for doing this. If you remain silent about them your friends will do the bragging for you. Either you can discuss or brag about your strengths openly and your friends will criticize you for doing so; or you say nothing and your friends will discuss your strengths amongst themselves. The latter is obviously far preferable. If your strengths are obvious, as they eventually will be, they will stand out like a lighthouse in a dark sea. Your open discussion of them can only dim the light. Your friends discussing them will brighten the light. Your actions will speak the loudest.

Conversely, to discuss openly under proper circumstances your weaknesses will bring forth the sympathy of your friends. They will be cheered by your honest admission and will diminish or "play down" these weaknesses. They will urge upon you the thought that your weaknesses are not nearly as devastating as you portray them to be. To discuss your weaknesses openly is to invite the sympathy and empathy of your friends and acquaintances. One further advantage of this is that you might overcome them.

Known strengths not openly discussed become a powerful tool with which to fight the battle of life. Open discussion of them ruins their effectiveness. A further tragic result of such open discussion is to invite envy and jealousy. These emotions become devastatingly harmful when directed against an individual. Envy and jealously turn into hate, and to be hated complicates life enormously. On the other hand, an open discussion of your weaknesses, under properly selected circumstances, invites the goodwill of your friends and the act of confession is also good for your soul.

When you follow this pattern, your strengths are not envied and your weaknesses tend to be diminished, if not turned into outright assets.

PROBLEMS

The trauma is usually greatest when we first discover that we have a problem. The nerves get tense, the blood pressure rises and sleepless nights ensue as we look only at the problem. Frequently, the reaction of people is to ignore the existence of the problem requiring positive action in the mistaken belief that this approach will somehow reduce its impact or lessen its trouble making potential. This type of person exists in a world that is filled with fright and tension oftentimes resulting in ill-health. The problems continue indefinitely or worsen in character due to in attentiveness. Ultimately, their damage is much more extensive and costly. Prompt attention (once the extent of a problem is ascertained) frequently will shorten its duration and lessen its impact. We are far better advised to "spring into action" which tends to resolve the problem than merely to sit frightened and insecure while worrying and losing sleep.

Before we "spring into action" however, we must be certain that we understand as much as is possible of the exact nature of the problem. We can't act hastily in fear, anger or anxiety without first taking the time to analyze the problem. Remember most problems at "first blush" appear more serious than they really are and to take precipitous corrective action of the wrong nature often can increase the severity of its consequences. When reacting to a problem, always engage your brain before you engage your "mouth" or your "brawn." It is important to start dealing logically with the problem.

It is important to understand that every problem, after its existence has just been discovered, has two sides. The "worrying" side and the "effective understanding" side. Some people never get beyond the worrying side. They seem incapable to taking the necessary effective action. One must leave the worrying side and penetrate the problem by objective analysis and thereafter, having worked yourself through the problem mentally one must take effective action. Recognize also that after a careful study and analysis of a problem, the best thing to do in many cases is nothing. Under such conditions, the understanding side would require nothing to be done. The mere passing of time and nothing else will solve many problems. The important thing is to start dealing with the problem objectively; and doing those things that a careful analysis suggests should be done.

In a more opportunistic vein, all problems can also be called challenges that contain growth opportunities. The size of our problems is usually related to the level of responsibility that life has placed on us. If our position in industry, for example, is highly placed, then it follows that the size and amount of our problems are more numerous and of greater severity than are those of a person of lesser industrial stature.

I suspect that life would be very boring if we had no problems. Problems lend an uncertainty to life that adds excitement and relieves boredom. We should evaluate all our problems in this philosophical light and everything will become more bearable and less frightening.

The less time we spend worrying about our problems and the more time we spend dealing with the problems of others will cause our level of personal happiness to rise. While dealing with the problems of others, we should not fail to take direct action (if such is warranted) on our problems and then go on with our life. Always remember that time resolves all problems one way or the other. Action by ourselves may change the ultimate resolution, but be assured that whether we act or not, time will resolve all problems. Remember that some problems are unsolvable and must be accepted. They sort of "go with the franchise" so to speak. They are simply part of the reality of life so do the best you can, then sit back, relax, and enjoy whatever happens.

UNPLEASANT TASKS

Every day of our lives, we are confronted with the necessity of doing certain things that for purposes of simplicity can be described as being unpleasant. These include getting out of bed in the morning; taking exercise; going to work; confronting unresolved problems, borrowing money; etc. No one is exempt from these experiences. The only difference is in how people react to these unpleasantries.

Let's take the first illustration dealing with the necessity of getting out of bed. I suggest when you first wake up and while you are still in bed, be thankful that you are still alive. Once this thought penetrates your mind in all its significance, the idea of having to get up is not so bad after all. Next, if it occurs to you, think of the people who are bedridden due to illness and are unable to get out of bed.

After you slowly rise, don't think of everything you have to do before you go to work, but take one segment of your arising ritual at a time. Maybe you should splash some cold water on your face or put on the coffee or get the newspaper. All these acts or any one of these acts start to get the adrenaline flowing and all parts of your body start to awaken. Be sure that you get out of bed early enough so that you don't immediately have to rush madly through your bath, breakfast, and dressing to get to work on time. I can think of nothing more traumatic and unpleasant than starting your day behind schedule or having to hurry. The important thing to remember in accomplishing unpleasant tasks is that you should start dealing with aspects of the tasks that encompass less than the whole. Single out the least unpleasant part of an unpleasant task and start dealing with it. Let's assume that you don't feel like exercising on a particular day. Assume further that certain parts of the exercise routine are more pleasant than other parts. Under those circumstances, start with the pleasant parts and in so doing gradually work into the unpleasant parts of the routine. You will probably find that the entire procedure will become less unpleasant as you proceed through your exercise routine.

Remember, even unpleasant tasks can be broken down into more desirable and less desirable parts. The important part is to get started. Don't just sit back and commiserate. Get the wheels turning. Start dealing with various aspects of the unpleasant task.

Soon, you will be caught up in the actual work rather than in worrying about doing the work. Usually, most experiences are never as unpleasant as they first appear. Most of the distastefulness is often in our minds.

You are far better off working to accomplish an unpleasant task than in sitting idly by and worrying about its existence.

ANGER

Anger is one of our most dangerous emotions. It is dangerous because it often results in violence causing immeasurable hardship, both for the one angered and the victim or the object of the anger. Uncontrolled anger has ruined many lives, though the time involved may have only been seconds or minutes. After all, it takes very little time to pull the trigger of a gun, stab someone, to hit someone, or to say something unforgivable. Most anger flares up quickly and almost as quickly, disappears. If you possess a temper learn to control anger in the first moments of its existence. To control it then is to eliminate all the disastrous consequences resulting from its uncontrolled expression.

Always remember, when you confront a situation which causes anger to swell up within you, what is happening is either for the best or the whole incident represents an opportunity to grow and become wiser. The perpetrator of the act causing the anger is no doubt doing the wisest thing possible in view of his intellect or the facts available to him. Most people tend to do that which to them represents the wisest course of action, even though their judgment may be faulty, their information may be erroneous, their mind may be clouded by drugs, or they may possess a very wrong system of values. In any event, their ultimate action, which resulted in your anger, was taken after all possible actions were considered and that certain course of action which angered you was decided upon. The party committing the wrong acquires a problem. If you let this wrong result in undue anger by you, then you too have committed a wrong which now results in you also having a problem.

When you let your anger explode without control, you wind up looking foolish. By this display, you have hurt yourself more than you've hurt the object of your anger. Your anger will not convince the other person that you are right. It will merely reveal you in an unfavorable light while convincing no one of the correctness of your views. An angry person can convince no one of the merit or truth of his argument. All he can do is convince his listeners that he is immature.

If you allow yourself to become angry with a person who you are convinced acted wrongly, you may decide not to talk to him. But when you do this, you hurt yourself again. You now have to spend much time and effort avoiding contact with the other person. In so doing, you limit the "space" in which you can travel. Why hurt yourself when you've done nothing wrong.

The far wiser course is to try to understand why someone acted as they did. Don't get angry at them. You might well feel sorry for them, but to get angry is to hurt yourself. If you truly understand, you never get angry. Wisdom diminishes anger. Conversely, excessive anger is evidence of ignorance.

Courtesy

"It is always wise to be courteous and thoughtful in all situations."

Strive to be courteous in all dealings with people. As our world gets more and more crowded, contacts become more frequent and inescapable. If you do not develop an inherently courteous style, your mannerisms will develop a great deal of unnecessary friction. When this happens, a pathway that should be smooth and untroubled suddenly becomes difficult and unpleasant. The difference may be no more than your failure to say, "good morning" or even more subtly, in the tone of voice with which you said, "good morning."

In Europe they have developed what they call "Continental Charm or Mannerisms" This involves the logical outgrowth of different cultures living virtually "on top" of each other. Since contacts are so frequent between people of different languages and cultures, the successful survivors are the super diplomats who are constantly solicitous of another's welfare. This method of conduct has become known, for want of a better description, as "Continental Charm." Bear in mind that it's essentially superficial and should never be taken for true friendship. Nonetheless, Americans are fascinated by it and seem to be a bit envious. We Americans have neither had time nor to some extent had the necessity of developing courtly mannerisms. After all, when America was still a frontier with vast expanses of nothingness, Europeans were already living on top of one another. While they were perfecting Continental Charm we were developing the cowboy epitomizing straight-from-the-hip rugged individualism. In Switzerland, for example, French, Italian, German, and Swiss dialects are all spoken. It becomes necessary for someone who travels all over this small nation to speak four languages. This necessary European multi-lingual capability adds to the aura which surrounds Continental Charm. Americans traditionally have not had the need to speak more than one language, although this condition is changing fast.

A courteous person is nothing more than a person who takes the time to consider the other fellow. This habit can be readily detected by the discerning individual. Along with the habit of being courteous, you should develop the quality of sincerity. It is devastating to affect an air of courteousness and make it obvious that you are totally insincere. If this be true, then you are better advised to remain your normal self, because hypocrisy and deception are resented and detested above all else. If you can't be genuine, don't get into theatrics because the price of detection is very high.

Genuine, sincere courtesy involves nothing in the world but considering the next person's problems and feelings. An exclusive preoccupation with your own problems is nothing but the mark of a selfish human being. It is utterly provincial to exclude the problems of the entire world and to dwell exclusively on your own. The rest of the world is really not interested in your problems, so why bore them with a litany of your trials and tribulations? You will get a lot more sympathy if you keep your own problems to yourself. "He who complains the least gets the most sympathy." So train yourself to be considerate of the next person's problems. Be genuine about it and not superficial. A shallow and insincere display of concern and empathy breeds contempt. So cultivate sincerity or forget the whole effort.

Once you have taught yourself to put the next person and his problems ahead of your own, you will find great success, tranquillity, and happiness in your life. How can you be depressed about your own problems if you only worry about your neighbors' tribulations? Your own cares will pass with time, and true happiness will come your way.

BE AWARE OF HOW YOU IMPRESS PEOPLE

"If you have a strong personality, and a better-than-average intellect, you probably intimidate most people."

Most people are shy and unsure of themselves. They need to be reassured constantly that they are acceptable and performing adequately. While they were in school, they received grades which informed them of the quality of their performance. Since they left school, no such convenient yardstick is available.

As a consequence of the facts discussed above, people are easily intimidated. An individual who has a positive, intelligent, and strong personality will tend to frighten or intimidate most people. Such a person has to be purposely "low key"; otherwise, he will harm himself and his chances for success. After all, people don't feel comfortable with people who overpower them with the sheer force of their personality. They don't want to deal with or be associated with them. People feel jealous of these types and are often very critical of them. The average person likes to work with someone they can relate to on a person-to-person or ability-to-ability basis. People want to play ball in their own "league." They don't want to get in the "major league" when they only feel qualified to play in the "minor leagues."

Therefore, if you have a forceful, intelligent personality, learn how to operate on a "low-key" basis. Deliberately downplay your strengths and be quiet about your accomplishments. You needn't discuss them publicly because people will know about them soon enough. Your problem is too much ability, not too little. Therefore, you have to darken some of the luster surrounding yourself. You need to let a little "dust" collect on the "diamond." Don't polish or embellish it because it shines too brightly already. Life tends to be competitive, and this is especially true in the areas of work or career. If you shine too brightly, people will be afraid to compete with you. When this occurs, your chances of success are unnecessarily reduced.

Purposely maintain a low profile and downplay your accomplishments. If your abilities are discussed, let others discuss them. The truth will reveal itself making it unnecessary for you to flaunt it before a jealous world. If they can't match you, your peers will attack you. This is especially true if you maintain a high profile. If you adopt a quiet, nonverbal posture, your peers will do the "bragging" for you. Once this occurs, your acceptance will be much improved. The overachiever's success becomes his biggest problem. He must deal with it intelligently or the underachievers of the world will gang up on him and make life very difficult.

The important thing is to recognize that a problem exists and also to understand the exact nature of the problem. No problem can be solved if it is not recognized. Once identified, the rest is easy. The solution is easy to arrive at once the situation is understood. A feeling of isolation grips all overachievers. They do not feel a part of their peer groups. Their peers do not identify with them, only resent them. *A special gift of intellect and ability carries with it somewhat of a curse, the curse of being isolated, of being looked upon as somewhat of a freak.* This condition can devastate an overachiever. An understanding of all the undercurrents involved will go a long way toward alleviating and making the whole situation more tolerable. This in turn will lead to more contentment and happiness for everyone affected by a strong, intelligent, and forceful personality.

SEARCHING FOR THE TRUTH

"Search always for the truth, and when you think you've found it, accept it as a part of reality."

The world does not really want to hear the truth. A politician knows that the public does not want to hear "unpleasant" news. It wants to be told that the president is in the White House, the governor is in the State House, the mayor is in City Hall, and all are well and functioning. A citizen votes for the harbinger of good times. A voter doesn't understand a messenger carrying unpleasant news; one who dwells predominately on unpleasant news can be nothing but a precursor to unpleasant happenings. Consequently, the "Good News Charlies" of the world are the ones who get elected.

I say the above to warn that one who seeks to find the truth and pass it on to his fellowman is frequently not very popular with his acquaintances. Remember, the last thing the world wants to hear is unpleasant news. Now if this unpleasant news happens to be the truth, that fact really makes no difference. If "junior" is intolerable and a brat, "mama" does not want to hear it. In her eyes her son is a "darling" even though he may be a veritable "monster" to the rest of the world. A bearer of unpleasant tidings is frequently a very lonesome person. These types of people worry others, and humanity would rather be around someone who makes them smile.

A search for the truth as a way of life is nonetheless the wisest course of action for a human to pursue. After the truth is known, it depends entirely on the individual as to how widely he may wish to disseminate this knowledge once it is acquired. The objective of philosophers has primarily been to find out the truth about as many subjects as possible. It is significant to note that the average longevity of philosophers far exceeds the normal population. This would seem to suggest the fact that the truth is better than ignorance and that it is also better for your health. Even though its possession may result in barbs and criticisms from our fellowman.

We can train ourselves to discover the truth more quickly or more accurately. Our powers of observation can be increased so that our ability to see the truth is appreciably enhanced. Many people seek to find as the truth what they wish it to be in their hearts. They believe the "rose colored glasses" through which they look at the world. Ignorance leads to much unpleasantness eventually. Therefore, a happy person is one who looks for and finds the truth in everything and everyone within his powers of observation.

Merely to discover the truth is quite inadequate. Once the truth is known about a person or a situation, one must learn to act on this evidence. To know the truth and not act on it is to be a fool. Unused wisdom is probably the greatest waste in human endeavors. If I know that cigarette smoking causes cancer and I still smoke, I am committing a grievous wrong against myself and my loved ones. What good does it do to know something and then do nothing about it? The answer is you'd probably enjoy life more if you never knew the truth in the first instance. The ability to act fully on all truths does not occur overnight. It takes considerable training and intellectual growth before this practice is always followed.

The truth is always the best. It is better than an untruth or ignorance. Truth has its own special beauty. It creates a unique inner peace and tranquillity for the possessor. Never fear the truth and always be grateful to the person who brings it to you, even though it may hurt and shock you initially. If you are wise, ultimately you'll know it was better that you were informed. Once you learn to act on the truth, your life will be richer and happier.

MEANINGFUL EXPERIENCE

"It is completely erroneous to look at the ebb and flow, the achievements and the failures in life in terms of winning or losing: It is far wiser and less productive of misery to look at the incidents of life as meaningful experiences."

We have all heard it said that a certain individual is a "loser" and another individual is a "winner." This is nothing more than a very simple answer to a complex process. The final appraisal of a life cannot be accurately made until it has ended. If you compare life to a poker game, then it becomes evident that the winners cannot be determined until each participant has "cashed in his chips."

Christ was crucified; Mahatma Gandhi, Abraham Lincoln and John Kennedy were assassinated. Were all these individuals "losers"? Joseph Stalin was given a state funeral in the Kremlin; does that make him a "winner"? Adolph Hitler, Napoleon Bonaparte, and Benito Mussolini all reached the heights of great acclaim. Did that make them "winners"? When these questions are asked, it becomes evident that looking at life in terms of "winning" and "losing" is a very simplistic approach to a very complex process.

Life, rather than being expressed in those simple terms, should be thought of as a never-ending series of experiences. The wisest of men are usually those with the greatest number of expe-

Franklin D. Roosevelt. UPI/Bettmann Newsphotos

riences behind them. Some of the great men of history went to jail (Mahatma Gandhi); went bankrupt (Harry S. Truman); or were severely handicapped (Franklin D. Roosevelt). Some of our most successful and greatest politicians lost a number of elections

(Abraham Lincoln). Physical deformities and handicaps have been overcome by great men and women on their way to success. Remember Jimmy Durante's nose?

Great lives frequently represent examples of individuals who rose above bitter personal experiences to achieve great success, both of a personal nature and in their efforts to benefit their fellowman. *People grow in hardship and decay in luxury.* Individuals become more successful and wise through problems which they have overcome. One of the surest ways to grow is to experience hardship. Knowledge gained in the crucible of adversity is less likely to be forgotten than anything learned in the spotlight of success.

The tendency of mankind is to immediately brand someone undergoing misfortune as a "loser." It is far wiser to consider that such an individual is undergoing an opportunity to mature and develop as a human being. Every problem anyone ever has contains within it the seeds of his next opportunity. Looked upon in this light, an individual with six problems, for example has in his personal inventory six opportunities to grow. Whereas, a person who is luxuriating in the "lap of luxury" has only the opportunity to decay. Problems, when properly handled, become an asset. Attained goals become very dangerous pitfalls.

SELF-APPRECIATION
"A well-balanced person has to learn to be happy and contented with himself as a human being."

Happiness begins deep within our souls. We cannot be happy unless within ourselves we are quiet and peaceful. We must have a feeling of tranquillity and contentment that can only come after we adhere to those values and rules that we believe to be important. In short, we have to be true to our own spirit. If we believe that something is repulsive, we can't outwardly proclaim its praises. To do this is to lie to our own spirit. This we cannot do because we know the truth and we are not fooling ourselves. We may fool everyone else, but we know the truth about our own feeling.

When you lie to your own spirit or project on the "outside" what you do not feel on the "inside" you are creating serious tension within your own body. This tension carried on for sufficiently long periods of time can cause high blood pressure, ulcers, tension headaches, depression, and probably far more serious diseases as yet not fully understood by science. When you adopt an untruthful life style or talk and act hypocritically, the principal party being hurt is yourself. The truth of whatever you are misrepresenting will eventually be known. Meanwhile you have to live with your hypocrisy and lies, which will cause you to dislike yourself and force you to combat all sorts of ailments that can seriously threaten your health. *Be truthful with yourself and the world using the most diplomatic techniques possible.* Bear in mind that an unpleasant truth will be unwelcome by the person it concerns. But an unwelcome truth properly stated is always far better than lies or deception for everyone concerned.

If you are truthful with yourself and the world your whole body and spirit and mind will be better because of it. Your friends will value you for what you really are—a truthful person. Truth has its own beauty; it is refreshing and exciting. Anyone who follows a policy full of lies and deception in his dealings with the world is really not a very unique or exciting person. The withholding of vital information in a given situation is just as deceptive as an outright falsehood. Total truthfulness couched in a diplomatic demeanor is unsurpassed in its beauty. Such a person is indeed an asset to mankind and his personal knowledge of his character traits will bring him much happiness and contentment. He is the man you see with a steady look to his eyes, a smile on his face, a warm handshake, and usually a healthy body. Such a person likes himself.

A truthful person is usually a wise person. One who learns to deal only with the truth soon learns to apply this knowledge to his work and his recreational hours. He is able, by his habit of recognizing the truth, to learn about love and life and science and any field of knowledge he is inclined to pursue. Knowledge is nothing more than knowing the truth about a certain proposition. Obviously one who dedicates his entire life to the pursuit and determination of the truth is better equipped to learn than is one who deals in lies and deception. Such a "truth-seeking" person is happy and contented with himself. With this happiness contained within himself he will have no difficulty in favorably affecting all his loved ones and friends. He will be like a bright star in a dark universe. Everyone is benefited by his existence. Such a man can only be happy and wise.

SELF-KNOWLEDGE
"The beginning of happiness is to be honest
with ourselves about ourselves."

Oh, what magnificent pictures we paint of ourselves in our minds! We fool ourselves into thinking that we are far greater or far wiser, far more beautiful or far more desirable, far more hardworking or far more respected, or far more popular than we actually are considered by our peers. We mentally construct a hallucinatory creature that does not, in fact, exist. When the inevitable happens which brings us back to reality, we are deeply hurt.

If we take the time and have the wisdom, we can develop a fairly accurate image within ourselves about ourselves. Start with your mental prowess. Most of us are just average in intelligence. We may have more intelligence than we have wisdom or we may have more wisdom (common sense) than we have intelligence. We may be good in mathematics but poor in reading or vice versa. We may have a natural talent in foreign languages or a special ability in science and related subjects. We should determine whatever areas of intellectual achievements command our abilities and these areas should be catered to in our planning. We should in effect "play the game in our strongest suit." By an analytical process we should find out what our strongest intellectual areas are and plan our life in such a manner as to take advantage of our special abilities.

It may be that our principal abilities lie in working with our hands. If this is true, we should recognize it and plan our lives around these facts. Craftsmen make a vast contribution to the human condition and are adequately compensated for their knowledge. The mechanic who fixes the automobiles in the neighborhood makes a tremendous contribution to the welfare and contentment of the people. The real question is, what is the extent of your contribution?

Having considered what our intellectual and physical abilities are, we should next consider our personality and how our acquaintances react to it. Is our personality such that people inherently like us, or do they detest us? Or do we fall somewhere in between? It may be that our personality is such that people ignore us. Whatever the facts may be, we should make an accurate judgment, and after so doing, we should alter our life accordingly. For example, if your personality is such that people dislike you, then you should not try running for public office. Since politics is a game where people have to like you to vote for you, you shouldn't consider it as a profession unless you have a compatible personality. Occupations such as club manager, preacher, or salesman also require a compatible personality. If you are the quiet, retiring type, occupations such as bookkeeper, bank auditor, stockroom clerk, or many other vocational fields of this nature should be considered as your potential profession.

Remember, in approaching this whole subject, that everyone has natural abilities in some field. If apples are selling, why should you push oranges? Do what comes naturally. Tragedies occur when people go into an incompatible line of work just because someone else wants it. They lacked the intelligence or self-confidence or courage or willpower to pick their own line of work. How tragic it is when people spend their life in the wrong type of work.

This often happens because many people do not stop long enough to try and analyze themselves and evaluate their abilities. The happiest people spend their lives at work in vocations for which they possess natural abilities. Remember, everyone is good at something or, at a minimum, is better at some line of work than at another. Find out where your strong abilities lie and pursue that field as your life's work. People usually enjoy what they're good at and vice versa. If you do this, your chances for happiness will be greatly increased.

GOALS

"One of the most difficult things to learn in life is how to keep yourself on the correct path while seeking to accomplish a goal."

Let us assume that your goal is to acquire a four-year college degree. In order to accomplish this objective, one has to sacrifice many things that are tempting but would tend to prevent us from attaining our objective. The constant watching of television, for example, carried to the extreme that many people do, would prevent us from studying and making the grades necessary to obtain a degree. Gambling, womanizing, golf, excessive alcohol, or drug consumption and many other practices would rob us of the time and energy required to be a successful candidate for a college degree.

Wisdom will tell us what we can do and still enable us to put forth the effort and time necessary to obtain the goal we desire. Life at best involves a trade-off. You give up "this" and eventually you get "that." To be a successful college student is a very difficult undertaking. Sacrifices have to be made. Intelligence will suggest what course your life can take and still keep yourself on a college oriented pathway. How many nights a week can you date? Or how many hours can you work? How many classes can you not attend and still learn enough about the subject to pass the course? Judgments will have to be made on many subjects relating to interferences with your college life. Figure out how many social activities your schedule will permit related to college work; such as working on the college newspaper, etc. While these activities are honorary in nature and may add to your overall prestige as a collegian, they will not help you pass your examinations. Study and familiarity with the subjects alone will do that.

It becomes important always to bear in mind, for instance, that you are a young person going to college in pursuit of a college degree. Always keep this in mind. Remember the highest undertaking of your life, during this period, is the acquisition of a college degree. For this reason, it becomes important to do those things that will enable you to reach your goal and to eliminate those things that will prevent it.

The principle of being "goal-oriented" applies to every goal any person can ever have in life. The higher the goal, the more sacrifices will be required. To be a surgeon, or a scientist, or a theologian, etc., would require more personal discipline than to be a desk clerk at a motel. I speak of the preparatory study required.

Nothing worthwhile comes without an effort. No pain, no gain seems to be the operating principle. The pain increases the pleasure later on when the goal is achieved. All goals require work. Work keeps more people happy than does leisure. Most hardworking people are happy people, while many idle people are unhappy people. So don't let the fact that work is required in order to attain your goal dissuade you from it. After all, work done with the right attitude is a pleasure. The harder you work and sacrifice to attain your goal the greater will be your pleasure when victory is obtained.

Don't drift through life without a plan. Set reasonable goals for yourself and plan carefully how you will reach them. Recognize in advance that your lifestyle will be altered while you strive to reach your goal. Do what is necessary joyfully and cheerfully and your whole future will be enjoyable. After all, this type of activity is what any worthwhile life is all about. Be happy and get on with your life's work. Your personal happiness is involved.

CONSISTENCY

"Develop a quality of sameness about yourself, whether at work or play. Your acquaintances will appreciate consistency in your demeanor."

Some people bubble over with friendliness one day when you meet them and won't even say "hello" the next day. When this type of inconsistency creeps into your behavior, your friends, if you have any, will be perplexed and hurt by your actions. If you know someone and meet them on the street, say "hello" to them every time you meet them. Don't change your conduct from day-to-day. Try to be and act the same because it will better enable your acquaintances to understand you. Excessively violent shifts in one's personality are sometimes indicative of mental illness. If this is your problem don't hesitate to see a doctor about it. Some people are simply moody and allow their feelings of the moment to completely change their behavior. Always remember that no matter how great, or competent, or unusual you may be, you will still be judged by your humane qualities and not by some intellectual, athletic, or artistic abilities you may possess. Human beings are judged alike regardless of their wealth, position, or uniqueness. So learn to develop consistent, predictable social habits. Your friends and acquaintances will be better able to understand you.

This quality of sameness should also enter your job or profession. Whatever your work may be, you will soon learn techniques that result in a more successful accomplishment of your tasks.

Once you have determined the best methods to accomplish your tasks successfully, use those tried and proven approaches over and over again. In the routine of your work, don't adopt a plan of endless and meaningless experimentation. If there is a "best" way to do something, then do it that way. Don't adopt another less successful method.

Consistency can be seen to be especially successful in the field of sports. Golfers go through a unique set of motions before they strike the ball. Jack Nicklaus addresses a golf ball the same way every time. He swings at a golf ball with the same high arc every time. And so it is with Julius Erving in basketball or Muhammad Ali in boxing, or Bjorn Borg in tennis, or Terry Bradshaw in football. All these sports stars, through a system of trial and error, have worked out what to them is a physical technique that seems to work the best. Having developed this, they then do with "muscle memory" that which enables them to be exceptionally successful in their chosen athletic careers.

Inconsistency is very harmful to us all. If our friends cannot predict what we'll do in a given set of circumstances, we may find ourselves alone and untrusted. Our children need to know what our predictable response will be to a given act on their part. They need to know in advance whether we will approve or disapprove of their conduct. Our business

Julius Irving. UPI/Bettmenn

229

associates, our supervisors, our subordinates, all need to know where we will stand on issues that affect them. We cannot speak one way and act another way. Our actions have to match our words. When they don't, people lose faith in us; they no longer trust or respect us. So learn to be consistent socially, at work and at play.

HUMILITY

"Be humble in all things you do and say. If you have great achievements, be thankful for them but remain humble."

Sincere humility is the outgrowth of wisdom. True humility breeds love and peace. Hypocritical humility will soon be detected and deeply resented when discovered. Insincere humility, in order to obtain praise, is the lowest, most detestable form of pride. The more a person thinks and understands, the more reasons we discover to be humble. When a sincerely humble person is discovered, we can be sure that he is a wise person. Proud people are universally ignorant. Humility only comes after severe experiences with life, which leads to a deep understanding of who we are and how truly insignificant we are in the scheme of nature.

Every man you will ever meet will have something superior about him as compared to yourself. If he is older, the probability is that in addition to living longer than you, he has probably done more good in his life than you. If he is younger than you are, you have probably sinned more than he. If he is richer than you, he has probably given more to charity than you. If he is poorer than you, he has probably suffered more than you. If he is wiser than you, you should honor this superiority; or it he is more ignorant than you, you should honor his great struggle to achieve. If he's a "country boy" he probably knows a lot more about animals than you. If he's black and you're white then he has probably suffered far more from racial bigotry than you. The point is that anyone you will ever meet or compare yourself with will have one or more characteristics in which he is superior to you. When you think of yourself in this fashion you have a lot of reason to be sincerely humble.

If you are a beautiful woman, you should thank your parents and those features which you inherited that account for your beauty. The list is endless. If you are a great athlete or have an unusually high intelligence quotient or any one of a million different human characteristics you should be thankful for this superiority and not proud of it.

In the broad sweep of the universe we are truly less than a grain of sand on the beach. For one thing, a grain of sand was here long before we were and will be here long after we're gone. Pride produces needless tension and anxiety. Humility invites love and compassion. Our destiny is to be eaten by worms or to be cremated. When you think of it this way, we have nothing to be proud of and everything for which to be thankful.

When you are thankful instead of proud, you have nothing to prove to anyone. Proud people tend to have to prove whatever their boast may be. If I tell you I will shoot a 72 on the golf course and I actually shot a 75 you will consider that I exaggerated. However, if I tell you that I've been shooting fairly good scores lately— between 100 and 75—and I shoot a 75, you will consider that I have told you the truth.

Learn to be sincerely humble. Think deeply about yourself and you can't help but realize that *there is nothing concerning you which gives you a reason to be arrogant.* You have no reason to be proud, but every reason to be thankful. The difference will have a powerfully beneficial effect on your life.

DETERMINATION

"Once you have logically and reasonably convinced yourself that a certain goal is attainable, never, never, never quit until you have achieved success."

Every worthwhile goal you can set for yourself in life has a certain price tag attached to its attainment. Nothing of value comes without a sacrifice. An unbelievable amount of success is available to anyone who is willing to pay the price. The quitter never reaches his goal because when hardship rears its ugly head, he turns from his goal and goes in the other direction. You will encounter barriers of varying degrees of difficulty in your climb to attain any worthwhile goal. A dieter may lose ten pounds in the first two weeks of a diet and then go an entire third week without losing another pound. If such a person will just "hang in there" he will break through the ten pound weight barrier and lose as much as three more pounds overnight. This breakthrough will only come to the persistent person. The golfer may practice and practice to get his "tempo" correct with no success. If he persists, he may suddenly understand how to achieve the correct "tempo." The quitter will never experience this. Thomas Edison ran experiments as many as 5,000 different times before he arrived at the right combination for the dry-cell battery. Clark Gable knocked on studio doors for seven years and was told that his ears were too large for acting before he achieved success. Helen Keller was deaf, dumb, and blind; her struggle to communicate with the outside world is a classic example of success after persistence.

Remember, you must first be convinced in your own mind that success is reasonably attainable. Once you have arrived at this conclusion, then don't quit. If you quit when the first barrier appears, you will develop a pervasive feeling of failure that will permeate your entire outlook on life, and, what is more important, your self-image will be very poor. You have not failed until you decide to "quit." By the act of quitting you have determined that you either want to fail in reaching a particular objective or goal or you are unwilling to pay the price for success. If this is the case, you have nothing to blame but your own weak resolve.

Victories are very important in one's life, for example, making passing grades in school, finishing high school, getting a college degree, or getting a raise on a job. Human goals represent victories or failures in individual lives depending upon whether they have been attained or not. One thing is certain, if goals are worthwhile they have a price tag attached to them. *Sacrifice and hard work are required.* Successful people are nothing more than goal-oriented people who decided they had the ability to attain a certain goal. Having made the decision, they struggled through all the hardships necessary to reach success. Many times along the way they could have quit. Sometimes faith alone keeps them going when logic tells them to quit. Success finally comes after you have paid the price.

Remember, quitters never win and winners never quit. The price tag or sacrifice makes the achievement all the more enjoyable. This technique produces a life of happiness and enjoyment. It only comes after a struggle. *So don't quit!*

The principle of being "goal-oriented" applies to every goal any person can ever have in life. The higher the goal, the more sacrifices will be required. To be a surgeon, or a scientist, or a theologian, would require more personal discipline than to be a desk clerk at a motel. (I speak of the preparatory study required.)

Nothing worthwhile comes without an effort. No pain, no gain seems to be the operating principle. The pain increases the pleasure later on when the goal is achieved. All goals require work. *Work keeps more people happy then does leisure.* Most hard-working people are happy people while many idle people are unhappy. So don't let the fact that work is required dissuade you from your goal. After all, work done with the right attitude is a pleasure. The harder you work and sacrifice to attain your goal, the greater will be your pleasure when victory is obtained.

Do not drift through life without a plan. Set reasonable goals for yourself and plan carefully how you will reach them. Recognize in advance that your lifestyle will be altered while you strive to reach your goal. Do what is necessary joyfully and cheerfully and the future will be yours. After all, this type of activity is what any worthwhile life is all about. Be happy and get on with your life's work.

THE ART OF COMPROMISE

"Strive for 100 percent in all of your endeavors, but be prepared to settle for 75."

Planning makes up a very important part of all lives; we tend to expect a perfect ending to our endeavors. It's easy to sit down with pencil and paper and arrive at a 100 percent solution for many of our problems. However, the execution of these plans is carried out by fallible human beings and the final results usually fall quite short of the "paper and pencil" plan. This is life, and it is to be expected. What we should realistically strive for are the best possible results obtainable after taking into account that humanity with all its weaknesses will be the executioner of our plans. Thus, when actuality falls short of paper planning, we will not be excessively distraught by the outcome.

New leaders are especially vulnerable to the gap between planning and actual results. This "gap" causes the inexperienced immense pain and mental anguish quite needlessly. Remember, error is an important part of the human condition. If you don't want errors, do not rely on humans to carry out your plans. Since we have nothing but humans to rely on, we have to live with human shortcomings and the attendant disappointments.

If we obtained perfection in this life I'm sure it would be quite boring. Envision a game of golf in which the participant gets an eagle on every par four and par five hole and a hole in one on every par three hole, or a baseball game in which every hit was a home run, or a football game in which every play resulted in a

234

touchdown. This ultimate perfection can readily become a very boring experience. The imperfection of us all lends itself to the ultimate unpredictability of human behavior and adds to the human experience. This experience involves joy-producing achievements as well as sorrow-producing failures. This interplay of our fortunes is what life if all about.

The expectation that we will attain near perfection in all we do is sometimes caused by an individual's pride or greed or ego, or combinations of all three. He is saying to the world that in his case only perfection (or near perfection) will suffice since he is very different from the rest of mankind. When such a person's results reach only 75 percent of his goal, he becomes infuriated and creates much inner tension and unhappiness, all of it quite needlessly because this is part of life. No one really sympathizes with this type of individual. His emotions and anger are needlessly wasted on unsympathetic ears and hearts.

Be realistic by striving to do well in all your undertakings. Never forget that everyone involved is human and will not carry out to perfection their assigned role. When this happens there will be a "shortfall" in the results. Learn to live happily with them.

SELF-CONFIDENCE

Will we be able to do something or will we completely fail? Can we endure the emotions and fears of giving a public speech or of an unpleasant meeting or a confrontation with any form of reality? Can we successfully survive the fears caused by a trip to the dentist's office or a plane flight or the loss of a loved one? Can we pass an examination? Will we be able to handle ourselves properly during an interview for a job? All these questions raise the issue of our "self-confidence." Do we believe that we can do these many things in life which test the confidence that we have in ourselves?

There are many things that can be done to greatly alleviate that destructive feeling of inadequacy that we all have in varying degrees when we are faced with difficult tasks. The objective is to absolutely convince ourselves that we can successfully do what has to be done. Note that I said that we must "absolutely convince ourselves," etc. I'm not suggesting some weak-minded belief or some weakly held conviction. The difference between certainty and uncertainty is simply a mental process. We have to learn how to convince ourselves—the rest is easy. Once our conviction is firm and unchangeable, the greatest portion of our anxiety will disappear. We then will be able to more suitably perform our duties under emotional conditions that are more relaxing and enjoyable.

The difference between confidence and the lack thereof is the difference between joy and misery; between pleasure and drudgery; between night and day. This difference permeates our entire life and affects everything and everyone that we contact in our lives. Favorable results are obtained simply by a mental process. The battle is fought entirely in the mind. Don't expect to win the first battles. But by persistence and practice, the victories will come more frequently and with less effort. It is important to recognize when the battles should be fought and over what issues. The power of the mind, once its forces are brought to bear on a given problem is almost unlimited. It remains for each of us to recognize this great source of strength and to learn how to use it to improve the quality of our lives.

Usually the culprit we are talking about when we discuss the lack of self-confidence is fear. The mind properly used is the greatest enemy of fear. A trained mind can be victorious over fear. It is literally waiting to be used for positive purposes. By intellectual processes that are unique to everyone, fears can be overcome. The first thing we have to believe is that fears can be overcome. We have to believe this with a deep conviction. Then we have to believe that it is fear that is a largely responsible for keeping us from reaching our potential in everything that affects our lives and fortune. Once we learn to use this awesome weapon to establish our self-confidence, we will become the "best that we can be." After all, that is all anyone can ever do with his life.

HUMOR
"Learn to laugh at yourself."

Whenever we start taking our role in life too seriously, we are immediately beset by all kinds of problems. If we start thinking inwardly and encounter some of life's difficulties, we become depressed. If we place our self-interest above all other considerations in life, we are headed down the path to unhappiness. Remember, we are not unique. What we do has been tried before. There is really nothing original about us or the thinking that we do. Even Albert Einstein admitted he only had one original thought in his entire lifetime and that was his formula for the theory of relativity. All the responsibilities that we have can be readily assumed by many others. When we die, we will leave no appreciable impact on subsequent life. Even the greatest among us are soon forgotten. Twenty-five years after his death, Gandhi of India did not have as many followers as are officially attributed to him.

If our influence is temporary, we should approach all of life with this realization uppermost in our minds. We should perform the tasks that life brings our way to the best of our abilities, but we should also remember that the world does not depend on the successful completion of our duties. What we do has importance, but it is limited to the same importance that surrounds the duties of billions of other inhabitants on this planet. The world will continue whether we function properly or not. However, we should always bear in mind that we will be much happier if we do our work to the best of our ability. We must strive to do this for our own well-being—as much as for the well-being of our fellowman.

It is only when we attach an exaggerated importance to our

work, or to anything else about ourselves, that we encounter the resentment of our acquaintances. If we do important work we do not have to brag about it because the world will recognize our contribution. When we in effect tell the world, "Hey, look how smart I am" or "Look at what marvelous work I have done" the world will soon resent us. Our achievements will speak louder than anything we can do or say. Additionally, it is important to know that once we start boasting, the world will start criticizing. Once we become truly humble, the world will begin praising.

Since we are all human, we all make mistakes. Learn to accept mistakes as being common to all men. If you try your best and still make a mistake, learn to laugh at the result. Learn to laugh at yourself. If you do not want to make a mistake, then you had better stop living, or at least stop performing. If you live and perform, you will make mistakes. When it happens to you, consider that you have only shown that you are human. Jealous people may laugh at you, but even under these circumstances you should readily admit your error. Everyone understands mistakes and will think highly of you for readily admitting your error.

All humanity tends to follow the same pattern. We are born; we get some education; we usually marry and raise a family; we work to help support ourselves and our family; and we die. What we do between birth and death has a remarkable similarity for all of us. When we truly understand this aspect of life, it tends to make us very humble. When we have arrived at the proper level of humility, we will have no trouble in laughing at our foibles and errors. It is far better than crying or becoming angry. After all, the rest of the world will hardly notice our error, and will certainly not remember it for any significant length of time.

EMOTIONS

Emotions are a real part of all our lives. Feelings of happiness, love, hate, sadness, jealousy, greed, pride, insecurity, and fear are a part of everyone's mental makeup. All of us have to learn how to be the master of our emotions, rather than let our emotions control us. Emotions can only be controlled by wisdom or logic or a deep understanding of the truth.

None of us can go through life without emotion. Emotions give our lives excitement and richness. You are by your very nature an emotional creature. We all have the capacity for joy and sadness, love and hate, pride and humility, self-assurance and insecurity, tranquillity and excitability, fear and bravery, generosity and greed, selfishness and unselfishness, jealousy and trust. Whether we like it or not, we all have to deal with our emotions; therefore, a deeper understanding of our emotional makeup can only help us.

All of us are products of our environment. Our past history largely determines our emotional reaction to any experience. However, the degree to which we can control our emotions depends largely on our understanding of the logic and truth inherent in any situation. A penetrating analysis of the logic and truth in a given incident will enable us to deal realistically with the emotional fallout. People do things for a reason adequate for their purposes. We must always try to understand their reasons. To do so will prevent an emotional overreaction.

Emotions can be very illogical. Many times, they are the opposite of logic. Wisdom and understanding will lead to deep emotions consistent with logic and/or the truth. Your course should always be set by logic. The direction of our lives, to the extent that we are in control, should be based on our sense of truth and logic. Having embarked on a logical course of action, we will then find that our normal human reactions of emotion will have many opportunities for expression.

To live a life based on truth and logic does not suggest that we have to live a life devoid of emotions. Logic and truth must be the master of our emotions—not the slave. We should proceed by our understanding of truth and logic and not by our emotions. If the controlling force behind your activities is emotion not tempered by logic, you will exhaust yourself physically. With our emotions in total or substantial command, our bodies will respond beyond our capacity to endure. Its energy will be artificial and not based on inherent physical vitality. A person thus controlled, will frequently discover that his "motor is running" too fast. If this continues too long, the body (or "motor") will soon be destroyed.

A far better course is to let our understanding of truth and logic control our lives. Emotions should be complementary in a subservient capacity, ever ready to lend meaning and richness to our existence.

EMOTIONS AND LOGIC
"Always remember that emotions are the opposite of logic."

Most of mankind are guided exclusively by their emotions. Decisions made on this basis may or may not coincide with logic. Man selects his mate on the basis of emotion. He votes on the basis of emotion. He chooses his friends, insurance agent, real estate agent, lawyer, doctor and most every other associate in his life on the basis of his feelings or emotions. A decision arrived at in this manner may not be logical; but if there is a conflict between emotion and logic, emotion will govern. A man may talk logically about any problem he has. However, if you want to find out how he is going to act, discover first how he "feels" about a given subject. Once you know this, you will then be able to predict his actions. The overwhelming probability is that he will react according to his "feelings." These feelings, in all likelihood, will conflict with logic.

All people have four corners, or parts, to their personalities. Try to envision a square tilted to a position that is poised on one of the corners. Label the top corner as the higher ideals or aspirations which all humans possess. Attach to the bottom corner the label of negative or evil forces, another characteristic all humans possess. Label the left corner as logic or "sense"; and label the right corner "feelings." Contemplate this, and you will see that man is constantly buffeted by four opposing forces, namely: good, evil, logic, and emotion. If you want to know what an individual is going to do in a given situation, determine what his feelings are; and the probability is that this will reveal the course of his actions. Man is governed by his emotions, not necessarily by his logic. This explains his inability to avoid predictable pitfalls or trouble spots in his path. It also explains his ability to withstand severe hardships once they are encountered; but which by the use of logic, could have been avoided in the first instance.

In no area of human activity are feelings more in control than they are in the field of love. This includes not only man-woman love but also parent-child love and family love of all kinds. Mary is in love with Johnny. She knows Johnny has a terrible, uncontrollable temper. Every bit of logic suggests that she should not marry Johnny. Yet, her feelings are such that she overlooks his terrible fault and marries him because of those feelings. To no one's surprise, Johnny's temper wrecks the marriage. Drinking, gambling, womanizing, and many other faults are overlooked because of feelings. Likewise, men do the same with women. While the fire of love burns, all logic is discarded before the onrush of feelings of love. Once the initial flame of love has somewhat dimmed, the fault looms larger and larger and ultimately wrecks whatever relationship existed.

Parents tend to overlook faults in their children because of their love or feelings. Little Mary or Winston uses terrible profanity, will not work, is a spendthrift with money, is exceedingly selfish, will not study in school, skips school, and/or is rude to his parents. If disciplined, the child says to the parent, "You don't love me" or "I'm going to run away." So, in the name of love nothing is done on a timely basis to correct the fault. Later in life, a creature has evolved with so many faults that he or she, as an adult, is incapable of coping with the many disappointments of life and ultimately becomes very unhappy. This error was committed in the name of love, when in the name of logic, it could have been corrected. The habit becomes so ingrained and a part of the child's personality that it takes a major tragedy to correct a tragic problem.

People tend to conduct their business on the basis of feelings. As mentioned earlier, many associations such as with insurance agents, lawyers or doctors are based on an emotional selection. In the field of medicine, for example, people choose a doctor for his "bedside manner." Or their lawyer may be a friend for whom they have feelings, and who may or may not have the necessary competence. In other words, selection is based on personality. People will go to the church of their choice because of how they feel about the minister. The minister with the most overall effective personality has the largest congregation. People even tend to vote for a candidate whom they like even though his political views differ more from theirs than do the views of the opponent.

Because the world tends to operate on the basis of emotion rather than logic, style is often more successful than quality. Entertainers who have a nice style are frequently more successful than are entertainers with greater ability but less style. Clothes with a nice style are bought rather than those clothes with greater quality. Politicians with "style" enjoy a larger following than those politicians who may have greater competence and more character but less style. This is particularly true with the advent of television where make-up, appearance, and body language are significant factors. How many times have you heard "I like his style." The world pays more for style than for quality. This is due to the fact that feelings or emotions are generated by style; and ultimately govern most of the decisions of mankind.

These feelings or emotions are often the opposite of logic,

242

and frequently result in decisions which are illogical. In any conflict between emotions and logic, you can almost be assured that emotion will be the victor. So, if you want to predict an individual's reaction or decision, first discover what his feelings are—the rest is easy.

PERSONAL EXCELLENCE

Every person wants to be successful and happy while leading a useful life. These desirable goals are not achieved accidentally without focus and effort. The usual rule in life seems to be that all worthwhile achievement comes at a price. Nothing worthwhile can be achieved without a concerted effort. It all seems to start with an individual being or becoming the very best person he can be. The higher the caliber of person he becomes will cause the higher types of individuals to be attracted to his causes and objectives. Foremost among these would be the caliber of mate such a person would attract and with whom he or she can share their life. It all depends on the caliber of goals an individual establishes. Without high standards, a person will cast away any opportunity to extend his or her persona above the teeming masses of people.

The first thing a person has to do to be noticed as one who "is on the way up" is to achieve superior results in all his work and personal standards. Putting this in simpler terms, a person desiring to attain success, should do everything that affects his work and his personal life in the best manner of which he or she is capable. As the old timer said, "Anything worth doing, is worth doing right or don't do it at all." Some people stumble through life doing everything in a haphazard and careless manner and thereby achieve substandard or mediocre results. These same people then wonder why the "Gods of Fortune" never smile on their efforts. They wonder why they never get good grades in school or why they never meet a worthy love interest and simply blame it all on their bad luck. These same people will bemoan their acquaintances good fortune and never have the least idea of what forces and principles are at work in making these vast differences. We all tend to wind up with the type of fate that is exactly predictable by the standards that we set for ourselves in our personal and professional lives. If you want to elevate the level of your life, your acquaintances, your success, and your friends then start out by lifting your own level. *Remember people tend to attract as friends and acquaintances people of like caliber.*

Change the caliber of your tomorrow's by installing a standard of personal excellence in every phase of your life, today. If you are in school then dedicate yourself to a superior effort in all aspects of your school life. Do everything as well as you can, don't settle for mediocrity or less than your best. At work apply the same high standards to your work product. This includes both the quality and the quantity of your work product. If you are going to do something, then do it as well as you can or don't do it at all. Remember every day of your life you write the next installment of what will become part of your persona. This standard of excellence applies especially to your personal social life. Keep your habits clean and wholesome and protect your health and your reputation. You will attract a high caliber life-mate if you have set and maintained high standards for yourself. People of like caliber and kind tend to gravitate towards each other.

PART IV
Your Relations with Others

INJUSTICE

"Permitting injustice to go unchallenged in one's own arena of life is tantamount to assenting to the existence of injustice everywhere."

Frequently one hears an acquaintance forcefully denounce the practices of the United Nations or a foreign government or of a political leader in the nation's capital or in the state house or in city hall. The impression is often gained from listening to such a conversation that the speaker is fearless and quite discerning in his appraisal of people and events. Admiration and respect for such a forthright and seemingly courageous person can often follow from these type of remarks. Frequently this same type of person will stand by silently when a gross injustice is perpetrated against someone in his or her workplace or club or neighborhood. The question might well be asked, "why can such an outspoken person do nothing to fight injustices that exist in the very world or arena or neighborhood in which they live or work or socialize?" It is obvious that one can do very little if anything about what happens in the United Nations or in Washington, D.C., or in the state capital or even in "city hall." One can however do very much about an injustice occurring "close-up" in the very world in which one works, lives or plays. What's the difference?

The principle difference is that one perpetrator of injustice is "face to face" while another is remote and doesn't even know of the forceful denunciator's disapproval. The "close-up" wrongdoer has to be dealt with on a personal basis and consequently any attempts to correct, resist, or condemn will be known to the wrongdoer and will result in negative consequences to the "do-gooder." Remember it requires no great courage to condemn an injustice that is remote and where the perpetrator doesn't even know of a speaker's resistance. However when the evildoer "is right in your face," all sorts of consequences ensue. Social stigmatization or economic damage can often be the price attached to a struggle for justice in one's own arena of life. This is the struggle that separates the brave souls from the braggarts.

In Germany during Hitler's rise to power German citizens and foreign governments turned "a deaf ear and a blind eye" when it came to overlooking the many portents of evil frequently exhibited by the Hitler "juggernaught." No one seemed to struggle against the evil simply because their "ox was not being gored." However when everyone's ox was finally being gored there was no one to turn to for help. War was inevitable because the evil had become too powerful.

In you condone injustice in the world in which you live by doing nothing when your actions could have a positive effect you are telling the world that it is alright. You are saying by your actions that injustice can exist everywhere in so far as you are concerned because you are condoning its existence in your own "backyard." If a nation is to stand for justice then the battle against injustice must be fought on the local level. If a nation has injustice on a local level than it cannot be a just nation. Always use your voice and influence to fight injustice where you live, work and play.

MARRIAGE

"Marriage is an institution in a state of flux."

The author recently asked 20 young lady friends of his granddaughter, who were all high school students, "What are your life plans once you graduate from high school?" They all wanted to go to college and thereafter pursue careers. None of them wanted to be a mother and a housewife. Subsequently the author, while lecturing to a high school class on "career day," asked the same question to a class of 30 girls and 30 boys. Again the answers were that everyone, with the single exception of one girl, wanted to go to college followed by a career. None of them seemed to want to play the traditional role of a woman in a marriage. They didn't seem to want the life that their mothers were experiencing. Incidentally the author got the impression from her speech and manners, that the girl who opted for becoming a housewife and a mother was on the bottom of the intellectual scale in her class.

If one considers that marriage is an essential building block to a successful and peaceful society, one has to wonder what do these facts foretell for America's future. Today many career women solve the problem of procreation outside of the marriage contract. They either go to their favorite "sperm bank" or they simply get impregnated by a "'favorite lover" who then conveniently fades out of the picture. If the career woman doesn't need a husband in her life, it seems that we have far too many men around. For example, this problem is solved in the wild by having open seasons on bucks. Of course this is not a viable solution for humanity.

In a divorce prone society, such as California for example, there really is no incentive to solve marital problems. The marriage contract alone is sufficient to establish great wealth in the hands of a new husband or wife under modern community property laws. This type of "romance" unfortunately soon turns to "finance." Actually the practice in California is to "trade up" by divorcing spouse number one and marry spouse number two who happens to be wealthier than spouse number one. This "trading up" process can continue as long as the trader has sufficient appeal to attract another "customer."

The result of all the changes in the marital situation has been to leave many people, especially women, middle-aged and all alone in their twilight years. Is this a good or desirable result? The original idea behind the concept of marriage must have been to unite the explorer or adventurer (the male) with the nurturer or nester (the female) in a loving lifelong relationship. This arrangement capitalizes on the fundamental characteristics of both sexes by uniting them for the purposes of procreation and for building a useful, productive and peaceful society. Is there any better system on which our future can be based?

All young people contemplating marriage need to carefully consider what they are bringing to the marriage plate. If the value of their contribution is minimal or nonexistent, they can be almost guaranteed that their marriage will be of a short duration.

THE JUDGMENT OF OTHERS

"Your acquaintances are often more critical of your virtues than of your vices."

Superiors are usually envied and subordinates are usually loved. This statement is not always true, but it applies more often than does a reverse statement, i.e. that subordinates are envied and superiors are loved. John was unfortunately a victim of the habits of gambling, alcohol consumption, and womanizing. He practiced all three vices to excess. He was a "sure-fire" source of conversation dealing with his foibles. All his acquaintances got many good laughs out of the antics of poor, dumb John. Eventually, John's lifestyle led to so many problems that he decided to eliminate all three vices after his wife divorced him. It took three years of great effort and willpower, but he finally stopped gambling, drinking alcoholic beverages, womanizing, and for good measure he stopped smoking. He met a nice woman and they were married. John's life took a dramatic turn for the better. He soon found that he had almost no problems. Unfortunately, he no longer served as the "butt" of derisive jokes by his acquaintances. They started looking at him in an envious manner. They were jealous of his newfound happiness, and they really did not like the person John had become. They even told John that they liked him more the way he was before he reformed. Actually, they did not like him more; they simply resented losing the "court jester" or "clown" in their midst. They envied John's ability to eliminate his vices and secretly wished that they could do the same with their own negative habits. John was perplexed at his acquaintances' reaction. Actually, the story is quite typical. Practicing Christians are constantly derided by non-Christians for their Spartan and happy lives. Great efforts are made to prove that they are less than perfect. Constant criticism is expended on any person or group whose ethical standards somehow emerge a notch above their fellowmen.

The principle involved in this discussion is that a person who "cleans up his act" or one who eliminates his vices should not expect the praises and exultation's of his friends. This may be quite perplexing to the "newly reformed" but actually the rationale is quite logical. The reformed person has, by his lifestyle, acquired a certain "image." All his acquaintances have learned to accept his image based on previous indulgences, and they all enjoyed his antics as he went from one self-created problem to another. Actually, they liked him for the levity he furnished. Suddenly the "court jester" is no longer providing laughs for everyone. He now has to be taken seriously. The cynics believe that he will soon revert to his old lifestyle. During the period that his image is changing from that of a "fool" to that of a serious member of society, a reformed person will know many disheartening moments. He must always keep in mind that he didn't "clean up his act" for the purpose of receiving applause from his acquaintances. He reformed in order to enjoy his life more fully and to increase the happiness of his loved ones.

Once a reformed person stays on the path of the "straight and narrow" for a protracted period of time, he will become accepted on the basis of what his new lifestyle represents. The cynics will have been proven wrong, and he will be forgiven for the previous error of his ways. In this way lies the greatest hope for everyone in the world who does not like the current direction of his life. One can start a new life with each new day. This profound truth must be clearly understood by everyone. If it is clearly comprehended, then hope, optimism, and happiness will dominate everyone's life.

EXPRESSING FEELINGS

"Important relationships are damaged by failing to express feelings about a subject or a person."

Do not be afraid to show love. Love is the greatest force on earth. Love brings beauty to an otherwise ordinary existence. It makes all the difference in life. If you love someone, then communicate this fact to them frequently by your actions and by your words. Just to feel love and affection is not enough—these emotions need to be expressed and "acted out." Tell your family that you love them. You may believe that they already know that you love them, and this may be true. Nonetheless, a verbal expression makes a great and beneficial difference. The mere verbalization that you love someone has an enormously beneficial impact on a relationship.

Feeling love and affection without an outward expression or verbalization of these emotions is most often done in the case of a spouse and children. It is tragic to think of the marriages that have failed because the spouses failed to express openly and frequently their feelings of love and affection for each other. Tragic beyond description are the lives of people who have been destroyed because they did not receive love and affection during their formative years. Too many people reach adulthood believing they were not loved as children. This conviction produces disastrous results in their mental stability. One of the most readily available examples of a person who felt unloved as a child is a typical product of an orphanage. Somehow this child cannot escape the belief that his parents did not adequately love him. The child fails to consider unique circumstances that may impel an adult to surrender a child to an orphanage.

Just because a person may inundate a spouse or a child with material gifts does not mean he fulfills the requirement of expressing love and affection. Expensive gifts may be nothing more than pacifiers intended to eliminate the need to deal more personally with the donee. There are far happier children sitting on a riverbank with their parents, fishing with a hook and line on a home-made pole, than there are happy children driving around in new sports cars. The former feel loved in a meaningful way while the latter feel abandoned by their parents. I have never seen a child who truly felt loved by both his parents that got into serious trouble. By loved I mean love in a truly beautiful and proper manner.

It is equally important to express calmly and lovingly your feelings on subjects such as food, clothing, automobiles, entertainment, and others too numerous to mention. Properly expressed opinions can add to the depth of understanding and commitment between individuals. Never fail to express an opinion just because it may differ from someone else's viewpoint. What you must learn to do, however, is to express it without using a contentious or emotional manner. Learn to convey your views with a faint suggestion of a smile on your face, if possible. If smiling is not possible, at least do so with a calm, unstrained voice and in a pleasant manner.

INDIVIDUALITY

"The sovereignty of each individual's mind is a reality that needs to be appreciated and respected."

The human mind is an incomprehensible "computer." All of us are given a mind at birth. This mind controls everything about our life. We are happy only if it decides we are happy and vice versa. We work if it decides we are to work. Our body is its slave. We can accomplish nothing of value except that it originates and is orchestrated by our mind. I'm sure many of us have not thought of the "mind-body" relationship exactly in that fashion but upon reflection we must surely conclude: the mind is the "captain," so to speak, of our ship.

Many people try to control the minds of their adult children, who by virtue of their age, should be considered emancipated. When this happens, many unpleasant events begin to occur. If the children themselves are normally developed, both mentally and emotionally, they will resent parental domination once they are mature. If a young man permits his mind to be controlled by his parents, then his wife will not only resent such parents' control, but she will begin to lose respect for her husband. The only method a parent should use in raising children is to try and train the child's mind to grasp and resolve problems. If this method is successful, presumably the child will be able to cope with the adult world on his own because of the training he received as a child.

The wisest course of action is to respect the sovereignty of each person's mind. Concede him the right to do what he pleases. Everyone must understand that improprieties always carry with them their own punishment. The age-old law of cause and effect operates in all our lives. We must recognize that we can't protect anyone from damage they do to themselves by virtue of bad habits, or vices, or other improper conduct. We might advise against, but the option to act remains with the sovereignty of each individual's mind.

This principle of allowing everyone to "be their own person" becomes especially difficult when it comes to our children and their children, our close friends and our spouse. Oh, how desperately we want to prevent them from coming in harm's way. We are disillusioned when, with the best of intentions, our advice is resented and not followed. Realistically, everyone wants to experience life on his own and above all else he wants the right to decide his own course of conduct. He doesn't want to live out a format devised and proposed by someone else. This would take all the surprise and freshness out of his life. He wants to step out into the darkness not knowing what to expect. If he fails, he expects you as a friend or a parent to help pick him up and treat his wounds. He doesn't want to be told, "I told you so." All he needs and wants is your support, love, and understanding. He doesn't need your pontification.

Respecting the sovereignty of everyone's mind is very important for a smooth interchange of human relationships. Give your advice if you deem it appropriate, but remember the individual should cast the deciding vote for matters affecting his own life. Remember this and your chances for happiness will be greatly improved.

ASSERTIVENESS

"Do not be afraid to defend your beliefs even if it involves making enemies."

One of the great fallacies of the modern world is the belief that we should go through our entire life being popular and loved by everyone. There is supposedly something really terrible or wrong with us if we have an enemy. This makes us controversial and we are judged to somehow lack something in our makeup if we have even a single enemy. So people go around smiling at each other and keeping their feelings to themselves or whispering them to a select few. This practice, which is hypocritical in nature, creates an artificial environment of amiability when, in fact, much discontent and ill-feeling seethes just beneath the surface.

What the world desperately needs is well-intentioned people who defend their logical, proper, and moral viewpoints. Ignorance only triumphs when wise people fail to act. Whenever you express views which may be unpopular or opposed to another's viewpoint, you are bound to incur resentment. But what is the life of a person who never defends his beliefs? It is a life of cowardice and depression. People who are ostensibly your friends only because you have kept your beliefs to yourself are really not your friends. *If you ex-*

press intelligent views in a proper manner, good people will respect you even if you disagree with them. It's too high a price to pay for a friendship never to express your opinions. Many times in life it becomes necessary to oppose openly and vigorously something that is being done. As one becomes more and more successful, frequently such a person may be the only one who possesses sufficient facts to oppose openly a person, a plan, or a policy. When this is done, people may turn from neutral acquaintances to actual enemies. This, however, is the price one has to pay to speak up and be counted on the side of wisdom.

One of the best ways to judge a person is to examine the type and caliber of his enemies. If his enemies are undesirable people with improper lifestyles and motives, then you can be assured that you are probably dealing with a wise person. If, on the other hand, a person's enemies are wise, wholesome people with proper motives, then you better question the character of such an individual since he has the wrong kind of enemies. Another way to judge a person is by the caliber of his friends. Generally speaking the criterion is wise friends, wise person and ignorant friends, ignorant person.

The most despicable type of person is the kind who will not openly express his views on important controversial subjects because to do so would incur someone's wrath. Such a person reasons that if he incurs anyone's wrath, this will hurt him; therefore, he fails to speak out when he is morally bound to do so. Such a person is the epitome of self-centeredness. Yet the world tragically misjudges this type of person. He is often held in high regard by everyone, when in truth and in fact, he does not deserve respect.

The greatest people who ever lived all had enemies. These are people who spoke the truth and acted on their beliefs: John Kennedy, Martin Luther King, Jr., and Joan of Arc to mention but a few. These people were true to themselves and their beliefs. Mankind respects them, yet in each case their enemies put them to

Martin Luther King, Jr. UPI/Bettmann

death. Look to these immortals as your guiding light. Let them guide you in the direction of defending your beliefs and speaking out against impropriety when it is proper to do so. Don't worry about incurring wrath. The right type of enemy is nothing but a

Jesse Jackson. UPI/Bettmann Newsphotos

badge of honor. Your self-pride will be enhanced when you have openly defended your beliefs.

SENSITIVITY

"Everyone's feelings or sensitivities have to be considered in our daily dealings."

We are all sensitive creatures. Some people are more vulnerable to sensitivity than others, but all of us have areas in which we are sensitive. When we deal with people we should try to learn their areas of particular sensitivity and do our best to avoid doing anything that would cause them emotional harm. If someone is bow-legged or obese or bald headed, for example, we should avoid these areas in our conversations with them. No wise person deliberately sets out to injure another person's sensitivities. It is counterproductive to the perpetrator's self-interest. There are hundreds, maybe even thousands, of possible points of sensitivity. These areas, if known, should be broadly by-passed.

Some people are incredibly or excessively, even neurotically sensitive to almost everything that comes along. Life simply becomes too much of a hassle and experience for these types. If you feel that you fall in this category you should take a careful look at yourself. The probability is that you are terribly immature. You may be thirty years old, for example, but you could be reacting to life's problems at the level of a fifteen-year old. Perhaps you should seek psychiatric help to determine the cause of your immaturity. Your oversensitivity may be related to selfishness on your part. Perhaps you place your feelings above all other matters and become very upset and depressed when the slightest injury is inflicted upon your emotions. Unless you learn to discontinue this selfish practice, you will be in for a long and unhappy life. Remember that life "jerks" all of us around. You are not the only person who suffers because of these characteristics. Learn to flow with the drifting tides. Understand that your problems are not unique.

It is possible to diminish greatly the damage to one's sensitivities if we acquire a deeper understanding of life. A person does not intentionally decide to single you out as the target of all their emotional abuse. What usually happens is you simply get between someone and something he wants, so he strikes out in the only way he understands. In the process, some of his actions may inflict harm on your emotional tranquillity. Remember, you just happened to be in the wrong place at the right time. It could just as readily have happened to someone else. This greater understanding will add immensely to your emotional well-being.

Your best cure for all this inward thinking is to forget yourself and your pride and sensitivity and concentrate on the problems of other people. It is impossible to become overly depressed if all your thoughts are directed outward to your fellowman. Most selfish people tend to be overly sensitive and consequently live miserable lives. If you extend your heart and thoughts outwardly to others, you will forget about most of your problems. Time solves the greatest majority of them anyway. Most problems are only a problem for a little while. The mere passing of time will cause most of them to disappear. When they are at the zenith of their destructive force, don't overreact.

Be wise. Teach yourself to understand, to the maximum extent possible, the usual motivations of people. Usually, their destructive or harmful actions are not directed toward you. The impact of their conduct may affect you, but be assured that it was only coincidental that you were affected. It could just as easily have been someone else. Knowing this to be the truth you should learn to subdue your sensitivities to harmless and manageable propositions.

SEARCHING FOR THE TRUTH

"Your life should be a constant search for the truth. When you find it do not be offended when people who have erroneous views resent having the truth presented to them."

Humanity everywhere has many beliefs on many subjects, a surprisingly high number of which are erroneous. The beliefs people have become a part of their very soul. Just because they have the truth pointed out to them doesn't mean they will change or appreciate hearing the truth. To destroy a person's beliefs can be a very shattering experience. It may very well be what makes them happy. When you change their beliefs, their happiness may change to unhappiness. For this you will be resented.

The simple truth is the very last thing many people want to hear. Children do not want to be told that there is no Santa Claus. Parents do not want to be told that their child is ignorant, or is a troublemaker in school, or is a thief, or is taking drugs. If you happen to be the carrier of such truths, be prepared to "duck" or at a minimum be prepared to prove your statements convincingly. People do not want to hear their work is substandard, or that they are not liked by their peers, or any one of a thousand different bits and pieces of bad news. People tend to fantasize a world that is attractive and suitable. They like their "nonexisting" creation just the way their fantasies have constructed it. When truth confronts this "dream" world, truth loses the battle.

People who resent the truth do so for many and varied reasons. Philosophically, everyone should love only the truth. But we see in reality that is not the case. The truth which would reveal an erroneously held opinion could clash head-on with a massive ego. Many people are insecure enough that when you start shattering their professed beliefs they get defensive. Though they may ultimately change their views to coincide with the truth, you who pointed out the error of their beliefs may never know their appreciation. Resentment might also stem from jealousy. The erroneous believer may simply resent the messenger's superior views. Whatever the reason, a surprisingly large percentage of people resent the messenger who brings unwelcomed truths.

Whatever the consequences, after due regard to reasonable diplomatic proprieties, one should learn to love the truth. Truth alone is the principal track on which your life should travel. The truth ultimately will govern. Your life should be a lifelong quest for truth.

As you search for the truth it is far better to do so quietly. Don't flaunt it around your fellowman. Don't use it as a tool, but rather as a means of quietly improving the quality of your life and the lives of those dear to you. The truth is the most beautiful possession you can have. Never fear it. Make it welcome.

FALLIBILITY

"Remember that all our acquaintances possess, in varying degrees, some of the weaknesses of mankind."

No man possesses 100 percent integrity, loyalty, truthfulness, sincerity, honesty, or any other desirable human quality. We all fall woefully short. Because of this it is very dangerous, and this is especially true of younger people, to place someone on a pedestal and make a hero out of them. Truly wise persons have no heroes. They have people whom they admire more than others, but they have no one they believe to be a perfect hero. Young people especially have the psychological need to elevate someone too high up and too far away. Young lovers and immature people of all ages are especially prone to do this. They look upon their loved one or hero as being absolutely perfect. By so doing they place the one who is the object of their adulation at a severe disadvantage. Whenever such a person proves by some act or deed to be all too human (or shall we say "less than perfect") the "hero-worshipper" is totally crushed and absolutely devastated. The truth is their hero or lover is probably just a very normal human being. Their blind adulation was the cause of the problem not the hero's or lover's imperfection.

In keeping with the belief that no one is perfect, we should remember, "To err is human, to forgive is divine." This statement is true up to a certain point. Anyone who stays in a relationship in which they are doing all the giving and the other one is doing all the taking should question their wisdom after a reasonable amount of time has passed. We should not immediately jump to precipitous conclusions; but if the flow doesn't change after a protracted period of time, only a masochist would continue such a relationship. This doesn't imply that the "giver" should be angry at such a person. Rather the "giver" should feel genuinely sorry for the apparent ignorance of the "taker." Such an unfortunate person will have difficulty maintaining any meaningful relationship with any normal, intelligent person. In terminating the relationship the "giver" is not being unforgiving but is simply saying, "I've had all I want of this unpleasant affair."

Even the best of people make serious errors in their dealings with their peers. Maybe they lack loyalty at a critical time. Maybe they lack the candor required by the circumstances. Maybe they lack understanding very much needed by a friend. Maybe they fail to give emotional support which should be given. Maybe they repeat an unkind statement about an acquaintance that, whether true or not, should be more wisely left unsaid. Maybe they rejoice at another's misfortune. Maybe they are envious or jealous or have too much to drink or tell a lie or commit any one of the million acts that make up the myriad of human weaknesses. All the above indiscretions are nothing more than a litany of some of the things of which we are all guilty.

Recognize that none of us is perfect. We all fall far short of perfection. Don't expect it in your loved ones or your friends. After all you yourself are not perfect. What right have you to expect something in your loved ones or your friends, your parents or your children, that you do not possess? To do so is nothing more than an act of immaturity. Don't "overexpect" and you'll never be disappointed. When someone does something nice for you, be thankful. When they do something thoughtless or unkind, be forgiving. Remember they are human just like you.

APPEARANCES

"Do not decide a person is friendly just because he smiles at you."

Some people's faces are so constructed that they are constantly showing their teeth. To the untrained observer, it might appear that these people are smiling. Conversely, other facial structures are such that it appears the owner is frowning at you or looking very grim. This outward impression created solely by facial structure can be a very great asset if you appear to be constantly smiling, or a very great liability if you appear to be constantly frowning. Most acquaintanceships in the fast-moving, mobile world of today are limited to brief contacts. During these fleeting moments, people make economic decisions of vast importance, based exclusively on a hurried impression of a salesman. They are not together long enough to have any greater opportunity to know each other. Consequently, this first impression is frequently the basis of success or failure.

The irony is that the one who appears to be smiling all the time, may be a very selfish, unfriendly person. On the other hand, the one who appears to be grim and unsmiling may be a very warm and friendly person. Therefore, you should bear in mind that just because a person shows his teeth, he may not be smiling at you. True nature lies much deeper than the superficial appearance of the face. Look behind the face and observe the other indicia of a person's feelings. It is not hard to tell if a person is compassionate or not. This characteristic can be determined in subtle ways from unguarded moments. How does he treat his own family; his wife, children, his mother and father? How does he treat animals? How does he treat his subordinates at work? How does he react to an acquaintance's misfortune? Does he appear to be loyal or disloyal to his other friends and acquaintances? These examples are but a few of the "little" ways you can measure the type of person you are observing. Never stop at his facial expression. Go beyond this feature and try to find the real person.

The tragedy of not knowing exactly what type of person you are dealing with is that you will lack the confidence to place your trust in anyone. Since you lack the criteria to judge, you will find it difficult to trust anyone. Yet in life, it becomes absolutely necessary to trust other people. The greater our responsibility, the greater the necessity for you to place your trust in others. Here are some rules to use for judging people:

— (1) Beware of a man or woman who flatters excessively.

— (2) Beware of a man or woman who criticizes his or her

friends to you.

— (3) Beware of a man or woman whom you see steal from or cheat others.

— (4) Beware of one who is not faithful to his or her wife or husband.

— (5) Beware of one who takes too many mind altering substances (such as alcohol and/or drugs).

— (6) Beware of one who blames others for his or her problems and won't assume responsibility for his or her own mistakes.

— (7) Beware of one who always "takes" but never "gives."

— (8) Beware of one who lacks the capacity for righteous indignation.

— (9) Beware of a man or woman who is miserly and lacks normal generosity.

— (10) Beware of one who lacks empathy and compassion.

— (11) Beware of a man or woman who trusts no one.

— (12) Beware of one who makes money his or her "god."

— (13) Beware of a man or woman who gossips and will not keep a confidence.

— (14) Beware of one with an unsavory set of friends.

— (15) Beware of a man or woman who makes everything overly simple or overly complicated.

— (16) Beware of one who can't control his or her vices.

You should watch for these attributes in people, in addition to whatever impression you might get from their facial features. So much of your happiness depends on your ability to judge your acquaintances accurately. Start practicing early in life and never stop working at it.

MORE ABOUT APPEARANCES

"A man who is always paying compliments is insincere."

An insincere compliment is the greatest form of insult possible. It amounts to deception and constitutes the one commodity with which the world is tragically oversupplied. All relationships tend to be based to some degree on fraud and deception. There never was a relationship that was based entirely on the truth. All relationships contain elements of deception and truth. As is the case with everything in life, it becomes a question of degree. One of the easiest ways to detect deception is to be alert to the person who literally drowns you in flowery rhetoric or praise. If done rarely, then one might believe the sincerity, but if it is a frequent habit, you can be sure that you are dealing with a person who seeks to gain personally from a fast, favorable impression. This impression is superficial because it is created by his flowery words of praise in hopes that everyone believes and is flattered by favorable assessments of himself as an individual.

The wiser course of action is to question the motives of anyone who bestows praise and flatters far beyond your true worth. You should ask yourself just what causes this individual to be so unnecessarily complimentary in his remarks. He is probably seeking some personal gain from these statements. It may be nothing more harmful than a neurotic desire to be loved. It could also be more sinister if the "praiser" is looking for personal benefits of a monetary or social nature by his insincere remarks.

Excessive compliments leave a person of average intelligence quite ill-at-ease. A typical compliment concerns the proud parent who constantly insists that his child displays some musical, athletic, or scholastic ability. Though these compliments are sincere, they still leave the child embarrassed and to some extent embarrass the audience for whom the performance was given. The discomfort increases when the compliment is not earned and is patently insincere. It is, in fact, quite irritating to an intelligent person. An intelligent, beautiful woman knows she is beautiful and needn't be constantly reminded. A brilliant scholar knows that his intelligence far exceeds the average human's and is embarrassed to be constantly reminded of this. A great athlete or orator or entertainer who is wise is in the same position. Why dwell on the obvious? An individual who possesses unique talent would much rather be regarded as a whole human being than merely being appreciated for his area of unique ability. All these people are human beings first and anything else second. They get weary and tired of being overly praised for certain abilities or assets. They want to know what you really think of them as humans separate from their talents. This broader appraisal includes, in addition to their great talent or asset, the same qualities of fear, jealousy, pride, insecurity, success, failure, and other human traits.

In your own life, be slow to flatter. Most wise people are very cautious of those who flatter excessively. If you have something of this nature to say to someone, call them aside and mention it personally. They will believe it far more. Even under these circumstances, don't do it too often. The same line of flattery repeated excessively becomes very unwelcome. Be conservative but truthful in your appraisal of your acquaintances. Nothing stated in this book is intended to imply that you should never flatter or praise. The occasion which calls for sincere praise arises frequently in life, especially for someone in a leadership position. Just remember that you have to handle the entire subject very carefully. If you do, your personal relationships will be strengthened.

FRIENDSHIP

"Friendship, while a precious human experience, produces much unhappiness because people have not learned to recognize when it exists."

Acquaintanceship and friendship are quite different and produce a lot of human suffering and misunderstanding. Acquaintanceship is plentiful and everyone knows many people whom they meet frequently through their common interests. Golfers often meet people who share their love of golf. Horsemanship attracts great numbers of people who share a common love of horses. At work, we all know many people who work with us and greet us with a warm smile and a "hello" every day. And so it is with the millions of types of human activities in which we share a common interest or love. We acquire numerous acquaintances who share our same objectives and interests.

These acquaintanceships can be warm and friendly or they can be distant and cold. We will encounter no heartbreak or difficulty in our acquaintanceships as long as we recognize an acquaintanceship for what it is and what it is not. An acquaintanceship, essentially, is knowing someone in any number of variable possible degrees. We may know almost everything about some people and not even know the names of others and yet both are acquaintances. An acquaintanceship is not a friendship. A true friendship is a very rare relationship. Most people go through their entire lives and never experience the first friendship.

When we start trying to make a friend out of what is merely an acquaintance, we are asking for heartache and trouble. In our desire to be loved by everyone or at least to be popular, we look desperately for friends. We start applying a very loose definition to the word "friend." We broaden its meaning so that in our "dream world" we can deceive ourselves into thinking we have a lot of "friends." Soon we have deceived ourselves so much that we start believing that mere acquaintances are, in fact, our friends. Consequently, when their actions seem hostile to our interests, we become hurt and disillusioned. Actually, a realistic appraisal of the relationship would not have classified it as a friendship in the first instance. But in our desire to make our world secure and happy, we created something in our mind that never existed. Out of our imagination grew a situation that caused us great hurt and emotional injury.

The fact is that a true friendship is very, very, very rare. Most people are concerned with their own problems and with anyone who can help them. A surprising percentage (probably even a majority) of all husbands and wives, while they may be lovers, are in reality not friends. Brothers and sisters and parents and children are very often not friends. All one has to do to confirm the lack of friendship in many parent-child relationships is to go to a nursing home and witness the number of abandoned parents.

A friend is one who will do a great favor for another such as giving him $10,000 knowing that the recipient will never be able to return the favor or the $10,000. A friend is one who supports another all the time, even to his own detriment. This support has to be forth-coming in bad times as well as good times and has to be there even if it is in opposition to the entire world. Do not expect to find even two or three people like this in your entire lifetime. Everyone else you know is merely an acquaintance.

THE CONTROL PANEL

"People tend to do and say the wisest things they can, based on their judgment and intelligence."

The final product of our past experiences includes: Environmental factors, educational, religious, ethical, nationalistic, and philosophical statements or actions which constitute our considered response to a given situation. People think before they act or say something. They may not think clearly or they may not think long. They may act out of conditioned reflexes that require almost no thinking, but you can be assured that it all starts in the mind. The mind is the "control panel" for the rest of the body. The mind is where you think.

The mind retains the residue of all of life's prior experiences. It stores our fears, our hopes, our aspirations, our failures, and our victories. It is the repository of the total residue of everything that has happened in the past. It contains the intangible remains of our past life. When a new situation develops that requires affirmative action, the mind examines that situation, influenced by all it has experienced in the past. Every mind is influenced, yes, even scarred, by traumas of the past. Latent fears and anxieties enormously influence the conclusions our mind reaches. The point we should never forget is that the end product of all this mental activity is a statement or an action an individual makes or performs. We may wonder aloud at the seeming idiocy of the individual involved, but his past may cause his mind to look at a situation entirely different. For him his actions or statements are correct. They are the wisest choice he is capable of making. The search is always for that which is appropriate considering the million factors that influence everyone. People don't attempt to make or perform the worst or most inappropriate statements or actions possible. They at least try to do or say what to them is the wise thing.

Let's take one element that has enormous influence over our minds—alcohol and/or drugs. The mind is altered by these evil influences. Alcohol and drugs so influence the quality of our mental decisions while driving automobiles, for example, that they are responsible for some 50,000 deaths on the highway each year. People who are "breezing" along the highways on the "wings" of a mind-altering drug are really doing what their drug-influenced mind decides is best, or at least appropriate under the circumstances. Granted their actions are totally improper, but you can be assured that their foggy mind does not agree with this conclusion.

We really start having difficulty understanding people's words and actions when we leave the field of alcohol and/or drugs and enter areas of neurotic behavior. Remember that the totally healthy, normal mind has never been discovered. Our fears, hatreds, jealousies, bravery, ego, insecurities, pride, humility, greed, lust, covetousness, work ethics, and patriotism influence our words and actions. This influence is different than in the drunk who staggers all over the place and whose words and actions are readily discounted because of his obvious intoxication. The influences mentioned in the preceding sentence are difficult to detect and far more subtle to the casual observer. Whenever someone does or says something you simply can't understand, just ignore the entire matter to the extent that is wise and remember that he probably did the most intelligent thing that he knew to do.

When you deeply believe that this is the wisest course of conduct in your dealings with people, your life will be more tranquil and happy. I suspect if we were "all-wise" we would never become angry at anyone regardless of what he did. Remember, the mind (which is the "control panel") is malfunctioning for a lot of people.

FALLIBILITY

"Remember that no one is 100 percent right all of the time, or 100 percent wrong all of the time, or 100 percent anything all of the time."

Mankind has always been part honest and the complementary percentage dishonest. If a man tells you that he's 100 percent honest all of the time, be cautious in your dealings with him because he told you an untruth. Don't even expect an acquaintance or a friend to be completely loyal or honest, because if you do, you are in for a disappointment. Even Adolph Hitler, for example, was a favorite of the children of his close associates and he loved dogs. Ergo, even Hitler wasn't all evil. It is in the very nature of men that we are all imperfect. It is all a question of degree. The question becomes, "Are we honest enough that our acquaintances care to deal with us?" While our noble ancestors such as Thomas Jefferson and others were proclaiming to the world their startling new theory that all men were created equal, they owned slaves which they clearly did not regard as equals. While Karl Marx and Frederick Engel maintained that their communist ideals grew out of their compassion for the suffering masses of the world, their followers, Mao Tse-tung and Joseph Stalin, slaughtered an estimated 100,000,000 people while attempting to install this "Utopian" paradise in China and Russia.

More accurately, all men contain bits and pieces of all the foibles and strengths of mankind. We are all good and evil; we are all happy and sad; we are all energetic and lazy; we are all kind and cruel; we are all bigoted and tolerant; we are all religious and irreligious; we are all beautiful and ugly; we are all generous and miserly; we all love and hate; we are all disciplined and undisciplined; we are all correct and we are all wrong; we are all wise and ignorant and so continues the list endlessly of all the human traits. The point is that no one is totally perfect or totally imperfect. In our personal lives, we should strive for perfection, realizing in advance that it can never be attained. When we possess this wise viewpoint of ourselves and our fellowman, we will neither let our failures overwhelm us nor the imperfections in our peers disillusion us. Always bear in mind that we live in an imperfect world. This especially includes our loved ones such as our parents, our spouses, and our children. When you keep this truth in mind, you will find it easier to deal with the uncertainties of life. When meeting a stranger who appears perfect at first glance, you will know as you meet him that he contains imperfections; it is just a question of where these imperfections lie, and not a question of whether or not they exist.

What we must do is strive to do the best we can in everything we attempt, knowing that we will not achieve perfect results. In some areas of life, our successes will be greater than our failures; and in other areas, our failures will be greater than our successes. This random result, which is neither perfect nor imperfect, is the range wherein all humanity operates. We may look across the fence at our neighbor's "greener pastures" and be inclined to forget this, but you can be assured that it applies to everyone, all the time.

Success is not difficult to accept. Do so with grace and humility. Be thankful for your good fortune. Remember always that failure is a part of life. Shrug your shoulders and accept it with grace. Always remember the struggle itself is what makes for a full and interesting life. Not the achievement—but the struggle. When you look at all your activities in this light, everything about life is so much easier to accept, and you actually are exhibiting a very deep grasp of the realities of living.

MORE ABOUT THE JUDGMENT OF OTHERS
"The judgment of one's contemporaries
is not necessarily accurate."

Mao Tse-tung of China is revered by hundreds of millions of people, yet historians calculate that he was instrumental in the slaughter of as many as 65,000,000 Chinese. Joseph Stalin of Russia was revered as a leader, yet he is considered to have been the governing factor in the annihilation of some 35,000,000 Russians. Adolph Hitler was so popular in Germany that he was elevated by the German people to an almost "god-like" status. Women by the hundreds threw their undergarments at him at public gatherings. Yet, the world has seldom known a more demoniacal or ignorant figure than Hitler. He practiced genocide against the Jews and the Gypsies and to some extent against the Polish people. The contemporaries of Gandhi, Christ, Martin Luther King, Jr., John F. Kennedy, and Lincoln assassinated these towering leaders of world history. Each leader, in his own way, contributed mightily to the alleviation of human suffering. Yet the last verdict of his contemporaries was a bullet through the head or a nail in the hand or a sword in the side. Yet, when it came time to bury Al Capone, an arch criminal of the first order, his contemporaries gave him a great funeral. These few words should illustrate how woefully inaccurate is the judgment of contemporaries.

The usual reason for the erroneous appraisal of another's true worth is that the masses do not have accurate information on which to base their opinions. A carefully orchestrated scenario of lies and deception can fool large numbers of contemporaries. If the world knew the truth, it would make few mistakes in this area of human activity. The sad fact is that the world seldom knows the truth about its leaders, especially in a dictatorial society. The controlled news media are issued only that information which is acceptable for public consumption. Woe be unto that individual or newspaper that deviates from the "official line." By a carefully constructed house of lies and propaganda, a cruel, worthless leader can be altered to present a fatherly image of justice and love.

This game of deception applies equally to individuals in their dealings with their acquaintances. A "reputable" member of the community was being tried for selling stolen black market cigarettes without paying the applicable federal and state taxes. This criminal's activity had been going on for years. Doctors, lawyers, businessmen, and community leaders were paraded into court as character witnesses all testifying as to the defendant's good reputation for truth and veracity in the community. The wise old judge asked each character witness, "If you knew, that all the time you thought he was an honorable citizen, he was actually stealing black market cigarettes and selling them, would you still be here as a character witness in his behalf?" Each, of course, answered in the negative. The point is that deceptive people very carefully build false reputations of honor and successfully fool their close associates for a long while. When this happens, the judgment of contemporaries is woefully inaccurate. These problems, like most human aberrations, can be combated only by that illusive thing called "truth."

When dealing with people, it is possible for the exceptionally discerning individual to accurately judge an acquaintance by close observation. The true person usually becomes visible in the "unguarded moments" that even the cleverest individual exhibits. You can be sure that as an individual's cleverness increases, his "unguarded moments" decrease. Nonetheless, no one is perfect and the true nature of a person is discernible if you train yourself to watch for the truth.

All this discussion lays the groundwork for a problem that all of us sooner or later must face. We all feel we are not appreciated or listened to by our contemporaries to the proper extent. Remember that individuals far greater than ourselves had the same problem. Our effort should be to set the best example possible in our lives and having done this, we will have fulfilled our reason for existence. We have little control over whether the world listens or not. Our happiness comes in leading a life "well-lived."

DISCRETION

"The most capable or deserving people in a given endeavor often do not display their superiority in public: instead they seek to make their contribution in other less publicized fields."

In 1950, I was at Valley Forge Army Hospital where there lived a certain doctor's wife who had been Miss America two years previously. At social functions at the Officer's Club I noted seven or eight women out of three or four hundred whom I thought were more attractive than was the former Miss America. The point is that the best-looking and talented women frequently do not chose to "go public" with their beauty and talent.

In a democracy, the types who run for public office are almost always not the best examples of political leadership the community has to offer. It seems the really capable ones sit back and maintain a low profile. This failure to use its best "raw material" in the form of political leadership is tragic for the democratic process. Extremely able people simply do not want to put up with the "hassle" of a political career. They don't want to subject their families to the unpleasantness of political leadership. Often these superior types simply do not have the need to bolster their ego in the "glory" that fleetingly accompanies political victory.

What applies to politics and beauty contests is equally applicable to the whole field of sports. You meet physical specimens who clearly could have excelled in football or baseball or boxing, but who chose to pursue a life of contribution and reward in some "low-profile" field of human endeavor. The reason for this reluctance to "go public" is many and varied. Sports, in the final analysis, are really nothing but another form of entertainment. Nothing a football player does, for example, in any way affects the human condition or the future of civilization. It is thoroughly logical and understandable that a naturally gifted athlete would forego the glories of professional sports for the quiet achievement of his selected field of human endeavor. He may altruistically believe that the field of medicine, for example, may be more important, both for his own well-being and the well-being of humanity. Additionally, a lot of people who have the athletic ability are reluctant to grow old crippled from traumatic arthritis and other ailments which seem to result from a career in professional sports.

There is nothing wrong, in my opinion, with not "going public" with superior ability of the type described above, if the individual elects to pursue a significant career in another field. The tragedy occurs when someone of superior ability elects to make no contribution and instead flounders in a sea of self-indulgence and negative personal habits. The classic alcoholic (or drug addict) is an example all too readily available to illustrate this point. How great a grievance it is to waste great talent. Hell's Kitchen in New York is a frequent repository of intellectual giants who have abandoned all legitimate human pursuits for the numbing comfort of an alcoholic stupor.

On the other hand we are refreshingly treated each day to the spectacle of an individual with very average ability exceeding and contributing in excess of his natural levels. These people are the real heroes. They are the persons whose families can be truly grateful for the example they provide of the fortitude and industriousness so readily available.

Remember, recognition of one's contribution, while good for the ego, is really not the important aspect of our life's work. What is important is that we know in our hearts we have contributed to the overall human condition by our efforts. Recognition is often a very accidental thing. Brave acts in wartime, for example, often go unrecognized by medals while far lesser acts are excessively recognized and rewarded. The main thing is the contribution, not the recognition. Happiness is what this game of life is all about; and when an individual silently recognizes his own contribution, that is all that is necessary.

INSINCERITY

"If a man is smiling when he should be angry,
you are dealing with a cunning person."

Truth is the one thing the world hates to hear. Wisdom suggests that truth is the best foundation on which to base relationships. Yet the world seems reluctant to hear the truth. The messenger who brings unwelcome truthful news is frequently disliked. If a person displays anger to you regarding some incident, you are probably getting a truthful reaction. Truth in dealing with another is the best indication of honorable intentions. Now the truth may necessitate a display of anger but at least it is reality; it is the truth. The highest compliment one can pay to his neighbor is to be honest in their relationship. Dishonesty or deception is degrading. It means that one's regard for another is not great enough to command truthfulness in their relationship. It is strange that people would rather hear a pleasant untruth than to hear the unpleasant truth. Progress cannot be made unless the solution involves intelligent action based on a truthful analysis of a given situation. Ultimately, truth is the best foundation on which to base our actions. A "fool's paradise" will only lead to disastrous results. So learn to love, respect, recognize, and search for the truth. Also respect the bearer of truthful tidings.

Beware of the deceiver. Beware of a person, who by the very nature of an incident or situation should be angry and responds instead with an "angelic" smile. You can be sure you are getting a dishonest reaction. This type of person cannot be trusted. You may call this diplomatic, but in truth he cannot be trusted. Considering the state of world affairs based on "diplomatic" maneuvering, it is not necessarily a compliment to be described as a "diplomat." Diplomats seem to be "masters of deception." If there were more honesty and forthrightness in international dealings, the world would be closer to peace. Instead, we are constantly treated to a panoply of diplomats bowing and smiling to each other one day and declaring war on each other the next. You are far wiser to appreciate an honest reaction of anger than a deceptive one of smiles and solicitude.

Most relationships are based unfortunately on a substantial degree of fraud and deception. People react to others for many complex reasons. People enter relationships for a wide variety of reasons. Don't be afraid to accept friendship and love, but always be alert to the possibility that your acquaintance could be "coming from a different direction." For example, in a love affair, you may be interested only in traditional reasons for falling in love. You may want love, friendship, and someone to share your life with, while your partner may have ulterior motives such as financial gain or social prestige. People seldom enter into relationships for exactly the same reasons. Hence, a majority of relationships, be they love or friendship or both, are based to some degree on fraud or misrepresentation. This is a reality with which we all must deal. Since the incentives for relationships are so complex and difficult to understand, you are well advised to be truthful in explaining your position in all relationships. When you base your life on the truth, you will find much satisfaction in your relationships. People will understand and appreciate your feelings if truthfully expressed. They will allow for the fact that your reasons may be different than theirs.

People deeply resent being fooled and deceived in a relationship. Deception may work well for a while, but the truth will eventually emerge and when it does the consequent feelings generated will be bitter and lasting. So be truthful and seek the truth within all your relationships. Unless a relationship is based on truth that is acceptable to you, it has little value.

MORE ABOUT INSINCERITY

"Beware of a man who pictures himself as perfect with no visible vices. You must know that he is not perfect; therefore he is either a fraud, a hypocrite or is deluded."

Richard Nixon and Spiro Agnew convinced a majority of American voters that they were super-patriots with the welfare of their country as their only objective. Almost every time they were photographed, the American flag was somewhere in the picture. In addition, they wore a miniature American flag on their lapels. They wanted America to return to those "old fashioned values that made our country great." They wanted to "get crime off the streets and put the criminals in jail." Their stated objectives were so lofty and noble that if you disagreed with them it was almost tantamount to being against the Deity. You were looked upon as un-American if you were opposed to their candidacies. They looked "perfect" on the surface, hiding, as was later revealed, very corrupt and fraudulent characters. These men went to great lengths to protect an almost perfect media image. The voters were fooled, though either choice they could have made during the election was woefully inadequate.

It is comforting to be able to observe a few visible vices or weaknesses in any acquaintance. When you readily detect defects, you are probably looking at the worst part of this person's character. If his negative traits are the type you can tolerate, you probably can feel quite comfortable in the relationship.

A "con artist" or a "crook" goes to great lengths to hide his most unacceptable characteristics. He trains himself to present his personality in the most favorable light. This type of crook is usually guilty of "overkill." He projects himself as being perfect on the surface. A cursory examination of him will reveal no visible apparent defects. This is the type of person you must be very wary of trusting. You know he is not perfect. If he appears so on the surface, the important question becomes, "just where and what are his defects of character?" Always remember, a thief or robber or swindler can hide his deficiencies a lot better than can a drug addict or an alcoholic. The latter vices are somewhat difficult to hide. Some of the greatest thieves and scoundrels in our society parade around well-covered by the cloak of respectability and propriety. Some black-hearted villains have white and pure exteriors. Hence, the need to be especially cautious of the seemingly "perfect" individual.

Many so-called honorable people have undeserved reputations that have been obtained by clever public relations and purposeful orchestration. On the other hand many people of comparatively low esteem and reputation, if the facts were known, would enjoy a much higher regard in the eyes of their acquaintances.

Know that no man is totally wise and further know that no man is totally ignorant. Everyone has some wisdom and some ignorance. Accept this as part of life and you won't be disappointed in your fellowman. Wisdom causes a man to have integrity while ignorance frequently results in a person of low moral character.

ACTIONS VS. WORDS

*"Good and/or glib talkers
are usually poor performers."*

Always beware of an individual who by his conversation seemingly has all the answers to any problem you may wish to discuss. His fast and easy answers may make "mince meat" out of any problem that to you seems reasonably difficult. By the time this "type" finishes verbalizing away your difficulties, you feel embarrassed that you brought the problems up for discussion in the first place. His solution seems so obvious and easy. The reason for his apparent ease of solution is quite understandable. You or anyone else can readily work out the answer to a given problem verbally or on paper. The ultimate solution is more difficult than the planning or verbalization because implementation is far different than verbalization. When you start implementing the solution to a problem, you have to begin dealing with human beings. At this point, all sorts of complications arise. People don't follow instructions. They fail to carry out their assigned tasks. For reasons associated with human weakness, implementation is a different matter than is verbalization.

Fast, articulate talkers tend to rely on this ability alone to guide them successfully through life. The fact is, a "good talker" can fool a lot of people some of the time and some people all of the time. Although many lead successful lives, these types often become very lazy. In reality, "jawboning" will seldom get a job done. To "wrap up" an assignment requires someone to go through the tedious stage of persistent implementation. Unrealistic people believe everything is no more difficult than setting forth a solution on paper. In their ignorance they believe once you have set forth a solution on paper or formulated it in your mind this fact alone constitutes 90 percent of what it takes to be successful. Nothing could be farther from the truth.

The real art lies in implementing the solution to a problem. One has to pick people who will carry out the details necessary to solve a problem successfully. This requires patience, understanding, leadership, and close, persistent supervision. Without implementation, the most appropriate solution to any problem is meaningless.

Whenever you are in a position of hiring assistants (in any field) beware of the smooth talker. Beware of the man who orally solves all problems with total ease. You can be certain that problems are not that easy to solve. You can be certain that his "level of performance" is far below his "level of conversation." Experience will demonstrate on whom you can rely and whom you should disregard. For example, in an initial conversation regarding prospective employment, you are looking for a person with a reasonable, logical, low level of conversation. Under these circumstances, such a person's level of performance will probably be higher than his level of conversation. This kind of person is more believable. In short, what he says makes more sense.

Investigate a stranger. Chances are that your experience with him will approximate his experience in his past relationships. All one has to do is check with his past acquaintances. That will give you a fairly accurate measure of what to expect from him. Generally, people don't change much once they reach adulthood. This approach makes it unnecessary to judge a person on the basis of his conversation and appearance alone. An interview alone, without checking into background, is a very unsatisfactory method of deciding a person's desirability for your commencing a new relationship—be it personal, professional, occupational, or social. Always use the best tools or sources available, especially if the contemplated relationship is important. You will never regret the extra trouble it took, and could be saving yourself much hardship and heartbreak.

Obfuscating

"Beware of a man who makes everything unnecessarily complicated."

Life is complicated enough without attempting to complicate it by the way we think or act. While many aspects of living are inherently complex, you should always strive to unravel life's problems and not to add to their complexity by your mental approach.

Place very little trust and reliance on a person who is always stressing how involved all his problems are and who appears to have no solution to them. His conversation ranges unendingly along lines where nothing seems to have a solution and he himself suggests no remedy for whatever situation he is discussing. He leaves all his "ends" hanging in mid-air and suggests no method whereby he can escape the malaise of his troubles. Regardless of the nature of a problem, there is always an intelligent course of action that commends itself to a careful thinker, even for a criminal who is going to be electrocuted in the morning. The night before there are things he should do and things he shouldn't do. Probably the best thing for him to do, would be to take a powerful sleeping pill and shorten his wait by a drugged sleep. Problems may not have a solution, but there is always a wisest course of action available out of many alternatives.

We get into trouble when we seek a "solution" to each and every one of our problems. Many of the problems facing us have no solution. They have only alternative courses of action that are preferable, one over another. Only a dreamer looks for a solution to all of life's hardships. The one final solution to each of our life's problems will occur when we are buried. Problems associated with living will cease at that time. We may have new problems confronting us in the "hereafter" but our problems associated with living on this earth will definitely be over. While we are living, we should seek only the wisest alternative to follow for each and every problem. Once we have selected our "route of travel," thereafter we should relax and enjoy life.

People who are constantly raising their hands in apparent despair in a seemingly endless recitation of their "unsolvable problems" are either very ignorant, very frightened, or are trying to make themselves indispensable to a certain job or position. Ignorant people despair of the apparent complexity of life. If they would just stop and think, they would realize that problems are associated with every life. To live is to have problems.

Once this is fully understood and appreciated, these same people would take their problems in stride and live a happier and more complete life. It is only through confronting problems that we strengthen our character and grow as a person. With this thought, we should even welcome problems. Frightened and insecure people literally panic and recoil in terror at the average problems life sends their way. They are mentally unable to cope and eventually despair. These people are sick and need medical help. Lastly, fraudulent people habitually overstate the complexity of whatever their work or career is so they can overcharge or make themselves indispensable. These people usually do this for the limited purpose of personal gain.

For the reasons given, beware of one who overstates the complexity of his problem. Usually an intelligent course of action is discernible for any problem and the discovery is not that difficult to make.

INJUSTICE

"Beware of anyone you observe inflicting an injustice on another, because given the opportunity or necessity he will do the same thing to you."

Certain character traits go a long way to describe a person and make his actions quite predictable in a given situation. A liar

283

will lie to anyone if it serves his purpose. Usually a liar will also steal. Lying and stealing go hand in hand. While no man is completely honest, the propensity towards imperfection is more pronounced in some people than in others. When you associate with people, observe their little habits. Watch them in their unguarded moments (and observe the subtle manners about them) and you should find no surprises in your relations with them. People are either essentially honest or they are not. If they are essentially dishonest, this trait will be reflected in all their dealings and will exhibit itself at any time which serves their purpose.

If in your observation of your acquaintances, you see them inflict cruelty on their fellowman or even an animal, you should be very reluctant to get involved with them. If they will cheat someone else, they will also cheat you. If they will lie to someone else, they will lie to you. If they will steal from someone else, they will steal from you. If they get caught by the police in the commission of a crime, they will inform on you if it serves their purpose. Character is either wise or ignorant. As a consequence, one's character is either oriented in the direction of integrity or it is not. You cannot go down two different paths at the same time. Either one can be either on the path of honor and integrity or on the path of corruption and dishonor. There can be no middle ground.

Nothing herein is intended to suggest that we look for "perfect" men with which to associate and bargain. There is no perfect man. All men have weaknesses and compulsions to do dishonorable and wicked things against which some people put up a more successful battle than others. What we all should seek in the people with whom we associate is a firm habit of pursuing an honorable course in life. It all boils down to a question of degree, since no man is completely honest. What we seek are the most honorable men we can find, knowing ahead of time that we will never find perfection.

Most important to this whole subject is the quality of our own character. To associate with honorable people, we first have to become the best person of which we are capable. Decent people will not associate with crooks. So as an initial requirement, we should "clean up our own act." Once we get our own house in order and get our own life on the correct course, all sorts of good things will start happening to us. It will be largely due to such age-old truisms as "birds of a feather flock together" and "water will find its own level." If you are an honest, alert, hardworking person, the overwhelming probability is that honest, alert, hardworking people will be attracted to you as friends and acquaintances. Therefore, if you have the wrong set of friends and acquaintances, you probably have defects in your own character.

FEELING NEEDED

"Remember, people like to believe they can be of help to you in some way. This gives them a feeling of being needed."

The "helpless" woman who constantly wants to know if some big, strong, "macho" man will help "little ole me" out of some dilemma is a classic example of an appeal to the instincts of people to help others. As soon as one feels that he is in a position to help someone else, he suddenly becomes more secure in the relationship. People are attracted to those they can help. They do not hate, but they certainly do not feel very close to someone who has never let them help him. They fail to feel important in such an overly independent person's life. He doesn't seem to need anyone. Therefore, if he needs no one, his acquaintances tend to leave him alone. Since he can exist by himself, why bother to get acquainted with him?

In truth and in fact, we are a part of everything we see and everything we see is a part of us. We all exist interdependently one on the other. When you adopt an ultraindependent stand, you somehow interrupt this natural flow of interdependency. It is as if you suddenly raised your head above the crowd and told the world, "Hey, listen I don't need anyone, I can take care of myself." You can be assured that with that attitude the world will soon find a way to totally avoid your doorstep. Isolation will come your way much quicker and with more severity than you imagined.

When others offer you help, accept it with grace. Even if circumstances are such that you really did not need anyone's assistance. Sometimes people have a need to help others; it is their way of showing their friendship. If you reject their offer of help, you somehow reject their friendship. People reject assistance on the grounds that they don't want to be indebted to anyone. Help offered for the proper reasons carries with it no obligation for reciprocity. Any normal human being would want to help another in need, whether such person previously helped him or not. A refusal to permit others to help you implies that you do not want to be close to them. All sorts of deductions can be made from such a refusal. One might conclude that you are hostile, that you are selfish, or that you are unfriendly. Any of these conclusions are harmful to you.

We must always remember that we are human, and that we live with and amongst human beings. We have to act with our peers in such a manner that no one can judge us to be aloof or conceited. This does not mean we have to be a doormat for every con artist who comes along. It does not mean we have to surrender our dignity or individuality in order to blend into the masses surrounding us. It does mean that we have to act as a functioning part of our peer group and acquaintances. We sort of have to be "one of the boys." We have to approach others and be approachable by others on a smooth and relaxed basis. We cannot refuse to deal with our kind. We cannot walk around in circles ignoring the normal offers and supplications of our acquaintances. We have to conduct ourselves so that we truly become part of everything we see and make everything we see a part of us.

MOTIVATION

"Some people are exclusively dedicated to the advancement of their own fortunes while other people are exclusively dedicated to the advancement of issues. Most people are partially dedicated to both themselves and issues."

Beware of a person who is a friend to everyone. Such a person is probably dedicated to his own selfish interests and will not confront others with his position on issues. This person is not at all interested in harming his self-interest by adopting a conflicting position on any ethical, moral, political, or religious question. He is only interested in advancing his own fortunes and cares little about righteous indignation emanating from ethical, moral, political, or religious questions. This person fools everyone and is usually quite successful. He has no enemies; he flatters and cajoles everyone to further his own ends. Such people are actually very selfish and greedy. Their motives are, in fact, questionable and their true character is not very moralistic. Yet they continue to fool the world; everyone seems to love them.

There is another type of person who is often very idealistic and who can best be described as a "crusader." He cares little about his own well-being; he is forever advancing myriad causes, often to his own detriment. He has legions of detractors; consequently, he is often alone and without friends. Such a person often has a very beautiful soul and/or character. His motivations are usually based on very noble and unselfish considerations. One of the best examples of this type of person provided to us by history is Socrates. As you know, he was finally forced by his countrymen to drink a cup of hemlock, resulting in his untimely death. These brave souls go through life embattled and forlorn and actually create much unhappiness for their families and friends (if they have any). Morally, ethically, and philosophically they are very wise people. They are seekers of the truth; they react noticeably to lies, deception, fraud, and crime whenever and wherever they discover its existence. These "harbingers of truth" are not very welcome to mankind.

Most people are a mixture of the two extremes described above. Most people are interested in advancing their self-interest; and occasionally, under proper conditions, they will advance causes that are in varying degrees harmful to their self-interest. The latter situation arises in a democracy when people get involved in an election campaign. Whenever you start supporting one candidate over another, you will incur the wrath of people supporting the other candidate. The same principles are at work when you support causes. If you, for example, support an antinuclear movement, there will be many people who will resent you for the position you have taken. This type of ill-feeling will be created once you leave the universally admired positions of "apple pie, motherhood, and country." Notwithstanding the harm incurred by supporters of various causes, most people sooner or later get involved in issues.

It is not my purpose to advocate an issue-oriented or a self-oriented life. It may be profoundly disappointing at times, but it is always interesting to lead an issue-oriented life.

I believe that certain people are better equipped to advance issues and causes than are others. Don't go through life advancing only your own self-interest. Every once in a while take a stand for something or someone other than yourself. Even if you are not successful, you will improve your self-image in the process and obtain considerable personal satisfaction. Additionally, during this experience, you will have directed your mind and thoughts away from your own selfish interests. This alone can be a very enriching experience.

INSINCERITY
"Never accept a stranger at 'face value'."

The world population from Mother Theresa to Adolph Hitler,

runs the gamut from good to evil, or more appropriately, from wisdom to ignorance. In between these two extremes exist people of every character trait and deviation of which mankind is capable. The problem is that when you are being introduced to a stranger, you can't tell whom you are meeting. Some people are "up front" with all their traits and habits and what you see is pretty much what you get. Others, however, are quite devious and adept at fooling people or hiding their true personalities from the casual observer or stranger. Some people reveal their true nature after a brief encounter and others are able to hide their true character for a lifetime. Some people are able to masquerade as reputable members of the community, occupying leadership roles in the church and civic clubs while clandestinely engaging in organized criminal activities. Some people will go to any extent to hide their true nature from their acquaintances. They are like an iceberg floating on the sea with ten percent exposed and 90 percent submerged.

A wise person is more proficient and trained at evaluating strangers than the average individual. *Even the wisest human being is unable to recognize all undesirable types; only association over a period of time may tend to reveal the truth about someone.* Sometimes a golf game with a dollar wager or a poker game with minimal betting will reveal as much about an individual as any other method. Casual acquaintance over extended periods frequently does nothing to reveal a person's true character. After all, anyone can act quite proper under pleasant, ideal conditions. It is only when the "going gets rough" that the true self tends to emerge.

Never place your confidence in a stranger if you can possibly avoid doing so. Surely, in most situations, one's fortune, or life, or well-being does not depend on a stranger. Ways can be found to avoid the necessity. Let everyone earn your trust; don't give it away blindly. An honest stranger with proper motives will understand this approach. It is only the person with devious intent who will raise objections.

The lifestyle and life purpose of many people in this world is to make a quick and favorable impression on a stranger and take advantage of him in the process. Their whole plan is aimed at this goal and they are masters of their trade. *The so-called "confidence man" is truly an artist.* He is schooled to know all the subtle workings of the human mind and answer all your questions before you have a chance to verbalize them. The best yardstick to use in judging the intentions of a stranger is the extent of reasonableness of his conduct when you seek to use certain safeguards in dealing with him. For example, your refusal to cash a check for a total stranger, if met with outbursts of indignant anger, should serve as a warning that you'd better watch this fellow. He is not being reasonable. An honest person would understand your caution.

In a fast-moving world where people are constantly on the move, strangers are constantly meeting. A wise person will always let a little time and experience pass between himself and a stranger before he places any substantial trust in a relationship. To do otherwise could cause great tragedy and unhappiness. Why unnecessarily risk this occurrence? Know someone before you place your trust in them. Do not judge on the basis of an initial impression. It is probably erroneous.

FUNDAMENTALS

"Small minds concentrate on the behavior of people while great minds are concerned with why people believe and act as they do, and with the forces that control our lives."

The activities of man seem to control the thinking of certain people to the exclusion of all philosophical, political, or any other type of thinking. Exclusively watching people (or letting your mind dwell on them entirely) will create a picture that is almost predictable. Every human has the same desires, and the only question is how well a given individual is able to control them. Almost every human being has all the weaknesses of every other, and the only question is how well he has been able to overcome them. Nearly every human has a tendency to the same vices, and it is simply necessary to determine how well he has been able to control or eliminate them. Putting it another way, each human eats, sleeps, goes to the bathroom, and has a sexual drive. Most of human conduct is in furtherance of these habits. While following these habits, people get in trouble with each other and the law. So much of "people watching" deals with excesses occurring in furtherance of basic human drives. Sometimes people will have sex with people they should not have, and troubles will ensue. Sometimes people will rob others and burglarize property to further a need for food or security.

A small mind is exclusively interested in the behavior of his fellow acquaintances. His interest stops when he has found the answer to the question of "what" someone did. A far more important question is "why" someone did a certain thing. "Why" becomes much more important in this context than "what." It is more interesting to find out "why" a boy shot his parents than to stop with the discovery that he did, in fact, shoot his parents. "Why" young people have turned to drugs becomes a far more relevant question that the confirmation that they have turned to drugs.

"Why" crime has increased in America is a far more consuming and meaningful answer than is the discovery that crime has, in fact, increased. "Why" has such a tremendously high percentage of black youth been unable to find employment in America? A pursuit of the answer to this question is far more relevant than establishing the fact of high black unemployment and letting the inquiry end there. "Why" is there so much unrest around the world? The answer is far more important than it is to know that there is, in fact, vast unrest around the world.

The great mind asks "why" something happened. *The small mind is content to find out that a certain thing happened.* Advances have always occurred when great minds found out the answer to "why" something happened. The vaccination against smallpox was discovered when it was noted that milkmaids in England who contracted cowpox were immune thereafter to smallpox.

Man's progress up from the caves, as painful and treacherous as it has been, was made possible by those great minds who dared ask "why" and were not content to simply know "what" happened. By questioning the great movements that control humanity they made the human condition more pleasant. Within your own life, never stop your inquiry once you have learned that a certain thing has happened. Go beyond the fact of an occurrence and ask "why" it happened.

DIFFERENT METHODS

"Wise people accomplish the same worthwhile goals by different methods."

If an instructor were to watch Ed Furgol or Miller Barber or Doug Sanders hit a golf ball, he would tell them their swing is wrong and should be changed. Yet all three of these gentlemen reached the zenith in golf using a swing that was not normal. If you watched Stan Musial stand at the plate in baseball, you would say that his stance was all wrong. Yet he was one of the greatest hitters in the history of the game. This same unorthodox approach to a million different life situations can result in your reaching the same desirable goals as the person who uses the orthodox methods.

One person may manage a restaurant with 50 waitresses by kissing everyone on the cheek when they come to work and telling them how pretty they look, while the other manager may be reserved, officious, cold, and humorless. Yet both managers, using completely different techniques, may run excellent, first-class restaurants.

When you ask anyone to do something, you may be inclined

to disagree completely with their initial approach to the task. You may be unable to see how, with such a beginning, the stated goal can be reached satisfactorily. It is important to be patient in this situation because your method is certainly not the only way to do the job. If you have selected a wise person, you will probably be surprised to learn that his method will produce just as good results as would yours.

Pride, or simply that old devil "ego," will not permit certain people to let others deviate from the former's way of doing something. These people are most unfortunate because they function with a "closed" mind and consequently will learn very little from anyone else. These types make bad leaders because they stifle creativity and demean the ability of others.

Public speakers use a thousand different techniques which are equally effective. No two actors will portray a character exactly alike and yet their performances may be equally brilliant. No two politicians may use the same vote-getting techniques, yet both can be consistent winners. Divergence and variety are two consistent features found in all of nature, especially in humans. One of the unfortunate consequences of mass communications and rapid transit is that the world is losing its uniqueness. Cultures are converging into a "sameness." When cultures were isolated, common problems of many cultures were solved in vastly different ways. Even though the approaches were far different, citizens of each culture lived out their lives with about the same degree of happiness. Children were raised to be healthy and happy though the rules were quite different.

Each man has his own style. Accept this fact and learn from it. Your way of doing things is not the only way. If you are patient and watch the other man, you may learn something. Remember, you can learn more with your mouth closed than with it constantly open. Let the other fellow express his views; let him give his opinion. Anyone who never changes his mind is ignorant and has stopped learning. One should never stop learning so long as his mind is functioning properly. Open your mind and eyes and study the world around you. Discard what you may, but at least listen. Almost any destination or objective can be reached by different routes. Yours may not be the best.

LOYALTY

"As you mature you will learn to value loyalty far more than cleverness."

A clever person readily attracts attention in a crowd or gathering of people. Some people "wear their cleverness on their sleeve" and it becomes immediately apparent to strangers. People who make a minimal commitment in their relationships usually rely on cleverness to succeed. There is no question that a clever person shines brightest on brief examination. It is a flashy quality that is detected before other more subtle attributes. If you can sing or tell a funny story, imitate someone or play a musical instrument, or if you are a good athlete, you will attract attention. The problem is that many people are attracted to these clever abilities and overlook the less "flashy," but more substantial qualities of humanity.

Frequently, people who have a surface attractiveness based on being clever hide a very shallow and selfish personality. They have learned how to get by without making a serious commitment of any sort. People accept them for their surface appearance and never bother to examine them more carefully. These flashy persons can go through an entire lifetime in this fashion; but in order to be really successful, they have to keep meeting new people. Since they meet and impress people so fast, they never have to stay around long enough to allow their new acquaintances to evaluate their true worth as a human being.

The truth: an ounce of loyalty is worth a pound of cleverness. Loyalty is something not noticed immediately. It is the sort of quality that emerges slowly and with little fanfare. It is something only demonstrated over a period of time. The loyal person is often not noticed in the fanfare of a gathering. His qualities are not apparent, and he may be considered a nondescript individual who is rather dull and, therefore, largely unnoticed. This loyal person no doubt carries more happiness in his heart than does an outgoing, clever person who is noticed by everyone but who is disloyal.

Loyalty is usually returned in kind. Disloyalty is also returned in kind. Therefore, if you've practiced living a lifetime of loyalty you will eventually possess numerous friends who are loyal to you. Again, if you have been disloyal all your life, you will arrive at your advanced years unloved and without loyal friends.

Success usually comes to those people who have a well-developed sense of loyalty. Employers consider loyalty one of the most desirable traits in an employee. Once they discover an employee has this quality, they will usually promote him before they advance a disloyal employee with more ability. After careful thought, you must agree that if a relationship doesn't involve loyalty, then it is undependable and worthless. Wise people look to loyalty as a necessary quality in their marriage partners. The wiser you become, the more you downgrade cleverness and the more you upgrade loyalty.

Learn to be fiercely loyal in your relationships. If you are loyal to a person, you must be loyal all the time. You cannot defend him 50 times and denigrate him one time. Your failure on one occasion ruins your value as a friend. Once you learn to be loyal, you will receive loyalty in return from your friends. This will beneficially affect your life and the lives of your loved ones.

BUSINESS RELATIONSHIPS

"In investigating a possible business or occupational relationship with another, determine as much as possible about this person before you commit yourself. Personality

and character traits will have a profound influence on whether you will succeed and whether such success will bring happiness."

One of the great errors of mankind in dealing with one another is to make a commitment while in possession of incomplete or inaccurate information. We have all been hurt by this practice. Some, by the very impetuousness of their emotional make-up, are adversely affected far more often than others. On occasion we have all made this error. Everytime we do, we necessarily pay the price. Sometimes in our preliminary investigation we only listen to those elements which lend favor to our desires. We ignore the negative factors.

Since most business or occupational relationships involve close contact with other human beings, we must make carefully planned efforts to find out what sort of person or persons we will be involved with in our new relationships.

Are they honest people? Do they tell lies? If they lie, then they will also probably steal from you. *Lying and stealing seem to be fellow travelers.* You seldom find a person with one of these traits who does not also possess the other.

How has this person or persons dealt with their previous relationships? Whatever may be the answers to this question, you can be assured that they will be duplicated in your dealings. People don't change very often in this regard unless they undergo a profound religious and ethical metamorphosis.

What is the stability of your new associate's personality? Many men have a profound problem in dealing with their ego or pride. They literally destroy themselves and their relationships by never quite learning how to deal with this destructive monster. If these new people have unresolved ego problems, your relationship will be turbulent. *How do they work under pressure?* Are they graceful or do they shout and scream and panic? If they do, you will have to overlook an awful lot to remain successful.

What sort of willingness to change will your new associate display if presented with a newer and better way to accomplish a given task? Will he resent you for even suggesting it? Will it be necessary to do things the wrong way in order to "keep the peace"?

What basic intelligence does your contemplated associate possess? Is he an intelligent person? If he is intelligent in the sense of being wise, you will be able to work peacefully. Ignorance brings with it many problems.

Are you new associates generous or are they miserly and greedy people? The latter are usually unfair in their dealings. If they are miserly and greedy, it will become impossible to maintain a good relationship. These traits form parts of men's souls and are not easily discarded.

What are the drinking and drug habits of these people? Are they consistent in their approach to problems or do they have a new approach every day? Are they sincere in their dealings? If not, beware.

These are but a few of the questions an intelligent person should ask before starting a new business or occupational relationship. Failure to do so (and to arrive at the correct answers) will subsequently create severe hardships. This approach can avoid much misery for everyone concerned. A wise person can go a long way towards accurately predicting the success or failure of a new understanding. Be wise yourself.

MONEY

"People who live above their means or who spend more money than they earn, tend to be insensitive and unhappy."

When I say people are living "above their means" one shouldn't consider this in relation to life's bare necessities. This is not meant to apply to the need to eat or to be clothed or to be housed. People who spend more than they earn for these bare essentials of life cannot be condemned or criticized in any way. This truth applies to those people who, having life's bare essentials, seek to upgrade their living habits at a time when they do not earn sufficient funds to pay for this extravagance. These are the people who (for ego and other reasons) try to keep "up with the Jones's." They are intent on doing this regardless of the logic or wisdom of this approach. Their value systems virtually demand they put on an air of importance which they believe they can achieve by acquiring material goods. Their aspirations can never be fulfilled because once someone starts trying to impress his neighbors, there is no limit to how far the charade can be carried. This approach to life is destined to leave the practitioner forever unfulfilled. The more you get, the more you want. The objective should always be that once life's necessities are achieved, any extravagance thereafter should be strictly on the basis of affordability. You should "move up" in the world of material possessions as your ability to pay increases. To do so artificially invites unhappiness and eventual exposure.

A caring person will not incur obligations for luxuries beyond his ability to pay. The creditor is entitled to collect his accounts without experiencing a bad debt. It takes a very insensitive person to incur a debt for a luxury knowing the creditor will probably not get his money. No ethical person could possibly enjoy any material goods obtained in this manner. This practice cannot (and will not) be left confidential and will severely injure the guilty party in the eyes of his acquaintances. People do not accept or forgive ethical transgressions of this nature. When this practice is exposed, one's esteem plummets dramatically. The reason, of course, lies in the fact that *people do not forgive others for unfair tactics.* No matter how great or famous one becomes, he is always judged on the basis of age-old concepts of ethics and duty.

After debts from extravagance mature and remain unpaid, creditors will leave the debtor with few moments in which he is not being reminded of his failure to pay. The harassment of a debtor will disturb the life of anyone close to him. All his family and loved ones will have the quality of their lives diminished by the debtor's unethical conduct. Embarrassment and humiliation will follow. All of this will result in unhappiness to a debtor and his loved ones.

For these reasons a person is well advised to live within his financial means once he has acquired the bare necessities to maintain life. Any other approach will eventually result in emotional disaster.

MATERIALISM

"As you reduce the amount of material possessions needed to survive and be happy, you correspondingly increase your security and happiness."

Birds, for example, have the greatest security since their survival does not depend on economic prosperity or the continued existence of peace or the preservation of any particular government. They have security everywhere. They are indeed far more secure than man is, for example.

Humans have developed, throughout the advance of civilization, an incredible array of items that are classified as necessities. The list continues to grow and in the process the vulnerability of man increases. Instead of working to reduce the size of the list of necessities, every force in the modern world seems to operate in the opposite direction. The obvious danger lies in the disruption of world commerce and the consequent disappearance of these necessities from the shelves of merchants.

A wise person constantly strives to eliminate or reduce the list of material possessions that are necessary to his personal happiness and/or survival. For example, cigarettes are not necessary to a nonsmoker. Alcohol is not necessary to a nondrinker. Expensive clothing and jewelry are not necessary to a modest dresser.

Expensive cars and homes are not necessary to one who lives conservatively. By the exercise of conscious effort and willpower, the list of what is essential to our survival and our happiness becomes amazingly small.

The more we depend on material possessions for our personal happiness, the more vulnerable we become. Anything of a material nature can be taken from us. This can be done by a criminal or by the fluctuations of economic conditions, or by war. The happiest person the author has ever encountered in his life was a monk in a trappist monastery who slept on a board; who took the oath of silence; who never ate meat; who never drank alcoholic beverages or smoked, and who did not own the cloak on his back or the sandals on his feet. Contrariwise, some of the unhappiest people the author has encountered were extremely wealthy people who possessed everything a human could desire and far more than they would need for survival.

The spartan existence, in the long run, makes for the happiest existence. Children who have excessive material possessions never seem to be happy. Their frivolity seems to be shallow and short-lasting. Many of them are subject to spells of depression. They frequently cause disciplinary problems and often turn to drugs and alcohol for their "kicks." In short, their pleasures are unnatural and are of the type which lead to serious problems in their lives. The child who does not possess all the material things that are supposed to represent the "good life" somehow seems to have more enthusiasm and capacity for wholesome enjoyment of activities that are more vigorous, optimistic, and goal oriented towards the useful life. Somehow, it seems that if you give a child too many material things, too early, you rob him of his dreams; the dreams that are ultimately attained by hard work and the useful life. The spartan and conservative life is the one that ultimately leads to the greatest benefit to oneself and one's fellowmen.

WORDS VS. ACTIONS

"One who has a high conversational level
exuding confidence and ability usually does
not match this with his or her performance."

People who are absolutely confident of their ability tend to be quiet and self-assured in their demeanor or conversations. They have nothing to prove; consequently, their conversational level is subdued and conservative. This person usually has a level of performance which far exceeds his level of articulation in a conversation. All he wants is a reasonable chance to prove himself by his actions. After all, a wise person knows no one can prove his competence by "jaw-boning." He also assumes the listener knows this; consequently he does not try to persuade another of his ability through his verbiage. The final proof is in the "doing" not in the "discussing." If this is true, and it is indeed, why waste a lot of time on a senseless undertaking? Simply wait until you have a chance to perform. If you have the ability, this demonstration will provide all the necessary proof.

Verbose or overly articulate people make everything excessively simple in their conversation. Nothing is difficult. Everything can be readily and easily accomplished. They will forcibly and quickly point out that they are superbly qualified to do this or that. They exude confidence and endlessly reassure their listener that they are the ones who truly possess the rare talents needed to accomplish whatever task is at hand. *Beware of these people for they are hiding incompetence in the majority of cases.* They are covering up for their own deep-seated feelings of inadequacy. Do not believe what you hear. Wait and see them perform before you make any judgment whatever. *Do not make a final judgment until their performance has been consistently competent over an extended period of time.* Some people have everything it takes to be successful except "staying power." They start out like a veritable powerhouse, but they soon fade out and disappear. One should wait until their persistence has stood the test of time.

A fast, hard "starter" cannot keep up such a speedy pace. Much of this type of approach is showmanship and has no true lasting value. Consistency is the most valuable trait any person can have. *Quietly competent people work with a pace that is unhurried but effective when measured against a time clock.* Whirlwind performances usually just touch the surface and do not result in quality results. Some people work quickly because subconsciously they actually hate their work and by hurrying they believe they can get away from it sooner.

The real "winner" in life is usually the quiet, matter-of-fact person who does not seek to overwhelm you by his talk. He does not need to impress you with his genius nor does he try to do so. He would enjoy having your approval but can live without it. He is content and happy with himself. He knows himself quite well and is content with what he knows. In your travels through life seek out these people to be your close friends and acquaintances. Learn to recognize them. They all tend to fit a recognizable and identifiable mold. Practice and observation can make their discovery quite simple. The more of these types you take into your life, the more enjoyable your life will be.

MORE ABOUT WORDS VS. ACTIONS

"Do not judge people totally by the tenor of their conversation, but put greater weight on their actions or deeds."

In 1948, when Harry S. Truman was touring the country on his whistle-stop train tour, he visited New Orleans, Louisiana. Hale Boggs, then House majority leader, later stated to me, "When President Truman came to New Orleans campaigning for reelection, the only two people who met the President at the train station were myself and the tax collector. Everywhere you went in New Or-

Harry Truman. UPI/Bettmann

leans during this campaign all you could hear was 'Dewey, Dewey, Dewey.' " Everyone was saying that he or she was going to vote for Thomas Dewey for president. At cocktail parties the conversation ran 95 percent for Dewey, and only a few brave souls publicly stated that they were going to vote for Truman. In 1948, you must remember that Truman was advocating the enactment of a Civil Rights Act which would have had profound sociological reverberations, especially in the South. Anyone listening to this one-sided support for Dewey would have believed that on election day Thomas Dewey would overwhelmingly defeat Harry Truman for president in New Orleans. Not so. The result was quite the opposite. Harry Truman soundly defeated Thomas Dewey in New Orleans for president in 1948.

This seemingly inexplicable conduct on the part of the New Orleans electorate is not as rare and incomprehensible as it might seem at first glance. Never forget that people want to "belong." If all their peers are headed in one direction, they will follow the crowd even though they may secretly want to go in the opposite direction. Most people do not have the courage or fortitude to stand up for their beliefs when the whole world seems to be in opposition; hence the tendency of people to go along with the crowd at least in conversation. Therefore, it is unwise to make an important judgment about a person solely on the basis of conversation.

If you really want to find out where a person is "coming from," watch and observe the subtle nuances of his unguarded and spontaneous actions. Herein lies the secret to a person's soul. Those actions are not necessarily accompanied by corroborative words. Words are cheap and often meaningless. Actions are affirmative, positive and require the expenditure of time, energy and often money. Actions or deeds tell almost everything important there is to know about another human being.

Words come very easily to articulate people. Almost any excessively articulate individual has a level of conversation higher than his level of performance. Quiet, uncommunicative people frequently have a level of performance higher than their level of conversation. Do not rush out and act on the basis of a person's conversation. First, observe more closely. To do so will give you far more insight and a more accurate appraisal than would your failure to be more thorough.

This in-depth analysis of a person should be done only when you have a significant reason for knowing the facts about a person. Someone you will meet once and never again can be dealt with solely on the basis of his verbiage. In-depth analysis should be done when a significant transaction or relationship in involved. It will reduce your amount of "people error."

PRIMA DONNA
"Remember, everyone is a prima donna."

One of the most important considerations in dealing with your fellowman is to consider his feelings in all your contacts. Without being devious, self-centered, or greedy, but purely from the standpoint of your personal happiness, *always* consider the other man's feelings and your pathway through life will be a lot smoother. Most (if not all) people are terribly sensitive; everyone who offends their sensitivities, does so at their own expense and peril. Once the offense occurs, a lot of negative "vibrations" have to be overcome in order to reestablish a favorable relationship. The easy principle to follow is always to consider the other person's feelings in all your words and actions; then you will never have to reestablish or completely dismiss any relationship you have. Think about how many relationships you had in the past which were needlessly destroyed, probably because you temporarily lost your temper. An angry moment can destroy a lifetime relationship. If you make a mistake, do not be too proud to make a sincere apology. It is the wisest course to follow and you will find that most people will accept a sincere apology. When you have done this, you will feel a lot better "inside," where it counts!

It benefits your fellowman when they feel somewhat better because they had contact with you. No one is perfect. We all have good points, and we all have less than desirable qualities. *When dealing with your fellowman, find some good quality he has and stress it as a means of making him feel good and of making your relationship pleasant and happy.* Why not use this approach? Everyone involved will be better off. It does not cost money, nor is it being deceitful. It merely constitutes the truth as you perceive it to be. No one is completely bad or completely undesirable. Everyone has desirable qualities. Learn to look for them and stress them in your contacts. Life will be much more pleasant for you and your acquaintances.

Whenever one stresses the good qualities in a person, the very practice will cause the person to try to become an even better indi-

vidual. An employee will try to become a better employee. A girlfriend will try to become a better girlfriend. A son will try to become a better son. A wife will try to become a better wife. A friend will try to become a better friend. A boss will try to become a better boss. A daughter will try to become a better daughter. All kinds of magical things will begin to happen to you and to all your relationships. You will start to get help from places and persons you never dreamed would help you.

This does not mean you should excessively (or insincerely) toss around one compliment after another. This is transparent and never appreciated by an individual. Insincerity is one of the first qualities recognized by an individual. It has devastatingly harsh results to the perpetrator. As previously stated, everyone has qualities which are good and valuable. Using this reasoning, pick out the good qualities and stress them. In so doing, you will be accepted as sincere and your compliments will be graciously accepted by your listeners. As a result your whole world will change.

Everyone in this world has negative qualities. There are people who search out these qualities in individuals and see nothing else. With this approach, one sees negative qualities in everyone. Such a person will probably lead a very unhappy life. He will tend to discuss negative qualities in other people with his friends. Soon his friends will note this tendency. They will realize that when they are absent, his critical approach will be aimed at them. Consequently, they will tend to give such a person a very wide berth and divulge few confidences to him. This type of person will probably be unsuccessful in all his endeavors. If he has a supervisory position, he will have much difficulty trying to get loyalty from his subordinates. This person makes a very poor leader or supervisor of any nature. His career opportunities will be severely limited, especially if he has to deal with people. His critical approach will drastically reduce any chance for happiness and serenity.

One of the usually prerequisites for success is to be a leader of

306

people. One way or the other, a leader must demand loyalty and expect a conscientious performance of his instructions in his absence. Half-hearted attempts by subordinates to perform a given task usually indicate that there exists a problem of leadership at the top. *Subordinates who do not like and respect their leader usually find ways to sabotage that leadership effectively by the nature and quality of their performance.* A legal secretary sends out a poorly typed letter. A cook does not keep the kitchen clean. A telephone operator does not relay messages. A soldier does not take pride in his appearance. Under some circumstances, a subordinate learns not to care about the quality or quantity of his work. Disloyal conversation or "behind-the-back" criticism is rampant. This atmosphere spreads throughout the entire organization and has a detrimental effect on the efficiency, morale, and ultimately the very success or survival or an organization.

Subordinates of a strong leader make that extra effort to do a good job. Their conversation is optimistic and cheerful and this attitude is reflected in the quality and quantity of their productive efforts. This positive thrust within an organization usually guarantees the ultimate success. This same principle of leadership applies not only to an economic, professional, or career organization, but it also applies to family, church, school, or friends. A good leader gets unsolicited support from all directions whereas a poor leader gets unsolicited hindrance from all directions. *All good leaders tend to have one thing in common—they know how to treat people.* They do not necessarily use the same means, but they recognize that each person has feelings which have to be considered above all else. They know that every person has a certain "prima donna" tendency within and they treat each person accordingly. Poor leaders tend to run "rough shod" over the hopes, feelings, and aspirations of their acquaintances; the result will do great harm to such a poor leader. His goals are almost never accomplished. He never ceases to blame his misfortune on the weak qualities of his associates. He blames everyone else for his failure and never blames the right person—namely himself.

Consequently, if everyone has this tendency to be a "prima donna," it is certainly intelligent to recognize this and act accordingly. All people love to hear about their good qualities; and most people already know about, or at least suspect, their negative qualities. They do not need to be, and do not want to be, reminded of them. If negative qualities need to be pointed out, at least start the conversation by pointing out the person's good qualities first. With the good will generated by this approach, an individual becomes more receptive to constructive criticism. If you will only use this tactic in your relations with peers, your life will become a lot simpler and happier. Why not do it this way? It is certainly a wiser course of action.

PART V
Morality

COERCION

"Modern life emphasizes the dominance of force in the affairs of mankind. This has caused young people to lose compassion for the plight of their fellowman."

Almost all popular shows on television exhibit in their plots the principle that force alone dominates. While the "bad guys" may consistently lose to the "good guys" the principle is quite evident that only the use of superior force enabled the "good guys" to win. This theme being used in almost all television shows cannot help but leave the impressionable viewer with the conviction that the only important determinant is force.

This same scenario is repeated daily in the newspapers. Regardless of whether it is right or wrong, the fact remains that newspapers all over the world search for news of violence and the use of force so that it can be displayed on the front page. The reader is treated daily to a litany of terrorists who strike down an unsuspecting victim or to a belligerent dictator who forces his will upon a helpless neighbor or who tortures his subjects. The theme is always the same—force, force, and more force.

Children today are exposed to a criminal environment by the simple practice of going to elementary and high schools. The use and/or sale of drugs is a crime in every state. People who use or sell drugs are criminals since criminals are people who violate criminal laws. Drugs are used and are being sold in every elementary and high school across this nation. Anyone who may purchase a marijuana cigarette, for example, understands in no uncertain terms that his source of supply must remain confidential. "Mafia-type" tactics are used against the informer in the form of intimidation through the threat of physical harm. Just think of what this pervasive environment does to the student who engages in habitual illegality. It is also bound to profoundly effect the nonparticipant who simply observes but who is equally intimidated by the "enforced" confidentiality of the entire scenario. Justice is frustrated by this "force" arrayed against informers.

Once a child starts using drugs, he then becomes a habitual criminal. Just think of the sociological implications of all the young people in this country who use drugs who, therefore, can be correctly described as habitual criminals. Start with the fact that a "drug user" can have no respect for the law. He then can have no respect for his parents or guardians because his usage of drugs demands that their future relationship will necessarily be based on fraud and deception. These "types" tend to associate with fellow "drug users." You now have a young person who habitually breaks the criminal laws and who associates with many others who also habitually break criminal laws. Instead of simply a young person getting an education and trying to find his niche in life, you also have a criminal who associates with criminals.

These startling facts concerning drugs, aided by news media exposure, television, and unprecedented violence in the movies, have created a new breed of young person; one who is cunning, close-mouthed, intimidated by wars, violence, and the drug culture and psychologically hardened to the realities of life. This is a far different environment than that which existed for young people thirty or more years ago. Upon careful reflection, it is not surprising that young people today tend to be "hardened" and lacking in compassion. They are the victims of their environment.

This book is intended to be a powerful statement that ethics and righteousness constitute an enormous motivating force in the affairs of mankind. It is not aimed exclusively at the young, for the older generations have also been affected by this pervasive reliance on force. It is my belief that the forces of wisdom, choosing as they invariably do the paths of goodness and righteousness, constitute the most powerful force on this planet. People everywhere have to be shown that the superior influences in the affairs of men are ethics and goodness. The Nazi concentration camps are an eternal testimony of what is left in man once ethics, values, and goodness vanish.

GOOD VS. EVIL

"It is important to know and believe that the forces
of good or wisdom are more powerful and will
ultimately dominate the forces of evil or ignorance."

Cynics have little faith in the ultimate justice of life. They do not profess to believe that right or truth will prevail. Their predictions are gloomy and they readily concede that evil or ignorance will prevail and be the ultimate victor over the forces of good or wisdom. They are instantly ready to believe any negative facts about governments, institutions, and people. They concede that crooked politicians will forever reign over honest politicians. They don't believe that it pays to be honest and forthright in your dealings. Their warped minds have concluded that honesty and integrity are really the first symptoms of insanity. They actually believe that all honest people are "losers" and are following an ill-advised course of conduct.

Ultimate wisdom will lead us to a life based on ethics and morality. An understanding of the forces of life will cause us to conclude that the most powerful force is wisdom. Ultimately, wisdom and goodness merge into one and have no separate identity. They are one and the same. If you conclude that it is wiser to work for your money rather than to acquire it through robbery, you will act the same as a person who arrives at the same conclusion out of a desire to be good. This same interplay of wisdom and goodness occurs throughout all of life. What is wise is good and what is good is wise.

Just as goodness and wisdom are synonymous so it is with ignorance and evil. What is evil is always describable as being ignorant. You can name any evil person in history from Ivan the

312

Terrible to Adolph Hitler and you must conclude that they were also ignorant people. A professional robber would be far happier if he would change his life to legitimate endeavors; a murderer if he were not ignorant would not find it necessary to murder in order to fulfill his desires. A cheat or a swindler would find an honest life far more enjoyable. All these types of people can be described as being evil or can also be accurately described as being ignorant. Jails and penitentiaries are filled with evil people who in every instance can also be described as ignorant people.

The world has a great need to increase the level of wisdom. If all the peoples of the world were very wise the troubles of the world would vanish. The trials and tribulations and wars are all based on the incredible ignorance of people. Eliminate this ignorance and the forces of "evil" existent throughout the world would be vastly reduced by the forces of wisdom which are productive of goodness.

The only way this battle can be won is through education and a consequent lifting of the level of wisdom in the world. As long as the forces of wisdom are on the increase, the forces of good will be winning the war against ignorance or evil. Wisdom suggests that the so-called forces of good will ultimately overwhelm the forces of ignorance or evil.

HABITS

"Undesirable habits or vices are easily acquired
or adopted while desirable habits are difficult
to acquire without a lot of determination."

Life seems backward when it comes to the commencement and the cessation of habits. For example, take a drink of alcohol or light a cigarette at 3 p.m. for four consecutive days and on the fifth day whether you like it or not you'll be fighting an intense desire to do the same thing again. You have already picked up the emotional desires of an undesirable habit in just four short days. *Authorities say that if you take heroin ten times you will be a hooked heroin addict for the rest of your life.* So you can believe that undesirable vices or habits or addictions are the easiest things in the world to acquire. It can be done with absolutely no effort.

Conversely, it is a very difficult undertaking to discard undesirable vices or habits or addictions. To be successful one must expend an almost superhuman effort and willpower in order to overcome the addiction of cigarette smoking, alcohol consumption, overeating, or drugs. You really have to get yourself in a solid physical and emotional state in order to have the persistent will power to overcome. It is not easy but the results are worth many times the effort. As long as you are addicted to anything, you in effect are a slave of that particular practice. To think that a cigarette is your master is a very humiliating admission.

Actually the continued practice of habits that destroy your health either physically or spiritually is nothing but a display or ignorance. Overcoming your vices is nothing but the exercise of wisdom. We all know quite well what habits are undesirable and should be discontinued. Knowledge that is not used amounts to ignorance. Wisdom necessarily involves the exercise of the intelligence that we have. A man has truly not developed as a human being until he overcomes his major vices. Knowing what to do is meaningless unless you in fact do it.

An acquisition of good, healthy habits is more difficult to accomplish but one can truly become "addicted" to good habits. These include such things as taking physical exercise, eating the correct food, occupying yourself properly in your leisure hours, having good practices in your relations with your family, your co-workers, and your fellowman in general. It is readily possible to develop a whole series of "positive addictions" that have become deeply ingrained in your emotional and intellectual makeup. Once these type of addictions are acquired, you will not be happy unless you continue these on a consistent basis. The acquisition of "positive addictions" is an intellectual exercise. Just because you know what you should be doing doesn't solve your problems. Wisdom will cause you to put this knowledge to work for your benefit. The wisest person has the greatest number of positive habits that are beneficial to his emotional, physical, and spiritual welfare.

In order to discard the worthless and acquire the worthwhile, you need to take a very private and thorough look at yourself without the benefit of rose-colored glasses. Try to see yourself as you really are. You needn't disclose your program to anyone else. In a very quiet and private way simply get started doing what intelligence suggests. If you are overweight, change your eating habits; if you lack exercise, begin a program that will benefit you. Whatever you lack in your personal life, begin the corrective measures that intelligence and wisdom suggests are needed. Your personal benefits will be great.

GAMBLING

"Gambling for money with cards, dice,
roulette, horses, dogs, sports, etc., is a very
destructive vice and brings much unhappiness."

The love of something for nothing, of attaining money without working for it, is just one of the factors which leads people into the vice of gambling. The results are universally very negative to a gambler and his loved ones. Aside from the fact that gambling is illegal in many states and its practice constitutes a crime, the overwhelming majority of people are ill-advised to gamble. If you gamble with your friends much ill will is generated against you if you win. People don't like to lose to their friends. If you lose, they consider you a fool.

Professional gambling such as occurs with a "bookie" on sporting events or in gambling houses such as exist in Monte Carlo,

315

Jimmy "The Greek" Snyder. UPI/Bettmann

Atlantic City, and Las Vegas has odds overwhelmingly in favor of the professional. Over a period of time, the law of probability is almost 100 percent in favor of the professional winning and the "customer" or amateur losing. One might win on a single gambling trip or in a single gambling "session" but over an extended period of time probabilities say that 100 percent of the amateurs will lose. This is true of baseball or football or basketball as well. In football, for example, the amateur knows less than the professionals who set the odds. The amateur may be betting, for example, on the basis of a certain quarterback or a certain running back playing. Unknown to the amateur, but known to the professional odds maker that quarterback or running back may be injured; and if he plays at all it may only be at 50 percent of his capacity.

After considering that the amateur knows less about important details, the amateur in effect says to the "bookie," "If I lose I will pay you 110 percent of our bet; but if you lose, you only owe me 100 percent." This single fact ruins any chance of the amateur winning over a period of time.

If you work as a professional gambler, your gain will be at the expense of human suffering and misery. No personal happiness can come to you out of the wreckage of lives caused by gambling. After considering that to win from your friends creates ill will (if you win and do not in fact, lose) and that your chances of winning are nonexistent over a period of time from a professional gambler, one is harmed even more seriously in the areas of the heart and mind. If your thoughts are dominated by gambling activities, all the sensitive niceties of life are overlooked and not appreciated. Gambling, being such a brutal occupation, desensitizes man's feelings about his loved ones, his career, his friends, and his fellowman in general. It is such a dominating physical and mental force that all the beautiful nuances of life are swept away in the unstoppable onslaught gambling represents. Economic devastation results when the "addict" loses his money. Families are ruined and promising careers are discarded before their potential is ever reached. The mind eventually becomes so totally preoccupied with gambling in all its evil aspects that many "addicts" can talk about nothing else.

When you consider all the mental, social, and economic aspects involved, there is really nothing you can win by gambling. It wreaks havoc on your health in addition to its other negative aspects. This business of getting something without working for it is a fool's dream. What you get for nothing is worth no more than what you paid for it. The far wiser and happier approach is to resolve that you will have to work for everything you get. When advancements are made this way, they are appreciated. Diligent work produces lasting relationships, it produces the trust and reliance of your fellowman and the love and respect of your friends and family. Thoughts of profiting from a gambling activity are the products of a fool's mind and should be dismissed.

VICE

"Always keep your vices under reasonable control."

No one who ever lived is perfect. We all have weaknesses or vices that crept up on us, which if not resisted will dominate and possibly destroy our entire life. The most common vices that people have are the consumption of excessive drugs or alcohol, tobacco smoking, gambling, criticism of others, overeating, laziness, sexual promiscuity, gossiping, dishonesty, hypocrisy, greed, jealousy, and covetousness, to name but a few. These types of moral flaws are possessed in varying degrees by all people. Any one of these carried far enough can destroy a human being. It can wreck his reputation in the community and disrupt the lives of his loved ones.

A mature intelligent person takes inventory of his vices and sets out to systematically eliminate them. A regular plan of attack must be formulated and followed closely and consistently. You can be assured that for every vice you get rid of, your happiness will increase. Ignorant people say that they enjoy their vices and have no desire to get rid of them. Somehow they feel that life would be less enjoyable if they abandoned a vice. Actually, the void left after a vice is eliminated is quickly filled with substantially pleasant emotions and contentment. *New pleasure replaces the old pleasure obtained from the vice.* The great difference is that the situation leaves everything on a high plane permanently. One who has consumed an excessive amount of alcohol no doubt goes through a period of euphoria which to the ignorant is enjoyable. After the "bout" with alcohol is over, the euphoric feeling soon vanishes and is replaced by feelings that are not so pleasant. The victim may be guilt ridden or depressed or in legal or domestic trouble or in varying combinations of all four. This aftermath of a "drinking bout" depends on the ability of the drinker to control his behavior while drinking. Even if he can perfectly control his behavior, excessive consumption of alcohol is harmful to the health and can harm, or in the extreme, destroy his life. Therefore, when a vice such as the excessive consumption of alcohol is discarded, the joy and happiness replacing the vice far exceeds any joy or happiness the alcohol ever brought. This is true of all the vices mentioned above. I speak, of course, only of those moral flaws that are carried to an extreme, thereby causing harm to the individual and his loved ones.

When we carry on our lives amidst numerous uncontrolled vices, we are setting a bad example to the world and to our friends, acquaintances, and loved ones, especially our children. By our conduct we are diminishing the quality of life around us rather than increasing it. Our example is negative in its impact rather than positive.

Intelligent, wise, and mature people learn to control their vices. I would say that the happiest person would be completely vice-free. However, since we are all human and none of us are perfect, this condition will never be attained by anyone on this earth. But surely many vices can be totally eliminated as a factor in our lives and the others reduced in prominence until they are totally controllable. After all, we are not the "Captain of our own ship" when our "addictive" vices or "compulsive" vices control our behavior. We then become a slave to moral weakness and our entire effectiveness as a human being is greatly reduced.

So become what you can be by getting your vices totally under control. Eliminate them where possible (such as tobacco smoking) and reduce them to manageable proportions where their elimination is not possible (jealousy for example). When you've done this you have truly begun to live and to reach the highest rung possible on life's ladder of happiness.

RULES

"The morality of the royalty of yesterday has crept downward to the masses and consequently, we no longer find rigid and absolute rules of morality and general behavior."

The royal families of the world hid their vices from the masses by a rigid set of rules for thousands of years. Though keys might have been swapped at the Balmoral Castle of Queen Victoria on Saturday night, you better believe this fact was never communicated to the masses. Though a married couple who were members of royalty may not have spoken for thirty years or had sex, you can be assured that they never got a divorce or in any way let their problems be aired in public. The one sure way to be "blackballed" by the private "club" (royal circles) was to air your dirty linen in public. Actually a massive fraud was perpetrated on the masses in that the "blue bloods" did anything and everything to portray a perfect image to the world. They hid every vice known to mankind. The whole social structure was a sham. The truth was kept hidden.

While the royalty of the world played their little wicked games in secret, the great masses of the world were rigidly controlled by religion and laws which were very restrictive in nature. The masses were largely ignorant and submitted to a surprisingly high standard of conduct by virtue of the various controls placed upon them by the governing classes.

As a result of these rigid rules, most women who married were virgins. Families held together and tended to operate effectively for the common good. Parental respect was high, as was respect for elders in general. Children were taught to work at an early age and thereby became an economic asset early in life. Crimes were severely punished. Routine offenses such as larceny carried a penalty of the severance of the hand. Adultery in some areas caused the guilty party to be stoned to death. Punishment for relatively minor infractions was horrendously severe.

Modern civilization now has the morals formerly possessed by the ruling classes. Rules have been relaxed if not totally abolished. Marriage to a woman who is a virgin has become relatively rare. More than half the marriages end in divorce. Mental illness and crime are experiencing a startling increase. Murder occurs everywhere. Drugs are a problem of severe proportions. Alcoholism is the most rampant it has ever been. Pornographic movies are shown in the home. Anything goes.

All one can do in this permissive world in which we live is to try to live by those age-old principles of morality that have proven worthwhile. Do not worry excessively about those things over which you have no control. Just try to keep your own person in order. Set the example. If the little niche in the world that you occupy is proper, then the whole world has benefited by your existence. Man will one day want to return to an orderly society. After all, it's no fun to live in filth and dirt. Keep yourself clean and your morals high and in so doing be assured that your peace and happiness will be great regardless of the condition of the world surrounding you.

BEAUTIFUL ACTIONS

*"By your actions, make life more beautiful and
meaningful for everyone with whom you come in
contact. Create your own sunshine. Add to
the beauty in the world; don't subtract from it."*

If you only take care of your own problems to the exclusion of anyone else's the world really doesn't need you. It might be said that type of individual does not "pay rent" for the space he occupies on our planet. Only by one's surplus effort going to alleviate the needs of others is human existence justified.

The manner in which this effort is expended becomes very

important. If one robs people and institutions and gives this wealth to the poor, the beauty of life is not increased but is drastically decreased. Hence, the ethical nature of the efforts expended to create the surplus available for the help of others is also quite pertinent.

All of our lives should be lived in such a manner as to add to the ethical and moral climate of the whole human race. The very conduct of our lives is noticed in minute detail by all who know us. Young people especially, who desperately need ideals and principles in which they can believe, watch older people for meaningful signs. It's not so much that youngsters do what older people say, as they tend to follow older people's conduct. The value systems of the older folks generally tend to be passed down to the next generation. We can lecture and sermonize until we're "blue in the face" but our peers, and especially younger people, will judge and emulate us by our deeds and forget entirely our words. Therefore, if we are intent on adding to the beauty of life and to enhance its quality and meaning for everyone, we have to "clean up our own acts."

We can't sell drugs to schoolchildren and donate the profits above our immediate needs to charity, for example, and thereby add to the beauty and meaning of life for our fellowman. These activities ruin too many lives or they pollute too many lives to be worthwhile. Our entire life must have ethical stature and moral integrity. We don't have to be perfect, but we must strive always towards perfection. We have to stay all our lives on the highway of self-improvement. An alcoholic pollutes the human condition, as does a thief, murderer, coward, crooked politician, prostitute, homosexual, and on and on throughout the whole spectrum of human weakness. Life has less beauty and meaning because these faults exist. Hence, the need for a constant self-improvement plan.

The real stars of the human condition are those people who stand taller than all others because of their good character traits; their dedication to work; their control over their own personal habits such as: eating, drinking, use of profanity, drugs, alcohol, etc. They are a constant beacon of light for the weak and confused people on this earth. Because they once trod the earth, they left more beauty than existed at their birth and added a more beautiful and deep meaning to life. The river of their life flowed freely into the ocean which makes up all of the human conditions and because that river was relatively pure and unpolluted it improved the overall quality of life on this planet. Such a person led a very successful, happy, and contented life. You can be such a person if you try.

HONESTY AND DIRECTNESS

"Never do or say what you think is necessary to make friends—rather do what you think is right by taking the position dictated by judgment in any given situation. Don't bend to suit everyone."

One of the best ways to travel through life with the greatest peace of mind is to do and say what your best judgment dictates for any given situation you may encounter. Your judgment should be based entirely on the facts as you know them to be and what justice would then demand in a given situation. If you use this criteria in all encounters throughout your life, you will be well regarded by your peers. Additionally, your life will remain relatively uncomplicated.

It is when we twist and turn in an effort to please everyone else or to do what we think they want us to do that we start getting into trouble. First and foremost we are living a lie. Under these circumstances we lose our self-respect. Once you lose your self-respect it's very hard to be happy. After we practice the art of doing what is expedient and not what is proper we soon lose the respect of our peers. Again, it is not possible to be happy if we do not have our own self-respect and the respect of our peers. Always remember, people may disagree with you and respect you. The ultimate issue is whether or not you are sincere. Opinion changes with the wind. If you constantly take positions that are not based on simple justice and fact, but on whatever popular opinion is at the moment, you will be left alone as soon as popular opinion changes. So with this in mind, always stick to the facts and base your judgment on what constitutes simple justice. In short, do what you believe is right and proper and your relationships with your peers needn't bother you. Ultimately, you will be accepted as a man who does and says what he thinks is right.

Before you take a firm position on any issue, be sure you know the facts. Only a fool takes a firm position when he is not in possession of the facts. One of the hardest objectives to achieve is to obtain the simple facts about a situation, a happening or anything else. People are not very observant. They sometimes mean to tell the story as they see it, but many are not accurate. Nothing can make a person look more foolish than to take a strong position on a firm set of "facts" only to realize later that he didn't have his facts correct. Ten people can see the same things happen and give ten completely different honest accounts of what they saw. If you don't have the facts, say so, and act accordingly. Don't give a firm opinion about something when you know you don't have the facts.

Above all else be true to yourself. If your position is in opposition to friends who are dear to you, state your opinion in a calm and respectful manner. If you deem it appropriate, give the reasons behind your decision. Don't be argumentative in your tone or imply by your demeanor that you alone are correct and that everyone who disagrees with you is wrong and ignorant. Learn how to disagree without being disagreeable. When you've mastered this technique you will have learned something quite valuable. It will make an enormous contribution of happiness to your life.

FAITH AND IDEALS
"Have faith in as many concepts and beliefs as possible."

The more absolutes in which you believe, the more regulated your life will be and the richer will be its meaning.

The ingestion or injection of mind-altering drugs by a healthy human being is harmful, and one should *absolutely* avoid their usage. The consumption of alcohol by a healthy human being to the point of legal intoxication is *absolutely* wrong and should not be practiced. The beating or striking of another human being, except in self-defense, cannot be justified and is therefore *absolutely* wrong. A life of no work or meaningful endeavor is worthless and *absolutely* improper. To abandon one's children is *absolutely* improper. There are many acts which form a part of human conduct that are *absolutely* wrong and should not be perpetrated by anyone.

Conversely, there are many actions and concepts that are valuable and work *absolutely* for the betterment of mankind. Physical exercise for a healthy person is *absolutely* beneficial. A proper education for a young person, capable of learning, is *absolutely* essential to such a person's future happiness and well-being. The works of nature are *absolutely* more awesome and beautiful than anything man has created. A normal relationship between a man and a woman is *absolutely* the best sexual and social arrangement available to mankind. The practice of a high degree of ethics and integrity in all our actions is *absolutely* the best way to conduct our affairs. Love is *absolutely* a very important part of the happiness of mankind. So it is that one can go through the whole myriad of human beliefs and activities and find thousands of "absolutes" that can be relied upon as deserving of our deepest and most positive convictions.

We should accumulate negative and positive "absolutes" as early in life as possible in order to guide us relatively trouble-free down life's pathway. Nothing is more tragic than to meet someone who believes in nothing *absolutely*. They may have fainthearted convictions or mild suspicions that certain things are right and certain things are wrong, but they have no "absolutes." In the final analysis, they are not really sure. Their guideposts are vague, uncertain, and often missed. Consequently, their lives follow painful and tortuous pathways with no real destination in mind. These types of people can be detected by the confusion and tension easily seen in their faces.

Once we have "thought out" many of life's situations to the point that they have become "absolutes," we can put these particular matters to rest. We need take no time in resolving their worth in the future. This very condition of having many strong convictions already decided is productive of much tranquillity, contentment, and happiness. Resolve finally that which lends itself to absolute, categorical treatment. Recognize that most conditions cannot become an absolute belief. If this is true, do not treat them as "absolutes." Remember, we are trying to increase as much as possible those things in which we believe *absolutely*. Most of life does not lend itself to that treatment. Therefore as to the grey areas of which life is largely composed, "play those by ear." Nonetheless, erect as many "absolute," or "guidepost," or "highway directional signs" as possible, pertinent to your existence. It will simplify your life and increase your happiness.

PART VI
Cause and Effect

PERSONAL APPEARANCE

*"Personal appearance forms a very
important basis by which we are judged."*

The first impression a stranger gets of anyone is his personal appearance. There is usually no other basis on which to make an initial impression. By appearance I refer to the overall person. This includes weight, clothing, and all aspects of his personal grooming. The manner in which his hair is groomed is very important. Since first impressions are very important in the fast-moving mobile world of today, it is only wise to make as favorable a first impression as possible. Decision makers do not like to advance people in their careers who do not keep their personal appearance acceptable. Subordinates do not tend to respect a superior who does not have a well-kept personal appearance. Customers, patients, parishioners, and clients do not regard a sloppy appearance as being very desirable. People like to do business and socialize with neat appearing people. A neat appearance is synonymous with a successful appearance. Tidy, well-groomed people tend to reach the top of the success ladder in their careers.

In the 1960s and 1970s, young people were rejecting the values of adult society and attempting to turn the world closer to the truth and away from hypocrisy and war. In this attempt, they started disregarding their personal appearance. They wore dirty, tattered clothing and long hair and beards. They did everything possible to let the older generation know they were rejecting their value systems. Unfortunately, the entire movement veered off into drugs and cultism leaving great opportunities largely unexploited. These people were rejected for employment by businesses that had to serve the general public. The customer resented being served by a long-haired youngster whose entire appearance bespoke an attitude of arrogance and insensitivity to established customs and morals. Eventually these same young "hippie" types got married and soon realized that personal grooming was very important in the world in which they had to make a living. Those who had not destroyed their health on drugs or their character with criminal convictions soon discovered they were only a haircut away from joining the establishment. As this book is being written, the youth revolution of the '60s and '70s is largely a thing of the past. Today, young people for the most part, are very concerned about their personal appearance.

Since grooming is so important to success and happiness, it is wise to establish good habits that affect the way you look. Your hair should be trimmed on a regular basis. Do not let it grow too long; when a convenient opportunity presents itself, go in and get it cut. Schedule this on a regular basis and do not neglect getting your hair trimmed on a timely basis. Your fingernails are an important part of your appearance. Therefore, you should make sure that they are clean, and together with your cuticles be certain that they are properly trimmed. Your physical fitness and body trim are an important part of your appearance. I recommend that you follow the physical fitness program outlined elsewhere in this book. Watch your weight and make any sacrifice necessary to keep your weight at acceptable levels. Wear clothing that is clean and stylish but not overly ornate. "Far-out" styles are resented by most people. Do not "over dress" since this is frowned upon by people everywhere. Buy those clothes you can wash rather than those that require dry-cleaning. The cost of the latter is prohibitive today. If you want to be crowned with acceptability and success by your peers, you must do that which is pleasing to them in the area of personal appearance. Once you develop the habit, you will find that you enjoy looking neat and trim yourself. By doing this you will add to your success and happiness and set a good example for those whom you love.

THE MALE EGO

"The 'male ego' if left unchecked can destroy a
man or at least render his life very unpleasant."

Men have this phenomenon known as the "male ego." This characteristic, which all men possess in varying degrees, has a profound impact on the lives of all humans. Wise women learn to take into account the reality of the "male ego" in their relationships with men. They learn not to confront it "head-on" but to work around it in such a manner that peace and tranquillity prevail. They learn to convert it into a tool for their own well-being and the well-being of all the affected lives. Actually, the existence of this "childlike" monster, more appropriately called the "male ego," makes men very vulnerable to the wiles and machinations of everyone—especially women. Carried to extremes, it almost converts a man into a child. It makes him so vulnerable to insincere praise and adulation that a clever manipulator can wrestle anything he may want from such an individual. The irony of the "male ego" is that even if praise is manifestly insincere to a disinterested bystander, the object of the flattery does not detect the "sham" because of the exhalted opinion he holds of himself. Women are not free from susceptibility to insincere flattery, especially when they are told they are sexy or beautiful. They want to believe this is true and all too often, accept the flattery as being factual and sincere.

The unwritten rules of the "male ego" syndrome demand that a man remain "cool and calm" at all times. The scenario requires that the male remain seemingly impervious to tragedy and fear and a whole assortment of other normal human feelings. The ultimate taboo is for the male to weep in public. This foolishly violates the code of the "male ego." Tender feelings are supposed to be hidden and suppressed, at least in public. Women have a far healthier approach to this subject. It is universally accepted as proper for women to openly weep for any reason that affects normal sentiments. Men, on the contrary, are usually expected to remain unperturbed throughout most of life's turbulence. Actually, suppressed emotions will necessarily find an outlet. If they are not allowed to surface in a normal manner through an open display of feelings, then their emergence will be disguised in more harmful ways. They could emerge as hypertension, alcoholism, ulcers, depression, or in a thousand different ways. I am not saying that these drastic results would occur as a consequence of a single incident of suppressed emotions. However, I am saying that the cumulative effect of unreleased emotions is devastating to a person's health.

Men should become acutely aware of the existence of the "male ego." They should know that it can be very destructive; and as consequence, they should learn to recognize its existence in themselves. Once they understand the manner in which it operates, they should learn to "downplay" it as a dominant force in their lives. They must understand that it can be very destructive, and that it can disastrously affect their lives if allowed to reign uncontrolled by logic and wisdom. This factor, more than any other male trait, has ruined men's lives. It is based on foolish pride, a presumption that the male is supreme, and that he is far more durable than the female. This latter statement is being disproved more each day with statistics showing that women can endure more tribulation than can men.

Do not be afraid to show your weaknesses in public. It is ridiculous to try to present an inhuman image of infallibility and imperturbability to the world. Every wise person knows this is not possible. When you admit your fallibilities, you become more human; and as a result, more lovable. This, in turn, will make your life more filled with friends and love and happiness. By controlling this "monster" residing in the breasts of all men, you will lead a longer, healthier, and happier life.

LOW SELF-IMAGE

*"A low self-image is usually caused
by a history of nonachievement."*

Some people approach life and its duties in a totally undisciplined and undedicated manner. The majority of their efforts are aimed at avoiding as much work and responsibility as possible. As a child they delight in being able to fool their parents in the areas of their homework and miscellaneous tasks around the house. Mother being a loving creature, overlooks her child's irresponsibility and the average father is probably not even aware of his child's worthless habits. This scenario continues to the point where the child perpetually borders on failure in his schoolwork and everything else. If father is wealthy enough, the child goes to college; but due to his lifelong habit of lethargy, he fails to complete college. He then enters the real world and fails at one job attempt after another. In this modern society, this type of individual probably started using drugs and/or alcohol by the eighth or ninth grade. This, of course, was done without his parents' knowledge. He is cunning enough to keep his drug habit a secret unless he's unfortunate enough to get arrested for his activities. Even then his parents are naive enough to pass off the entire incident as an unfortunate break for their child.

Eventually this person has indelibly impressed upon him that he's quite worthless as a human being. Actually, his self-appraisal is accurate because his life history is a sad series of failures and parental disappointments. In short, he has every reason to have a low self-image. In fact, he has been a "taker" all his life and has made no contribution to anyone. In the truest sense of the situation, the only person he has harmed is himself. This person can turn his whole life around by following the advice in the next paragraph.

First he must understand exactly what has caused his problem. The answer, of course, is that he caused it. His low self-image is well deserved. All he needs to do in order to change everything is to simply become a "giver" instead of a "taker." He needs to start solving problems instead of creating problems. This whole procedure should start with his awakening in the morning. He should start by going through the exercise program outlined in the article entitled "Physical Conditioning." Having done this, he will feel "great" and be able to chalk up his first "victory" of the day. It will be a "victory" in that he did something very wise. Secondly, he should complete his full bath including a shave and neatly groom his hair and he should leave the house neatly dressed. When he gets to work "looking good" he will have chalked up his second "victory" of the day. Before he leaves his home, he should hang up his clothes, clean the bathroom, put his bath towel and anything else into the clothes hamper, take out the garbage, clean his breakfast dishes and take clothes to the cleaners if necessary and any other task that he can perform. If he does these types of things, he will have chalked up yet another victory. This attitude of helpfulness should carry over into his work. He should do his work thoroughly and be as helpful to his co-workers as possible. If he does this, he will chalk up another victory. When he returns home at night, he should go through the same exercise program again and continue to be helpful around the house throughout the evening. These types of activities will add another victory to a day already filled with them.

A low self-image is caused by failures. Start filling the days with many little victories, and the day in retrospect becomes one huge victory. After he has continued in this new lifestyle for six months or so, his self-image will start to change. He will have "earned" a more pleasant opinion of himself. It will be something that he had to work for, but not really that hard. The big difference will be his change in attitude and the great happiness that has come to him as consequence.

POSITIVE ATTITUDE

"Any task we willingly perform or any hardship we willingly endure becomes far easier because of our attitude."

A recalcitrant attitude to any necessary act makes the performance thereof more difficult. The simple act of getting out of bed in the morning becomes pure torture for some people who have never cheerfully resigned themselves to its necessity. The need to work can be made pleasant if we willingly and cheerfully approach the undertaking. In all our lives we have a myriad of duties and obligations that we alone must accomplish. The whole subject can become pleasant and quite tolerable if we approach it with a cheerful and willing approach. Some of these duties are pleasant and others can be described as relatively unpleasant. Everything becomes easier if we use the correct mental approach.

Going to a dentist bears terrible implications for some people. They cringe in fear at the very thought of a needle and the dentist's drill, or at the extraction of a tooth. Actually with your outlook geared to the right approach the whole subject is really not that unpleasant. Every conceivable duty falls in the same category; for example; firing a subordinate, admitting a mistake, getting fired yourself, enduring pain, or worry, or financial hardship. Your attitude determines whether your spirits will be up or down.

Marriages can succeed or fail depending on the willingness of the parties involved to tolerate the "rough spots." Every married couple is going to have some problems from time to time. A willing approach on the part of both parties to work out the differences will frequently make the problems disappear. Certainly, it will at least reduce their disruptive effect to a minimum.

Look at the brighter side of a problem. Let's assume you planned to do something quite enjoyable that can only be done outdoors in dry weather. Let's further assume that at the time and date there is a torrential rain which deprives you of your enjoyment. If you willingly accept the deprivation, its effect will not be severe. After all, rain does water the flowers as well as the farmer's crops. Surely something that important takes precedence over whatever little activity you had planned.

We are constantly being asked to do something for other people. If we're perceptive, we can see things that other people need done for them. A willing, cheerful approach to these types of undertakings makes the whole procedure fun. Additionally, the recipient of the favor will greatly appreciate your generosity and also your attitude. Great joy will fill your heart in knowing that you did something for someone else. Later on, these good deeds rebound to your benefit when you least expect it. People do not really want you to do something for them if you have a begrudging attitude.

Services willingly given can lift your spirits and change your entire life. As a means of testing the accuracy of this statement, perform all your duties in a twenty-four-hour period in a willing and cheerful manner. You will find that you will enjoy every minute of such a day and almost nothing becomes drudgery. Everything is easier, including each of those daily tasks that you normally hated. Not only that, but the attitude of your peers towards you as a person will delight you in every way. Their response to you will improve in direct proportion to your cheerful and willing attitude. Your mind is all that has to change. It is very easy and the results are amazingly positive.

INDEPENDENCE

"Learn to develop as many ways as possible to be happy alone without depending on another human being. The more successful you are in this endeavor, the more secure will be your physical and emotional well-being."

Most of our life involves extensive contacts with other human beings. People are judged by how popular they are with their contemporaries or by how many friends they have. Most of us think only in terms of the company of others when we seek recreation and joy. It would be unthinkable to enjoy ourselves all alone. If we did that the entire world would leave us at the "starting gate," so to speak.

Yet many of us, while in the company of a great and varied numbers of people, feel a pervasive loneliness that even a crowd cannot dispel. In order to get rid of this alienated feeling, we have to get into ourselves. We have to quietly probe the depths of our own feelings all alone. We have to think things out by ourselves. Those quiet moments we spend alone are the most productive of ultimate happiness of any time we may spend anywhere. At an absolute minimum, if we're going to enjoy this inevitable experience called life, we have to get our own thinking straight. This can only be done alone. The more we do this the greater progress we'll make in self-knowledge. The more self-knowledge we acquire the greater will be our tranquillity and subsequent happiness. Brief periods should be set aside each day for self-communication. They don't have to be long, but they do have to be quiet and alone. If we don't do this consistently, we begin to lose an understanding of ourselves. Our spirits begins to disintegrate. In these moments, begin to ask yourself what kind of person you really are; what you really believe in; if you are fulfilling your obligation to your loved ones; or a thousand questions that we all must answer about ourselves if we're to experience happiness.

Frequently, in this fast-moving world, our reliance on other people to entertain us, or simply to make us happy may prove or appear to have been misplaced. When this occurs, as it must to all of us sooner or later, we have no back-up system on which to rely unless we are capable of spending lengthy periods by ourselves in a happy and contented manner. This training should go on while all goes well. Don't wait for a major crisis to find out whether you can live with yourself. The very practice of communicating with yourself will tend to improve your personality and increase your acceptability to mankind in general. After all, if you can't live by yourself, or if you can't tolerate yourself, the overwhelming probability is that your fellowman has the same views. Solitary contemplation is at once a refuge and a self-improvement method and necessarily serves that function for all of us. By this type of thinking, answers will begin to come to us which will begin to benefit our emotions and mental well-being. Don't wait for a major crisis to develop; do it while all goes well. Your rewards in upgrading the quality of your life will be enormous.

SELF-IMPROVEMENT

"If you want to upgrade the quality of your life, you have to stress self-improvement."

A mother does not want her outstanding daughter marrying an alcoholic, a drug addict, or a convicted criminal. The daughter, if she is intelligent, would not want to marry one of these types. Most outstanding young people generally tend to marry someone close to their own ethical, moral, and attainment level. Golfers tend to associate with golfers; gamblers tend to associate with gamblers; crooks tend to associate with crooks; politicians tend to associate with politicians; athletes tend to associate with athletes; scholars tend to associate with scholars; religious people tend to associate with other religious people. People tend to socialize with others who have their same habits, both moral and social.

If you examine your circle of friends and conclude that they are lacking in qualities that you admire, the probability is that the problem lies with yourself. Since "water seeks its own level" it is probable that your friends have the same values you possess. If all your friends are excessive consumers of alcohol the probability is that you fall in this same category. If you eliminate your habits with reference to the consumption of alcohol, then you will soon find that your new set of social friends do not drink excessively. Since people tend to associate socially with those who enjoy doing the same types of things, if you upgrade the quality of your habits, your entire life will be improved. By a process that is as subtle as it is certain, you will gravitate toward those people whose quality of habits will be on the same level as yours.

The entire pattern of our life is determined by our habits. Our habits decide our lifestyle. If we hang around bars or taverns, the probability is that we consume excessive alcohol. If we stop consuming alcohol, we will no longer frequent bars or taverns. While we were frequenting bars or taverns, we met numerous people who similarly frequent bars or taverns and consume alcohol. When we stop visiting these types of places, we soon lose contact with people who frequent them. If we love to bowl, the probability is that we will spend a lot of time at bowling alleys. When we bowl frequently most of our friends will be people who love to bowl. If we are a drug addict, then most of our friends will come out of the drug culture. Eliminate the drug addiction and we will soon lose contact with other drug addicts. The scenario of habits determining friends and lifestyle is so predictable that if a person simply describes his habits one can describe his lifestyles and friends without firsthand knowledge of either.

From this brief discussion it should be obvious that we determine the quality of our own lives. We can change the entire pattern of friends and lifestyles by simply changing our habits. The objective should clearly be to acquire positive or desirable habits and eliminate negative or undesirable habits. The more we improve ourselves the more will be the improvement that occurs in our entire life.

When we decide that we don't like our lifestyle or our friends we are simply saying that we don't like ourselves. We reflect, or mirror ourselves in our friends and in our lifestyles. It is a cheerful thought to realize that we have so much control over our own destiny. All self-improvement requires discipline and hard work and wisdom. Nothing worthwhile comes easy. Everything has a "price tag" or a penalty attached to it. Basically, if you want good things to start happening to you, then start examining yourself continually and honestly. If you are wise enough, you will be able to lift yourself upwards by the simple process of self-improvement. Once you've eliminated your more serious flaws, then good things will start happening in your life.

PERSEVERANCE
"Before we can succeed at anything that is worthwhile,
we have to learn the art of perseverance."

Clark Gable knocked on directors' doors for seven years, always hearing that his ears were too large, before he finally was allowed to begin his climb to stardom. The life of Franklin Roosevelt with his paralysis, or of Helen Keller who was deaf, dumb, and blind are examples of perseverance that come readily to mind. The world of art, entertainment, politics, industry, sports, and religion are full of examples of people who succeeded after great struggles. One of the greatest speeches Winston Churchill ever gave was on the occasion of addressing the graduating class of one of England's esteemed universities. He was in his eighties and as he walked to the podium the audience settled back in anticipation of hearing the great man expound extensively on his wisdom. He spoke as follows: "Never give up; never, never give up; never, never, never give up." Having thus spoken he sat down, concluding what was probably his greatest speech. Those 12 words delivered with the emphasis of which he was uniquely capable told a powerful story.

Any objective or goal that is worthwhile usually requires dedication and effort to attain. If it was very simple and easy to achieve everyone would accomplish it and it would be rendered relatively worthless. No, something truly worth striving for only comes after perseverance, hard work, and sacrifice. The greater the effort, the greater the pleasure upon the attainment of a goal. Even though one should never gloat over victory, an inner feeling of self-satisfaction is bound to occur once a hard fought battle has been won.

One of the criticisms frequently heard today is that wealthy parents give everything to their children without making them work for it. The same children being thereby deprived of the joys of self-achievement are frequently depressed and unhappy. This fact surprises a lot of people. They seemingly do not understand how a young person, luxuriating in the lap of luxury, can be unhappy. Actually the answer is quite obvious. Being literally "buried" with many luxuries their lives lacks a challenge. They have nothing interesting or worthwhile to work towards; only the pursuit of pleasure. This is not fulfilling even to a young person. Hard work and challenges make life interesting and exciting. The relentless pursuit of personal pleasure has never made anyone happy. One has only to study the lives of the idle rich to realize this is true. It is also true that one seldom sees a hard working person who has excessive depression, whereas one sees a lot of idle people who are depressed and unhappy.

If you want to be happy establish worthwhile goals. Study the situation very carefully before you decide upon your objectives. Make sure that they are worthwhile. Determine that they are what you really want. You must believe that they are attainable by you. You will find you can do anything that you can convince yourself you can accomplish. Once your goals are established in the proper way outline your plan for their accomplishment. Be sure that those people closest to you, especially your spouses and children, wholeheartedly support your plan. Once all these hurdles are crossed then "roll up your sleeves" and quietly go to work. There will be many moments when you will question whether or not you can be successful. It is in these moments especially that you must persevere. Remember, if it was too easy the goal itself may not be worthwhile.

It is this type of activity which occupies the minds and hearts of successful and happy people. These types of people, who can be described as goal oriented, are interesting people to know. They don't have time to be jealous of their neighbor. They are too pre-occupied with their own thoughts and actions. They are truly happy people. They are the achievers of the world.

ENVY

"Envy is a mysterious and terrible disease.
Envy causes the possessor to suffer, therefore,
learn to envy no man for his good fortune."

There are many people in this world whose only, or whose greatest happiness, comes from the misfortune of others. Addition-ally, this type of mentally diseased person actually begrudges another's good fortune all the more if he is particularly close to such an individual. Sibling rivalry is rampant with examples of malice based on envy. This type of passion causes the possessor untold suffering and ultimately turns to hate. Most types of hate are cur-able except that type which flows from envy. Envy is a totally nega-tive passion and is productive of nothing positive or enriching.

Much envy is based on the fact the "grass looks much greener" in the other man's pasture. Another man's morsel always seems to taste better or smell sweeter. In making these types of judgments we see only the cheerful and positive aspects of another's posi-tion. We do not take into account the many negative forces which make up all lives. Consequently, an envious person over evaluates the worth of another man's possessions. He then begrudges that person's good fortune and often does so in a malicious manner. Frequently, the revenge a holder of good fortune gets against an envious person is the damage inflicted on that envious person by his malicious reaction to the former's good fortune.

The only cure for envy is wisdom. One should readily understand that the fact of envy changes nothing as far as the one who is blessed with good fortune is concerned. It certainly does not transfer his good fortune to the envious person. So the only effect is to ruin the contentment of the one whose heart is filled with malice growing out of envy. Since one only hurts oneself by envy, a wise and intelligent person would not waste his time on such a negative pastime.

The cure for envy is to learn to be satisfied with yourself and with your fortune. Learn to look introspectively at yourself and seek ways for self-improvement. If you get busy with such a positive program, you will have little time to spend envying others and their apparent good fortune. One should be especially careful not to envy another's material possessions since it is not readily apparent what price in peace of mind or morality or ethics another might have "paid" for such material possessions. His gains could well be ill-gotten.

Whether this is true or not, be satisfied with yourself. After all, you are the only thing you have going for yourself. Spend your time on self-improvement rather than self-destruction through envy. Your life will be a lot more contented and happy.

Jealousy

"Jealousy is an emotion we all experience. Basically it is caused by fear of losing something we have. How we control this green-eyed monster within us all determines the extent of the happiness and contentment of ourselves and those dear to us."

Jealousy is a normal emotion possessed in some degree by everyone. Unlike pride and envy, it is not all wrong. Many very proper and normal people experience jealousy from time to time in their lives. The real evil of jealousy occurs when it becomes unreasonable and/or uncontrollable. Carried to extreme, jealousy can destroy any relationship against which it is directed, ruining in the process the happiness and contentment of everyone involved. Jealousy must be distinguished from envy in that the former arises out of a fear of losing what we have, whereas envy is an emotion which begrudges or covets in a malicious manner what someone else has. Jealousy is normal, malicious envy is totally negative and is usually the product of a diseased mind.

It frequently occurs that an insecure person will deliberately provoke jealousy in an acquaintance or mate, in order to prove their desirability or popularity. This practice is contemptible and indicts the provoker. Nonetheless, the victim of such deliberate provocation has no right to become unreasonable or uncontrollably jealous. Ultimately the victim has to very logically decide whether or not the relationship is worth the constant pain and suffering of deliberate provocation. After all the provoker has the right to terminate totally the relationship if he so chooses. In such event the victim can only assent to the wishes of the provoker. Any relationship requires the assent of both parties to make it continue on a worthwhile basis.

One should never forget that although love is blind, sometimes jealousy sees too much. The act by the provoker could well be totally innocent or at the least unintentional. Jealousy also tends to be a question of degree. It has been said that any man who loves without the slightest trace of jealousy is probably not really in love. The evil lies in the excess. Excessive jealousy tends to read things into a situation which in fact do not exist except in the mind of the victim. Thus, if you are a jealous person by nature, get your facts straight first and then consider whether your mate's actions were purely innocent and also whether they were intentional or unintentional. If they were intentional you may very logically want to terminate the relationship. Anyone who continues a love relationship based on sex which is productive only of suffering raises serious questions about their wisdom.

It has been said that we anger our fellowman by our virtues. The anger of our fellowman exhibits itself in the form of jealousy. As a consequence of this universal human trait, all achievers in any field of endeavor must understand that they always live surrounded by the jealousy of their fellowman. It is part of the imperfection of mankind so don't let it worry you.

In short, if you want to be happy and contented, learn to control your jealousy.

HELPING OTHERS

"Whenever you help someone, in the greatest number of cases, you will be benefited far more than the expenditure of effort or resources required of you in the process."

Philosophers have pictured the entire population of the world as standing with arms outstretched and crying "help!" Wherever one looks, there are many opportunities to be of help to someone. Each one of us in our daily lives has hundreds of opportunities to help. Each one of these opportunities is in reality an opportunity to help yourself. For when you help someone else, in the greatest majority of instances (since the actions and reactions of nature and one's fellowman always have to be stated in terms of probabilities) the one who gave the help will be benefited the most.

The lady in the supermarket who has several large bags of groceries to carry out to her car will be most appreciative of any kind person who is thoughtful enough to help her with the task. Not only will she be grateful, but the probabilities are that when she gets home or when she talks to her friends, she will recall the story. In the recalling, whoever performed the good deed will be benefited by the good will towards him which will be generated in the hearts and minds of the listener. The result of such good will inevitably help the benefactor far more than any effort

344

expended in the performance of the deed.

A kind act towards fellow human beings is the surest way to communicate in an effective, helpful way. Words are cheap and in the cynical world of today, for the most part, are not believed. Acts are unmistakable and since they by themselves are mute, they are recognized for their true purpose.

A lonely, perplexed, or depressed person is always in great need of help. One can brighten such a person's day immeasurably by talking to them or helping them straighten out their thinking or by performing an act designed to brighten their day or lift their spirits. An unattractive girl can be cheered if someone will take an attractive feature of her looks or personality and compliment her on it. An angry person can be helped if one will take the time to simply point out that perhaps every thought they have isn't necessarily well thought out or correct. An angry person is helped when something is done to diminish his anger. A sick person needs any sort of reassurance that their illness is temporary, or not as bad as they think it is, or, if it is terminal, many things can be done which show love, thoughtfulness, or concern. Young people of all kinds are desperately searching for answers to all sorts of perplexing questions associated with life and the process of growing up. Hours spent in this manner with young people, helping and guiding them through the maze of life's problems and hurdles, are very rewarding to the thoughtful person who will take the time. The benefited adolescent will never forget the guidance or helping hand in his hour of need. Many people are terribly worried about life and corruption and crime of all sorts to the extent that they no longer see any logical reason for the very continuation of life itself. These people can be immeasurably helped by pointing out some of the worthwhile features of life and people. Their thinking has become so clouded and twisted that they fail to spot anything of value that life has to offer. Their only search is for those things, or persons, which tend to confirm the preconceived notion that life has no meaning. This type of person becomes disastrously cynical to the point that his acquaintances start to avoid him, thus increasing by geometric proportions his cynicism and its consequent bitterness. Time spent helping such a person see some of the worthwhile things in people or life will be appreciated and very beneficial to both people involved.

Those who are looking for employment are in great need of help. Many people, by a minimum expenditure of time are frequently able to be of assistance in helping a deserving person find gainful employment—to the eternal gratitude of the person helped. The handicapped person is in continuous need of help that is rendered in a subtle manner and which does not deprive him of his dignity. Handicapped people have trouble finding employment, yet in a job that complements their handicap they are a most loyal, efficient, and trustworthy servant. All of us have contacts and know of opportunities that would enable such a person to be self-sufficient. Any help given will render to the giver far more blessings than will enure to the benefit of the recipient.

Old people are constantly in need of help of all sorts. They are lonely; they have difficulty shopping; they have trouble getting to a doctor; buying prescriptions; sometimes their children need to be reminded that they should go to see their parents; sometimes a meal prepared and given to them answers a great need; sometimes their grass needs cutting. All the above and many other items too numerous to mention present opportunities to be of assistance to others, especially old people.

People in jail or about to go to jail are in great need of assistance of all forms. Such persons are frequently abandoned by their friends and acquaintances and are left utterly alone. A quiet voice saying that they are not totally forgotten and followed up with a helping hand can be of immeasurable assistance to such a person in a time of his greatest need.

People who have come upon financial misfortune sometimes

to the extent of bankruptcy have a great need to have their personal sense of security buttressed and their self-confidence restored. A relatively small act offered in a graceful manner can be of immeasurable assistance at a time when they are in their hour of greatest need.

People in all walks of life throughout the world are in need of help of some sort. The person who, as a habit of life attempts to answer those needs, benefits himself or herself directly from the goodwill created by these acts. The recipients of his or her good deeds tell their friends, who tell others, which creates an aura of warm feelings toward a giver. This cloud of goodness creates a happy heart and soul in the giver which will keep his life bright and cheerful. A giver also carries with him the best wishes of all those people who have directly experienced the benefits and help of his or her good deeds. Such a person is indeed a rich human being in important ways, and what's more, he or she will have a life of happiness.

Thinking outwardly, or to put it another way, thinking of the problems of others, will cause one to forget his own problems; and if they are forgotten long enough and consistently enough, the vast majority will disappear. The mere passing of time, if nothing else, either solves most problems or makes the individual realize that the only place they ever existed was in his own mind.

Selfish people tend to think inwardly or only of their own problems. Selfish people tend to be unhappy. All the kindness you show to others comes back to you multiplied many times over. When you think only of yourself and your own problems, your fellow-man will soon recognize this trait in your personality and treat you accordingly. You will find yourself friendless and not treated very nicely by your acquaintances. You may be sure that your peers will recognize whether or not you have a kind heart. You will receive what you give.

Never speak unkindly about your neighbor; visit someone who

is ill; refuse to further communicate unkind remarks or rumors; be cheerful and optimistic rather than remorseful and pessimistic; help someone who is slow to learn rather than to call them stupid or ignorant; never be critical of others unless it is directed towards them in a helpful, understanding manner; look for the good qualities rather than the bad qualities in your acquaintances; help people overcome a lack of confidence in themselves; decrease animosity between antagonists; terminate relationships in a gracious manner; make people feel better because you met them; increase the love in the world by your actions; be always a part of a sensible solution rather than a party to increasing a problem; smile instead of frown; reduce the fears of the frightened; the pain of the sick; the hunger of the hungry; the depression of the mentally ill; the disorder in the world, or in your city or county or block or your own household or business. Replace madness with reason, hopelessness with hope, hate with love.

If you lead such a giving life, you will create so much "lift" for yourself from your fellowman that your own problems will disappear—"lift" being that which one's fellowman does for someone else as opposed to "push" which is what one does for himself. A giving person's life can be literally borne upward on the wings of assistance provided by others, or plunged downward by the opposition of one's peers. If you want good things to happen to you, perform good deeds for others. Make your choice depending on the results you want.

History reserves a very high place for those outstanding humans who spend a great portion of their lives answering the needs of others. Notable among these are such people as Dr. Albert Schweitzer, Abraham Lincoln, Florence Nightingale, and Mahatma Gandhi, to name a few. All your acquaintances, on a much smaller scale, will reserve an equally high place in their hearts for you if you give of yourself for others. This process will bring much happiness and serenity to yourself. However, to receive, you must first give.

INJUSTICE

"Whenever someone does another person a great injustice, the offending person will be punished by forces other than the victims."

Retribution and recrimination are the most needless undertakings of mankind. Whenever one suffers an injustice at the hands of others, the ugly face of anger and revenge appears in the heart of the victim. This feeling of anger and revenge does more damage to the victim, both emotionally and physically, than was inflicted by the transgressor.

The victim of such an injustice should consider that there are forces at work which will punish the wrongdoer far more effectively than anything the victim can do. First, consider that if this practice is engaged in against the victim, the overwhelming probability is that it has been inflicted on many others. This being the case, word-of-mouth conversations by other victims and the repetition of this by the listeners will soon downgrade the culprit immensely in the eyes of his peers and in his community in general. This thrust will prevent such a person from living in peace and harmony in his environment. This, in and of itself, is a severe price to pay.

Secondly, no man is so callused that he does not have occasional pangs of guilt and conscience. One who inflicts harm and injustice on others as a part of his lifestyle will have many doubts and guilt feelings concerning his activities and relations with others. His conscience will not let him rest. He will eventually find it impossible to think of himself as a good person. This will prevent him from living harmoniously within himself, which constitutes the most severe form of punishment.

All of this punishment will have been inflicted without the slightest effort by the victim.

RETRIBUTION

"Whenever you intentionally hurt someone, you will be hurt far more than any harm you may have inflicted."

The qualities of pride, jealousy, fear, greed, lust and ambition are intermixed in all of us. Outward exemplifications of these traits cause one to inflict harm on his fellowman. When the cycle of harm and retribution has run its full course, the one who inflicts the harm in the final analysis is hurt the most. A happy person is one who has learned to control these characteristics, to understand when they are causing distasteful action, and to avoid the disastrous results they inflict on one's fellowman and finally on the individual involved.

John works with Bill and they are both ambitious and seek to climb the ladder of success within their organization. John, in an effort to keep Bill from advancing, does everything he can to cast Bill in a bad light by constantly pointing out Bill's weaknesses; by directly and indirectly sabotaging in any way possible all of Bill's work and work products. In this manner, John hopes to advance over Bill. By his actions, John will inevitably reveal his own character; his own inadequacies and weaknesses. His motives will become apparent to his fellow workers, and when this happens, the initial harm inflicted upon Bill will be visited upon John, multiplied by geometric proportions. John would be far more assured of attaining his goal if he concentrated on his own self-improvement, making it clear by his own efficiency that he clearly deserves a promotion. With this approach, mentally and emotionally, he will be in a far healthier frame of mind than if his heart is filled with vindictiveness and connivance against the best interests of Bill. If he can't advance by his own abilities, then clearly it is to the best interest of all concerned, especially John, that he not do so. For if John has responsibility beyond his capability, he will be the unhappiest of all.

Centuries before anyone living today, our forefathers inflicted a terrible evil upon the black man. For reasons of greed he snatched him out of his environment in Africa and forcibly brought him to America to perform all the backbreaking labor that needed to be done on the farms and plantations of North America. He separated mothers from their offspring at public auctions; he dealt cruel punishment to anyone who failed to follow his rules; and for all purposes, he treated the black man as an animal. For these sins of our forefathers, the United States fought a Civil War which resulted in 620,000 casualties. To this very day, racial unrest and rioting are the price we are paying (the full bill for which we have yet to receive) for the sins of our forefathers.

In the 1920s and '30s, Germany allowed itself to be hypnotized by a demagogue named Adolph Hitler. He was supported and financed by Germans knowing full well that he represented evil and ignorance. Yet the German people gave him support in the form of millions of votes. They allowed him to be their leader. The result of this alliance with evil and ignorance resulted in the total destruction of Germany in 1945, together with the loss of millions of lives.

The principle that you can't hurt someone lest you hurt yourself more, while applying to nations, applies even more noticeably to individuals. The greedy, selfish businessman soon finds it difficult to find anyone who will do business with him. The person who hurts other people with his derogatory remarks about them will soon find it impossible to find anyone who wants to be close or friendly with him. They soon realize that this type of person will talk derogatorily about them as soon as their back is turned.

Vengeful people spend their greatest amount of energy trying to get even with someone for a real or imagined wrong. Their mental processes are preoccupied with thoughts of revenge and are not free to engage in useful pursuits. Just avoiding a single enemy takes a lot of effort and energy. Life can be so much more enjoyable if this sort of activity is eliminated totally from one's pursuits. Chances are that a frank conversation with the individual will eliminate all the emotion and tension required to keep a feud of this sort going. Once eliminated, one can turn his attention towards useful pursuits that are far more productive of happiness and tranquillity.

Pride keeps an individual from praising his fellowman for his skill or a job well done. Jealousy causes an individual to constantly berate one of whom he is jealous. Fear causes an individual to react violently towards the actions of others whom he believes threatens his physical or economic security. Greed causes an individual to inflict all sorts of harm on his fellowman and ultimately in larger proportions, upon himself. Lust for seconds of pleasure has ended many otherwise pleasant relationships and ruined the lives of thousands of innocent children and adults. Ambition has caused individuals to hurt their fellowman without regard to the resulting consequences.

In every one of these cases where harm results to your fellowman, the harm that is visited upon you as a direct consequence of your initial action is far greater than any pleasure one can possibly derive from a harmful act. All these acts eventually come back to haunt the perpetrator and a price is exacted for each one of them.

An unkind remark circulated about one's fellowman will eventually be heard by the subject himself or one of his friends. When this happens, the originator will be cast in an unfavorable light not only with the subject but also with his friends. When this happens, the originator has negative goodwill to overcome, which will exhibit itself in ways that effectively limit his worldly success, and what is more important, his happiness.

One of the surest ways to be lonely, friendless, and unhappy is to spend your time trying (or for any reason whether intentional or not) to hurt someone else. It is totally nonproductive of happiness.

Ancient literature, philosophy, folk sayings, and the Bible, representing the accumulated wisdom of mankind, are replete with advice on this subject. If you live by the sword, you will perish by the sword; as you sow so shall you reap; when you frown the world frowns at you, are but a few of many examples. A mind that gives a minimum amount of thought to the subject is bound to conclude that there is no gain of a permanent nature possible from inflicting harm on one's fellowman. Just as the laws of physics tell us that a motion or force in one direction creates a force in the opposite direction, so it is with the philosophical laws of mankind. When you hurt someone, you get hurt in return far more than the harm you inflicted on that person originally. History is filled with outstanding examples: Al Capone, Joseph McCarthy, Richard Nixon, Benedict Arnold, Adolph Hitler, and Napoleon Bonaparte, to name but a few. Contrariwise, when you help someone, you are helped in return and will be remembered in a grateful way such as Florence Nightingale, Albert Schweitzer, Abraham Lincoln, Mahatma Gandhi, and Dr. Martin Luther King. While it is true that the last three mentioned were assassinated or executed, history forever through future ages will ring with their praises.

HARDSHIP
"A life without hardships or challenges results in unhappiness."

A deprived person can be thought of as one who was never allowed to meet his own challenges; one who conceivably had his doting parents solve every problem for him before he had a chance to do so himself. Such a person never knows the joy of achievement. He never builds up the confidence in himself which can only come from obstacles successfully surmounted. Lacking the self-confidence that only a successful confrontation with past hardships can produce, such a deprived person becomes an insecure, frightened, and consequently unhappy individual.

A smooth sea never made a good mariner. A clear day never

made a good pilot. Steel can only be forged by holding it in fire. All these truisms were thought of by someone in the past, but are manifestly true in their application to anyone. One of the building blocks of a secure individual is the successful solving of past problems. I don't refer to problems which were solved for you by someone else. I'm talking about problems you solved yourself without anyone's help. These are the sort of experiences that mature an individual. This valuable ingredient of knowing in advance that you can solve tough problems only comes from having done so in the past. One cannot acquire this character trait by reading or by watching others. It can only be learned in the crucible of life. Once an individual gets some real tough problems behind him, he can then learn to face life and its certain problems with optimism and self-assurance.

We should learn to be thankful for all the problems life sends our way. Immediately, upon spying a problem, we should rejoice in the fact that we are being presented with yet another opportunity to learn. For it is only through problems and their subsequent solutions that we learn about life. Progress is somehow always painful. If we dig deep enough into a new problem, it won't be long before we can detect within the core of this new challenge the seeds of our next opportunity. Now this new opportunity may be very well concealed. However, we should know in advance that all problems contain an opportunity for learning. With this knowledge, we should approach all problems with vigor and optimism, secure in the knowledge that it is yet another opportunity for personal growth and advancement. We shouldn't allow ourselves to be intimidated, discouraged, or frightened. Problem-solving is bound to leave you wiser.

The surest method of self-destruction is to luxuriate in the lap of luxury. The easy life makes for a lazy, dull individual who is, or will become terribly depressed and unhappy. Try to build some rigid discipline into your life. It will prepare you for the inevitable hardships that will come your way. When you are physically and mentally seasoned, you are better prepared to resolve difficult problems. Idle people who follow the "good" life and let others solve their problems make no contribution to their fellowman. The world really doesn't need them. They are takers and not givers. Ironically, the person they take the most from is themselves. They take from themselves the opportunity to be happy.

Welcome all challenges and hardships. Leadership always advances to the forefront in all problem-solving situations. Actually, if one stays busy working at a solution to problems, then no time will remain to be bored. This type of scenario—of staying busy in constructive pursuits—will leave no time for self-doubt, and self-pity.

Remember that if you are living, you are bound to be experiencing problems. Always remember that everyone faces essentially the same types of hurdles. None of us is unique. So cheerfully accept what life brings your way. Plunge into each day with vitality. Dispel fear as a dominant element in your life and happiness will soon "move in" as a "permanent companion."

LOYALTY
"Loyalty or disloyalty is almost always returned in kind."

Some wise person once said, "Give me an ounce of loyalty and I'll give you a pound of cunning." Ability doesn't mean much unless accompanied by a reasonable degree of loyalty. The world is full of cunning and trickery and when this is accompanied by innate ability, it still doesn't represent a situation in which a wise man would place his reliance. After all, the world is full of treachery and to discover this again in an acquaintance is somewhat depressing. What is refreshing is loyalty.

Certain people, by their very personality, command loyalty from their associates. John Kennedy is an example of a fortunate type of person who somehow received a high degree of loyalty from his associates. Richard Nixon, on the other hand, is an example of a leader who had a difficult time obtaining loyalty from his associates. Usually loyalty is returned to those people who by their nature are loyal. Most people will not be loyal to someone who is disloyal. Loyalty and disloyalty are usually "two-way streets." One is foolish to be loyal to a disloyal person and also to be disloyal to a loyal person. Many people receive loyalty who do not deserve it. When this happens, it is just a quirk of character or personality. Generally speaking, however, we will get back in the realm of loyalty pretty much what we dispense. To this extent, loyalty is similar to a "boomerang."

It is very wise to develop the quality of loyalty within our own lives. People seek out loyal types with whom to establish friendships. As you act and react to life's problems, people are quick to detect the type of person you are with reference to loyalty. Your progress in dozens of life's areas depends in no small measure on your reputation for loyalty. All sorts of desirable characteristics usually accompany the quality of loyalty. People know this and reward such a person with the best that life has to offer. For example, a loyal person will keep a confidence if requested to do so. Knowing this, people will place their reliance on him. Loyal people are usually good company men, which allows them to be promoted in their life's work. Loyal people are good family members and this quality radiates in all directions amongst their family. When this occurs such a family is close-knit and helpful to one another. This almost ensures a happy, successful family life. Loyalty is a treasured quality in love affairs between wise adults. When loyalty is radiated from one's personality, this quality is soon detected by the object of love and is normally returned in kind.

Loyalty is not always reciprocated and this is justification to some people for not extending loyalty to their acquaintances. One must learn to accept those unfortunate people who don't know how to be loyal. Because of their ignorance, one should not abandon a wise policy for living just because another person is igno-rant. It is far better to be loyal and be deceived than it is never to be loyal at all. Disloyal people live very unsuccessful lives. They are soon discovered; and thereafter, they start paying dearly for their disloyalty. Such a price comes in the form of few friends, minimal economic success, shattered family relationships, poor relations with a loved one, little recognition by one's peers, and in many other ways. Do not let ignorant, disloyal people affect your lifestyle adversely. Dispensing loyalty is the best policy even if it is never returned in your day-to-day relationships. This latter condi-tion almost never occurs.

So be wise and be loyal. It will enable you to look your loved ones, friends, and acquaintances in the eye knowing full well that you have done what a loyal person should do. Always remember you can't be loyal 99 percent of the time and disloyal to the same person 1 percent of the time. No, loyalty requires 100 percent con-sistency in your actions. When you act this way, you will set good examples for your loved ones and bring much happiness and suc-cess to yourself.

SELFISHNESS

"Selfish people tend to be unhappy:
unselfish people tend to be happy."

The above truth, upon close observation, can be verified by anyone as he studies his fellowman. Everyone has known a per-son who thinks only of his own selfish interests—always asking what's in it for himself and never considering the needs, wishes or aspirations of his fellowman. This type may gain temporary ad-vantages, but they do so at a terrible price to their own happiness and to the position they enjoy in the eyes of their acquaintances. Being constantly selfish and self-centered leaves such a person with tension and guilt feelings engendered by the knowledge that his gain has been at someone else's expense or effort. This type of person loses one friend after another until it culminates in his living in a friendless world, alone and unhappy. It is possible to be selfish and live constantly among new acquaintances and escape the harsh judgment of one's peers. But if one's contact is repeatedly with the same people, then the pattern of selfish behavior will be discerned by all and such an individual will soon be isolated by his acquaintances. No one will seek his company socially or in business. His social opportunities will gradually diminish as will his business opportunities. The only way he can continue to function is to constantly seek new contacts on a social and business level. Repeated contacts with the same person are bound to result in his ostracism. A selfish person cannot function successfully very long in the same locality amongst the same people. He needs a high turnover in his total environment.

Unselfish people have a warm heart and a happy mind. They are blessed with many friends and loved ones. The better they get to know people the greater are the bonds of respect and affection that are created. These people never seem to lose a friend. Once they meet someone and become their friend, they maintain the relationship for the rest of their lives. The life of an unselfish person is filled with very little tension. Since all their acquaintances have a warm and friendly regard for them, they seldom encounter friction. Their whole world is filled with love and affection. They are aided in many unseen and unsolicited ways by the efforts and sentiments of their peers. Everyone wants to see them succeed and have pleasant things come their way. They are able to make great strides with a minimum of effort. Their great qualities become known to everyone and no one is jealous or envious of them. At the least, their unselfishness has reduced jealousy and envy to a minimum. With most of the negative forces removed from their lives, they are able to achieve great heights of love, friendship, and material success. All these desirable possessions are a natural consequence of their unselfish character. This characteristic will make life pleasant for everyone close to them, especially their family. At the conclusion of their life's journey, their existence on this earth will have benefited everyone with whom they came in contact. Certainly no one can spread this much joy without receiving a greater amount himself. In short, it is wise to lead an unselfish life.

GREED
"Greed, in the greatest majority of cases, hurts the greedy."

The most boring and unpleasant person to be around is the one who continually asks, "What's in it for me?" or "What can I get for myself?" If I can't benefit myself somehow, then I'm not interested." This type of person fits a predictable profile. He is a very cynical type. He literally trusts no one. Like all thieves, he sleeps with one eye open. He has an abnormal love of material things. He has few friends. He really doesn't love anyone but himself. He is not a very wise person. He may have a lot of "street smarts" but he is not wise. There is a vast difference. He values money above human relationships. As a consequence, he is not a loyal person. After all, his only loyalty is to material gain. This type of person is usually unhappy, if not depressed. Such a person usually has very few sincere religious convictions. He is not very exciting to be with since his whole reaction to everything is utterly foreseeable in advance.

A greedy person, through his greed and avarice, will no doubt accumulate inordinate amounts of material gain. It is not hard to do this when your every waking thought centers on the acquisition of material wealth. What such a person does accumulate will necessarily have to be through his own efforts. Others who truly know him will hardly lift a finger to help him. Thus, while his accumulation of wealth may be substantial, it will be hard won gains. A generous person, on the other hand, will often receive great help from his many friends. The greedy person will usually not know how to enjoy his material benefits since his entire life is aimed at their acquisition and not at their dissipation. Usually, this type is left alone to count his wealth and no one will applaud his victories. His achievements of a material nature will be insignificant in their contribution to his happiness and emotional well-being.

We all have the need to feel secure in a world of starving people. The tendency to be greedy and to store away material possessions is great in a world that is insecure. The practice of putting yourself first is widespread and is usually an outward sign of inward insecurity. Be assured that if you approach life from the standpoint of the "giver," all the things you require to be secure in this world will come your way without the asking. People will constantly push you into leadership positions that carry with them excellent remuneration. The world requires many leaders to function properly and leaders are picked amongst acquaintances or peers. People do not pick as their leaders greedy people whom they invariably dislike. No, they pick generous people whom they invariably love. Keep in mind further that the world handsomely rewards its leaders.

The leadership of which I speak exists on every level of life. Social, political, economic, philosophical, and religious. In all of these categories of human endeavor, the generous types emerge predominantly as leaders.

So if you are truly wise, you will analyze yourself with the idea of reducing any greedy traits you may have. We all have streaks of greediness in our character and it is necessary for the wise man to recognize where it exists, and having discovered it, to find ways to eliminate it. It may hurt at first to eliminate a greedy trait. But I can assure you that the replacement will be far more valuable and enjoyable.

It is hard to be happy in life when you greedily place too much value on material things. First and foremost, by your inordinate love of wealth, you place yourself in an extremely vulnerable position. Wealth can be easily lost and since this is true, the greedy person is constantly worried about this possibility occurring. If, however, you recognize that your most valuable possession is your generous heart, then you alone have control over its continued possession. No event or person can take that from you. Only you are the master of the single most significant element of your happiness. This makes you a very fortunate and wise human being.

GENEROSITY

"Generosity, in the greatest majority
of cases, benefits the donor."

Whenever we place ourselves in a position of giving of our time, love, energy, or material possessions, we are fulfilling the highest mission that life has to offer. Giving means that you are contributing to the welfare of someone other than yourself. By your act of giving, you are lending meaning and substance to life. You are adding to the goodwill amongst men that exists on this planet. You are engaged in a wholesome activity. You are easing the human struggle. You are adding to the sum total of love and understanding which is so necessary to make the overall human condition more enjoyable. By contributing, you are making it worthwhile that you were born. Your life assumes far greater meaning and purpose when you use your energies to help some creature other than yourself. Such generosity is an act of unselfishness. In an otherwise dreary, and too often ignorant world, your acts of generosity introduce kindness. All your acquaintances draw strength and purpose from your actions. Everyone is enhanced by your existence.

What many people do not realize is that when you perform an unselfish act of generosity for others the greatest beneficiary of such actions is you. Once you give, your generosity creates all sorts of positive vibrations that radiate in all directions. People familiar with your conduct immediately respond with affection towards you and your noble act. The acts of which I speak must be truly unselfish. You surround yourself with an aura of love, respect, and affection that will warm your heart and add great depth and contentment to your life. By the simple act of giving, you have received something of far greater value than anything you might have given away. Givers are the happiest people. Takers are the saddest and most depressed people.

With these consequences in mind, we should always be on the lookout for kind actions we can perform for others. By others, I mean all creatures and do not intend to limit the targets of generosity to human beings. However, a good place to start giving is within your own family. Start by doing your share of the work around your own household. Don't just throw your dirty clothes on the floor, but put them in a clothes hamper. Don't leave the bathroom dirty in the morning, but wipe off the basin and clean up the bathroom floor. If trash needs to be taken out, do this as you leave for work. If clothes need to be taken to the cleaners, do this also. If you fix yourself a bowl of cereal for breakfast, for example, clean the kitchen before you leave. Obviously these tasks have to be performed by someone. Everytime you do them, instead of leaving them for someone else to do, you are telling such persons by your actions that you love them.

This type of giving can be continued once you arrive at the place where you can earn your living. A generous spirit can be displayed in subtle ways at your place of work. Little tasks can be performed for your fellow workers that are really not your duty. However, your accomplishment of these acts is indeed an act of giving.

Giving, of course, can take the form of material contributions also. Whichever form it may take, the ultimate result will be to benefit the donor far greater than any good received by the donee. First and foremost, giving will enrich a person's life beyond anything else he can do. It will relieve boredom and put a "song in one's heart." A habitual giver is warmly accepted by his acquaintances. The very habit of giving of oneself makes it possible to describe such a person favorably, even though you may not be acquainted with him. You can be sure of one thing and that is that such a person is happy.

CHARACTER AND DESTINY

"Your character will be a dominant
factor in determining your destiny."

Most of the things that happen to people are a logical consequence of their habits and lifestyles. A close study of an individual will enable a discerning person to predict a great amount of things about such a person. For example, a habitual liar does not have the trust of his acquaintances. Once one determines that an individual is a habitual liar, it then becomes predictable that no one who knows him will believe what he says. All alcoholics tend to have similar problems. Once we determine that an individual is an alcoholic and we know the extent of his alcohol addiction, we can just about predict what his personal relationships will be like, and certain other problems that are traditionally associated with alcoholism. One who habitually disregards traffic laws will no doubt receive summons for traffic violations in the future. One who habitually breaks any criminal laws will no doubt be arrested for such violations at some time in the future. A habitual gambler will probably die broke.

One who goes around looking for trouble will find it frequently. If one speaks derogatorily about his "friends," then such a person will have few friends. The simple rule that unwise actions in the present will ensure an unpleasant or undesirable destiny is quite true.

Conversely, the statement that a good, or sound, or wise character will ensure a pleasant or desirable destiny is also true. If one does everything he can to help his friends, he will have many friends. Life is just that simple. If you take care of your health by performing exercises and watching your diet, then it is predictable that you will probably enjoy good health in the future. If you work hard and effectively and consistently, it is quite predictable that your efforts will meet with success. If you have good personal morals and health habits, it is quite predictable that substantial people of good character will be attracted to you as friends. As you sow, so shall you reap. Now, there is nothing very difficult or illogical about these truths. Surely they are all foreseeable by a clear-thinking person.

Once it becomes obvious that the level of a person's character determines in large measure the quality and level of his destiny, the course we should take in our lives becomes quite obvious. We should all try to improve our character and wisdom. We should sit down and in our quiet moments, reflect carefully on ourselves. For these purposes we should take off the "rose colored glasses." What we need to do is to take a realistic look at ourselves. This may be somewhat painful, but keep in mind the wisdom of our actions. We all have rough spots. Learn to observe the truth about ourselves. What are our habits with reference to eating, tobacco smoking, drugs, alcohol, truthfulness, work, speaking ill of our acquaintances, fidelity to our wives, etc.? The list is endless. A million factors are involved in forming our character.

Remember that no one is perfect. What we're trying to do is to bring the negative forces in our character within manageable or tolerable limits. Remember, if we were truly perfect, no one would relate to use. However, since perfection is always unattainable, our problem is always too much imperfection. Thus, our efforts should always be aimed in the direction of improving or uplifting our character. As we improve ourselves as individuals, we will slowly begin to see good things happening to us. The quality of our friends will improve. The direction of our life will take a more favorable turn and its improvement will be more consistent. Most of all, our day-to-day happiness will increase as our character improves.

INDULGENCE

"For every indulgence you permit yourself, there is
a corresponding penalty to be exacted in the future."

Many people live only for the present. The tragedy of this philosophy is that an excess committed today ruins unalterably the "present" that will come with future tomorrows. If we eat and eat and eat anything that appeals to our taste buds, we may be able to enjoy the present. Certainly it is not very difficult to exercise no willpower or restraint in what we eat at the present. Unfortunately, these excesses will fill a body with excess calories which will drastically alter weight and affect health adversely. Having indulged excessively, as days pass, the present that comes with future tomorrows can no longer be enjoyed. If we are 100 pounds overweight, for example, we will have difficulty walking without heavy breathing; it will become arduous just to tie our shoe strings. People will look at us in a different and less favorable way than if our weight were normal. Carried further, such continued excess weight can create heart trouble and other physical ailments such as diabetes that will positively make it impossible to enjoy the present in the tomorrows which have not yet arrived. Past and present indulgences will ruin the future. These penalties are inescapable and are frequently irreversible.

Cigarette smoking is "oh so enjoyable"; why should we give up the habit? We enjoy it, so why not smoke? Wisdom and experience would reveal that the joy associated with not smoking far exceeds any pleasures derived from smoking. Nonetheless, we live for the moment and "light up" everytime the urge "strikes." This indulgence carried on long enough will result in serious health problems that could include heart trouble, circulatory problems, emphysema, or lung cancer to name but a few. Let me emphasize that the pleasure comes first. The penalty comes later. Now, it is fairly obvious that the subsequent difficulties associated with cigarette consumption are largely incurable and irreversible in their progress. Once these ominous ailments arise, they tend to run their tragic courses unstoppable by medical treatment.

Drug addiction is for the guy who really wants to enjoy the present to its fullest. The high one gets in the present is worth any penalty that may be exacted in the future. So goes the thinking of a drug user. Unfortunately, those highs are harder and harder to recreate as one's drug habit progresses. Marijuana soon will not get the job done; hashish will do it better for a while; suddenly cocaine is discovered as being the supreme high; and eventually the granddaddy of them all, heroin, is necessary to send the addict into "never, never land." "Tomorrow" for the drug addict is an unpleasant thought. Drug usage becomes a bottomless pit. It is impossible to satisfy the craving. An addict's entire life is consumed in the acquisition and consumption of drugs. The penalty he must pay in his tomorrows is indescribably cruel.

These scenarios can be repeated using every indulgence in a negative or harmful habit that it's possible for a human being to practice. Enjoy the present and pay the price tomorrow. That's the way the game of life is played by many people. It is very deceptive and tempting, which explains why so many people destroy themselves by their habits. The exercise of thought and wisdom will enable you to escape this "tender trap." Think! Think! Think! Once you've done this, it is far easier to follow the correct course. You have no right to destroy your mind or body. Take care of it by following good habits. Good or positive habits create more pleasure than negative or harmful indulgences.

SACRIFICE

"For every sacrifice you make there is a corresponding reward."

It is ironic that any good result requires sacrifice first, while the benefits come later. Life would be "oh so sweet" if this process were reversed. Realistically the pain comes first and the joys come later. This rule of life keeps most people from adopting habits and practices that are beneficial to their emotional and physical well-being. The sacrifice is a voluntary thing that one can make or not make as his conscience dictates. It is so much easier not to make the sacrifice. It is so much more fun just to wallow in the sea of self-indulgence than it is to pay a "price" now for benefits that will occur or be realized some time in the future. The result is that most of mankind procrastinates and fails to adopt positive habits that will uplift their physical and emotional well-being.

When we sit down to eat, we love bread and butter, and pie à la mode, and steak, and a multitude of foods that will cause innumerable health problems in the future. Americans are overweight because they lack the willpower and wisdom to control their eating habits. They give in to the temptation to not only eat the wrong foods, but at the same time to eat too much of such food. The result is a nation of obese people.

Alcoholic consumption overcomes the willpower of many people who find it difficult to forego that unnecessary drink in order to have the pleasure of alcohol. The slightest exercise of willpower and wisdom will make it extremely easy to resist the temptation and forego the drink for benefits to be derived in the future. Alcohol deprives an individual of his health at a date subsequent to his excessive consumption. The sacrifice of not drinking has to be made in the present, the benefit will come later.

The great tragedy of America today lies in drug consumption. An unbelievable number of our citizens, especially young people, are throwing all precaution to the wind and consuming every form of mind-altering drug in prodigious amounts. Again, the exercise of wisdom and willpower in the present will enable anyone to discontinue such a ruinous habit. Drugs are destroying the very soul and body of millions of our citizens. The practice is so widespread as to represent an emergency of national proportions.

Exercise undertaken at the present, though it may constitute somewhat of a sacrifice, will tend to ensure a sound and healthy body in the future.

A student who pays the price of studying now will have less difficulty passing his examinations later.

Because a sacrifice has to be made first, at a time when the pleasures are as yet not realized, most people never develop positive addictions to healthy practices and habits. However, once a positive practice of self-denial or sacrifice has continued long enough for the subsequent benefits to be enjoyed, then such a person has no difficulty or at least far less difficulty continuing such wholesome habits. The benefits of not smoking cigarettes soon become apparent after one has stopped for a month; and so it is with exercising, not consuming alcohol or drugs; reduced eating habits and a multitude of other wholesome practices. Once the benefits begin to be realized, it becomes rather easy to become addicted to a positive habit. Our habits also make up our lifestyle. For example, drug users associate with other drug users, etc. So once you clean up your act and fill your life with positive addictions, your level of happiness will increase enormously as will the quality of your relationships.

POSITIVE ATTITUDE

"Your attitude makes the entire difference in
whether you fail or succeed in any endeavor
or in your overall goals for your lifetime."

One almost never exceeds his goals. Usually the final result is something short of our intended achievements. Many people make the mistake of setting their goals too low. People tend to under-evaluate themselves, thereby setting goals based on an under-valued self-worth. Most people are more expert, more competent, and more worthy than they secretly believe. In short, their self-image is lower than it should be based on a realistic evaluation of their worth as a person. This diminished self-image usually arises out of insecurities we all accumulate as we journey through life. People tend to exaggerate the importance of their failures and minimize the importance of their successes. The self-appraisals I'm talking about are not what people verbalize to each other, but what they think only to themselves in their quiet moments. Usually the louder the outward braggadocio, the more insecure is the inner person. This boastful characteristic is usually a wall erected by people to hide their inner feelings of inadequacies.

The first thing we have to decide about ourselves is that while we may not be perfect, we are at least as worthy of success and as capable of attaining our goals as are our fellowmen. Once we get over this initial and formidable hurdle, we then literally are limited in our goals only by our imagination. I believe that anyone can accomplish anything he can convince himself in his mind is possible. If you firmly believe you can do something, and you are sane and logical, then I believe you can do it.

This attitude of positiveness makes the entire difference in whether we fail or succeed. We have to adopt a positive mental attitude about our objectives once calm reflection convinces us that we can do a certain thing. The idea that success is ours for the taking makes all things possible. Now, it is important to realize that the attainment of any worthwhile goal requires hard work and sacrifice. If this were not required, then everyone would attain their objectives. The fact that each goal carries with it a price tag for victory, eliminates most of our competition. When the going gets tough, many people surrender. They want the good things of life without a struggle. Unfortunately, life doesn't work that way. A wise person realizes that the struggle to attain is really the elixir of life. Achievers often pattern their entire lives on this premise. If all valuable goals were attainable without work and a struggle, life would be filled with boredom and mental depression would be prevalent everywhere.

Enjoy the struggle, for it is what keeps humanity happy. Hard won victories result in the greatest feeling of well-being possible. Get your attitude in the proper mode and start "climbing the mountain." Your attitude determines whether or not you will be successful. Consistent hard work and perseverance are the usual characteristics of happy people. If, after giving it "your best effort," you fail, set another goal and start all over again. This scenario has described the life patterns of successful and happy people from the dawn of time.

INSINCERITY

"Whenever someone or something or some business proposition sounds too good to be true, the overwhelming probability is that in fact the person or proposition is not as good as it appears on the surface."

Man is wise never to let himself be swept off his feet in the emotional reaction to a new acquaintance, situation, or business proposition. Closer scrutiny will almost always reveal good reasons for caution or hesitation. A more penetrating look will always introduce another dimension or a different view.

This can best be illustrated by a man glancing at the skin and hair on his arm. If he holds a magnifying glass of sufficient strength to his arm, the hairs look like trees and the surface of his skin appears craggy, almost like the pictures shown of the surface on the moon. If one looks at his skin and hair chemically, he sees water and blood and a small percentage of solid matter. If he looks at his hair and skin subatomically, he sees molecules with atoms traveling 2,000 miles a second.

Epictetus (50-120 A.D.) advises: "Be not swept off your feet by the vividness of the impression but say, 'Impression, wait for me a little. Let me see what you are and what you represent. Let me try you.' "

If nothing is ever as good as it seems, it is also true that nothing is ever as bad as it seems. It depends on what the viewer is seeking. All people, for example, are a mixture of both wisdom and ignorance. The final judgment has always got to be made on the basis of whether the good outweighs the bad.

Shakespeare (1598-1600) in *Henry V* states as follows: "There is some soul of goodness in things evil, would men observingly distill it out." (IV, i, 4)

Every problem that may come your way and be recognized as such at first blush, may at a later date be looked upon as a great or fortunate occurrence; one that enables a human to grow and reach new heights of ethics and understanding. Since this is covered in depth in another chapter, nothing further will be developed at this time on the advantage of having problems.

This chapter tells one to be observant; don't overreact to your first impressions. Always let the penetrating light of close observation and study give a more complete picture of someone, something, or a business proposition. Closer study will never fail to add another dimension to whatever is being viewed.

Con artists down through the ages have always preyed on the impressionable, superficial observer to garner their ill-gotten gains. The naive person who doesn't observe closely is his natural victim. The fast sell, the rosy picture, the faultless proposition, almost always acquires another dimension or two, or three, etc., upon careful scrutiny.

Mankind in his pursuit of a mate with whom to share his life, violates most often the requirement of careful scrutiny which adds dimensions not otherwise noticed to a person. The person one sees "some enchanted evening across a crowded room" can look quite appealing and romantic in the rarefied atmosphere of moonlight, soft music, and champagne. Who wouldn't be at his or her best under these ideal conditions? Many people meet and get acquainted at a time when their only contact has been under ideal conditions of enjoyment and relaxation. What kind of person is left under difficult conditions—conditions of stress and adversity? Is this sexy, romantic creature still appealing under these adverse conditions, or has a metamorphosis occurred which has changed him or her into some kind of ugly, unappealing monster? Always take the time to see how a person reacts to stressful conditions. Ideal conditions don't exist, normally. Stressful conditions in modern life are more normal.

Girl meets boy. Girl becomes immediately infatuated with boy. Boy has terrible, uncontrollable temper. Beware! When the first bloom of love and sex passes, the only permanent aspect will be the boy's temper. This latter factor, if not controlled, will ruin the girl's happiness and destroy the relationship.

Boy meets girl. Boy is infatuated with girl. Girl is sweet, flirtatious, and loves diamonds and minks. Beware! Her flirtatious, materialistic tendencies will remain and ruin any relationship which may develop. The moral again is that the first impression is never accurate. The tendency of a person in the first blush of love is to overlook and forgive. Ultimately overlooking and forgiving "wears thin" and the relationship is destroyed. By careful observation much unhappiness can be avoided.

Always remember, everyone, everything, and every business proposition that can ever be encountered has many dimensions to it or them, and a superficial glance only reveals that which the observer can readily see. Subsequently, the other dimensions will emerge "loud and clear" and have to be dealt with or lived with, regardless of the desires of the observer.

OVERCOMING FEARS

"It is necessary to conquer all your
fears if you want to be happy in life."

A young lady walked casually into a Certified Public Accountant's office with a cat in her arms. Instantaneously, one of the accountants jumped on top of a desk and started screaming in a terrified manner. He was a man of 40 years of age. Everyone thought he had gone berserk, which of course he had. Finally, it was realized that the presence of the cat literally terrified this 40-year-old man. When the cat was taken out of the office, the accountant calmed down and everything was all right. This unfortunate man suffered with this terrible fear for many years. Long before he could have resolved and/or conquered this fear either on his own, through logic, or if necessary, with professional help. The point being he didn't have to suffer with it.

A stockbroker was invited as a guest speaker to a Lions Club for one of their monthly dinner meetings. All through the dinner and for days before, tension began to mount within him at the thought of having to address an audience of people. He was determined to go through with it since it was a good business thing to do, as well as something he needed to do for his own self-assurance. As the meal progressed, his heart started palpitating, his hands were perspiring, and his whole body was shaking. His host, seated to his left, attempted unsuccessfully to engage the speaker in a meaningful conversation during the meal. Several times the speaker started to excuse himself, but persisted in his determination to speak. Finally, while his introduction was being made, the speaker was literally panic-stricken at the whole prospect. With the introduction over, the speaker got up and started to deliver his speech. The audience was nervous because they sensed the extreme nervous condition of the speaker. His hands were shaking as he held a paper from which he was reading. Large beads of perspiration were popping out on his forehead. His voice was quivering, his throat became drier and drier, his sentences became disjointed, and finally he built up such a level of hysteria that he fainted and fell down. He was carried out of the room to the outside where he was soon revived and recovered. Again, this poor man was the victim of an unresolved, unreasoning fear which could have been conquered.

There are as many fears as there are avenues of thought open to the human mind: fear of failure, fear of embarrassment, fear of heights, fear of close places, fear of death, fear of humiliation, fear of lightning, fear of earthquakes, fear of being alone, and a thousand other fears too numerous to mention. President Franklin Delano Roosevelt put it best when he said, "... the only thing we have to fear is fear itself." It must be believed that all fear can be overcome. Fear is based on a lack of ethical principles and on ignorance possessed by an individual. A wise person with faith has no fear. Basically, if you get your soul right, it will automatically correct your thinking in regards to fear. Competent professional counseling can further assist one in overcoming his fears. Once all fears have been shed, an exciting fulfilled life awaits such a wise person.

WORRY

"Worry is based on fear and is nonproductive and harmful to everyone involved."

Everyone who is born will die. In between, he will have success and failures; sadness and joy; pain and good feelings. Now, if we know this ahead of time, why get into the habit of worrying about everything that could possibly happen? Do the very best that you can in any endeavor and let everything happen that's going to happen. The really great forces that govern your life are largely beyond your control anyway, so why worry about them?

Worry is a habit that some people are more addicted to than are others. It is just as much a habit as smoking or drinking, taking drugs or gossiping, or overeating or gambling. Notice that only negative habits are mentioned. Fear or worry is probably at the head of any list of negative habits. Studies have shown that people are able to endure the massive tragedies of life such as death, divorce, imprisonment, and bankruptcy. What kills people, or at the least what ruins their health, are the petty hassles and grievances that nibble at our health throughout our lifetime. These annoyances make a far greater impact on the well-being of a worrier than they do on one who tends not to worry. Worry itself is very harmful to a person's well-being. Now consider the fact that the greatest percentage of what we worry about never happens and you can see how much needless suffering a worry addict endures.

Habitual worriers will find that life's routine annoyances deprive them of their happiness. They develop ulcers, hypertension, angina, and a thousand other unnecessary ailments associated with the tension caused by worry.

The habit of worry can be defeated just like any other addiction. All it takes is wisdom and willpower. First of all, you must recognize that worry is a bad habit; that it isn't necessary that you worry. Understand that many intelligent, happy people go through life and do not worry. Believe that it is ignorant to worry needlessly and excessively. Know that worry deprives you of the energy and tranquillity necessary to confront problems successfully when they arise. Excessive worry not only ruins the worrier's life, but these negative traits are passed on to his children and they, in turn, have the foundation laid to ruin their chances at happiness. Also, an excessive worrier can ruin his relationships, be they marital, social, professional, or occupational.

One who is excessively preoccupied with his own problems

to the exclusion of everyone else's is also frequently a very selfish person. These are the types of people who suffer mental depression. One seldom sees an outgoing person, one who is always concerned about the well-being of his fellowman, suffering from mental depression. It is always the selfish worrier.

Fear also produces worry. Excessive fear produces worry and in aggravated cases can cause severe mental illness. It is possible to live free of fear. Fear of death, failure, embarrassment, pain, and a million other things that people can fear is nothing more than a bad habit. These fears can be overcome by wisdom and willpower. Fear, once it leaves your life, will take with it the habit of worry. Fear and worry are running mates. Eliminate fear and selfishness, and worry will soon leave and be replaced by good health and happiness.

HARDSHIP AND CHARACTER
"Hardship builds character."

To survive a hardship assists an individual in innumerable ways. The learning process almost always involves difficulties which have to be surmounted. We may be advised; we may read books; or we may be warned against—but nothing equals the actual experience as a lesson. The history of many great personalities lies in their ability to overcome personal hardships. Franklin Roosevelt and his paralysis; Helen Keller being deaf, dumb, and blind; Beethoven and his deafness, are but a few of the examples. Nothing in this world builds self-confidence more than real difficulties actually experienced. Until we actually go through the crucible of fire, we will have grave doubts about whether we can survive hardships. Once hardships have come and gone, we then know that we have the character and stamina enough to withstand reversals.

Experience is nothing in the world but a process of overcoming hurdles. Mankind tells us we have to have experience to succeed at anything. What they are speaking of is wisdom that is gained from living and not from a book. A good pilot, as we have said, never really learned how to fly until he flew through a few storms. If all his flying was in fair weather, then he lacks the certain knowledge that he can survive a storm. A sea captain is not experienced until he has survived a few gales. A smooth sea never makes a good mariner. It is only in foul weather or stormy seas that great sea captains are made. Abraham Lincoln was a country lawyer when he was elected president. Before he died on April 15, 1865, he knew that he could survive a terrible struggle as president of his country. Combat troops are not really relied upon until they are "seasoned" or until they have had actual combat experience.

When hardship comes your way, learn to welcome it. Don't panic and flee in fear. Remember, it represents an opportunity to climb to the next higher level of experience and capability. It is really the only way we have of bettering ourselves. We can't get experience in the form of reading material or advice from a well meaning friend. It has to come the hard way.

The wisest among us are the older citizens. The Oriental has always associated age with wisdom. Unfortunately, in America today, age is not afforded this respect. This works to our detriment in the form of society's upheavals and discontent. Younger people in America do not listen sufficiently to the older and wiser voices amongst us. Somehow we have become impatient with caution and wisdom that is not our own. We want to plunge forward into the maelstrom of life and forge our own conviction from our own experience. This young nation, blessed as it is with wealth and freedom, could lose all that it has that is worthwhile unless wiser heads prevail in its management.

One difficulty has been our incredible material success. We "force-feed" our young people with every type of gift that a child could want. We are determined that our children will have it better than we did. Unfortunately, once a society begins to luxuriate in the lap of luxury, it starts to decay and deteriorate. The oil rich Arab countries had a well-controlled younger population while they were impoverished. As soon as oil brought them undreamed of wealth, their young people lost their moral values and their discipline. It is awfully hard to control your young men when each of them owns his own Cadillac.

Don't be afraid of hardship and misfortune. It is really the only way we have to grow and become a better person. So, welcome it with enthusiasm and optimism. For it always presages a new and higher level of excellence in our lives.

SELF-LIMITING

"Most people consciously or unconsciously do what is necessary to obtain the results they either want or are prepared to accept."

Heavy cigarette smokers continue their harmful habit in the face of overwhelming statistics which reveal the dangers. They know what they risk, but they are prepared to balance the pleasures they derive from the habit against the risk and the ultimate suffering resulting from such a habit. Criminals ply their trade with full knowledge of the probable consequences of their activity. Their life of crime seemingly carries with it sufficient rewards to counterbalance the consequences of arrest, conviction, and incarceration. Terrorists around the world carry on their activities prepared to die for whatever beliefs they hold. All drug addicts do not sufficiently resist their desires to continue their devastating addictions. When the penalty arrives for their past addictions, they may not welcome the price they have to pay; but they certainly knew in advance of its probable coming.

Positive healthy habits carry with them the predictability of future good fortune. A life of discipline and deprivation carries with it the promise of future health, longevity, and happiness. The penalties of all subsequent good fortune must be paid in advance.

If you want to be slender later on, you must diet now. If you want to be physically fit in the future, you must guard your health now. If you want a happy family life in the future, you must forego your riotous conduct now.

All these principles are known by most people. What happens to them in the future as a result of their present conduct is pretty much what they are prepared to accept. They know the relationship between their present conduct and future happenings. When a heavy cigarette smoker contracts lung cancer, he knew when he was smoking that his present pleasure carried with it a grave future risk. It has even been said that such people have a desire for self-destruction or that they are suicidal.

Most hazards that people incur are done so knowingly and really represent a tradeoff. When the tragic probabilities occur, they have no one to blame but themselves. For this reason, it is so important for people to want good things to happen to them and their loved ones in the future. It is not enough to only want it; we must be prepared to do those things which will ensure their happening. The key to this scenario is wisdom, and from this wisdom will come discipline. Discipline is entirely within the mind. Willpower is built up and sustained in the mind. Once we make up our minds to do something, thereafter, the battle becomes easy. The mind controls everything. If we let our animal desires control our life, we are going down the road to disaster. Proper mental resolution will easily overcome addiction to any habit. The battle must be fought in the mind. You will be surprised how easy it is to overcome a harmful or negative addiction once the battle in the mind has been resolved in favor of its discontinuance.

People arrive in their twilight years in the condition that their previous habits and discipline created. If they led a Spartan disciplined life, the likelihood is that they will arrive at old age fit and mentally alert. If, however, they have indulged all their animal desires throughout their lifetime, if they arrive at old age at all, it will be in a deteriorated physical and mental condition. Learn restraint and discipline in your eating, drinking, work, and health habits. You will increase your own joy and the joy of your loved ones. Set the example of good practices and let others draw strength from you.

TRUST

"Cynical, untrusting people tend to be frightened, insecure, and ignorant and are probably untrustworthy themselves."

Frequently, the world believes a cynic has a quality he does not possess—wisdom. The cynic misleads the world by his fast answers to all situations, and he points out quickly the faults in everyone and in every situation. The reasoning then follows that if such a person can quickly find all faults, he must be wise. Such reasoning could not be further from the truth.

The only aspect of any person or situation that a cynic looks at is the negative one. His eyes are cast in only that direction. He has long ago turned off all the goodness in the world. He sees the world in the same light that he sees himself. Inevitably, he finds what he is looking for, which further buttresses his pervasive cynicism. A bee looks for flowers and finds them. A bird looks for worms and finds them. A cynic looks for the worst in everyone and every situation and finds it. The reason being that the world is full of both wisdom and ignorance. Every individual has ignorance and wisdom in him. The cynic has lost all confidence in his ability to make a judgment, which requires trusting someone or some situation. He is frightened and disillusioned. His fears have gotten the best of him. He has forgotten that there is any good in the world. He considers a good person to be ignorant. He thinks that only his thinking is wise and that goodness is weakness or at the least, very uninteresting. He gets to the point where he admires selfish, deceptive, cunning people. He has developed a completely false set of heroes. The likelihood is that all his "heroes" act and think exactly as he does.

Whenever an individual trusts no one, the probability is that he is completely untrustworthy himself. I do not speak of a person who is intelligently cautious of all strangers or people until they have had a chance to prove their capability and honesty. I speak of that individual who never trusts anyone; who is incapable of placing faith in his fellowman. Such a person judges the world by his own moral standards. Additionally, he doesn't even like himself. He doesn't have a very high regard for his own person or moral character. The likelihood is that he is fully justified in his own beliefs of himself. Yet the world frequently passes such an individual off as being intelligent. It is said of him, "nobody can get to him, he's too smart." The fact is that he is terribly ignorant. He has lost his confidence in his own judgment. He has "tuned-out" the world. He has built an impenetrable wall around himself for his own protection against a world that he fears. His lack of intelligence no longer enables him to make judgment decisions so he has summarily dismissed the entire world and its inhabitants as being unworthy of his trust. He is a sick, frightened, lonely, insecure, unhappy, ignorant man who deserves the pity of his peers.

There is another far wiser course on which to travel down the pathway of life. That course involves love and trust. You can take almost any individual in this world and if you only look at the goodness in him the likelihood is that this goodness will grow and grow, at least as far as his relationship with you is concerned. Your trust and confidence will make a better person of him. By your trust, you establish for him a criteria that expects, if not demands, the best that is in him. In so doing, you make him strive for greater heights; you bring out the goodness, and/or wisdom in him. By the warmth that you receive in return, your happiness will be increased and the net effect will be to increase the wisdom in the world.

TEACHING REALITY

"The sooner a child knows about life and its realities, the better prepared he will be to accept the ebb and flow of life."

Eventually, as much as parents may desire to the contrary, a child cannot be shielded from the trials and tribulations of life. Sooner or later a crossroads will be reached where life will be revealed in its total reality without the benefit of the "rose-colored glasses" applied by the parent in an attempt to "soften the blow." Sooner or later important decisions affecting health, happiness, and even freedom will have to be made by the child alone, without the interference or guidance of a protective parent.

With the advent of the drug culture mingled with sexual promiscuity and the automobile, the age at which important decisions must be made gets younger and younger. Children in early grammar school are being exposed to drugs. Without their parents' advice, they have to say yes or no to an individual who more likely than not is a peer leader in their group. When offered a drug they have to have the wisdom to reject the offer, even if it means resisting peer pressure, with the consequent peer group rejection that normally accompanies such a decision. These important decisions were not forced on earlier generations until they were in the late teens or later, if ever. Many times they include such decisions as whether or not to get in an automobile being driven by an intoxicated acquaintance; or taking a drug that could lead to an addiction; or becoming involved in a drug transaction that constitutes a criminal act; or engaging in a sex act that could result in pregnancy.

Influenced largely by television, children today have more awareness about life in general, gained at an earlier age. There is considerable evidence that they have no greater judgment than did their forebears at the same age. Though their head is full of facts about every aspect of life, their mind lacks the judgment to deal intelligently with these facts.

An intelligent parent will attempt to impart as much wisdom as possible to his child as fast as possible. Great efforts have to be made to find the correct way to get the message across to each individual child. If the child gets irritated with the parent's constant preaching, then clearly another method will have to be found to reach that particular child. When it comes to drugs, perhaps it is wise to take a trip to the jail to show an impressionable youngster what the law does to those who are convicted of dealing with drugs. Maybe a trip to the hospital to show a youngster what happens when intoxicated drivers get in accidents is advisable. Even a trip to a drug treatment center to show a child the suffering of a drug addict could have a positive effect.

It matters little how a parent conveys wisdom to his child, so long as the child is given a realistic picture about the dangers of certain types of human activities. The cruelest act a parent can perpetrate on a child is to send him out in the world with a wholly unrealistic view of life. They become "sitting ducks" for every vice that man has to offer. They totally lack the wisdom and judgment to make the correct decisions that they must make in order to survive successfully.

The child's happiness is at stake in this process. The only reality is the world and life the way it really exists. A fairyland dream world concept will only lead to disillusionment and tragedy. Get your child intelligent and wise at the earliest possible age. Don't pull punches. "Tell it just like it is" and forget the fairy tale versions.

CRITICISM
"Needlessly critical people are fear-ridden and jealous."

Criticism is easy to give and hard to accept. The one who criticizes is not a very popular person. Certain types of people are far more prone to criticize than are other types. Since most people do what they think is best, it is really not wise to criticize them. While there may be nothing wrong with suggesting to a person a better way to do something, it is an extremely negative endeavor to criticize someone with no goal in mind other than to voice discontent.

People are fearful of the success of others. They are afraid lest someone advance too far too fast and in so doing make the critic look bad by comparison. Such a person uses criticism as a means of retarding the progress of an achiever. Instead of accomplishing the intended goal, it frequently has the opposite effect. Every "knock" is sometimes a boost. A nonachiever is almost never the target of criticism. He constitutes very little threat to anyone. Occasionally, he may be the target of a sympathetic remark about his ineptitude but the real "strong criticism" are reserved for the achievers. The ones who, by their effort and wisdom, are able to raise their head above the others and thereby provide a target for all the people in the world who feel threatened or are jealous of their success. These people will try to surpass the achievers, but failing to so do they will try to minimize their prestige by criticism. Winston Churchill put it very well when he said, "The price of success is criticism." I'm sure Harry Truman had it in mind when he said, "If you can't stand the heat, stay out of the kitchen." Achievers soon get used to living with criticism.

All great people are viewed by the faceless masses of the world from the standpoint of their weaknesses, not their strengths. The whole world has elevated them to the status of greatness by virtue of their universally recognized strengths; so the search by the masses is for the weaknesses which all other humans possess. This practice tends to reduce great people to approachable dimensions. A free press is forever downgrading its leaders. Any area of fault or weakness is stressed and frequently enlarged beyond its true proportions. This tearing down through criticism goes on in all areas of human activity even when the achievers are known only locally or by their co-workers. The techniques applied and the psychological reasons are the same, whether it be a world figure or a student in a small class in a remote schoolhouse who made the only A on an examination. It is probably the same reason that in the "Old West" many people tried to outdraw the "fastest gun."

The far wiser course is to refrain from criticizing the foibles and weaknesses of your fellowman. Your remarks will be deeply resented by the people involved and will do harm to you. Know in advance that everyone has strengths and weaknesses; that no one is perfect. Praise if you will their strengths and ignore their weaknesses. If you start criticizing another for his weaknesses, you are inviting criticism of your own weaknesses. There may be occasions when duty impels you to tell the whole truth about an individual including his strengths and his weaknesses. When this happens, be truthful. However, why go into such a discussion when you are under no duty to discuss a person? I'm speaking of criticism that is motivated by fear or jealousy. Forget all about this type of criticism because it is completely negative and produces unhappiness for everyone concerned.

UNLIMITED GOALS
"Most men place a limit on their success
by artificial mental barriers."

Generally speaking, we can do anything we can convince ourselves in our mind that we can do. Once we are fully convinced that we can obtain a given goal, you can be assured that such a goal is attainable. Conceding the truthfulness of the previous statement then the only battle for success is the battle which goes on in our own mind. Our mental attitude has everything to do with our ultimate success or failure. Your mind is the beacon that guides you through the pathways of life. Therefore, a consistently positive, cheerful, and practical mental outlook is the greatest achievement which any of us can attain. Once we've reached this mental state, the rest of the battle is easy. The foremost victory lies in convincing ourselves that we can do anything we can convince ourselves we can do.

Look at Helen Keller—deaf, dumb, and blind; look at Ed Furgol with a disabled arm; look at Mel Tillis with his speech defect; look at Abraham Lincoln with his recurring depression; look at Franklin Roosevelt with his polio and his fear of speaking before an audience; look at Napoleon Bonaparte, who rose to the highest office in France though he was a Corsican. Life is filled with millions of examples of people who succeeded because they had convinced themselves that success was achievable. In most cases, this was done under conditions where no one else had faith that they would succeed.

One thing that we can all be sure of is that we will not succeed if we believe in our mind that success is not possible. First, under these conditions we will not expend the quality of effort required for success. Sometimes to succeed we have to persist on faith alone. Every logical thought may tell us that failure is just around the corner, but with faith in our ultimate success we have to persist beyond the normal bounds of human endurance. Now, if we've already convinced ourselves that success is not possible, we will simply fail to endure sufficiently to reach our goals. The great intangible in all success stories is that hard to recognize and identifiable quality of spirit that achievers possess.

Failures always attribute another's success to luck. This simple explanation excuses their own failure because they can simply say that they were unlucky. Nonachievers will blame everyone but themselves for their lack of success. The tragedy is that they convince themselves of the accuracy of their excuse. In reality, nothing could be further from the truth. They and their spirit and personality are the authors of their failure. Their pride and ignorance will not permit them to admit the truth.

The achievers of the world are the ones who literally carry all of the rest of humanity on their backs as mankind struggles up the "mountain" towards success. These types are easy to recognize. They never talk about failure; they don't let it become an element in their thinking, and a failure on their part would be a complete surprise to all their acquaintances. Their very personality and education are such that no one ever thinks of failure and an achiever at the same time. Any concept of failure is totally foreign to them. Their whole life projects success. They have goals that have been carefully analyzed. They have resolved in their minds that the goal is obtainable. Armed with this resolution, they march forward confidently towards their objective—prepared to make any necessary sacrifice without a whimper or complaint. From such a background success and happiness always come. Join the parade.

CONSTANCY AND CONSISTENCY

"Constancy of purpose and consistency of application form the surest way to attain a goal."

Any study or project, or exercise program, or love affair, or for that matter almost any human objective has to have applied towards it a constancy of purpose in order to be successfully attained. Starts and stops or an on-again, off-again attitude will not accomplish an objective.

If I want to be your friend I have to be one 24 hours a day. I can't limit my friendship to only four hours out of 24. I have to be consistently your friend. If I want to be appreciated for my sobriety I can't stay sober for 20 hours and intoxicated for four hours and be considered a sober individual. No, I would have to remain consistently sober. Remember, unfortunately, we are judged by our lowest levels of conduct and not by our highest levels. So we want to be judged on a high plane, we have to consistently conform to that standard of conduct which would warrant such a judgment.

If we want someone to believe that we truly love them, we must consistently show our love to them. If we react in a hateful fashion sometimes and a loving fashion at other times the object of our affection will have a difficult time deciding whether we love or hate them. If we play any sort of sports we must consistently put forth a great effort if we are to be considered a good athlete. We can't loaf 10 percent of the time and apply our best efforts the other 90 percent and be judged a good athlete.

If we are in a managerial position with numbers of subordinates, we have to adopt a consistent attitude in all our managerial efforts if we are going to succeed. We can't approve an act one day and disapprove the same act the next day and have our subordinates understand our policy. We have to treat one subordinate by the same set of rules by which we treat another. We have to be consistent in our treatment of co-workers.

As a parent we have an even greater need to be consistent in the disciplining and supervision of our children. If bedtime is 8 p.m., then this fact should be observed every night. You can't let a child stay up late one night and then condemn them for not going to bed by 8 p.m. the next night. You can't let them clutter their room one day and insist on a spotless one the next. The child will be harmed by your vacillation. He will not know exactly what your policy is with regard to his conduct.

Any personal goals that you have set for yourself can only be achieved by constancy of purpose and consistency of effort. The higher the goal the more need for consistency, usually over a longer period of time. Consistency is really not a difficult trait to cultivate. It can be readily achieved once we realize that everyone should do what they have to do. This simple statement handles the entire situation. If you seek a college degree, you have to study. If you seek advancement in your work, you have to be hardworking and diligent. If you want a happy home, you have to treat your family fair.

Once we realize what we have to do to reach our objectives, it becomes a very simple thing to consistently do what we have to do. Necessity need be our only guide. If it is necessary, then our choice is simple—one does what one must do on a consistent basis. If we follow this practice, our chances for happiness are greater.

OFFENSIVE HUMOR

"Humor that is attempted at the expense of others offends the victim and harms the one who tries it."

Most humor that is directed at the foibles, weaknesses, personality flaws or mistakes of others is frequently resented by the person against whom it is directed. Victims may manage to smile weakly while others laugh uproariously, but make no mistake about it—such humor harms the perpetrator much more than the victims. People don't want to be reminded of their weaknesses, their mistakes, or their incompetence, and they certainly don't want this fact highlighted in the form of a joke. Socially, about all they can do is to go along with the levity; but the resentment swells up inside and is not soon forgotten.

If you are fond of deprecating humor, let yourself be the target. If you do this, your friends will indeed laugh and no ill will should result. People somehow like people who put themselves down humorously. But no one really has the right to deprecate another person's prestige through the vehicle of humor or in any other way. If you want to get along with your peers and live harmoniously with them, don't criticize them humorously or otherwise. Some people only attempt humor which "knocks" their fellowman. Frequently, these same people become highly agitated when they find themselves the butt of such humor.

It is not hard to get a laugh when pointing to another's mistakes. The world somehow enjoys laughing at their fellowman as much as they dislike laughing at themselves. The truly great comedians make it possible for the world to laugh at them. The circus clown is yet another example. This type of humor leaves no unpleasant "aftertaste" in the heart or mind of the listener. Laughing, after all, is probably the greatest therapy available to man. So the person who makes people laugh is very much needed in a world that takes itself far too seriously. But direct the humor in the right direction. Let it be done in such a fashion that no one gets hurt.

Most of us take ourselves entirely too seriously. After all, we are essentially like billions of other people who have gone before us and who will live after we're gone. Our hopes, our fears, our dreams, our strengths, our loves, and our weaknesses are quite similar to almost everyone else who has ever lived or ever will live. As mortals, we seek love and understanding; and if we are wise, wc will give the same things to others. So the important first step is to keep our ego in check since we are really not that great or unique anyway. Now if we are more or less like everyone else, that means of course that we are far from perfect. People know this about you already so why not admit it publicly by occasionally revealing your own foibles, weaknesses, or mistakes? All it will do is make you more human in the eyes of your peers and they will love you for being secure and brave enough to reveal this sort of thing about yourself. In addition to everything else, they will get a good laugh out of the entire affair. Since people love to be around people who make them laugh, you acceptability in the eyes of your acquaintances will be enhanced.

Humor at the expense of others harms everyone involved whereas self-deprecating humor harms no one and causes everyone to laugh just as much. So if deprecating humor is your forte, then look to yourself as the butt of your jokes. It will immediately reveal to your listeners a humane side that will endear you to your peers. In the process you will have confessed publicly and confession is always good for the soul. So spread cheer by laughing at yourself and not at others.

RATIONAL LIVING

*"Men who live conceptually accomplish more
than those who live from incident-to-incident
or from emergency-to-emergency."*

It is a beautiful day and your friends call you up and ask you to play golf. You tell yourself that it's a great big beautiful day, your health is good, and you're going to play golf with your friends. Your concept of the whole game is such that no matter whether you win or lose, whether you play good or bad, whether your companions are courteous or not on the golf course, nothing, absolutely nothing, will cause you not to enjoy the game. You get on the first tee and you conceive of a ball going right down the middle of the fairway 230 yards towards the target. You hit your iron shots the same way. In your mind's eye you perceive the shot that you want to hit and do not excessively concern yourself with the details of the execution necessary to obtain these results.

You are a lawyer and you are getting ready to try a very difficult case; you are well-prepared. Your opponent has a habit or reputation of baiting his adversaries into anger and thereby lessening their effectiveness in front of the jury. You resolve in advance that nothing your opponent does is going to disturb your tranquillity. You are determined to stay calm and be patient. You are going to let your opponent go through his entire "bag of tricks" and not fall victim to his tactics. This concept thoroughly planned in advance will enable you to better represent your client.

You are a businessman with 100 employees. You resolve that you will not show favoritism regardless of the provocation. You are determined that you will be impartial with everyone in your employ. You plan this concept until it becomes second nature to you in your dealings with your subordinates.

Before good practices can be applied, studies have to be made within yourself to determine what the wise course of action is for a given situation. A careful analysis will tell you what is desirable in the way of broad principles to follow. These, for the lack of a better word, can be called a concept. It is from this type of conceptual thinking that good plans are formulated.

Many people operate without a plan. They react to each incident totally unrelated to any plan. They have no concept of what they should do or would want to do. They play each and every incident by ear and do not relate their reaction to an over all plan.

To be consistent and effective, one has to live by concepts. You have to decide that you are going to be punctual, or keep your body in good shape, or work hard, or study hard, or wear good clothes, or not gamble, or go to church, or teach your children the value of money, or live in a beautiful home, or live by the sea, or play a good game of golf, or get into politics, or stay out of politics, or keep your car clean, or learn how to play a musical instrument, or live on a farm, or any one of a thousand different means of living this thing called life.

If you have a concept, you tend to get further and to be more successful. Your life has organization; it is structured; it makes sense. After all, an animal reacts spontaneously to life without a plan. A human being should operate from the security of a concept. He should plan in advance the road he intends to take through the confusing network of paths which confront us all.

MORE NOTES ABOUT MOVING ON

"Never waste a lot of time once a realistic look at a love affair, a business proposition, or any situation convinces you that it is impossible to reach an acceptable conclusion. Do not live with dreams or strive for a goal that logic dictates is unattainable. To do so can only

lead to frustration, anger, and unhappiness."

We all want to do things or accomplish goals that for one reason or another cannot be done or are unattainable. Wisdom should tell us this at the earliest possible moment. Once we learn or discover the truth, in order to lead a happy life, we must alter our course to conform to these newly discovered facts. Goals that are unattainable are meaningless in our lives. We need to abandon these and deal with that which is possible. Our lives should be occupied with the possible, not the impossible.

We may want to be a professional athlete but physical restraints or limitations may forever bar us from such a life. We may want to be an atomic physicist but intellectual limitations may make this impossible. We may want to be a beauty contest winner but again our physical attributes may place this prize forever out of our reach. The sooner one's limitations are recognized the happier one will be.

The real goals that we should set for ourselves are those which are reasonably attainable. Therefore, an intelligent person searches for those undertakings for which he is suitable. This endeavor is not simple and remains unsuccessful in all too many lives.

The decision is an extremely personal one. It is personal to each of us, yet regrettably many people let other people's opinions dictate whom they will marry; or what home they will buy, or what school they will pick for their child's education. It is proper to listen to another's advice but having received it, do what you consider the wisest thing to do. Don't make these important decisions based on your fear of offending someone else. It is your life and you can spend it in the manner most suitable to yourself.

Many people spend their entire lives locked into one hopelessly unobtainable situation after another. They hang in there for no valid or intelligent purpose. If the surmounting of the obstacles is not worth the effort required, then forget it. If the objective cannot be obtained, even though you only found this out after several years of effort, abandon the undertaking. Head in the other direction. Throw yourself in reverse and change your goal. One's "reverse gear" should be in as good a condition as one's "forward gear" for the express purpose of changing direction hurriedly when newly discovered facts warrant. Don't be afraid to admit to people that your original judgment was in error or newly discovered facts or changed conditions dictate a change of direction. The sooner you "bite the bullet," the happier you'll be with yourself. If you eat enough "crow" after a period of time, it will begin to taste like chicken.

Live with the truth. Life becomes the art of dealing with that which is possible and not that which is desirable. Many things that we desire may not be good for us. Later events may prove this to be true. Remember, our decisions are based on the facts available on the day of the decision. Additional facts may warrant a change. If you do follow the truth and change; you'll remain far happier.

UNDERSTANDING

*"If you really understand a situation or a person, you will al
most never get angry or frustrated. Understanding reduces
friction and tension and increases your chances for happiness."*

Try throughout your life to understand as many different aspects of human activity as your intelligence will permit. Look for the facts in every situation. After you learn what has happened, ask yourself the far more important question, "Why did it happen?" Finding the answer to the "why" is far more important than is the answer to the "what." The more "whys" you figure out, the greater will be your understanding of life and people and the consequent increase in your happiness.

Always remember that everything that happens does so for a

reason. What you have to do is attempt to find that reason. Frustration and anger usually result from ignorance of the facts. The actions of people are thought out in advance to a greater or lesser degree by everyone. Remember that in this deliberative process, one can only use the intelligence he possesses. Maybe this process is further complicated by the fact that these deliberations may be occurring at a time that the mind is altered by drugs or fears, or insecurities or ignorance of the facts, or love or hatred, or any one of a thousand or more possible factors. The decision arrived at is usually the best that a particular mind is capable of at the moment of decision. The resulting actions of an individual can be understood only after determining all the background factors.

The world's newspapers and television stations have newsmen who seem to ask only the very shallow question: "What happened?" They seem to make no attempt to determine, or in any event to explain "why" something happened. This shallow practice of reporting world events leaves the public frightened, frustrated, and angry. It appears that if one seeks to get to the deepest truths discernible about life and people, one has to "dig" alone. No established forum will do it for you. It is a self-help concept and must be pursued individually to be effective.

Anytime one is confronted with a situation in which no understanding prevails, the immediate natural reaction is to become frightened, angry, confused, or combinations of all three. During this initial confrontation with a new reality, one should keep one's thoughts more intimately acquainted with the "why" and the "wherefores." It requires a keen and practiced eye and mind to penetrate the confusion surrounding any new reality. Look long and ask questions. Don't give answers, but ask questions. Think about what you have seen and heard. Judge everything and everyone in light of your knowledge of events and people. Be slow to form conclusions. Once you have reached a conclusion don't stop asking questions. Never stop questioning. Look for the reason that something happened. Be assured that everything happens for a reason.

Once you have discovered the facts don't reject the truth. Love the truth; don't let it frighten or confuse you. It is the most beautiful thing in this life. Practice over a long period of time will help you find it. It is far better than deception or ignorance. It will always make you the happiest in the long term.

KEEPING THAT POSITIVE ATTITUDE

"Never commence an undertaking with a negative attitude. Convincing yourself that you can successfully accomplish something comprises the greatest reason for ultimate success."

You can achieve anything that you can convince yourself in your mind, after careful thought, that you can do. Mental attitude is the greatest difference between achievers and nonachievers. Success comes to those who think success. Negativeness never aided anyone to achieve success. All it does is make attainment of any goal difficult, if not impossible. Believing that you can do something makes everything easier and more fun. If you convince yourself ahead of time that something is easy, chances are that it will in fact be easy. Conversely, if you can convince yourself that something is going to be difficult, it no doubt will prove to be difficult. Your attitude is everything. It makes all the difference in the world.

Just because something requires a little work or a little endurance or prevents you from doing something you would enjoy more doesn't make it difficult. In order to proceed cheerfully towards a given objective, all one needs is to have his priorities in order. If your objective involves a necessary achievement of your life, then get started towards its accomplishment. Forget all the moaning and complaining. If you've got to do something, then pay the price and go ahead and do it. Know in advance what is involved. If you know this, you can prepare yourself for the journey.

Most goals in life involve work. Work with the proper mental outlook can be enjoyed. Life without work and responsibility is nothing but boredom for a healthy person. Working people can help others and from this knowledge gain great satisfaction from their efforts. Work is the great anchor of life. It firmly moors most people to the straight and narrow. It gives their life direction and purpose. Working is the privilege of a healthy, normal human being. Since most necessary goals in everyone's life involve work, learn to love it.

Priorities affect everyone's life. One's priorities at age ten are different from what they are at age 50. A young person should have as his number one priority the need to get an education. He should start out by convincing himself that he can learn and that all it will take is hard work on his part. A young man out of school should have as his number one priority the selection of an occupation whereby he can support himself and his loved ones. He should convince himself that all he has to do is keep looking in the right places and he will have no difficulty finding the right occupation and so support himself and subsequently his family. Mostly, these priorities, once established, should be viewed as attainable with a reasonable amount of effort.

Positive attitudes make most of life's hurdles easily surmounted. Nothing is difficult if your mind believes this to be true. Reality, to a large extent, is whatever your mind makes it. The mind is the powerful and dominant force behind all lives. Through training and conditioning, turn it into a powerful weapon with which to attain your priorities. Be positive, think positively, and be happy. These conditions usually coexist.

PROGRESS

"Progress comes painfully slow. It seldom advances by dramatic leaps. It comes only after hard work and persistence."

Impatience causes most people to surrender their objectives

short of their attainment. Somehow most people have an idealized image of how success is attained or goals are reached. These dramatic leaps occur only in the movies—almost never in real life. If success came easily, everyone would attain it. The fact is that the circle of success occupied by the select few is dictated or governed by the principle that it only comes after a considerable struggle and/or sacrifice.

Learn to enjoy the struggle; learn to appreciate the sacrifice. In the achievement of any goal, the most time consuming part involves getting there. Arriving takes virtually no time at all. The struggle and the sacrifice take far and away the greatest amount of time. Therefore, if you are wise, you will learn to enjoy the struggle and the sacrifice necessary to attain any worthwhile goal. Most of our lives are spent in anticipation, not in realization. The anticipatory period is the struggling and sacrificial phase of our lives. This is the time-consuming part. This is the part that causes most people to surrender or give up short of their goals.

For many young people, the goal is to get an education. The struggle or sacrifice involves study, and the surrender or forfeiture of personal pleasures. One who is wise enough can quickly learn to enjoy the attainment of more knowledge. It may be that the goal is to receive a promotion at work. This promotion can only come after hard work and sacrifice. Wisdom will allow an individual to enjoy hard work. A job well done can be the source of tremendous pleasure to a goal-oriented or serious-minded human being. If you learn to enjoy the struggle and the sacrifice, the price you have to pay for progress or success becomes insignificant.

Progress is made in increments that are at times not discernible. After much work and sacrifice, we look around and conclude that our efforts have been in vain. That our work has not advanced our cause. In such circumstances, we have probably reached a barrier that will require continued and unrelenting efforts to surmount. If you are convinced you have the correct "game plan" and that your work and sacrifices are aimed in the right direction, don't try to measure your progress on a daily basis. Taking stock or inventory too frequently can be very discouraging. The novice dieter takes his weight daily and becomes very discouraged when it doesn't drop every 24 hours. That is why dieting counselors will tell the dieters to weight themselves only once a week.

Don't expect daily progress because some days you may drift further away from your goals. Just make sure you are headed in the right direction. Also make sure that you are putting forth the proper effort. Be aware that success doesn't come easy, for if it did, everyone would attain it. Pay the price, have the patience, and enjoy the rewards. They make life exciting.

RESPONSIBILITY

"Remember that the more successful you are, the more responsible you are held to be for all your obligations."

A bum never has to pay alimony, doesn't pay most of his bills, and isn't particularly condemned when he fails to fulfill a commitment or honor an obligation. The reason is not that he cares to escape these obligations free of any penalty, but is because he has already been relegated to a very low esteem by his previous conduct. His latest failure to fulfill his duties is merely consistent with his pre-existing image so severe condemnation does not result from his failure to perform. His low esteem is the penalty he has already paid for a life of irresponsibility; and he will go on paying for this until his whole life changes as a result of him changing his behavior and character for the better. If he persists long enough with his new and wholesome approach to his duties and obligations, eventually his fellowman's opinion of him will improve.

Contrariwise, a highly regarded citizen is expected to fulfill all his commitments and obligations to the letter; and his failure to do so will result in severe criticism. Such a person may regard his chastisement as excessive or severe but he must remember that everyone is not as highly regarded by his peers; therefore, his conduct must be above reproach. Those contemporaries who look up to another person by reason of his character and overall lifestyle expect a very high standard of conduct from such an honored person. Failure to perform in a manner consistent with such an exalted position will bring down the wrath of his "inferiors" upon him. This sort of thing is the price one must pay for honor and respect.

Those people who are not as highly regarded by their peers get real excited when they spot a weakness in a superior character. They will immediately seize upon a discovery as an opportunity to point out to their acquaintances that after all they are just as good as the honored individual because they are not guilty of whatever disrespectful act the exalted individual allegedly committed. This type of criticism is a continuous companion of anyone who seeks to lead an honorable and useful life.

In a very real sense, to be criticized in the above manner is actually an ironic compliment. What the critics are actually saying is that you are governed by a higher standard of conduct than most men. They are saying that by elevating you to a position of respect, you have also been charged with a higher degree of responsibility to carry out your duties and obligations; others will not tolerate the same failures in you that will be overlooked in people of a lower esteem. This type of judgment may be unfair, but it exists throughout the world.

One who leads a thoroughly honorable life should welcome being judged by these elevated standards. They will tend to keep him forever alert to his obligations, to himself, his loved ones, and his fellowman. This type of high moral conduct uplifts the whole human race by its inherent integrity and honor. To be judged in this category of humanity along with the attendant high standards of expected conduct is to be paid the supreme compliment by your peers.

HEALTH

"The fewer poisons you put into your body, the healthier you will become and the better you will feel."

We all put negative substances into our body. It is usually a question of how much. These substances include salt, sugar, caffeine, nicotine, alcohol, all other drugs, chlorine, red meats, and other things too numerous to mention.

The age-old villain is cigarette, cigar, and pipe smoking, commonly known as the nicotine habit. Most of us get hooked on this habit in our teens; and if we don't die prematurely from tobacco usage related illnesses, we tend to keep up this habit for the greater portion of our lives. It is an increasingly expensive habit. It is a filthy habit which dirties, or contaminates our clothing, our car, our offices, and our homes. It is highly repugnant to nonsmokers and deeply resented by many people. It is a habit that is being more and more socially rejected in the more respected circles. Everything you read and hear tells you it is harmful to your health. It sets a terrible example for your children, who do what you do, and not what you say. All it really takes to quit is that you make up your mind to do it. Once the decision is made, the rest is relatively easy.

Salt is a poison within your body, if taken to excess. We are taught early in life to put salt on almost everything we eat. It is a habit that is totally unnecessary, because one can be taught that food tastes just as good without salt. All the processed foods we eat already contain too much salt for our own good. Chinese foods such as soy sauce are devastatingly filled with salt. Once you get used to it, food tastes just as good without salt. Excess salt in your system is very harmful to your physical well-being.

Another way to poison your system is to eat too many sweets or use too much sugar. Coffee, once you get used to it, tastes just as good without sugar. It is merely a bad habit that is continued by most of us for no valid reason.

Tap water that we get from our municipal water supply is a serious source of poisoning in the form of chlorine. American health authorities supposedly "solved" our vast demand for potable water by a system of chlorination. We are now finding out that this water contains harmful carcinogenic materials. Purchase mineral water in the grocery store or get some from a friend who has a well. City tap water is pure poison for your system.

Caffeine is very harmful to your system. Decaffeinated coffee and tea are available, and once you get used to them, their taste is as satisfying as the old-fashioned coffee or tea. It all depends on what you get used to consuming. Developing a new taste does not take long and is very easy if you approach it with an open mind.

Red meats are increasingly being discovered as being harmful to your health and should be avoided. Eat chicken, fish, fruit, nuts, and vegetables.

Drugs such as cocaine and everything else in this related drug field are unspeakably harmful to your health and should be totally avoided. Their usage is declared illegal and condemned by the representative governments of all of mankind. This fact alone speaks clearly enough for a wise person. All the above poisons must be avoided if you want to lead a healthy life. Their consumption will cause every form of serious illness known to mankind. It is relatively easy for a wise person to avoid their usage.

INDULGENCE AND SACRIFICE

"For every indulgence you allow yourself now,
you will pay a corresponding penalty in the future;
and for every sacrifice you make now, you will
receive a corresponding reward in the future."

What we are really talking about here is the universal law of cause and effect; the application of which is totally inescapable by anyone. Whereas not too many events in life are predictable, the inexorable operation of the law of cause and effect is a notable exception.

If you watch what you eat and exercise will-power you have paid a penalty or made a sacrifice. The benefit of this will result in your having a slimmer and more shapely body, and a healthier body in the future. If you fight the desire to smoke tobacco now, you have made a sacrifice; or putting it another way, you have paid a penalty. However, the reward is most pleasant. You have reduced your chances appreciably of contracting lung cancer, or having blood circulation problems, or of having emphysema in the future. If you work really hard and try your best to give your employer an honest day's work while trying to learn as much about your job as possible now, you have paid a price or made a sacrifice. In return for this, you will no doubt be rewarded by advancement in the future. Your future will be more financially secure and you will be better able to provide for your loved ones. If alcohol presents a problem in your life you have to make a severe effort to forego completely its consumption now. The future reward for this sacrifice will be manifold. You will regain the respect of your friends and loved ones. More importantly you will regain your own self-respect. If you forego many material things now that you would like to purchase on the grounds that you need to save the money for your child's education, your reward will come in the form of an educated child. The scenario is always the same, pay now; enjoy later.

Conversely if you indulge yourself in pie à la modes or a lot of sweets or too much starch, or in short, if you exercise no restraint in your eating habits now, you will pay later for these indulgences in the form of a misshapen body and very probably ill health. If a nation attempts to solve all social problems now, by the expedient of printing more paper money and paying this out to nonproducers, the penalty for the nation in the future will be inflation and a devaluation of its currency. What in the long-run will probably be more serious will be a loss of belief in the work ethic on the part of its citizens. If you lie in order to hurdle a certain barrier of the moment now, your falsehood, when subsequently discovered, will result in your having lost respect and having considerable ill-will directed towards you in the future. If you treat your family badly now, later on you will lose their love and companionship.

There is nothing complicated about this whole subject. Sacrifice now and enjoy later. Ironically, all good results in life require a sacrifice up front with a reward in the future. All bad results follow the pattern of enjoy now and pay later. Life would certainly be far more enjoyable if you didn't have to make your sacrifice up front, and instead could have your enjoyment first. However, nature has dictated that you pay your penalty first. So if you are wise, this is what you will do.

CHARACTER AND FATE

"What you do today will determine to a significant degree where you will be tomorrow. Your character will largely determine your fate."

How you spend the present, what you do and what you say, will quite thoroughly determine the nature of your tomorrows. To a large extent we are the designers of our own future. Most of our tomorrows are quite predictable when we study how we spend our present moments. To a great extent we get the kind of future we obviously want because our present actions make certain events quite predictable. Karma, as the Buddhists call it, results largely from our present activities. Therefore, it might be said that we are the architects of our own future. Our fate will be largely determined by our character.

If, as a child, we refuse to study or do those things necessary to receive an education, such a person's fate will be that of an uneducated person. If we are lazy and refuse to get up and go to work in the morning and take no interest in our work when we get there, then it is quite predictable that our future will be filled with many jobs of an unfulfilling, unprofitable, and unimportant nature. If we eat anything we want all the time, regardless of its caloric content, it is quite predictable that our future will be that of an obese person with all the ailments attendant to obesity. If we use vulgar and profane language all the time, whether in a mixed crowd or not, our presence at future social gatherings will be quite undesirable. If we constantly drive in excess of the speed limit, our future will probably not include a driver's license. If we take mind altering drugs, which constitute a criminal offense, our future will probably include a prison sentence and ill health.

Some people, whether they admit it or not, really seem to want a diminished or unpleasant future. Their present actions leave no other predictable outcome. Man seems filled with an in-born desire to suffer. Masochism is prevalent throughout the human race. How else can you explain a person who smokes four packs of cigarettes a day; or drinks a fifth of whiskey a day; or takes mind-altering drugs which damage the health and threaten personal freedom? The fate of these people is highly predictable. There can be no outcome except an unpleasant one.

Therefore, if you want your fate, your destiny, or your karma to be pleasant, you have to "clean up your act now." What you do now determines whether you will enjoy your tomorrows. To the extent that you need to eliminate negative habits to which you have become addicted, just remember that the pleasure you'll quickly experience in their abolition will exceed any pleasure you ever got from their practice. In addition, you will feel much better about yourself. Your tomorrows will present a brighter prospect.

The "now" is "where it's at." Your whole life depends on how you deal with it. If it is well-spent, your future will tend to be rosy and bright. If it is ill-spent, your future will be dark and depressing. The entire option is yours. The correct practice is pleasurable and not difficult to follow. The one leads to a bright, happy future and the other to darkness and sadness. Wisdom suggest only one answer and that is to upgrade the quality of your present moments.

PART VII
Love and Hate

ROMANCE

"The relationship between men and women
occupies most of the thinking of mankind."

What a terribly dull world we would live in were it not for the motivation and excitement created by the relationship between the sexes. A man can be great and powerfully affect the lives of his fellowman; yet, for his life to have depth and happiness, he has to share it with a partner and to "normal" men, this means a woman. Conversely, a woman can be a greater achiever in may respects; but, unless she shares her life with a partner (and to "normal" women this means a man), it will be empty and have little meaning. In short, for normal human beings life was not meant to be lived alone. It is much better to share your life with someone of the opposite sex.

Women and men have power over the opposite sex for different reasons. Simply, it can be broadly stated that women decide when men have sexual intercourse and men decide when women eat. In other words the age-old arrangement of women being the sex partner and homemaker, and men "bringing home the bacon" still holds true in the modern world. Now, the power to decide when men have sexual intercourse is a powerful lure and weapon. This is especially true when you consider the surface readiness of men of the general subject of sex. This scenario gives women a lot of power over even the most powerful of men. Men, by their ability to compete more successfully in the world for wealth and shelter, possess an equally strong weapon in their attempts to control women. Actually, the distribution of the weapons of control between men and women makes the whole relationship equal. It makes the oft-referred-to "battle of the sexes" a relatively even contest, with both sides holding powerful weapons. The result has been that down through the ages the relative positions of both sexes have remained essentially unchanged.

Man, by his affection for women, has created a position that is unparalleled in human history. The "office" or "position" of "motherhood" has been honored and esteemed throughout history by all people. Motherhood has always been regarded as the highest position in life. A mother, by the very nature of her position, is esteemed above all other offices created by mankind. A mother surrounds herself with the love of her children. This is far truer with mothers than it is with fathers.

A father frequently finds himself alone and without love in a divorce case, for example. The children and even the friends of a married couple almost always sympathize with the woman, or mother. Consequently, men frequently do not do as well in a divorce situation as do women. While women are surrounded by the affection, sympathy, and companionship of the children, relatives, and friends, a man usually feels he is alone and friendless. In this situation it is usually the man who remarries first. He usually does this because he is lonely. On the other hand almost every woman has a lady friend with whom she shares those innermost secrets she has tucked away in the private corners of her soul. She is able to feel less lonely because of the intimate sharing of her secret problems with another human being. Men, on the contrary, almost never share their problems with someone else, at least not anywhere near the extent that women do. Consequently, they are far more vulnerable to loneliness in a divorce situation than are women.

The arrangement of the relative positions of men and women as found in nature is no doubt the best possible scenario imaginable. It could be no other way. Whereas women are physically weaker than men and unable to compete in commerce as successfully, their tremendous sexual appeal to men and the power derived from this fact makes the entire contest an even match.

PREJUDICE

"The practice of hating someone who is different than you, without even knowing such a person as an individual, is my definition of human prejudice."

We tend, all too frequently, to hate someone because he is a Jew, or a Catholic, or a born-again Christian, or a Greek, or an Italian, or a Negro, or an Oriental, or an Indian, or a Shriner, or any one of hundreds of different categories separating him from ourselves. This negative aspect of human nature has been responsible for more suffering than any of the myriad of negative characteristics possessed by man.

Hate usually damages the hater more than the subject. To carry hate around in your heart for an entire class of people, releases all sorts of poison in one's system which limits severely his opportunity to enjoy life. Prejudice simply does not bear up when analyzed against logic. There are wise and ignorant people in all races and groups of people. Why hate everyone in a group or class? All one does by bearing hate or prejudice is to create needless tension within himself, which ultimately reverberates throughout his contacts in the world.

I want to take a minute and examine three prejudices that exist in the world today, the ones against the Jew, the Negro, and Americans in general.

In the case of Jewish prejudice, we are dealing with the oldest prejudice which exists on our planet. Jewish people are like all other humans, only more so. They enjoy their families, worry about their children, value education, like good food, like a home and security, follow their religion, and want a homeland. They are hardworking, industrious, and value material possessions; they are intelligent and they enjoy sex. As I said earlier, they like all these things as does everyone, but it might well be said that their intensities run a little deeper in all these areas. Prejudice has forced

410

them to band closer together than most ethnic and religious groups. The world tends to envy the "togetherness" of the Jewish people and the overall achievement of the Jew and envy doesn't exist very long before it turns into hate—hence, the so called Jewish prejudice with which mankind is afflicted.

The Negro, coming from the hot, dark continent of Africa is immediately distinguishable by the color of his skin. Whereas, the white man has enjoyed an advanced civilization for 5,000 years, the Negro has lagged far behind. This cultural gap is due to climatic conditions in Africa and the fact that early civilization centered around the Mediterranean Sea and did not come into "the dark continent" until much later. Negroes in Africa are just now beginning to control their own governments, whereas the white man first started in Mesopotamia 5,000 years ago. Just as the early white governments were unjust and chaotic, so it is with some of the early Negro governments. Basically, the white man fears this emerging black giant. This fear forms the basis of black prejudice.

Americans have been, as a whole, the wealthiest, most free, most successful, most arrogant, most wasteful, and most self-confident people on earth. A championship American athletic contest winner immediately is dubbed a world champion. This flagrant display of excess causes the world to envy our nation. This envy has in no small way turned into hatred. Consequently, a pronounced prejudice has been created around the world against anything American.

The above illustrations reveal the true basis for all prejudice. It is either based on fear or envy. To be happy and enjoy life, you must rid yourself of prejudice.

BAD MARRIAGES

"People are often driven into the wrong marriage by peer pressure, insecurity, and fear."

411

The desire to share in life's experiences to the fullest drives many unmarried people into precipitous romances. When you are single, the whole world seems to be paired off in twos. Everyone seems to have a mate. This fact looms very large around major holidays and to a lesser degree on weekends. The art of learning how to spend your time alone is mastered by few people. In the desire not to be alone, people make the wrong commitments and in so doing, miss opportunities for more ideal relationships that would otherwise be available to them.

In order to avoid ill-conceived romances and subsequent marriages, one has to come to a peaceful understanding with himself. Incredibly, people know many of their acquaintances much better than they know themselves. Americans have a mania to be "popular." This is often taken to mean that if you are home alone and the telephone is not ringing off the hook, then there is something wrong with you.

The world is passing you up and you fear isolation. In order to avoid the onus of being left out or alone, unfortunate relationships are nurtured, when, wisely, they should be abandoned and left to die. The secret is to realize that being alone can be a very enriching and happy experience. It is very good for the soul to become introspective and for you to really think about yourself and your relationship with your creator and your fellowman. During these periods of introspection, you should read materials of a worthwhile nature that will further your understanding of life and your place in the overall scheme of things. Every library is filled with great books which discuss philosophy, religion, morals, ethics, and all the other deeply significant issues which need to be thought about and focused on to develop a strong sense of the value and purpose of life.

Once you have learned to be happy by yourself, you can then wait for happiness to alight on your shoulder like a butterfly instead of actively searching for it. True happiness comes to those who introspectively prepare themselves for it. You don't find it; it just happens. The effort should constantly be directed at making yourself a better person. Once you have improved yourself, good things will start happening to you.

A frightening percentage of marriages (judging by the divorce rate, if nothing else), seem to be entered into for the wrong reasons. Women and men seek marriage as a means of securing their future or pleasing their friends and relatives. While there is absolutely nothing reprehensible about this, the tragedy is that many grab at the first "straw" that comes along. It is easy, by wishful thinking, to upgrade a relationship into something it is not, if you seek love and marriage strong enough. If the relationship is not what it should be, trouble will soon rear its ugly head.

The truth cannot be hidden about something as intimate as love and marriage. Once the "I Dos" are uttered and the honeymoon is over and the serious business of marriage begins, any serious defects in the relationship will soon come to the forefront and predominate.

No, don't let a wish and a dream cause you to elevate a relationship beyond what it should be considered. Don't let fear and insecurity cause you to rush into precipitous action. Be realistic and truthful about something as important as love and marriage. If you're not true friends, the likelihood of the marriage lasting is quite remote. It has to be based on something more solid than a bottle of champagne and dancing under the stars. Life involves successfully handling the hard problems that we all must face. When this is done, happiness is yours.

SEX AND LOVE
"The sex drive if often erroneously taken for love."

Sex is probably the most beautiful expression of love between two human beings. It is by far not the only expression of love, but it is certainly the most intimate means available to mankind. Sex is a drive that humans share with all animals. It does not prove the existence of love any more than it does when practiced between other animals. It is basically one of the needs humans possess along with eating, sleeping, and discarding our waste materials. Modern literature and song seem to equate sex with love. The idea seems to be that sex is love. This misunderstanding of the role of sex in human relationships probably leads to more broken hearts and unhappiness than any other factor in the area of human dealings.

Love between a man and a woman has to answer a need for both of them, otherwise the love will not last. One of the most normal needs that humans have is the need to share their life with someone. Life was not meant to be lived alone. To be truly happy, we normally have to share it with a compatible partner. While it is awfully easy to get along during the sex act, the greatest part of life does not include the sex act. It involves such activities as working, eating, traveling, socializing, relaxing, and a myriad of other human pursuits. If minimal compatibility does not exit in these areas, then the life that is shared between a man a woman probably won't last. It is imperative that activities be mutually shared and enjoyed. Shared sex alone will not fulfill two lives. There has to be something else. In attempting to evaluate your love's chances of succeeding, look to the other things. There have to be some activities that you mutually enjoy other than sex. In many cases, a great sex drive, when carried to an extreme, is nothing more than an animalistic relationship. It becomes under these circumstances the opposite of love. Sometimes a morbid and uncontrollable sexual desire is found in neurotic impulses that are nothing more than indications of mental illness. How can anyone consider this abnormality to have anything whatsoever to do with love? Carried to extremes, it has nothing to do with love, and it even becomes dehumanizing. Sex that occurs in connection with

414

overindulgence in drugs usually has nothing to do with love.

The tragedy in many human relationships today lies in the fact that in our sexually permissive society, many people, while partaking of what is almost free love, suddenly decide they should get married. Without the sexual relationship, they never would marry each other. Only their sex drive brought them together. Now this great attraction called sex only retains its luster for a year or two. After that, in order for a relationship to continue, there has to be compatibility in other areas. People have to enjoy doing other things together such as dining, reading, socializing, or any one of many possible types of human activity. When the great sexual drive is gone, a marriage is in trouble if there isn't something substantial to replace it. This is often the case in the modern world where sexual intercourse is frequently one of the first things couples do together when they meet. This in previous times was usually way down the list of shared experiences.

Just because you may be initially, extremely compatible in bed sexually, don't believe for a moment that you have found your life's partner. Remember that some people are very good at sex with anyone, just as some golfers, for example, are very good at golf regardless of whose clubs they are using or which course they are playing. Ideally, when you love someone, you should first be their friend. This wild passionate love is going to end. It cannot continue at such a torrid pace. When it ends, there had better be enough other areas of common interest to replace it. Otherwise, you are facing unhappiness and another divorce statistic is about to be recorded.

HATRED
"Hate destroys the one who hates."

It is so easy in life to cross your arms, cross your legs, place a frown on your face, and announce that you hate everything and everyone. It won't be too long before you have no one who will listen to you. After all, people are not interested in being around someone who is totally negative in everything he says and does. Such a person is filled with unhappiness; and if you associate too much with him, you too will become unhappy.

People who hate everything and everyone really hate themselves. They have no confidence in their own ability to associate successfully with their fellowman. They lack the proper attitude to succeed in any of the normal goals we all must have to lead a happy life. As a consequence, out of fear and frustration, they simply condemn everything and everybody and this justifies their failures in their own minds. These types of people have few friends and almost all their relationships are of short duration and they usually do not live long lives. Since they are so miserable, fate is really being merciful in making their lives short.

Bear in mind that an intelligent, wise person can find plenty of reasons in life to love and be happy. If this be true, and the author submits that it is, the people who are filled with hate and consequent unhappiness are abnormal and are seriously lacking in important aspects of their character. These types of people are usually filled with jealousy, fear, distrust, greed, self-pity, slothfulness, cowardice, negative habits, self-hate, and many other characteristics too numerous to itemize. The reason it is really not necessary to itemize each individual defect is because one big word really covers all the items. Such a person can best be described as being ignorant. None of these aberrations would exist in a wise person. A hate-filled person has given up on the world. He has decided, whether he knows it or not, that he no longer wants to learn anything new. The last thing he wants is a new idea. His pride has closed his mind. He fears a new idea because it may shatter all his beliefs. He has somehow learned to accommodate himself to his limited and darkened world and his ignorance will not permit him to proceed towards the light at the end of the tunnel. Tragically, this type of person has stopped the learning process entirely. He is ready to die. He knows all he wants to know. The last thing he wants to do is to have his beliefs shattered by the truth. He has been literally consumed by his ignorance. Some people live out their lives in this self-constructed prison.

Fortunately, these types of people do not live long. They develop illnesses ranging from heart trouble to hypertension, from ulcers to migraine headaches, to mental depression. After all, the mind controls the body and a hate-filled, warped mind will destroy our body. Tension is the normal companion of a person filled with hate. Tension is the great killer of men; tension-related illnesses are probably the greatest of all killers. Some medical authorities even believe that tension causes arthritis and some ulcers. What is perfectly obvious is that a heart filled with hatred does not help such a person's physical health.

To overcome pervasive hatred, learn to look deeper at life. Once you do, you will become wiser and wisdom dispels ignorance on which all hatred is based. Once wisdom overcomes ignorance, happiness will overcome sadness and health will overcome illness.

LOVE

"Love helps the lover."

To fill one's heart with love is absolutely the wisest possible undertaking of a human being. Love is evidence that a person is wise and has great understanding. There are objects everywhere that one can love, and if they are not loved initially, our effort of study and understanding will soon lead to love.

Think of the nobility of a dog for example. Consider his loyalty. He cares not whether his master is a king or a beggar; the loyalty from the animal is as great regardless of his master's station. Careful thought about these characteristics of a dog will teach a perceptive person to love dogs.

Consider the sunrise in the morning or the sunset in the evening. Who hasn't been awed by these events and the many beautiful sights that both bring almost daily to all of humanity? Think of a mother duckling proudly displaying her newly hatched ducks, or a mother hen with her newly hatched chicks. Observe the protectiveness of these animals. How they stand between their brood and perceived dangers of any sort. In placing themselves in danger, they abandon every natural instinct of an animal for its own safety. Consider the beauty of a fresh snowfall blanketing everything in sight. The purity and freshness lifts the spirit and eases the mind. A snowfall almost seems to purify the air and enhance the level of our environment. Who hasn't seen a stream filled with fish darting back and forth in the water, or with beaver or muskrats following the instincts they are given by nature?

The incredible order of nature and the predictable pattern of animal behavior is one of the great blessings we all enjoy.

Most of all, in order for us to be happy we must learn to love our fellowman. This latter object of love is often the hardest matter for most of us to resolve in favor of love. It is so easy and convenient for us not to love most of our peers and acquaintances. It is so much easier for most of us just to sit back and find those characteristics about our acquaintances which make them vulnerable to criticism.

Upon deep reflection, we should understand that everyone tends to do the best he knows how to do in any situation or set of circumstances. His actions come about as a result of a thought process that may well be tainted by a diseased mind. After all, there is no such a thing as a perfectly normal mind. Life leaves all of us with distortions in our thought processes caused by traumas experienced throughout our lives, but especially in our childhood. It therefore follows that our actions will tend to deviate from an ideal norm because of our fears, insecurities, hope, loves, hatred, and a thousand other factors too numerous to mention. When we set out to love our fellowman, we have to take those negative forces into account in evaluating our neighbor's actions. When we do this, we may feel sympathy for him because of some abnormal reaction, but we will still find it possible to love him even though his actions may be against our best interest. If we take the time to study our acquaintances and if our wisdom is great enough, love should fill our hearts towards all creatures. When we do this, happiness will come our way.

MARRIAGE

"In any love affair between a man and a woman that may culminate in marriage, consider very carefully your prospective mate by time-honored principles that govern all human character and relationships."

Your system of values may not be the best, but if there is a great difference between yours and hers, you will have lots of trouble. The only way you can succeed with substantially different value systems is for one or the other, or both, to change their values. This is unlikely. By values, I refer to such things as striving constantly to "keep up with the Joneses" or tithing to a church, or being active politically, or agreed educational levels for the children, etc. What is important for one must necessarily be recognized as such by the other one, or trouble will loom quickly in the relationship. What is one's record of fidelity towards a mate? What attitude does each party have towards a marriage? Does one approve of an open or adulterous marriage? Unless they both agree, the marriage or the relationship won't last long. How does each feel about the so-called "women's lib" movement? What are your opinions on this vital subject? Do your views coincide? If not, then your relationship is doomed from the start. What idiosyncrasies do each of you have? Does one, for example, smack their lips real loudly while eating; or belch in public; or use excessive profanity;

or hate the opposite sex because of childhood problems with his or her parents? Does one or both lack self-confidence? Was the man raised to be a mama's boy and forever tied to his mother's apron strings? Does the woman realize that marriage involves placing her husband ahead of her family and does the husband realize this also applies to placing his wife ahead of his family? Whether the husband or wife can live with a mate who lacks self-confidence will become a very important question. Settle it early. What habits do the partners have when it comes to dependability? Can you rely on their promise? If you cannot, will the other party be able to live with this trait? Each person should consider the other's habits with reference to the drinking of alcohol or the intake of other drugs. What are the views and the habits of both parties with reference to drugs?

The work habits of both parties are an important consideration. Does the woman expect a maid or is she willing to work? Will the man be a breadwinner or will he go from job to job and never really support his family? What are the views of both people on working wives?

What is the status of their sexual compatibility? This should be wisely determined before marriage since it will form such an important part of the post-marriage picture.

Temperament is very important to a happy relationship. Does either party have a violent temper and say hurtful things on the spur of the moment that hurt long afterwards?

Religious beliefs that are compatible are very, very important. When the children come along the question of what religion will be taught to them must be answered. This question should be dealt with in advance.

Ultimately, the above factors, while often overlooked in the first bloom of mad passionate love, will decide whether a relationship will last. It will also determine whether such a relationship will be enjoyable while it does last. These same traits discussed here are really important in all human relationships. In love affairs they are often overlooked to everyone's subsequent regret. Deal with these questions early and truthfully and your lives together will be happier.

WOMEN IN LOVE

"A woman is going to act more purposefully and deliberately when it comes to a man-woman love than is a man."

Women grow up and have as their principal fantasy or dream a picture or image of their home and husband well-developed in their mind's eye. This practice encompasses the main objective of most women's existence. A younger man thinks in terms of his career, but a younger woman thinks in terms of her home and husband, which traditionally has been a woman's career.

It is good that both men and women understand that this picture is both normal and proper. There is nothing wrong with their habits. They are exactly as nature intended them to exist. These natural priorities of home and marriage for a woman versus a career, then home and marriage for a man, make the whole human family function in the manner in which it does. It is these traits or practices that result in the natural establishment of the human family along the traditional lines of the woman giving birth to the children and maintaining a home while the man obtains the material wealth necessary to maintain the family. To the extent that families are not functioning along these traditional lines they tend to fail as a unit.

To the average woman, her marriage to a capable, breadwinning male secures her economic and social future. Her career becomes that of raising and caring for her family, which of course includes her husband. Therefore, the average woman in the premarital relationship is just as serious about love and sex as is a younger man who is trying to determine just what career he will

421

follow in life. To both the female and the male, a life's career is a serious subject. It is for this reason that a woman regards courtship and marriage far more seriously than does a man.

Basically the whole scenario can be stated in another way. A man usually falls in love while he's trying to have sex with a woman; while a woman falls in love while she's trying to impress the man for whom she will raise a family while caring for his and her home. A woman's heart has always been in the home. While a man's heart is there also, necessarily a substantial part of it is also wrapped up in his life's work or his career. Consequently, during courtship, a woman responds far more seriously than does a man. If he is average, he "likes the girls," but a big part of his soul is occupied with thoughts of his career.

Bear in mind that this difference is natural. There is nothing cynical or devious in the basic approach of either sex. Both are acting out the basic plan of human existence. Now, if the man could give birth to the children, etc., then this whole scheme might be changed, but until it is changed it would appear that a woman's place will be in the home and a man's place or function will be that of a breadwinner. Accept these principles since they are anchored in the very core of human life. Understand and accept these tendencies and the behavioral patterns they create in your life will tend to be happier.

PART VIII

Nature

HARMONY

"We should strive to learn how to live harmoniously with our environment, which includes our peers and nature."

Harmony is the oil which makes life flow smoothly and with minimal pain and suffering. It makes quite bearable that which under conditions lacking harmony would become quite unbearable. This doesn't mean that harmony comes from an object surrender and passivity to the wishes and demands of others. But rather if refers to the harmony that comes from a continuous effort to understand the conduct, motivations and substance of our peers and nature.

When you look at your peers, remember that all their actions are based on what to them is their best judgment in a given situation. Their final actions are based on a compromise between their fears; their emotional condition at the time; their problems; their condition with reference to society and literally a thousand other different factors that influence every decision made by man. What we have to do at a minimum, in order to live with a maximum of harmony with our peers, is to conclude in every case that all human actions are the manifestation of the wisest decisions a given person was capable of making at the time. I am not saying that their solutions were proper or correct, but I am saying that their thinking process dictated their conduct after concluding the correctness of a given course of conduct. If people do the best that they know how to do, then why not accept their conduct with compassion and tolerance? As a person, do not be excessively critical or judgmental. If retribution is required for a given course of action, society will exact its pound of flesh. It ill behooves us to right all wrongs. If an individual is grossly in error in his conduct, the isolation he will suffer from his peers will be punishment enough. If his conduct is severe enough, the state will punish him. As for yourself, your best course of conduct is to be compassionate and understanding. In many cases, it may be very difficult to be tolerant, but whether it is difficult or not, the effort should be made.

Lastly, we must live in harmony with nature and with all animals and plants that surround us in this veritable "Garden of Eden." All living creatures have their purpose on this earth. Do not destroy them unnecessarily. Be their friends.

Once your life has reached a harmonious level of existence, your joy and happiness will know no bounds. This great feeling will affect everyone with whom you come in contact.

BALANCE IN NATURE

"The balance throughout nature reflects an order to everything. Without balance nothing will survive for long."

For millions, even billions of years, the moon has remained approximately 265,000 miles from the earth. This distance remains relatively constant because a balance has been established between the gravitational pull between the two bodies, relative to their speed and mass. This relationship has survived because of the balance. If, over the billions of years involved, the moon had annually moved closer to or farther from the earth, it would have long ago either crashed into the earth or disappeared. This balance exists with the sun and all other bodies within our solar system. This same balance exists between solar systems and galaxies. The universe survives because it has balance.

Shorelines around the world remain comparatively stable from year-to-year because tidal erosion and accretion balance out over a period of time. Ocean levels around the world remain relatively stable because the relationship between evaporation, condensation, freezing, and melting remains essentially the same from year to year.

The balance between the hunted and the hunter has remained the same in nature at least until man started interfering with wildlife through chemicals and the destruction of their natural habitat. To the extent that man has disrupted that balance, we find certain species either disappearing or at the least being placed on the endangered species list. Left alone, any species that survives will strike a balance between births and deaths.

Nowhere is balance more important for survival than in our own lives. A happy person has to strike a balance between work and play; eating and exercising; laughing and crying; home and friends; sugar and salt; and all chemicals that we put into our bodies. We have to have the proper amount of sleep each day for our continued health. No matter what we do, we won't live forever. Yet the duration and quality of our life will be determined by the overall balance to our existence.

We should respect money, but not worship it. We may drink alcohol but not to excess. We may laugh but not constantly. We may love our children, but not at the expense of ignoring all their faults. We may have some vices but not to the extent that they dominate our activities and our thoughts. We may gamble but not beyond the bounds of propriety. We may smoke but not to excess. We may enjoy certain forms of recreation but not to the exclusion of our duty to work and provide for our loved ones.

Everything we do should be done with balance. If we let our lives get out of balance in any direction, it will ruin the quality of our existence and in many cases, it can shorten our life. Overindulgence in a myriad of activities or vices can destroy our lives and the lives of our loved ones. Our happiness depends on the balance which exists in our lives. From this balance we will experience tranquillity and inner peace. When our heart is filled with joy, we cannot help but convey this emotion to others around us. This reaction vibrates outward from us and beneficially affects everyone it touches. Therefore, to the extent that our life is in balance, we tend to reject the order of nature. When we become one with the order of nature, our life has been tremendously enriched.

NATURE AND MATERIALISM

"It is easier to be happy if you appreciate the beauty
of nature rather than appreciating the beauty of material
things as seen in the works of man."

Where in the kingdom of man is there a sight even slightly comparable to a sunrise over the beautiful snow-capped Matterhorn in Switzerland; or the constant roar of the white-capped surf as it crashes relentlessly on the shore; or a mother duck crossing a road with eight or ten ducklings marching in soldier-life precision behind her? Where in man's works is there anything remotely comparable to a full moon rising over the horizon; or the sun setting in the west; or beautiful white, fluffy, new-fallen snow; or a school of porpoises gliding smoothly in and out of the ocean; or the look on a mother's face while caressing her new-born child; or the new blossoms of spring; or a warm April shower? Nature is filled with thousands of situations which will remain forever unmatched by the feeble attempts of man for sheer beauty.

Yet, it is difficult to understand how man has consistently remained so preoccupied by his own works in his search for beauty when he is literally surrounded by beauty which is all over for everyone to see. All too frequently men seek beauty in a new car, or a new home, or a new suit. Along this same vein, women seek beauty in clothing, cosmetics, false eyelashes, jewelry, and thousands of material things which all decay in time and which, in their finest hour, totally lack in their beauty the varied works of nature.

Much of man's unhappiness is due to the fact that he concerns himself with the least attractive of two worlds. His entire being is focused almost exclusively on the works of man. Whatever he sees is necessarily nothing but a reshaping of natural ingredients. Whatever product results from man's efforts, can in no way begin to compare with the wondrous beauty of nature. Additionally, the products of man's efforts can only last for a brief period. What is natural renews itself through the rebirth cycle of nature. None of man's edifices can possibly have this characteristic, which is destined to be for all time the unique aspect of that which is natural. Nature renews itself while all of man's efforts are soon buried by the shifting sands of time. When the product of man's efforts vanishes, the only remaining feature is nature. The works of man are temporary, the works of nature are eternal.

Why then does man, given the opportunity to fall in love with something that is permanent, choose to fall in love with and dwell upon that which is temporary? The answer lies in the nature of man himself. Man, for all his so-called advances, remains a basically ignorant creature. He has never, with all his so-called intellectual powers, been able to escape the clutches of his nature. He seems destined to be forever limited by his greed, his insecurities, his selfishness, his lust, and all the other weaknesses that bring down on his brow the burden of turmoil and pain. Nowhere on the horizon does there loom the slightest scintilla of evidence that mankind collectively shows any sign of learning from its past mistakes or of understanding the reasons for having made the mistakes. Man lacks collectively the intelligence to avoid mistakes, while demonstrating considerable ability to endure the suffering caused by his mistakes.

These thoughts are not directed to mankind collectively, for to do so would be futile, but are addressed to you personally. They ask you to examine the direction in which your eyes and your desires are cast. Are they cast downward towards the works of man? If they are, you may have a pleasant surprise in store for you. You have but to lift your sights and desires upward towards the works of nature, and your whole life will be miraculously changed. Let your attachments be to something that is permanent, something that has lasting value; and in so doing avoid the heartbreak and misery attached to having your interest and affections resting on insecure and short-lived foundations. Loving that which is natural will bring you undreamed of happiness. Why not do it, for it would seem a very logical and wise course. Try to appreciate the beauty of nature; it will be there throughout your lifetime to enjoy. It may take an effort, but just remember that nature's beauty is all around you and it will never disappear.

ORDER IN NATURE

"There is a tremendous order to everything found in nature."

We live on an elliptical ball called Earth. Earth is part of a solar system comprised of nine planets, several thousand much smaller planets or asteroids, untold millions of rocky particles or meteors, and large bodies of flimsy rock and gas called comets. Some of the larger planets have moons or satellites revolving around them. The Earth has one—our own moon—which is really very important, and appears so glorious only because it is comparatively close to us. Jupiter, the largest of the planets, has twelve moons.

The Earth spins through space like a top. It makes one complete spin or revolution at 1,000 miles per hour every 24 hours and this is known as a solar day. The direction of the spin is eastward. Traveling 1,100 miles a minute, the Earth takes 365 1/4 days to make a complete orbit around the sun and it winds up where it started a solar year later. Annually, the Earth travels 600 million miles through space around the sun. Meanwhile, our entire solar system is circling within the Milky Way galaxy at a speed of 180 miles per second. The entire Milky Way galaxy is traveling through space at a speed of 170 miles per second. Our galaxy measures 20,000 light years through its center and 100,000 light years from side to side. Light can travel six trillion miles in one year. Yet there are approximately 100 billion stars like our sun in our galaxy, and some of them are 20,000 times brighter than our sun. There are billions of galaxies. Our Milky Way galaxy is but an infinitesimal part of the greater universe. All this celestial movement has been going on for some 4.5 billion years without a major collision.

For example, what keeps Earthlings from flying off into space as the Earth spins around? In fact, what keeps Earthlings alive in gravity? Gravity acts as a magnet beneath the feet of human beings to pull them down to the Earth's surface, and it is gravity that holds down the Earth's atmosphere of oxygen and other gases which we breathe.

This incredible scenario has been operative since the dawn of time. The gravitational pull between the Earth and the moon is so evenly divided that the distance between the two bodies remains at a steady 265,000 miles; the same factors keep the Earth's distance from the sun at a steady 90 million miles. The predominate feature of the universe is its tremendous balance and order. It couldn't last without it.

This same balance is found throughout nature on our planet Earth. Consider, for example, that the sun draws into the atmosphere, in the form of evaporation, quantities of water that are later released back to Earth in the form of rain. Over the eons of time, the exact amount of water which has evaporated into the atmosphere has been released in the form of rain. If more water had evaporated than is released, eventually the Earth would be dry since all the water would be in the atmosphere. However, a perfect balance exists between evaporation and condensation.

For anything to survive in nature there must be a balance. If more of a species die than are born, eventually that species would become extinct. The fact that a species exists is proof that it has found a balance. For a human to survive he must find a balance between work and relaxation, asleep and awake, love and hate, and hundreds of other areas of life. Balance and order seem to be the very pillars on which the entire universe rests. We should seek to let these qualities permeate and dominate our life whenever possible. The more balance and order we achieve the happier we will be, together with all the other humans our life touches.

PART IX
Media

Bob Hope. UPI/Bettmann

Youth and Age

"Youth and the youthful body are exalted in all media hype; however, we should never forget that the majority of wealth, experience, and wisdom are possessed by people over forty years of age."

We are a society that idolizes youth and one that tends to ignore the value of citizens beyond 40 years of age. Because of our incredible preoccupation with youth and the youthful body, we tend to undervalue the continuing contribution to our way of life by older citizens. Youth, being aware of society's tendency to over-value all younger people, is inclined to ignore the wisdom and advice of our senior citizens. The natural result of all this youth worship is to ignore and ill-treat our elders. This condition is contrary to that which exists in the Orient where the older citizens, together with the departed ancestors, are literally worshipped. Our nursing homes are filled with abandoned people who are carted off to die in a ruthless manner once they can no longer fend for themselves. This cruel and heartless practice has caused many of our older citizens to spend the last years of their lives in a depressed and heartbroken state of mind.

The sex-oriented world in which we live today has placed a great premium on the "beautiful people." These are the youthful people with the firm and shapely bodies. They are the ones who command the total attention of the media. Everyone admires the beautiful body. Very little emphasis is placed on a beautiful mind, heart, or soul, but every thought of the media deals with the beautiful body. These are the people who attract the exorbitant fees and salaries and who form the new wealthy class of this nation. Included in this category, of course, are the super athletes who also possess the beautiful bodies.

With the world headed for nuclear destruction, we would be well-advised to turn our thoughts away from the beautiful bodies

Jerry Lewis. UPI/Bettmann

and towards the beautiful minds, hearts, and souls. These are the people who will save this world if indeed it is destined to be saved. Youth needs to listen to the older generation more than they do. They need to be taught that older people possess greater wisdom and experience; therefore, they should learn to respect and follow the advice passed unto them by their elders. Youth is a time in life of great experimentation. It is filled with blind alleys that prove to be worthless and without redeeming values. If youth can be trained to listen to the voices of their elders, they can expect to avoid many of the attractive nuisances that will lead them to heartbreaks and disaster. Society needs to be reoriented towards greater respect for its elders. In the process many of the tragedies that now befall the younger generation can be avoided in the future.

The voices of reason and wisdom and experience need to be heard more clearly above the restless masses of the world. The present tendency of mankind seems to be to drift endlessly towards the annihilation of the world. The populists who holler the loudest and the longest seem to be the only types capable of attracting man's attention, if only for a fleeting moment. Wisdom, love, and tolerance have somehow got to come to the forefront if the world is to be saved from itself. This practice of listening to reason should start with the youth being taught the advantages of maturity, or age. Certainly, among those advantages are a tranquillity and understanding which can only come with years of hardship, turmoil, and judgmental errors. The latter tends to be corrected with experience. The impetuosity of youth should forever be managed by the restraints only age can provide.

ENTERTAINER INFLUENCE

"With the opportunities for widespread communication provided by television and other media, entertainers are able to exert influence far beyond their moral worth."

Consider the influence of the Beatles on an entire generation of young people. They represented every value that would have been best never exposed to an impressionable, emerging generation. Their emulation of mind-altering drugs probably had more influence in the '60s for drug addiction than any other single factor. These people should never be emulated or cast in a role of influence. Their values are born of ignorance. Their attitude on sex and proprieties of all forms were destructive of all decent values promulgated by humanity down through the ages.

When John Lennon was murdered, this fact was indeed tragic. Nonetheless, even more tragic was the attempt by the news media to upgrade him into some sort of martyr or valuable world personality. The same reflections that we make on the Beatles apply equally to Elvis Presley and hundreds of other personalities from the world of entertainment. These people are not heroes. Their influence should be nil. They exploit every situation for their own personal gain. Yet, with the notoriety provided by the media and the image manipulation performed by their public relations departments, they are elevated to exalted positions.

All athletes should be included in the term "entertainer." If they represent anything worthwhile, then they too should be considered as entertainers. Any activity that commands an audience the size of the one that watches Monday Night Football is certainly entertainment. Professional golf, tennis, baseball, skiing, hockey, and all sporting activities, when reduced to their essentials, are nothing in the world but entertainment. The only possible thing they do to ameliorate the human condition is to entertain.

With the overpowering coverage of television, we find more and more entertainers leaving the field of entertainment and entering the field of politics. The exposure they got as entertainers permits them to successfully pursue political careers. This fact alone is proof of the powerful influence entertainers exert over their public.

The sad fact is that these people—the entertainers—are all

Dominique Wilkins. UPI/Bettmann

too frequently neurotic, addicted, self-indulgent people who barely are able to hide their vices from a hero-worshipping, naive, and gullible public. Consider the tortured figure of Elvis Presley. While to his adoring public, he was a god-like figure of an entertainer, he was also a frightened, tormented drug-addict who destroyed himself by his use of mind-altering drugs. Consider John Belushi or Janis Joplin, or Jimi Hendrix, or many other entertainers who were in a position of great influence but who were terrible examples of

Michael Jordan. UPI/Bettmann

Eric Dickerson and Dexter Manley. UPI/Bettmann

moral character and irresponsible human beings.

Let's face it, whoever controls television is in an awesome position of power. They determine what you and I will see when we turn on our television sets. It is only natural that entertainers are the types of people who predominately appear on television. Once an entertainer begins to appear, he soon is recognized throughout the country. This adulation gives these vain creatures an exalted view of themselves. What is true of television is also true of Hollywood. The film industry is also controlled by a reasonably small number of people. These individuals determine what we see in the theaters and which actors will appear in the films. Once again, these movie entertainers adopt a position of preeminence in the nation. When we read the papers, we learn everything that is happening in their often sordid private lives. Thus we

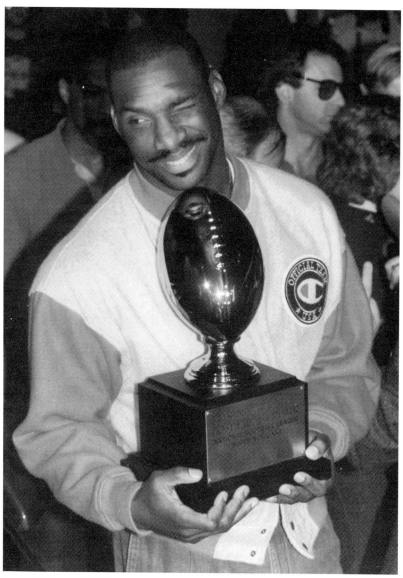

Doug Williams. UPI/Bettmann

are cast in the position of watching them as entertainers and thereafter reading about their lives as an item of news. Soon these same entertainers decide that they would make great leaders in other areas of our lives. When this happens, we have another entertainer turned government leader. There is nothing necessarily wrong with the scenario so long as we, the public, keep in our minds the entire background of just why and how such individuals gained notoriety.

NEGATIVE IMAGES

"The news media creates a negative image of America by exaggerating our problems."

The policy of American news media of concentrating on bad news becomes a powerful negative factor when it deals with our national political structure. The result of this profitable practice is to emphasize everything that is wrong with America to the exclusion of almost everything that is right. We tend to ruthlessly tear

Dan Rather. UPI/Bettmann

Bryant Gumble. UPI/Bettmann Newsphotos

apart the character of our leaders and our nation. Since good news
for Russia tends to be bad news for America, our news media emphasizes all Russian victories of an economic and political nature,
while at the same time emphasizing all the economic and political

failures of America. The net result can be devastatingly destructive to the respect and confidence Americans have in their political leaders and their nation.

One doesn't begin to see America in its true perspective until we travel across our nation and around the world. A young acquaintance, who spent an entire day in East Germany (a Communist social paradise), was particularly impressed with the fact that it was the only time in his entire life that he spent a day and never saw anyone smile. He was struck by the blank expressions on peoples' faces; by the drabness of life, and by the inevitable policeman on every corner. When he returned to America, he wanted to kiss the soil of his native land.

Our news media, while concentrating on Russian victories, doesn't advertise the quality of life in this "peoples' paradise." You are not told, for example, that to purchase a simple item like toilet paper you have to stand in a line for two hours and may or may not wind up with your purchase. You are not informed that the average Moscow resident has to spend an average of eight hours a week just waiting in lines for the bare necessities of life. Yet goods and services are far more available in Moscow than in the other parts of Russia—Moscow being a showcase for foreign visitors. You are not informed that 2 percent of Russian farmland provides 25 percent of all the food supplies in Russia. Remarkably, this 2 percent hap-

Howard Cosell. UPI/Bettmann

pens to be the same land that is farmed under the free enterprise system. You are not informed that 18 percent of all the internal commerce in Russia is carried illegally on the black-market with the fraudulent bribery of Communist officials. Russia could not exist without it. You are not told that those harbingers of future trends (the young intellectuals) are turning to religion and the love of freedom—totally in violation of communist teachings. You are not told that the average Russian is so disillusioned with the Communist police state that he drowns his despair in alcohol. Lastly, you are not told that the Communist dictators in Russia are not sure in which direction the Russians and their Eastern satellites will turn their guns in the event of war with the West.

In summary, America has far more going for it than our news media depicts. Conversely, Russia has far less going for it than our news media depicts. One would hope that a more balanced system of reporting news would eventually evolve. Meanwhile, don't believe everything you read in newspapers or hear on television.

TELEVISION

The newest technological advance with the greatest impact on the lives of people is television. It has permanently and profoundly altered war, our living habits, our politics, and our educational system. In sports, it has produced the athlete who makes over a million dollars in one year.

The private lives of many people revolve totally around TV programs. Children are so distracted by TV that they find it impossible to study. Parents who restrict their viewing find their rules difficult to enforce. Politicians who appear the most attractive on TV, predominately win the majority of votes. Wars are rendered more abhorrent when the folks back home can see the real horror of war on the six o'clock news. Crackpots of any ilk can get a mass viewing audience by merely making the TV news programs.

Don Johnson. UPI/Bettmann

Millions of people thus become instantly familiar with their cause. In short, TV, which first became commercial in the latter part of the 1940s, has infiltrated every part of our lives and the full impact cannot at this time be foretold.

Whether someone make a national news broadcast or not is

decided by one or two people in each of the major networks. Failure to have your cause broadcast results in continued anonymity and conversely, success in having your cause broadcast, produces instant notoriety. This power is so great that one shudders to think that it rests totally in very few hands. Yet the nature of the "animal" is such that no other system of space allocation appears to be superior. The opportunity to control the masses has never existed before to the extent that it now does with television. This opportunity rests in the few people who control the major networks.

Interestingly, it should be noted that in the realm of politics, TV has a devastating impact. In our 1980 Presidential campaign, we had President Carter, who came across the picture tubes appearing very "pious" in the 1976 campaign. This TV image, after the fraud and corruption of Watergate, was enough to throw the election to him. Yet, here was a man whose only qualification was his very mediocre governorship of the small southern state of Georgia. He possessed absolutely no experience with the tough issues that face our country internally and internationally. His opponent was Ronald Reagan who was a mediocre movie actor and who subsequently became governor of California and the leading candidate for president on the Republican ticket. The ability to project oneself favorably on television and thereby, get elected president, bears no relationship whatever to the ability required to run our nation. Our congressmen, senators, and other office holders are all beginning to look like the news commentators on TV whose every hair is kept in place by hair spray. Television has put the plastic man in positions of power. Maybe this explains why the last great president we had came to power before the advent of television. My choice for this honor is Harry S. Truman. He wasn't what you'd call a TV idol, but he sure was a good president.

DISTRACTION

One of the most difficult problems confronting everyone who tries to bring his energy and intellect to focus on a particular endeavor is the distraction that permeates life in the waning moments of the 20th century.

Through the incredible advances of communication around the world we are constantly being bombarded by every conceivable message of every action group on this planet. All that has to be done to spread a desired message is to perform an act outrageous enough to qualify for space in the communications network. This usually involves the destruction of life and/or property. The recent emphasis has been on the activities of terrorists.

The simple truth is that most of us are over informed; over-analyzed; overentertained; overeducated; overfed; overweight; overtaxed; overrelaxed; overdrugged; overly computerized; overly exposed to sports, news, medical data, medicants, and commercials of all types. We are constantly being bombarded by hype of all sorts, much of it so cleverly disguised that we do not recognize it for what it is. Almost everything we see in the newspaper and on television is orchestrated and staged especially for our consumption. Almost nothing is spontaneous and unrehearsed.

Literally the entire world is targeting its product and/or message for that big, fat, lazy, beer-guzzling American consumer. The result is that we have become so pleasure oriented that we find it very difficult to direct our intellect and energy towards worthwhile projects. In short, we are overly distracted.

To get some idea of how debilitating distractions can be, I refer you to the exercises outlines in the section entitled "More Notes on Exercise" in Part II of this book, "Your Health." Start doing these exercises with your eyes open. Having done them for several weeks with your eyes open, I now suggest that you start doing them with your eyes closed. By the simple act of closing your eyes you will find that your endurance to perform the exercise becomes much greater, while your mind and body are much more refreshed and relaxed once the exercise is completed. The difference is truly astonishing. All you have done by closing your eyes is to eliminate practically all distractions. With the distractions eliminated, you are able to concentrate your intellectual and physical energies more efficiently on the exercise.

Picture the student doing his homework with one eye on the television set and the other eye on his work. How can such a situation develop scholastic achievement that comes anywhere close to such a student's true capability? The answer is obvious. The work product in these situations is greatly reduced in quality. In many areas of American endeavor most of us are distracted in varying degrees just like the student described above.

We need to concentrate on ways to reduce distraction. We can't begin to perform at our highest level of capability if we are in an environment that is filled with distraction. Many of us are constantly afraid that we will miss something so we keep one ear tuned to gossip while attempting to concentrate on achieving some sort of task. The result is a work product of reduced quality. Train yourself to find opportunities to eliminate distractions. The quality of your life will greatly improve.

GULLIBILITY

"Most of what you see in the media is orchestrated for gullible minds and eyes; so, do not be overly influenced by it."

The fact that bad news sells and for the most part good news doesn't, plays an immeasurably significant role in the doubts and fears many Americans possess. There is tremendous profit available to the one who disseminates bad tidings. Consequently, our news media concentrates almost exclusively on what is wrong and almost never on what is right. When we watch the 6 p.m. news on television or when we read the morning paper, we are seeing what went wrong in the world over the last 24 hours. Almost no time or space is devoted to the overwhelmingly preponderant amount of actions or events that are good and proper. As a consequence, the impressionable reader can become quite depressed at the condition of the nation and the world unless he constantly keeps in mind that bad news is published simply because it is profitable.

Murders, robberies, rapes, tornadoes, earthquakes, and every other form of natural and human disaster is given front page billing to the exclusion of all the right things that happen everyday. People don't want to listen to good news. They almost seem to get bored with it. Bad news seems to be about the only way to get a person's mind off a selfish preoccupation with his own problems. Somehow one wonders if a certain pleasure is not obtained by reading or seeing someone in worse straits than ourselves. We can see the morbid fascination on the faces of people standing around a victim of a car accident on the highway, for example, or the victim of a heart attack in a crowded gathering. People have to be almost forced to step back in order to leave air for the victim to breathe.

One of the most popular themes in modern movies evolves around the "man in peril" theme. This can be best illustrated by such movies as *The Towering Inferno, Airport, The Exorcist, Earthquake, The Poseidon Adventure,* and many others too numerous to mention. This characteristic even seems to apply to the misfortune that befalls personal acquaintances or friends. Who has not heard people privately laughing at the misfortune of very close acquaintances? This is not indicative of the evil of man as much as it is of an age-old trait of human nature. Somehow those disasters seem to relieve the day-in, day-out boredom of human existence. These out-of-the-ordinary happenings seem to make easier and more palatable the humdrum of the constant repetitive cycle of everyday life. With this deep understanding of human nature, the news media gives people all the bad news they can discover around the world.

Lest we become overwhelmed by this avalanche of disaster, we must always bear in mind that to spread bad news is very profitable. As long as a profit is available, you can be sure that you will continue to get your daily ration of human and natural disasters. Remember there is far, far more unprinted good news any day than there is bad news. If you keep this in mind, you will maintain a proper perspective.

PART X

Government, Politics, and Business

SMALL BUSINESS
"An overview of problems affecting a small business."

The principal problems facing a small business (which for purposes of this discussion is considered to be any business which grosses less than $5,000,000 per year) are as follows:

1. Inability to have access to competent advisors on a wide variety of subjects, such as:
   a. Legal
   b. Accounting
   c. Taxes
   d. Government regulations of all sorts
   e. Buying practices
   f. Management practices
   g. Advertising techniques
   h. Employee relations
      1) Promotion policies
      2) Vacation policy
      3) Health insurance
      4) Bonus arrangements
      5) Retirement programs
      6) Proper pay scales
      7) Methods available to retain trained help
      8) Training programs
   i. Insurance program
   j. Banking relationships, and
   k. Raising capital

This inability to have ready access to competent advice on a wide variety of problems facing all small business hinders and often dooms to failure enterprises that would otherwise be successful.

Even when a small businessman searches for advice, he is

frequently not in a position to know whether the party he is seeking advice from is competent to assist him. In short, he even lacks the experience to intelligently pick his advisors.

2. Local governing bodies impose such severe regulations as curb cuts; parking requirements; sewer tap fees; building renovation fire regulations, etc., that render it impossible for a potential small businessman to even get started. The reason being that he lacks the capital to meet all the up front costs unreasonably required by local governing bodies. The days of starting a small business with $10,000 and a lot of hope are gone forever. Much of this is due to foolish requirements relating to start-up costs.

3. Small businessmen need to know how to raise capital for their venture. There are definite do's and don'ts to follow in this most important aspect of any small business. Banks should be encouraged to enlarge their effective assistance in this field.

Since not everyone is suitable to bear the rigors of being a small businessman, a standard profile of a potential small businessman should be formulated.

Another method of effectively helping small business is for the state (possibly through the Department of Labor) to advise small businesses on the wisest personnel policies available to such a venture. Success in a small business depends on people. An important question that the state should help the small businessman answer is "How do you attract and retain competent employees?" This would require advice on all the items listed in paragraph 1. (h) above and on other items not listed.

One way to combat this overall problem effectively is to teach in our state colleges and universities an accredited course on starting and operating a small business. Such a course should cover the whole range of problems encountered in a small business and be taught by actual businessmen who have dealt successfully with the whole range of problems encountered in a small business undertaking.

Potential needs for particular types of small businesses existing in a community should be developed by area Chambers of Commerce. Many communities have great needs for a particular type of small business.

COMMUNISM AND CAPITALISM

"The battle of Communism versus free enterprise capitalism continues unabated in every emerging nation around the world."

The future political shape of the world will be determined by which direction the emerging nations turn in their continuing economic and political evolution. The big question as thcy emerge from their oligarchical and/or dictatorial past, is which way will the struggling masses turn for help? Will it be towards free enterprise democracy or dictatorial Communism? Their decisions will be largely influenced by which of the two alternatives offers the most immediate benefits to the ignorant and impoverished peoples of the world.

Communism offers a plan which gives everyone a duty or job to perform. Their lives immediately assume a direction they never had before. Medical care, education, and a job represent three things most of these people never experienced. Instead of wandering aimlessly and forgotten, suddenly their lives assume direction and purpose. As soon as the revolution is over and Communism is installed, the machinery of the Communist government is put in motion with a plan for everyone. Now, behind every plan and governmental directive, there is the state, with gun in hand, ensuring the fulfillment of its decrees. Tragically for these same people, the previous government's decrees were also enforced at the point of a gun. So with both systems the gun was present; but under Communism, these people get an education, medical care, and a job.

The best example of how a Communist takeover works, is Cuba in 1959. Under Batista, the average worker in Cuba earned $60 a year, had no education and no medical care. The daughters went into prostitution in Havana, and the poor in the cities subsisted from garbage cans. Batista was a dictator and shot his enemies just as Castro does. However, under Communism these poor people now have medical care, education, and a job. Instead of wandering aimlessly with absolutely no purpose their lives now have direction. For this reason, the people of Cuba did not rise up at the Bay of Pigs and overthrow Castro.

Whether we like to admit it or not, in an ignorant, impoverished, chaotic, and revolutionary country. Communism is better equipped to make order out of chaos than is a free enterprise democratic society. In the past the Communist revolutionaries got their blueprints for establishing a government from Moscow. They had an exportable do-it-yourself kit complete as to all details. From this expertise, the surrogate revolutionaries were able to complete their tasks by converting the revolution to a Communist dictatorship. Once the government gets the "drop" on the population, calm soon follows. In this manner the precious chance for freedom was lost to yet another emerging country.

If our superior system of free enterprise democracy is to compete successfully in this evolving world, we have to likewise develop an exportable kit or blueprint for our surrogates in these emerging nations that includes a plan for the whole population. Such a plan necessarily has to include a job, an education, and medical care for everyone in an atmosphere of freedom. At stake is the makeup of the world of tomorrow. Will it be free or ruled by Communist dictators?

The upheavals in Russia through 1995 portend great changes in whatever appeal remains for the Communist system.

THE DRAFT

*"America has difficulty instituting the draft
because of its unique geographical status."*

The world has difficulty understanding America's reluctance
to institute the draft during the perilous times in which we live. All
the Communist dictatorships around the world have the equivalent of a draft, as do most of the Western democracies. Yet America
does not have the draft. Intelligence would suggest an inquiry as
to the reason for such a unique feeling in America against our
nation's safety.

Geographically, America's borders are uniquely secure. We
are a land that is essentially a rectangle measuring 2,000 miles
north and south and 3,000 miles east and west. On the north we
have the country of Canada, and on the south we have the nation
of Mexico. Neither one of these countries represent a threat to
the security of the boundaries of the United States. On the east
and on the west we have the geographical protection of the Atlantic Ocean and the Pacific Ocean respectively. When one considers
the accident of geography with which we are blessed, the conclusion that our boundaries are secure is logical. When America goes
to sleep at night we don't have to sleep with our rifles beside us.
The basic fact is that our boundaries are secure.

Whenever we have gotten into a world war in the past, the
scenario went something like this. Two foreign nations develop
differences. Their differences lead to an armed conflict. We then
take sides and support one of the parties and the offended party
attacks our ships or bases and we enter the war on the side of
our "ally." In 1914 (World War I), England and Germany started
a war. We shipped war supplies to England. Some of those supplies were on the *Lusitania*. Germany torpedoes our ship, the
Lusitania. The result was we declared war on Germany. During
the 1930's (World War II), Japan and Nationalist China started a

war. We supported Nationalist China. Our military personnel were discharged from our service and allowed to sign up in Nationalist China's forces fighting the Japanese, such as the Flying Tigers for example. The result was that Japan bombed Pearl Harbor, and we entered World War II.

In none of these conflicts was our territorial integrity threatened. We took sides in an armed conflict and we were attacked. The attacks were of such vicious nature that the American people were angered sufficiently to allow the President to declare war with the support of the people. The same technique was tried with the Gulf of Tonkin resolution in the Vietnamese conflict, but the American people were not sufficiently convinced of its validity to give our leadership wholehearted support. Hence the divisiveness of the Vietnamese War.

America will fight if its borders are threatened. Basically, we are normally asked to protect distant economic interests—not our own borders. This sort of threat is nebulous and quite remote. However, any would-be-aggressor who unites us in our anger has truly awakened a giant. Will this American attitude to world threats work in the next millenium? The answer will determine our national future.

CAPITALISM
"Free enterprise capitalism survives with a delicate balance."

One of the ironies of a free enterprise capitalistic democracy is that while it is without question the most precious system of government in the world, it is also the most difficult to preserve. It lies in the middle ground between totalitarian Communism on the left and totalitarian Fascism on the right. It is the one spot in the cycle of government where you have the least government; and as a consequence, freedom is the greatest.

The greatest problem in preserving this delicate balance between Communism on the far left and Fascism on the far right is due to the difficulty of packaging conservatism in as attractive a package as it is possible to do with liberalism. Liberalism can point to the wealth of a free enterprise capitalistic democracy and tell the people we have enough wealth to solve each and every problem facing our society. This incomparable wealth could only have accumulated in a society with a minimum of government controls. This very important point is either not mentioned, is overlooked, or not understood. The liberal seeks to solve all problems by more government. At some point in this process the goose that lays the golden eggs is killed. Down through history governments have proven capable of only one thing and that is to impose tyranny on their subjects. Nonetheless, the arguments of the liberal are very appealing. They are the ones who are pictured as caring for their fellowman. They are the ones who are able to excite the alienated and the discontented and well-meaning people who sincerely wish to improve the lot of mankind. Never forget that Karl Marx and Frederick Engel were genuinely distressed at the evils and excesses of the industrial revolution in the 19th century. Recognize the great evil of Communism that their compassion has unleashed on the world. Their solution was more government.

Governments are always controlled by power-hungry, greedy, and in all too many cases, sadistic people. The appeal of the intellectual liberal is undeniable and a great attraction to a majority of any society. Consequently, governments which have experimented with free enterprise democratic capitalism are constantly being pulled off center to the left by the popular vote. No one wants to vote against Santa Claus. The conservative, by comparison to the attractive promises of the liberal, can only say, "Hang in there, improve yourself, work harder, and your life will get better." In this never ending clash of political ideologies, the movement is inexorably to the left in such a society. When the movement goes too far to the left, the society either turns into a totalitarian Communist state such as Rhodesia recently, or a totalitarian Fascist state through a military coup, such as Chile recently. This process has been going on for 70-odd years, or ever since the Russian Revolution of 1917.

The point is that it is very difficult to let people know when they are well-positioned. Only education and still more education can improve the process.

GREED

"Human greed explains much of history."

The struggles going on in the world today can only be understood in terms of man's insatiable appetite for wealth and the power that goes along with it. Wars are sometimes attributed to religious differences, but I suspect that behind these surface religious shields, the accumulation of wealth and power are the real reasons. The very idea of war being used to obtain a religious goal is utterly inconsistent. All major world religions have, as a principal premise, the idea that one should not do to his fellowman, what he does not want his fellowman to do to him. I believe the history of the world can be explained more accurately in terms of the struggle for wealth and power.

Recent struggles serve to illustrate this point. In Cyprus the Greeks had the wealth and power, and the Turks wanted it. In Lebanon the Christians have the wealth and the power and the Muslims want it. In Ireland the Protestants have the wealth and power and the Catholics want it. In Portugal the farmers had the wealth and power and the city folks wanted it. The litany of wars which can be explained in terms of the struggle for wealth and power goes on and on.

Free enterprise capitalism's struggle against world Communism is again a struggle for wealth and power. World Communist leaders have no real feeling for the plight of the impoverished and downtrodden. They shoot anyone who disagrees with them. It has been estimated that the Lenin-Stalin era resulted in the extermination of 35 million "enemies" of Communism. In China, under Mao Tse-tung, it is estimated that 65 million were slaughtered as enemies of the "People's Democracy." If world Communist leadership cared for the downtrodden, the sad example of 100 million humans being exterminated would not be so readily available. Man has a very sad record when it comes to loving his fellowman. In Biblical times, infants were torn from the arms of their mothers and slaughtered before their very eyes. What is easily provable is that man will kill and be killed for wealth and power.

This greed lies behind today's struggle for world domination. Who will control the wealth and power in the world? Will it be Communist dictators, or will it be the capitalistic free enterprise societies? The free world can only begin to win this battle if the underlying issues are understood.

The downtrodden and impoverished are promised a redistribution of the wealth under Communism. What really happens is that wealth and power are transferred from the wealthy citizens to the Communist dictators. This wealth is soon dissipated under Communism by the inefficiency and bureaucratic structure of a Communist dictatorship. Soon the ignorant and impoverished realize that under Communism the wealth and power are in the same hands as the guns. Hence, the exodus from Cuba and Vietnam and the need for a wall in East Germany. Free enterprise capitalism can win the battle, but to do so they will have to drastically alter their tactics.

FREEDOM (CIRCA 1987)

"The forces of freedom are necessarily disorganized."

As one observes the scenario being played out by the Russians since World War II in the furtherance of their constitutional goal of spreading their evil doctrine of Communism around the globe, one has to admit that the Russians are currently winning. This vast monolithic giant which has no moral foundation whatever for its existence, is making frightening progress in its continuing goal of Communist world domination. Their abominable morals and techniques are justified in their acquisition of power and control over new territories.

Arrayed against this evil giant are the unorganized forces of freedom around the globe. The very process of democracy makes it difficult to unite the people in a common goal. Sacrifice by the populace is difficult if not impossible to attain. The leader who constantly preaches about the dangers of Russia soon gets the label of the "voice of doom and gloom." If one were to point out that the only difference between China and Russia is the contention over whose brand of Communism will govern the world, he would really be cast aside. A freedom loving population doesn't want to hear such realism. They vote for the person who promises a continuation of their present existence. The one who smiles and proclaims essentially that everything is great at city hall, the state house, and the White House is the one who usually gets the most votes.

Meanwhile, the Communist influence continues to spread around the globe. Their obvious current objective is to obtain the minerals of Africa and the oil of the Middle East. Once these two vital interests are controlled by the Communists, Western Europe and Japan would fall (to use the words of Lenin) like an "over-ripe plum from a tree." The economic chaos resulting in these two areas would make them "easy picking" for the Communist dictators. Meanwhile, the United States would lose its markets in Europe and the Far East. The Communist menace is spreading in the Western Hemisphere. Operating through its surrogate in Cuba, Russia has made enormous strides in the Caribbean, and you can bet it has as its main goal control of the country of Mexico with all of its oil. Meanwhile, in the province of Quebec in Canada, it has

461

obtained a substantial foothold. While all this goes on, China is busy importing our technology in order to catch up with the 28-year head start the Russian Communist party has in the industrial and technical field. You can be sure that once China advances technologically and industrially, it too will be present around the world selling its brand of human enslavement.

The big stumbling block is the United States. Russian leaders are far wiser than Adolph Hitler. When the U.S.S.R. runs into steel, she backs off. Hitler did not. When Russia encounters mush, she advances. To plunge headlong into steely opposition would spell disaster for the world and Russia. It would unite the forces of freedom against her. The Soviet Union's goal is to create economic chaos, and in so doing, gain world domination by capturing one country at a time. The forces of freedom must unite in a common policy aimed at stopping this process. The cult of Communism, once in world control, could remain so for thousands of years. History bears ample precedent for this fact.

MORE ON CAPITALISM

"Some thoughts on private enterprise."

The private ownership of wealth under reasonable governmental control has resulted in more advancement for mankind than any other system. Human love of security and material possessions has created the incentive for work and invention, which has advanced the lot of all people. Individual excellence has led the way. Government under this system necessarily has to be kept to a minimum.

The private accumulation of wealth has taken on a shameful or evil connotation. The reason for this is hard to understand when a complete understanding of human history impels the conclusion that the pursuit of wealth created most of man's advances. Call it free if you will, but the benefits are still there. Travel around the world and see how life in the United States of America exceeds what you find elsewhere. This is clearly due to the free enterprise system functioning more freely in America than elsewhere for the last 350-plus years. The facts are clear and simple. So what if most of the motivation lay in private greed? The benefits are still there for all of us to enjoy. Even the Communist frauds admit that the history of the world is essentially the history of economics.

The Communists use the negative human emotions of envy and jealousy to spread their evil system. They tell the downtrodden that they will take the wealth from the privileged few and harness it for the good of all. On the surface, this argument has vast appeal. Human envy and jealousy make it successful. In reality, the wealth under private enterprise is merely transferred to the leadership of a Communist police state. With the loss of private incentive and initiative under Communism, this wealth is soon dissipated. What remains of it is in the hands of the Communist dictators and their henchman. They are the new capitalists. The evil is enhanced when you consider that the wealthy or ruling or privileged class under Communism also controls the police. You now have the guns and wealth in the same hands. The most basic situation under Communism is that you simply have another police state. Another government where terror, persecution, torture, and all the other trappings of dictators down through the ages are now parading under the guise of a "People's Democracy." All Communism amounts to in relation to historical dictatorial governments is the same old "coon with another ring on its tail."

We should praise and be proud of the private accumulation of wealth. We should honor those who excel. After all, most human advances were made by a very few select and gifted people. Excellence should be honored and rewarded in our educational system from the earliest levels. No doubt, that is why these people were put on this earth—to help others while they pursue their own economic and social goals. Let us not apologize or be ashamed of this. It is what makes our country's contribution to the human condition so great and unique. We must broadcast this to the world and, in so doing, point out the fallacy and emptiness of World Communism.

DEMOCRACY

"Some thoughts on democracy."

"Send me your tired, your poor, your huddled masses; yearning to breathe free; the wretched refuse of your teeming shores, give these the homeless tempest tossed to me; I lift my lamp beside the golden door?"

Emma Lazarus, through the above words inscribed on the base of the Statue of Liberty, states the greatest case for America. Freedom is a rare and precious possession which we enjoy more than any other people on earth. We have enjoyed it so long that we take it for granted. Sometimes we forget that freedom is not a gift but something succeeding generations have to earn. As we complete the decade of the '90s, it becomes increasingly apparent that our way of life will again have to be defended. America, with more of life's creature comforts than any other nations, has more freedom to lose than any other nation on earth.

If the young people reaching adulthood are to live out their lives in freedom, they are going to have to get tough and disciplined. This same generation, which has been pampered by us more than any previous group in the history of the world, is going to have to clean up its act if our way of life is to survive. They are comparable to a wild animal raised in the softness of captivity and unable to survive in the wild. The product of our school systems will have to be improved. High school graduates will have to be better equipped to face and understand the nature of adulthood. They will have to be impressed with the serious nature of work and the need to earn a living. They constantly hear what their rights are under our system—they will now have to be forcibly informed of their obligations.

Our biggest problem lies in our leadership and our news media. Our government has become riddled with cynical opportunists who know how to get elected over and over again. The consequence of this accumulated incompetence is a tragic loss of faith in our system. Americans don't seem to believe enough. A free enterprise democracy can only survive on faith. A Communist or Fascist dictatorship can survive at the point of a gun. When a system of government is free and open, it has to have value to survive. The way our system is currently working raises a serious question of its inherent worth.

Some immediate changes aimed at constantly putting power in the hands of newly elected citizens with fresh ideas from the people are as follows:

— 1. Change the presidential term to one(1) six-year term only.
— 2. Change congressional terms to permit a maximum of two (2) four-year terms.
— 3. Change senatorial terms to permit a maximum of two (2) six-year terms.
— 4. Limit the tenure of all the judiciary to a maximum of ten (10) years.
— 5. Limit all other elected officeholders throughout the land to two (2) four-year terms.
— 6. Eliminate all private contributions for political campaigns. This will keep our politicians out of the control of special interests. Tax monies can be made available to those who have, for example, 6,000 signatures from registered voters in a congressional campaign to 25,000 signatures for U.S. Senate race. The money can be allocated in all elections, city, state, and federal, on the basis of those candidates who receive the required signatures.

— 7. Reorganize the overpowering influence of television. Steps should be taken so that both the liberal and conservative viewpoints could each control at least one of the national networks. The third network could be controlled by the government, similar to the British Broadcasting Corporation.

The above steps will greatly enhance the grass-roots support of and faith in our system. Our concept of freedom exceeds by far that of all other systems on this planet; it merely has to be updated to survive. We must never assume that our founding fathers could formulate a system which would be adequate for all time. Common sense suggests that it must be amended on occasion to solve problems not existing at the time our Constitution and Bill of Rights were written.

Of the 19 great civilizations that existed in the last 5,000 years, only eight exist today. Of those that perished, the main cause was always a period of poor leadership, followed by a decline in the will of the people to resist.

THE COMMUNIST AGENDA (CIRCA 1985)

"Communism has a careful plan for converting the world to its system."

Article Two of the Bill of Rights of the United States Constitution read as follows:

"A well regulated militia being necessary to the security of a free state, the right of the people to keep and bear arms shall not be infringed?"

In Dusseldorf, Germany, in May 1919, the Allied forces captured this document from a Communist activist—it reads as follows:

"Cause the registration of all firearms on some pretext, with a view of confiscating them and leaving the population helpless."

The following rules for a Communist revolution were secured by the State Attorney's Office of the State of Florida from a known member of the Communist party who acknowledged it to still be a part of the Communist program for overthrowing our government. The State Attorney's name was George A. Broutigam.

    a. Corrupt the young; get them away from religion; make them superficial; destroy their ruggedness.

    b. Get control of all means of publicity and thereby:

1. Get people's minds off their government by focusing their attention on athletics, sexy books and plays, and other trivialities.
2. Divide the people into hostile groups by constantly harping on controversial matters of no importance.
3. Destroy the people's faith in their natural leaders by holding the latter up to contempt, ridicule, and obliquity.
4. Always preach true democracy, but seize power as fast and as ruthlessly as possible.
5. By encouraging government extravagance, destroy its credit, produce fear of inflation with rising prices and general discontent.
6. Foment unnecessary strikes in vital industries, encourage civil disorders and foster a lenient and soft attitude on the part of government toward such disorders.
7. By specious argument cause the breakdown of the old moral virtues, honesty, sobriety, continence, faith in the pledged word, ruggedness.

This blueprint becomes quite significant when one realizes what the major governmental and sociological problems are today.

Communism teaches:
- a. There is no God.
- b. Man has no immortal soul.
- c. There is no after-life.
- d. Man has no personal freedom because he belongs to the state.
- e. Class warfare is necessary.
- f. Private property must be abolished.
- g. Religion is the opium of the people.
- h. All religions must be persecuted and abolished.
- i. World revolution, no matter by what means, is necessary for world domination.
- j. Any type of aberration, infiltration, infection, insurrection, or war on whatever is good to achieve a Communist world.
- k. If you act according to these maxims, there will be an earthly paradise.

Communism falsely promises to: abolish poverty; give everything everyone needs; bring prosperity and pleasure to all; do away with all inequality; do away with all discrimination; make women equal with men; free all people from all ties of whatever kind; create a classless society; abolish government; annihilate all abuses; abolish all child abuse; guarantee all freedoms; abolish war—in short, to create an earthly paradise.

In reality Communism does the following:
- a. Creates a super class.
- b. Enslaves the people.
- c. Builds up armaments at the expense of the necessities people require.
- d. Creates a society without even fundamental human freedoms of conscience, religion, family, speech, press,

assembly, etc.

e. Creates perpetual tensions of every variety.

f. Degrades women.

g. Destroys the family.

h. Indoctrinates everyone, especially children.

i. Persecutes all religions mercilessly.

j. Crushes all opposition pitilessly.

k. Abolishes all private property.

l. Makes the government almighty.

m. Murders millions.

n. Sends more millions to concentration camps.

By deceit and deception, it seeks to enslave all mankind perpetually.

GOVERNMENT

"Many people expect the impossible from
our system of government."

"Society in every state is a blessing, but government,
even in its best state, is but a necessary evil;
in its worst state, an intolerable one."
  —*Thomas Paine, 1776*

A country enjoying the unprecedented freedom that America does, creates by the very fact of its rare blessings, a problem that is as perplexing as it is unique. Americans, spoiled as we are, tend to expect too much of life's bounty from our society. One must bear in mind that since governments began to form and rule 5,000 years ago, the preponderance of mankind has existed in want and under tyranny. As one looks around the world today, freedom from want and freedom from tyranny do not exist in very many places. Nowhere today or in past civilizations has freedom existed to the extent that it does in America. Our revolution in 1776 was against government tyranny. Yet, the gripes and grumblings and the condemnations of our system are to be heard constantly. It is perplexing indeed to hear intellectuals condemn our society when there is no other system they can point to and honestly proclaim its superiority.

We must never forget that it is our free enterprise system and not the government that has produced a society which enjoys blessings unmatched elsewhere. To the extent freedom has ever existed anywhere, it has done so in spite of government and not because of it. The wealth in America was not created by government but by people interacting with each other and working to improve their fortunes. Governments destroy wealth—wealth that can only be produced or created by the work of the citizens. This experiment, lasting over 200 years, has created for each of us a life that knows no equal. Should our system of free enterprise be abandoned for any form of socialism, then our caliber of life will start a long decline into darkness. Governments have proven that they are efficient at only one thing and that is depriving citizens of their freedom. Historically, governments have shown that they are in the business of tyranny. All our efforts should be aimed at keeping government to a minimum and not increasing its scope and control over the lives of people. This great, free and open society was not created by government but by the free enterprise system, operating with a minimum of governmental control.

We constantly hear intelligent people seeking to cure all existing ills with more government controls. They expect too much. No system devised by man can cure all ills. No system can create a virtual paradise. Our free enterprise system has come as close as any society can come to perfection. Our problems should be solved through our free enterprise system and not by the extension of government control over our lives. This practice carried to an extreme can destroy the very thing that has brought us so far.

When we look at our society and its lack of perfection, we must remember that life at its best is imperfect and not expect too much. If we attempt to cure apparent inequities or problems, we should do it through a proven winner—the American Free Enterprise System.

DEMOCRACY (CIRCA 1985)

"It can be concluded that American democracy is a natural way for people to live."

One of the most predominate characteristics of American Democracy is the totally impersonal nature of our system. We are all subject to a system or structure of laws within which we must live. No one is above the law. We are all subordinate to this legal structure.

This method is quite different from a Fascist or Communist dictatorship. Under these forms of government, the people in positions of power are subject to a very personalized system of law. They are above the legal structure of their country. If they are close enough to the leaders, they and their friends can literally get by with murder. Hitler, Stalin, and Mao, for example, were above the laws of their respective countries. They and anyone else they chose to protect were above the law. The law only applied to the masses—not to the inner circle of the leaders.

In America, subject to small variations caused by the fact that justice is administered by human beings, all law applies to everyone. Even Nixon, Agnew, and Governor Mandel of Maryland, and others found this to be true. If you obey the laws in America, you can live a full and free life. If you don't, the probability is that you will spend part of your life in jail. You are free to spend your life either way; the system is utterly impersonal and does not care which way you spend it. The law applies without feeling or emotion.

This impersonal nature of our democracy bewilders a lot of

people. They seem to be waiting around for someone to tell them what to do next. Our system does not cover this aspect of human nature that some people possess. In America you can avoid going to work. If you do, you will be poverty stricken. In Russia, you either work or go to jail—not so in America. Our government foolishly hands out welfare and relief checks to the lazy as well as to the justifiable victims of poverty. This loophole places an enormous burden on our financial capability.

The laws of our democracy are very akin to the laws of nature in that the laws of nature are also utterly impersonal. If you walk off a cliff you are going to die. If you consume poison, you are going to die. If you diet and exercise properly, you will probably enjoy good health. If you go out in the rain, you are going to get wet. These examples illustrate that the laws of nature govern all our lives. No one is above them. They govern all our lives on an utterly impersonal basis.

It can be concluded that American Democracy is the natural way for people to live. It is as natural as the laws of nature. Contrariwise, Fascist or Communist dictatorial systems are totally unnatural.

RETIREMENT

"The free enterprise system has to develop a retirement method for the worker who spends his working life with various small companies which have no retirement system."

Two of the great weaknesses existing in our free enterprise system involve the millions of workers who are not covered by a retirement program and the difficulty of small businesses to retain competent help.

Many people work all their lives only to reach retirement age without a pension other than Social Security. No one, of course, can live off Social Security benefits. The tragedy is that these same people, upon reaching their nonproductive years, could have two pensions within the framework of our free enterprise system.

Numerous workers' productive lives never involve employment covered by an independent pension plan. In their teen years, such a person may work as a dishwasher, or at a car wash, or as a pool maintenance person, or as a bag checker in a grocery store, or in any one of thousands of different occupations not involving contributions to a pension fund. This same individual would probably never go to college and probably never finished high school. At age 21 this individual may get a job at a gas station or as a stock clerk in a warehouse or as a carpenter or sheet metal worker or in any one of a thousand fields not covered by a pension plan. At age 25, he may start switching jobs from one employer to another in the same or an allied industry. In so doing, many hardworking people spend 40 or 50 years working five or ten years at a time for various employers. Finally in their old age, they are performing guard duty or some less strenuous work in order to pay for life's necessities. Unbelievably, the only pension they get (Social Security) penalizes them for earning in excess of a minimum figure. These folks can only die; they cannot retire—even though they have worked all their lives. They made the mistake of always working for a company which had no independent pension plan. Millions of Americans are faced with this dilemma.

The solution is a "catch-all" pension plan for those workers who are not covered by another plan. Credits could be accumulated during each tenure of employment with a firm which has no independent pension plan of its own through the process of tacking on successive employment with different small businesses.

The cost of such a plan should be borne in part by the employer and the employee. This plan would force small employers to consider a pension plan of their own; or failing to do this, they would forced into a catch-all pension plan. The small employer would find that the catch-all pension plan would enable competent employees to stay with small businesses rather than seek a larger employer with a pension plan.

With this catch-all pension plan, every worker in America could realistically plan on an adequate retirement—Social Security plus another pension plan. This would do more to bolster free enterprise, by aiding its workers and its small entrepreneurs, than any single improvement possible.

Lastly, the entire program should be funded by a consortium of insurance companies rather than the federal or state government. Experience has shown that once the politicians get their hands on this money, they spend it.

DEMOCRACY AND INEQUITIES

"American democracy constantly readjusts inequities."

Our nations has survived for two hundred years despite numerous pressures and wars which have caused many powerful countries to forcibly change their governments. While Germany, France, Italy, Spain, Russia, China, Japan, Egypt, Chile, Cuba, India, Iran, Greece, African, and South American countries too numerous to mention, changed their governments, our republic forges onward with the same constitution originally drafted by our founding fathers. One might ask what it is about our system which has enabled it to preserve itself while numerous other systems have failed.

The single most important feature that has added to our longevity is our system's tendency to constantly adjust by peaceful means to inequities that emerge constantly in a thousand different ways and places. This continuous process is made possible by our First Amendment right of free speech, as exercised by individuals and the news media. It is further aided by our court system by our elective processes and by the executive branches of our government.

These adjustments are being made all the time at the local, state, and federal levels. No great inequities are permitted to remain unnoticed by our national conscience. No problem goes unnoticed long enough for it to grow into an explosion powerful enough to overthrow our government. The one exception was slavery, which fortunately did not destroy our system.

One of the features of the American character most frequently misunderstood is our constant airing-out of every problem confronting our society. Every day everything that went wrong is spread throughout our news media; nothing is sacred. Every improper act of public officials, each radical statement by groups of every political and economic persuasion is aired daily by our newspapers, radio, and television stations. Foreigners observing this kaleidoscopic interplay of democratic forces believe that our country is either on the verge of collapse or at best is in a terrible state of confusion and chaos.

Comfortable groups within our society are angered when less fortunate individuals scream for their share of the blessings of our wealthy country. They do not like to hear that anything is wrong so they look down on those less fortunate and hope that by ignoring their cries their voices will soon be stilled. However, the experience of our democracy suggests that if a dissident has a valid complaint, something will eventually be done about it. In the adjustment, another rough spot will be smoothed out and our democracy will be strengthened, thus ensuring the continuance of our form of government. Freedom is noisy but nice. Tyranny is quiet but ugly.

PART XI

Secular Humanism

*"A brief history of intellectual humanism
and the plight of America's youth in 1996."*

School statistics on any subject that reflect society's health
or moral conditions tell a depressing story. This is true whether
one looks at teenage pregnancies, drug-related crimes, arrests for
violent crimes, school dropouts, comparative public school comprehension data, federal and state prison populations, juvenile arrests, homicides, suicide rates, or the use of selected drugs by
age grouping or any of a myriad of data that is available through
the government printing offices. It's sad but true that American
society took a big downturn in the past twenty-five years.

The good old U. S. of A. is a very unsatisfactory place in which
to raise the leaders of tomorrow. Television, movies, sporting
events, the news media, advertisers, radio, internet, and entertainment of all types, constantly attempt to appeal to the public's pru-
rient nature. Everyone has a loftier and a bizarre side to which an
effective appeal can be made. If you want to entertain people you
simply direct your appeal to their animal instincts. These instincts
lie just below the surface in all civilized people. The modern com-
municator can profit immensely from this side of human nature.

Older, more thoughtful people around the world are concerned about the "cultural imperialism" that results when their
fellow citizens adopt the social messages contained in all things
"American." The public is bombarded by outrageous displays of
sex, violence, and almost every conceivable aberration of human
behavior. A normal citizen with his or her normal conduct simply
doesn't qualify as having entertainment value. This caliber of "entertainment" comes to the public in every form of communication
that the mind of humankind can devise. The world tolerates this
evil because it is always searching for ways to relieve boredom. Its
appeal does not lie in the fact that it is immoral or evil but because
it is used as a way to be "entertained," as an answer to the search

for happiness. From the statistics quoted in the rear of this book, it is evident that the American public searches for happiness in all the wrong places.

Meanwhile, the purveyors of filth, with evangelical fervor supplied by the American Civil Liberties Union, use the shield of the First Amendment to the Constitution for protection. They protect their "inalienable" rights to "celebrate" their particular brand of moral poison by branding it as "entertainment." We, as a nation, are indeed blessed with the First Amendment rights guaranteed by our constitution, but methods need to be created to protect our children from the terribly destructive message they receive from this type of "entertainment." The motivation for the continued projection of this filth is simple and it's called "profit." The problem is that its continuation robs our children of their innocence or their youthful naiveté. In many cases, it harms their chances of living a useful, normal, and happy life. It turns boys and girls, in their single digit years, into sexually aware and frequently sexually active children—all this at a time when they are totally lacking in judgment and discretion. The profit motive guarantees that "kooks" and their lifestyles will continue to be paraded on national talk shows or portrayed in the movies. As long as an audience and sponsorship are available the public can be assured of an endless parade of this type of "entertainment."

The American marketplace is the largest and most lucrative in the world. Promoters, of all sorts of filth and harmful ideas and products from around the world, exert their energies and resourcefulness to target this "mother load." The international drug trade creates the greatest problems resulting from foreign imports of this type. America is being deluged by every sort of mind altering substance that the creative genius of man can produce. Politicians, the judiciary, and the police departments are frequently involved in the protection of this evil trade. The large sums of money available for payoffs has compromised many a public official. America's young people are easy to victimize as consumers for this particular brand of human misery. It is therefore quite natural that many of our children are having their lives ruined by a hopeless drug or alcohol addiction or a tragically youthful pregnancy, sometimes even before they reach their high school years. It is unbearably sad to see babies that are born, shaking uncontrollably from a terrible drug addiction contracted in their mother's womb.

Phrases such as "Just Say No To Drugs" attempt to reduce drug addiction amongst our children. These types of efforts, while admirable, have proven wholly inadequate to negate the avalanche of hedonistic and permissive values instilled in our children. An amoral, profit driven entertainment, sports, and news media complex insures that this condition will not change at any time in the future. Published data on drug arrests, school dropouts, prison populations, teenage pregnancies, suicides, murders and other violent crimes by teenagers and preteens suggest that young people use more mind altering substances than ever before. Some form of alcohol is usually the entry level drug that introduces young people to this nether world of evil. They see their sports heroes and other attractive people in television commercials enjoying all sorts of pleasure. The media projects alcohol consumption as the necessary ingredient for such pleasure. Breweries go to great lengths and expense to sponsor activities at "spring breaks" in Florida and elsewhere. Everyone is laughing and having a good time. Classically designed beer ads on television peddle their products through senseless but very comedic plots. The message is loud and clear that the consumption of alcohol guarantees a good time. After all who doesn't want to be popular and associate with attractive people?

The consumption of beer and alcohol among our young people in high school and college has become epidemic. Logic seems to suggest that the "next step" is to turn to more powerful ways of reaching new "highs." This "next step" enters in the form of marijuana, cocaine, speed, LSD, acid, heroin, and other more powerful drugs of this genre. Since all these substances are banned, it now becomes a criminal offense to "alter the mind" with these substances. Consequently, the young children routinely using these substances are engaged in a criminal activity. This not only ruins the young people's self-respect, it also ruins their respect for the legal system and all legally constituted authority. These same young people become a severe problem to their parents, their school system, and society in general.

There is another factor that has to be considered before today's young people can be fully understood. It goes back to the era of the '60s that included Elvis, Janis Joplin, Charles Manson, Woodstock, Timothy Leary, Dr. Spock, Jerry Rubin and the Chicago Seven, Jerry Lee Lewis, Margaret Meade, and Haight Asbury, to name a few of the opinion-makers. Those people who were young and impressionable in that "hedonistic" era have become the parents of today's children. The parents of the "flower children" of the '60s were appalled at the morality, the drug usage, the songs, and the excessive consumption of alcohol that became typical conduct for that period. Along came Dr. Benjamin Spock, a pediatrician and a leader of the antiwar movement during the Vietnam War, and proclaimed that to use the rod was to spoil the child. Biblical wisdom told humankind that if you spared the rod you would spoil the child. Thus the idea of permissiveness or of a person not being held accountable for his or her actions or deeds became a significant part of society's thinking.

A majority of the younger generation experimented with illegal drugs and other hedonistic activities such as promiscuous or "recreational" sex. Consequently, the parents of today's children (1996), are not as shocked or bewildered by the practices of today's youth as were the '60s parents. Today's parents are more inclined to ignore their children's responsibility for their actions as were previous generations of parents. The result was more toleration and fewer prohibitions coupled with an enormous harmful inundation or contamination by this lowered level of morality. Consequently, young people today have fewer demands placed on their moral and social conduct than ever before in history. It's possible that today's parents are simply throwing up their hands in recognition of their inability to negate these messages. The tide being simply too strong to combat. There is no successful technique available to insulate the youth from the poisonous messages being forced down everyone's throat and into everyone's brain.

Sex and violence are the most popular formats around which to build an "entertaining" movie. This is a great place to indoctrinate the young people since they are the ones who go to the most movies. Love was formerly portrayed through hugs and kisses. It is now indicated by showing a couple in the act of copulation. Besides man-woman love, all forms of homosexual love are projected with increasing frequency. The message being, "Hey! Do your own thing, it's all acceptable, do whatever turns you on." Copulating actors are shown on television in the home and the subtle and not so subtle message contained in all this filth, is that sex, sex, and more sex is where the joys of living begin and end. The subsequent entry into the world of alcohol and drugs becomes an easy natural extension of this lifestyle, although it may have already been the precursor. Somehow drugs and promiscuous sex go very well together. Media communications teach young girls and boys that unless they are sexual creatures, actively displaying their sexual appeal, they are undesirable, prudish, and unfashionable. The dancers, with their slithering bodies, suggest the performance of the sex act while the dancers are in an upright position. Sexual promiscuity has become widespread at an increasingly younger age. The result of this promiscuity is widespread teenage pregnancies. Teenagers who become mothers and fathers are deprived of the normal joys of their childhood years by adult-type responsibilities that naturally flow from parenthood. These "grownup" problems occur at an age when teenagers are woefully unprepared to cope with the world of parenting. The result is a total breakdown in the normal human maturation process. This is necessary to prepare themselves to become self-sustaining, productive, and happy adults. Thus society by its permissive standards has contributed to the ruination of yet another life. Additionally, it has gotten another non-productive member who will probably appear on some government assistance role.

The entertainment entrepreneur defends his or her right to dispense cultural "poison" by invoking the rights guaranteed to all Americans by the First Amendment to our Constitution that reads as follow: "Congress shall make no law respecting an establishment of religion, or prohibiting the free exercise thereof; or abridging the freedom of speech, or of the press; or the right of the people peaceable to assemble, and to petition the government for a redress of grievances." These same entrepreneurs argue that no one is forced to watch their television shows or their movies or their other public communications. They fault the parents who allow their child to watch entertainment that is rated "R" or "adult." These arguments totally fail to consider the appalling breakdown in the American family structure as represented by "latch key" children, children from broken homes, or the children from dysfunctional families. The plain truth is that 18th and 19th century-type parental control and guidance have become a virtual impossibility in 1996. The moral poison and the "celebration" of all types of perversion have become too invasive and widespread.

Let's examine the historical facts that have contributed to society's present moral and ethical dilemmas. Prior to the 18th century, the "clerics" taught the faithful to live every day of their lives in preparation for their inevitable death. They were taught that an all-seeing Creator kept a record of all their deeds and sins and that the results, when tabulated, would determine their place in eternity. Heaven or Purgatory or Hell, one filled with eternal bliss and the other filled with fire and eventually Heaven, and the third with eternal suffering, were the only alternatives available to humanity. More importantly the clerics taught that everyone was personally accountable for their own actions to an all-knowing god. The age of permissiveness had not yet arrived. This theology so controlled the daily lives of people, for example, that King Louis XIII of France appointed Cardinal Richelieu as his chief minister to help calm a wave of civil unrest that was besetting France during his reign. In one instance in southern France, where a starving population was on the verge of a revolt, the Cardinal responded by sending a group of Jesuits to the area. From the advantage of the Sunday pulpits, Cardinals, with evangelical fever, reminded the congregations that the Bible commanded all people to render unto "Caesar" that which is "Caesar's." They further explained that Louis XIII was the biblical "Caesar" and that to revolt against the "crown" was to disobey the word of god. This "sin" would send them to "hell" for all eternity. These rules are very heady stuff for a true believer. Although the kings and their allies lived in unbelievable splendor and luxury, they could control a starving and impoverished population by playing, among other things, the religious card. This control lasted until the populace rose in arms and began the French Revolution. In 1793 King Louis XVI lost his head to the guillotine.

This type of control of the population of Europe, from a civic point of view, was in the hands of the governing bodies. The control of their religious lives was firmly in the hands of the Roman Catholic Church. The kings and the Catholic Church had a mutual understanding that caused them to work together for their mutual perpetuation. The Hapsburg dynasties had a similar agreement with the Catholic Church that lasted for a thousand years. This control, through religion, was only possible because of the deep religious faith of the vast majority of the populations of Europe. Thus the populace tended to lead legal and circumspect lives

Martin Luther. Corbis-Bettmann

although their indiscretions would have been known to no one but their creator. Historically immorality having been reserved for the royals and their peers, the kings and the popes supported this cozy arrangement because each understood that their continued power depended in large part on a continuation of this partnership.

However, ominous cracks began to appear in the centuries-old, impenetrable walls of authority carefully constructed by the crowns and the Catholic Church. The first major blow was delivered by Martin Luther (1483-1546). A Catholic priest, he began his theological career as an Augustinian monk. He became a professor of Biblical theology at Wittenberg University in 1512. In 1517 he attacked the Catholic Church's doctrine of selling indulgences and some of its other practices and teachings; by posting 95 "theses" on the church door at Wittenberg. This provoked major controversy and caused his excommunication from the Catholic Church. The Diet of Worms ordered his seizure but his life was saved by the elector of Saxony in Wartburg Castle. He began the German translation of the Bible (1521-2). The "genie" was out of the bottle and the Lutheran Church was off and running with its basic creed supplied by Melanchthon's Augsburg Confession (1530). Today there are about 70 million Lutherans scattered throughout Europe, Brazil, Canada, and the U.S.A.

The next major blow to the dominance of the Catholic Church came through the actions of King Henry VIII of England. His queen, Catherine of Aragon, failed to present him with a male heir to the throne. This lead him to ask Pope Clement VII to declare his marriage void (1527). In protest the King appointed Thomas Cranmer as the first Protestant archbishop of Canterbury (1533). Cranmer immediately declared Henry's marriage to Catherine of Aragon invalid. Cranmer ordered a revised English Bible to be placed in every English church and compiled much of the new Books of Common Prayer. Sadly, after the accession of Mary I,

King Henry VIII. Corbis-Bettmann

Cranmer was burned at the stake as a heretic. Unfortunately for Cranmer, Mary I, known as "Bloody Mary," the daughter of Henry VIII and Catherine of Aragon, had been raised as a Catholic. Henry VIII then married Anne Boleyn and the Pope refused to recognize this marriage. The English parliament passed the Act of Supremacy (1534) declaring Henry VIII the supreme head of the English Church. Upon the death of Henry VIII (1547), his son Edward VI caused England to swing to extreme Protestantism with the second Book of Common Prayer (1552) and the Forty-two Articles of the Church of England (1553). Interestingly, Prince Charles, the current Prince of Wales (1996), has announced that he will not take an oath as a defender of the Church of England but only an oath that he will defend everyone's freedom to practice a religion of his or her choice.

The two significant historical occurrences related in the preceding paragraphs (Martin Luther and Henry VIII), caused the populace to begin to question the legitimacy of the Catholic Church. They not only questioned the monolithic structure of the Church but also the "Catholic" Bible itself. In 1611 King James I published the "Authorized Version of the Bible." Here again, we have another crack in the monolithic "Wall of Faith" passed down from posterity. The most significant effect of a breakdown in the monolithic structure of Christianity, as it had been formulated by the Catholic Church, was a weakening in the faith of many Christians. This held ominous portents for the future strength and influence of Christian doctrine and theological teachings. The authority of Catholicism and Christianity had been given an immeasurable boost by Emperor Constantine (280 AD—337 AD). Before his conversion to Christianity, a Christian could not get a job and after his conversion a non-Christian could not get a job. Christianity and Catholicism had a long period of little competition for its influence over the teeming masses of the world. The doctrines of the Bible, of Christianity, and the traditional Churches were about to be confronted by the age of Secular Humanism.

By the dawn of the 18th century the intellectual and religious influence of the clerics, began to decline. They had been telling people how to live for 1,400 years. Unquestionably, all religions and especially the Catholic Church were guilty of extreme intolerance that resulted in terrible tortures being inflicted on the so-called heretics. In Ireland, for example, in the 12th century, 12 Catholic priests were roasted, while still alive. Their sin was that they argued that the consecration did not cause the actual body and blood of Christ to be present during the celebration of the Mass but that the "presence" was merely symbolic. This was contrary to the official Church's position which was that the actual body and blood of Christ were present at the consecration of the bread and wine. Besides these types of powerful negatives, which in reality constituted a departure from the teachings of Christ, the ethics and morals taught by the clerics, from the New Testament writings, created great societal benefits. Since the masses had no Bible, these authoritative teachings came from the clerics who preached their interpretation of the Bible's meanings. Not only were the masses told that they must live by these standards but that their slightest divergence would be recorded against them by an all-knowing God. The net affect was that the conduct, both civil and religious, of the vast portions of society was severely inhibited by their beliefs in and their fear of the doctrines of Christianity. Considering that this book is being written in 1996, for the 296-year period from 1700 to 1996, the vast portions of the masses would begin to lose their anchorage to the teachings of the Bible. Theological certainty was to be replaced by doubt and outright denial of the veracity and authenticity of the Bible and its teachings. The Western World had experienced domination by paganism and the clerics. By 1700 the age of Secular Humanism was about to dawn on this world. Secular Humanism would be controlled by the so-called intellectuals. The principal features of their age would be Utopianism or Communism, Hedonism, and Permissiveness. As of the date of this book (1996), all their grandiose schemes and theories lay decaying on history's scrap heap of tried but worthless ideas.

Starting with men like Voltaire (1694–1778), the so-called "intellectuals" began subjecting the Bible, Christianity, the Catholic Church, its hierarchy, and Protestantism, to the severest sort of fault finding scrutiny and criticism. Voltaire's clarion call was for a recognition of the dignity of man, coupled with free inquiry and equality. He was a great man of letters, but it has been said that instead of fostering a revolutionary proletariat, he fostered an ungovernable middle class.

He was a contemporary of Denis Diderot (1713-1784), another man of powerful intellect and together they incarnated the spirit of the 18th century. Both Voltaire and Diderot walked very softly on religious criticisms, since they were more fearful of retribution from the contemporary religious authorities than from a wrathful creator at death. They were both very aware of the experience of Galileo (1564-1642), who was forced to recant his support of the Copernican theory. Nicolaus Copernicus (1473-1543) advanced the then-revolutionary idea that the earth was not the center of the universe. He taught that the earth and the other planets orbited the sun, instead of the sun orbiting the earth as the clerics were teaching.

Jean Jacques Rousseau (1712-1778), a French writer with a keen mind, rebelled against many dominant values of his time. He advocated freeing the human intellect from the accumulated restraints of the clerics. He asserted man's rights to reject all or some Biblical teachings. His short and long-term influence was enormous. Many scholars hold him responsible for the start of the French Revolution which occurred years after his death. He was described as an interesting lunatic, "a monster who saw himself as the only important being in the universe, odious, deceitful, vain

Denis Diderot. Corbis-Bettmann

as Satan, ungrateful, cruel, hypocritical, and full of malice." He
deliberately abandoned five of his babies by turning them over to
an orphanage (Hospital des Enfants-trouves). He knew in advance
that, at this orphanage, two-thirds of its babies died in their first
year. He never bothered noting the birth dates of the children nor

Nicholas Copernicus. Corbis-Bettmann

did he bother to find out what happened to them. All this from an "intellect" who professed belief in the natural goodness of man and, who himself, was a terrible abuser of women or anyone else who befriended or loved him.

Galileo. Corbis-Bettmann

Jean Jacques Rousseau. Corbis-Bettmann

Percy Bysshe Shelley (1792-1822) was an English poet with a great intellect. He argued that enlightened man through his own unaided intellect had the ability and the moral duty to reconstruct

Percy Bysshe Shelley. Corbis-Bettman

society. He taught that poets, such as himself, were especially well positioned to lead this intellectual assault on a rotten society. He was known as the "Eton Atheist." Born into a well-positioned family, he became a lifelong absconder and cheat. He borrowed money he never repaid and fathered children he never bothered to see. He preached the total political transformation of society and the destruction of organized religion. He was a violent man and an outrageous womanizer who left female suicides in his wake. His own mother despised and feared him. Shelley died violently in a boating accident. The mother of Shelley's last child, Percy, when told that the child would probably grow up to be an "extraordinary" man responded, "I hope to God," she said passionately, "he grows up to be an ordinary one."

Karl Marx (1818-1883) published the *Communist Manifesto* in 1848. He founded the 1st International (1864) and published the first volume of *Das Kapital* in 1867. Freidrich Engels (1820-1895), a Marx collaborator, edited volumes II and III of *Das Kapital* (1885-1894), after Marx's death. The influence of these writings cannot be underestimated in their responsibility for human suffering and poverty in the 20th century. Estimates of as high as 135 million people died while the Communist utopia was being forcibly installed in China and Russia. Communism and its grandiose promises have been largely discredited at the time of this writing, although it still controls the governments of China and Cuba in 1996. Marx argued in his writings that he had discovered a "scientific" explanation for human behavior. He was a confessed atheist. His dialectic materialism coupled with his "scientific" approach made his appeal to the outspoken "intellects" of the 19th and 20th century all the greater. "Scientific" implied objective proof as opposed to the intuitive belief required by believers in Christianity and the Bible. Russia and China adopted his teachings and because of this powerful sponsorship, Marx became the most influential "intellect" of the 19th century and the first half of the 20th century. Karl Marx was known for his systematic misuse of sources for his writings. He freely misquoted or distorted the sources for his writings to buttress whatever point he was trying to establish. He was a proven intellectual fraud. His was an angry egotism that was probably connected to his personal life and habits. He constantly ate too much, was often drunk, and almost never washed or bathed. His excessive drinking caused constant liver problems. His once beautiful wife Jenny remarked every day, "I wish I was in my grave." His children were dying from the squalid conditions of their life, one in 1851 and one in 1855. They were expelled from their apartment for the nonpayment of rent. They could have lived well since Marx's inheritance was considerable and Frederick Engel gave Marx half his income. An insight into the character of Marx can be found in his pretended concern for the working person and his low wages. A stumpy little female named "Lechen" worked for the Marx family for 45 years without being paid a cent of salary. The entire family and "Lechen" lived in two rooms and besides her free labor she also served clandestinely as Marx's mistress. When she gave birth to a son, Marx not only denied his fatherhood, but he made Lechen remove the child from the household. She "farmed" out the child while she continued to live in the Marx household and work for no salary while furnishing free sexual services to Karl Marx.

Henrik Johan Ibsen (1828–1906) preached that the individual should follow his own intellect and personal notions of morality and pay no attention to the ancient myths and prejudices. He was a celebrity whose ideas had a tremendous influence on modern dramatists. His idea was that if it feels good and passes your own moral standards, do it and ignore society's preachments to the contrary. He was another milestone in society's march toward hedonism. His ideas were the precursors for the disastrous philosophies that help explain the Haight Asburys, the Woodstocks, and the Charles Mansons of the '60s. His intellectual thrust probably had more influence of the way people lived in the 19th and 20th century than any of the other "intellectuals" of this period. Ibsen was often drunk beyond his power to comprehend what was happening at receptions given in his honor. He ignored his parents who were experiencing extreme financial difficulties at a time that he had become an international celebrity. He avoided them

Charles Darwin. UPI/Bettmann

out of fears of their possible financial demands. He had not seen his father in forty years when he died in 1877. He abandoned his own illegitimate children, one of whom, Hans Jacob, was his exact likeness. At the age of 46, Hans, while totally destitute, presented himself at his father's door. This was the first time Ibsen ever saw him. He coldly gave Hans five crowns saying, "This is what I gave your mother." He never saw Hans again. He exploited women for his own purposes while having a long line of mistresses. Ibsen professed an undying love for the working person—a statement which was a complete misrepresentation of his inner feelings. His only love was for his career, himself, and his wallet. He was a self-ish, egotistical, greedy, intellectually dishonest genius who, again, was yet another example of a totally immoral person preaching a moral message to the world.

Count Leo Nikolayevich Tolstoy (1828–1910) came from a rich and noble family. He was a brilliant Russian novelist and moral philosopher. His great ego convinced him that he was part of a succession of intellectuals starting with Moses who were predes-tined to reform society. He wanted to form his own religion in which bliss would be attained in this life through Communism and So-cialism or through combinations of both. This opposed the cler-ics' promise of bliss in the afterlife if one conformed to the recom-mended conduct set forth in the Bible. Nonetheless, he recom-mended the practice of a "cafeteria style" of Christianity in which selected bits and pieces of the New and Old Testament and the churches' teachings that Tolstoy agreed with, would be followed. The portions of the Testaments with which he disagreed would be simply discarded. He considered the developing democracies of the United States and England to be the greatest dangers in the world. Tolstoy's influence in the promulgation of Communist doc-trine and the eventual 1917 Russian Revolution was inestimable. His efforts to improve the life of the average Russian peasant through the adoption of Communism became a joke. Millions of his "beloved" peasants were slaughtered by the Russian Commu-nist leaders. Leo Tolstoy was a homosexual who said, "I have never been in love with a woman . . . but I have quite often fallen in love with a man." However, his wife Tonya, because of his periodic sexual assaults, gave birth to five of his children. Throughout his marriage Tolstoy kept a diary of his sexual peccadilloes. His wife discovered his diary and surreptitiously read its contents without divulging her knowledge to her husband. His last days were filled with jealousy, spite, bad temper displays, hysteria, and petty meanness. After the successful Communist Revolution in Russia in 1917, Tolstoy was highly respected by the Communist leaders.

Ernest Hemingway (1898–1961) was a 20th century writer and intellectual. He rejected the religious beliefs of his parents as irrelevant to his life. He believed he had inherited a false world with false value systems. In his rejection of established values he allowed himself to be manipulated by the Communist Party. Here was yet another intellectual who allowed himself to be captivated by the false premises and promises of the Communist doctrine. He supported the Communists in the Spanish Civil War in the 1930s. He trusted and believed in the only truth he knew. This was limited to what he experienced through his sense of taste, smell, feel, and hearing. He had a great impact on society during the first part of the 20th century. Hemingway was a leader among the "intellectuals" of his time when it came to womanizing, creating a false public image, living a life of debauchery and alcoholism, while embracing Communist causes. He came from an unusually strict Christian family whose religion he totally rejected. He referred to his mother simply as "that bitch." Hemingway, like the rest of the "intellectuals" discussed in this book had an insatiable lust for fame and power. He cleverly developed the tough image of being the great white hunter, the great boxer, and the great womanizer. He hastened his age by encouraging people to call him "Papa Hemingway." He was forever available for interviews and photo sessions. His goal was simply to promote his own carefully crafted persona. He exposed himself to just enough well-publicized wars, bullfights, safaris, and fishing trips so that he could be familiar enough to write a novel on the subject.

Hemingway was a lifelong heavy drinker who eventually became a severe alcoholic. He was prone to having accidents all his life but especially when he was intoxicated. At his death, he suffered from diabetes, kidney and liver trouble, chronic insomnia, blood clotting, depression, and other ailments too many to mention. He committed suicide on July 2, 1961. He was survived by his fourth wife whom he met in Paris when she was working for *Time* magazine as a journalist.

Bertolt Brecht (1898-1956) was a German dramatist and expressionist. At school Brecht publicly repudiated religion by burning the Bible and the Catholic Catechism. He used his brilliant intellect to propagandize in the theater for Communist causes. He denounced capitalism and all its institutions. As a critic, he was feared for his rudeness, savagery, and cruelty. All ideologies crave for an intellectual to give credibility to their cause. Brecht was an ideal prospect and he was adopted by the Communist party as its star propagandist in intellectual circles. He became the theatrical functionary for the East German Communist Party. Brecht shared Hemingway's genius for self-publicity. As the star of the Communist party he had no difficulty getting publicity. The institutional backing of the party he supported for the last 30 years of his life gave him easy access to the media. He wore a "workers suit" which he personally designed. By 1949 Brecht had the best of all possible worlds, a West German publisher, an Austrian passport, East German government backing, and a Swiss Bank account. He obtained all these benefits by double dealing and outright lying. He was in all sorts of sexual relationships in which he was in total command. He fathered illegitimate children that he promptly abandoned. He had a heart of ice and because of his exalted theatrical and political position, he met many attractive women, whom he made love to and then left them without serious repercussions. He often did this with reckless abandon when it served his purposes. It was difficult to find a single redeeming feature in his character.

Bertrand Russell (1872-1970) was a British atheistic philosopher, mathematician, and political writer of tremendous influence. He spent his long life giving advice to humankind. His statement that god had not created man but that man had created god was widely accepted. At fifteen years of age, he became a nonbeliever despite his fiercely religious grandmother. Russells' parents, who died when he was four, were atheists and ultraradicals. They left instructions that he was to be raised according to the beliefs of John Stuart Mill (1806-1873). He published 68 books by most accepted accounts. He wrote mostly for fame and fortune that made him very typical of the "intellectuals" discussed in this book. Russell argued that humankind would behave decently by the simple application of logic, reason, and moderation. No man had greater faith in the power of the intellect yet he did not believe in educating the masses. He lived and died espousing atheistic doctrines. He established "The atheist's Creed" which he would chant in a clergyman's nasal tone. "We do not believe in God." But we believe in the supremacy of humanity. We do not believe in life after death. But we believe in immortality—through good deeds." He was totally lacking in the ability to boil water or to do hundreds of other simple menial tasks that ordinary humans had to accomplish simply to exist. Yet in other "intellectuals" Russell deplored a combination of theoretical knowledge and practical ignorance. Though he professed to be incredibly candid in his intellectual pronouncements to people, he was totally dishonest in his dealings with his many lovers. He simply exploited women for their ability to satisfy his sexual desires. The fact that his many affairs resulted in the birth of legitimate and illegitimate children were of little concern to him. He lied, cheated, connived, and manipulated to fool his various lovers thus placing him in the same moral category of the other "intellectuals" discussed in this book. He would chase anything in skirts, be they royalty or chambermaid, so long as they were young and pretty. He believed that women were inferior to men in every way—especially intellectually. Publicly he supported women's suffrage but privately he considered them a mere appendage to men. Russell was born into the Whig aristocracy and was a wealthy advocate of socialism. It was suggested to him that due to his professed love of the "common" man he should "give his great wealth away." His quick retort was, "I'm afraid you've got me wrong, I am a socialist not a Christian." In summary it can be said that "the 3rd Earl" Russell was a brilliant "intellectual," born with the proverbial silver spoon in his mouth, who was radical, hypocritical, and dishonest in his teachings.

Jean-Paul Sartre (1905–1980) was a philosopher, novelist, and playwright. In 1963 he was awarded but declined the Noble prize for literature. He was the principal exponent of Existentialism. The idea being that man is not apart of a metaphysical scheme, but that individual must create their own being, tailored to each individual's situation and environment. Women, whiskey, and debauchery of all forms were used as a substitute for religion. His ideas were particularly appealing to the youth of the 20th century. His main concerns were for the advancement of his own views and objectives. He could not establish a satisfactory relationship with a man that approached him in age or intellect. He used women for whatever sexual pleasures they were willing to dispense to him. His life and the philosophy of Existentialism were uninhibited by any adherence to religious dogma. He was a supreme egotist who tried to educate the masses by his plays and novels. He belonged to an upper-middle class family and received the best education that was available to his generation. He had a grotesque appearance caused by extremely thick glasses and a short muscular build. He was disgustingly dirty because he never took a bath. His ugliness prompted constant ridicule that turned him into a bittersweet character. His stated goal was to sleep with many women. His credo was travel, polygamy, and transparency. As with the "intellectuals" discussed in this book, women were attracted to his intellectual abilities. He became the archetypal male chauvinist of the '60s. His exploitation of Simone de Beauvoir, a leading, lifelong feminist was impossible to explain other than by her respect for his intellect. For over 50 years she served him as his mistress, surrogate wife, cook, manager, female bodyguard, and nurse. During this period he, of course, was notoriously unfaithful. He hated anything American. He went almost totally blind and his health reflected his lifelong excesses of drugs and alcohol. Sartre left no lasting body of thought that survived him. He was a Communist supporter and his philosophy, though confused, did represent an exciting way to live. His idea was that "if it's fun and enjoyable . . . go for it." He vaguely wanted to belong to the liberal left and to be appealing to the youth of his day. He died on April 15, 1980. Although the Catholic Church had branded him "an enemy of society," 50,000 people came to his funeral. With all his preachments, like Bertrand Russell, his ideas, obscure and disconnected, did not survive his death.

Edmund Wilson (1895–1972) was an American literary critic. He was born in an upper-middle class family, his father having been the attorney general for the state of New Jersey. He was brilliant having once read over 200 books in fifteen months. He was part of the massive swing to the left by the "intellectuals" following the 1929 stock market crash and the depression of the '30s. Along with the other "intellectuals," Wilson thought he would make the most out of the "last 24 hours of capitalism." He thought capitalism had failed and he announced in 1932 that he was going to vote for the Communist candidates. In the spring of 1935, he went to Russia to study under a Guggenheim grant. The experiences in Russia left Wilson totally disillusioned with the Communist system while breathing a bitter hatred of Stalin. To Wilson's credit, his eternal search for the truth caused him to denounce Stalinism as "one of the most hideous tyrannies the world has ever known." He continued, however, to believe in the Marxist principle, "from each according to his ability, to each according to his need." Wilson's attitude toward women was much like Sartre's; self-centered and exploitative. He married four times, drank excessively and when drunk, abused his various wives. Wilson displayed an unending hostility toward his fellow "intellectuals" even greater than Karl Marx. He almost went to jail for income tax evasion. A clever lawyer kept him out of jail by settling a $69,000 debt for $25,000 plus $16,000 in legal fees. Wilson retained his lifelong radicalism until his death in 1972. Typical of his genre of 18th, 19th, and 20th century "intellects," he ignored the "clerics" and sought a humanistic solution to mankind's ills. What he found were many "blind alleys" and nothing worth handing down to succeeding generations.

Victor Gollancz (1893-1967) was a British "intellectual" whose ultimate niche was as the publisher and founder of the Left Book Club, with a membership of 57,000. He limited his publications to authors who agreed with his left wing views. He did everything the Communist Party asked of him. He became man of extreme wealth with ten servants in his London townhouse and three gardeners at his country estate in Bershire. He came from a highly civilized Jewish family and married into an equally civilized Jewish family. He had a rare combination of innate intelligence, education, knowledge, and business ability. He went the way of the "intellectuals" of his era. First, he questioned Jewish orthodoxy, then Reform Judaism, and ultimately he had no religious faith. His publishing business gave the left-wing radicals a medium through which their ideas could receive widespread circulation. It is believed that he was responsible for the historic British labor Party victory in 1945. In his very profitable publishing business he hired only women because he could get the same job done for lower wages. He did not like men and men did not like him. Gollancz only loved women to the extent that they served his purposes. His wife Ruth was literally his slave who presented him with six daughters. She tolerated his many infidelities and his painfully disagreeable habit of "pawing" women. When he selected a Miss Dibbs as the supervisor of the female staff in his company, he compared her to a leader in a Russian factory. At his death in 1967, it could be observed, quite justifiably, that he served no real purpose other than his own desires. Finally and ultimately all his radical ideas and beliefs crashed on a scrap heap of "ideas with no value." Succeeding generations have been content to let his ideas decay on the same historical scrap heap with the discredited remains of Russian Communism.

Lillian Hellman (1905–1984) was an American playwright. She was born of middle class Jewish parents. Her great mentor was Dashiel Hammett, the mystery writer. Hammett was a severe alcoholic and a believer in the doctrines of Karl Marx. Lillian herself was instinctively a radical and was a member of the Communist Party according to Louis Bundenz, a former managing editor of the *Daily Worker*. She did everything in her power to assist the Communist Party in its penetration of American "intellectual" life. She was active with the Screen Writers Guild. In an editorial attacking the Un-American Activities Committee she asserted to the astonishment of knowledgeable people that, "there never has been a single line or word of Communism in any American picture." This was but one of many monumental lies Lillian Hellman uttered in her lifetime. She was a very shrewd business woman and became very wealthy when she purchased the copyrights to Dashiel Hammett's extremely valuable works for $2,500. Her sexual promiscuity, among other reasons, caused the Communist Party to keep her more or less as a secret member. She supported Henry Wallace for president in 1948. At her death in 1984, she left an estate of $4,000,000. Disbursements were to be guided by the political, social, and economic beliefs of Dashiel Hammett, a follower of the doctrines of Karl Marx. His beliefs coincided with Hellman's, whose hero was Joseph Stalin. Her well-attended funeral included such notables as James Reston, Katherine Graham, Warren Beatty, William Styron, Carl Berstein, Norman Mailer, and many others. History has documented her as one of the most prolific liars of the group of "intellectuals," who lead the world away from the influence of the clerics, beginning in the 18th century. Her contribution to this cause was enormous.

The "intellects" had replaced the "clerics'" starting with Voltaire and ending with Hellman who, for want of a better description, might be called the "humanists." They led lives of moral deprivation, they practiced uninhibited sexual promiscuity, they brought only suffering and death to their loved ones (if it can be said that they ever loved anyone or anything other than themselves). They were for the most part drug users and alcoholics; they were considered celebrities by their contemporaries; their relentless objectives were directed exclusively toward the advancement of their own careers; most of them really didn't believe in what they were saying especially in their promotion of Communism; they abused, exploited, and caused great suffering to those persons who were foolish enough to become their partners either as wives or mistresses or homosexual lovers; they considered women their permanent inferiors. At the end of their day, their preachments were worthless as a guide to the well-being of succeeding generations. Remember these are the same people who provided the intellectual platform and justification for the establishment of Communism. This single aspect of their utopian legacy accounted for the deaths of as many as 100 million human beings. The greater tragedy is the damage that they did to the belief of the masses in the teachings of the clerics as they espoused the ethics and values outlined in the Bible. They have created a world with little faith in ethics, values, morals, or simple goodness.

The frightening result of their pronouncements evolves around the body of public opinion that to this very day permeates our entertainment, government, news media, and our youth. This public opinion has been described as "political correctness." To be "politically correct," one has to pay homage to and abide by the teachings of these departed "humanists." Their vague principles involving an absolute faith in government administered programs generally formed the basis for the "Great Society" legislation of the '60s. This legislation has been vociferously defended in the media, courts, and Congress by such organizations as the ACLU, the NAACP, NOW, the NEA, and the unfailingly liberal media. Much of their teaching has been adopted by the liberal wing of the Democratic Party, the remaining elements of the Communist Parties, the Libertarian Party, and other fringe elements of society. These principles can be explained by such words as permissiveness, hedonism, and the constant application of the First Amendment rights. There is never the slightest reference to the individual obligations that beneficiaries of these rights bear to society in general. All one hears are rights, rights, and more rights.

It's in this climate that modern parents are attempting to raise children. The hope is that they will grow up to be useful, contributing members of society. Tragically the hopes and the dreams of parents are all too frequently shattered by children who fall through the cracks that a hedonistic society creates. The happiness of all the parties involved is then sacrificed on the altar of utopianism, permissiveness, hedonism, and "political correctness." It is not surprising that these young people have learned no absolutes or values that were useful in guiding them through the rocky and tortuous pathways of life. The argument is made by the "politically correct" people, that these values should be taught in the home by the parents. The pertinent questions are: What home? and What parent? The argument can be made that the deprivation of parental guidance applies to only a percentage of the children. While this is true, it is also true that a "few rotten apples can ruin an entire barrel." No, it's come to the point that society can no longer ignore the obvious need. We must address this problem in our schools.

The all-pervasive moral degradation, that confronts a child at every turn, leaves many parents with the inability to effectively counter this tidal wave of poison. The result is that yet another young human has slipped through the cracks, with the consequent destruction of the happiness of all those who are near and dear. This damage and suffering do not even consider the greater damage that is done to society, by having yet another non-achiever, or drug addict, or underage mother, or criminal, or uneducated, untrained citizen floundering around trying to scratch out an existence. Many simply learn to rely on government handouts and don't even try to compete or contribute to life in this country or on this planet in any meaningful way. The result is to further drag this country down toward a constantly lower quality of life for everyone.

It is readily conceded, that religion cannot be taught in a public school. Historically, the results have been catastrophic every time any government anywhere has grown too cozy with a particular religious denomination. The resulting zero tolerance for any divergence in religious thinking has caused indescribable tortures to be inflicted on many who resisted the official version of acceptable religious practices. History is all too replete with instances of people being roasted alive in the name of Christianity, for example, because of the slightest divergence from established dogma in their religious thinking. Religion and government simply have not mixed successfully. Yet, we cannot lose sight of the fact that all religions, except for their historic intolerance to dissidents, do teach everyday values and principles that will enable a person to lead a good life. The question remains: How do we teach our young people values, ethics, and morals for a useful, successful, productive, and happy life? It has become clear that we need to teach them more than reading, writing, and arithmetic. We must touch their innermost spirit, their deepest thoughts. Society has to do something to counteract the incessant stream of damaging values that the media in its many forms spews forth everywhere.

Young people need to leave elementary school, high school, and college or the university with a firm grounding in the basic principles of values, ethics, and morals. They will then tend to become a contributing member of society with an unshakable belief that goodness and ethical practices will inevitably prevail over evil.

Society has to add a significant addition or subject to the current school curriculums if the downside or dangers associated with the "age of Humanism" are to be successfully countered. Young people, during their formative years, must be taught some absolutes and guidelines that tend to result in a successful and happy life. The inevitability of the principles of cause and effect applying to all lives need to be indelibly implanted in their minds. They must leave their scholastic years believing in ethics, values, and morals that will stand them in good stead for the rest of their lives. These principles have to be of a nature that will permit them to successfully pursue their dreams—values, ethics, and morals that will help make them contributing members of the world in which they will live and die. The broad masses of the population, by their individual beliefs and actions, need to contribute to the improvement of the quality of life for everyone. If by a failure of the educational process, large numbers of young people are ill-prepared to meet life's challenges then everyone suffers. It takes an "all hands" effort to make this world and America a better place in which to live. Knowledge is power and that knowledge needs to include more than the insight obtained from a curriculum consisting simply of "reading, writing, and arithmetic." Elementary, intermediate, high school, college, and university courses should include several hours every week in which "values," "ethics," and "morals" or "cause and effect" principles should be discussed and/or debated. Call the course what you will but the idea must be incorporated in our educational process. What benefit has society derived from a person who is well trained in all the traditional subjects but has no concept of values, ethics, or morals?

This does not imply that we should teach religion in our public schools. Nothing of the sort is intended by this statement. Taking a page from the philosophy of Bertrand Russell who believed that "humankind would behave decently by the simple application of logic, reason and moderation," today's youth need to be taught, for lack of better words, "secular values, ethics, and morals." The argument is always made that these subjects should be taught in the home. Parental control, indoctrination, and education in the home had infinitely more achievability in the 18th and 19th century. Young people were almost totally controlled by their parents throughout their adolescent years. In today's world the parents start losing control when the children turn on the television set. The current argument, for example, is that "cyber-porn" depicting bestiality, homosexual and/or heterosexual acts, and every other sort of deviation are permitted under the First Amendment to the Constitution. Dissemination of all the other pornography through the rest of the media is likewise defended under the first amendment rights granted in the U.S. Constitution. The argument is made that it's the parents' responsibility to limit their children's access to this material. Again this argument would have made much more sense in the 18th and 19th century than it does today. American society is literally inundated with media of all forms displaying pornography and imparting values that are devastatingly harmful to children in their formative years and to young adults. The world of these young people is so totally polluted with pornography and harmful value systems, that parents trying to protect their children from this poison would have an equal chance of success in trying to block out the sun. There is simply too much filth out there. Positive steps need to be taken in our schools to counter these morally destructive messages. This can be done without entering the arena of religious teachings that cannot and should not be done in the public schools.

How then can we teach values, ethics, and morals in our public schools, and still observe the constitutional guarantees contained in the First Amendment to the Constitution of the United States? The answer lies in the techniques used in the dissemination of instruction relative to values, ethics, and morals. The schools should not teach that any one system relative to values, ethics, or morals is superior to all other ways. Classrooms should promote discussions relative to these ideas with the students left to draw their own conclusions after a free and open discussion. Let's borrow a page from the ancient Greeks who were known for their philosophical discussions. The ancient Greeks were notorious for "debates" on every aspect of living. No hard and fast conclusions were reached but in the process a great insight into the subject was gained by all the listeners. This really is the essence of all wisdom. A conclusion that is reached, after a full and free discussion, is far more securely held than one that is "force fed" without the opportunity of dissent. A relatively sound philosophy of living that will remain throughout life will emerge after these types of classes are held in the 12 grades of public school and the following four years of college or university. The beneficial part of this education will lie in the fact that after all these years of free and open discussion every type of human activity will be placed under the lamp of reason. It will help students decide how they want to live their lives. Imagine the deep convictions that will emerge from 12 years of philosophical discussions or 16 years when four years of college or university have finally been completed.

Most people lead their lives by reaction. Young people are tossed out in the world without the foggiest notion or without the slightest plan of how they want to live their lives. Most of them have never really spent much time dwelling on the subject. These same people under this plan would have spent many hours analyzing their feelings on this whole subject of successful living. Many people never really ever "bare" their souls. With the types of classes suggested in the book, they will have been doing this type of thinking for years. Consider how beautiful America would be if all our young people had been exposed to 16 years of introspection through classes dealing with values, ethics, and morals and the principles of cause and effect. America today is sending its young people into the adult world without a firm inner foundation concerning the most important parts of life. Those most important parts, include, but are not limited to, such questions as: What is the value of education? What is the wisdom of learning as much as one can while in school? How am I going to make a living? What will my guiding ethical principles be during my life? What qualities will I be looking for in a mate with whom to share my life? What will my work ethic be? What will my attitude be toward my country? How important is it for me to set a good example for my children? Is honesty a good policy, if so, then why so? What will be my tolerance toward differing ethnic groups? What will my tolerance be toward people who disagree with me? Yes, these and a thousand other questions can be discussed and analyzed during 16 years (12 years of grade school and high school and four years of college or university) of classes on values, ethics, morals and/ or cause and effect principles. At this point America's school systems will be turning out a far more satisfactory product.

For the serious student of the "age of the intellectual humanists" please note the following additional materials available at most public libraries.

Bertolt Brecht by Haas Willy; N.Y.: Ungar, 1970.

Brecht, as they knew him. Hubert Witt, Editor; N.Y.: International Publishers, c. 1974.

Living for Brecht: The Memoirs of Ruth Berlau; 1st U.S. Edition; N.Y.: Fromm International Publishing Corp., 1987.

Edmund Wilson, by Warner Berthoff; Minneapolis: University of Minnesota Press, 1968.

Edmund Wilson, by Leonard Kreigel; Carbondale: Southern Illinois University Press, c. 1971.

Edmund Wilson: A Biography by Jeffery Meyers; Boston: Houghton Mifflin, 1995.

Gollancz: The Story of a Publishing House, 1928–1978, by Sheila Hodges; London: Gollancz, 1978.

Victor Gollancz, in *Current Biography 1963*; N.Y.: H. Wilson Company.

Victor Gollancz in *The Dictionary of National Biographer, 1961-1970;* Oxford University Press, 1981.

Ernest Hemingway: A Life Story, by Carlos Baker; N.Y.: Scribner, 1969.

Hemingway: A Life Without Consequences, by James R. Mellow; Boston: Houghton Mifflin, 1992.

Papa Hemingway: A Personal Memoir by A. E. Hotchner; N.Y.: Random House, 1966.

Lillian Hellman by Doris V. Falk; Ungar, 1978.

Lillian Hellman: Her Legend and Her Legacy by Carl Rollyson; N.Y.: St. Martin's Press, c. 1988.

Lillian Hellman: The Image, the Woman, by William Wright; N.Y.: Simon and Schuster, c. 1986.

Henrik Ibsen by David Thomas, N.Y.: Grove Press, 1984, c. 1983.

Analyzing Marx: Morality, Power and History, by Richard W. Miller; Princeton, N.J.: Princeton University Press, c. 1984.

Karl Marx by Nigel Hunter; N.Y.: Bookwright Press, 1987.

Jean-Jacque Rousseau by Ronald Grimsley; Brighton, Sussex: Harvester Press; Totowa, N.J.: Barnes and Noble.

Jean-Jacque Rousseau, transparency and obstruction, by Jean Starobinski; Chicago: University of Chicago Press, 1988.

Rousseau—Totalitarian or Liberal by John W. Chapman; N.Y.: AMS Press, 1968.

Bertraund Russell; A Life by Caroline Moorehead; 1st American Edition; N.Y.: Viking, 1993, c. 1992.

Bertraund Russell: A Political Life by Alan Ryan; 1st American Edition; N.Y.: Hill and Wang, 1988.

A Commentary on Jean-Paul Sartre's Being and Nothingness, by Joseph S. Catalano; Chicago: University of Chicago Press, 1985, c. 1980.

Sartre: A Life, by Annie Cohen-Solal; NY: Pantheon Books, c. 1987.

Sartre: A Life, by Ronald Hayman; Simon and Schuster, c. 1987.

Percy Bysshe Shelley: a literary life, by Michael O'Neill; N.Y.: St. Marten's Press, c. 1990.

The Godwins and the Shelleys: the biography of a family, by William St. Clair; N.Y.: Norton, 1989.

Leo Tolstoy by William W. Rowe; Boston: Twayne Publishers, c. 1986.

Love and Hatred: The Troubled Marriage of Leo and Sonja Tolstoy, by William L. Shirer; N.Y.: Simon and Schuster, 1994.

Tolstoy by A. N. Wilson; N.Y.: Norton, 1988.

Conservative England and the Case Against Voltaire by Bernard N. Schilling; N.Y.: Octagon Books, 1976, c. 1950.

Voltaire, a biography, by Mason, Haydn and Trevor; Baltimore, Md.: Johns Hopkins University Press, 1981.

Appendix

The American Almanac, a Statistical Abstract of the United States has been published 115 times since 1878. It is "must reading" to the individual who is seriously concerned about social trends in the United States. The 1995–1996 Edition contains comparative statistical data on many subjects including the following:

a. Divorces–1950 to 1993

b. Births to Unmarried Women–1970 to 1992

c. Births to Teenage Mothers–1980 to 1992

d. Violent and Property Crime Rates–1980 to 1993

e. Child Abuse and Neglect Cases–1993

f. Crime and Crime Rates by Type of Crime–1983 to 1993

g. Crime and Crime Rates by Type and Area–1993

h. Forcible Rape by Number and Rate–1970 to 1993

i. Murder Victims by Age, Sex, and Race–1993

j. Murder Circumstances and Weapons Used or Cause of Death–1980 to 1993

k. Juvenile Arrests for Selected Offenses–1970 to 1993

l. Persons Arrested by Charge, Sex, and Age–1993

m. Federal Drug Seizures by Type of Drug–1990 to 1994

n. Child Abuse and Neglect Cases Reported and Investigated by State–1992 to 1993

o. Federal and State Prisoners–1970 to 1993

p. Prisoners Executed Under Civil Authority–1930 to 1993

ABOUT THE AUTHOR

L. Charles "Charlie" Burlage was born on a farm 3 1/2 miles from New Vienna, Iowa, of second-generation German parents on December 29, 1923. He was the fifth of nine children and attended St. Boniface School in New Vienna from September, 1929, until June, 1938, commuting by horse and buggy. Burlage moved to Dubuque, Iowa when the farm mortgage was foreclosed by the Federal Bank. At the age of 14 for economic reasons, he quit school to look for a job. With no employment available in town, Burlage began selling magazines from door-to-door throughout the Eastern part of the United States. When sales were lagging, as they often were during those depression years, food and shelter were available at the nearest Salvation Army.

Charles Burlage worked on farms and herded cattle on ranches before selling magazines. Thereafter, he worked as a carpenter, painter, plumber, sheet metal worker, roofer, automobile mechanic, shipfitter's helper, and was a crew member on ocean-going clam boats. He served in World War II, receiving four battle Stars for action in Europe on Omaha Beach, The St. Lo Breakthrough, The Battle of Falaise Gap, The Battle for Northern France, and The Battle of The Bulge. During these battles, he witnessed the death of as many as 10,000 human beings. After the Armistice in Europe, but before the end of the war with Japan, he operated a crap game in Marseilles, France, at Camp Lucky Strike, while waiting to become a part of the invasion force for the invasion of Japan. He also served in the Korean War and was the Chief Finance Officer for a 4000-bed mental hospital.

While returning from World War II Europe on a ship, Burlage won enough money in a crap game to go to college. He took entrance exams and was accepted by the College of William and Mary in Williamsburg, Virginia. Having never attended high school, he earned an Associate of Arts degree with Honors, A bachelor of Arts degree, and a Master of Arts degree in Tax Law. He passed the Certified Public Accountants Examination in 1951 and the Virginia State Bar Examination in 1956, after studying one year for what is normally a three-year course. During all of this, Burlage worked as a law enforcement officer, was an actor on stage, lectured against Communism, operated his own insurance brokerage firm, and wrote a column for three weekly newspapers.

Charles Burlage has owned, built and/or operated hotels, trailer parks, fast-food restaurants, clam boats, a paint company, and a golf course. He worked as an accountant on Wall Street, practiced public accounting for four years, and had his own criminal law practice for 16 years, becoming a multi-millionaire through his various business undertakings. He was appointed by President Lyndon Johnson to serve on the Board of Draft Appeals during the Vietnam War. He was also a candidate for the Virginia House of Delegates, for the Virginia State Senate, and for the Congress of the United States.

With exposure to literally every cross section of society, Burlage has been a member of, or an officer in, 16 professional and civic organizations and committees.

Considering such a varied and often tumultuous background, Burlage's acute awareness and understanding of human nature precedes his ability to impart that knowledge and understanding to the public through writing this book.

Charles Burlage resides in Virginia Beach, Virginia with his wife, Carol. He has two sons by a previous marriage and four granddaughters.

Burlage considers that the first third of one's life should be spent getting an education and maturing, the second third should be spent working and earning a living, and the final third doing that which brings the most pleasure. In his case, he is embarking on the final third and considers writing to be the most pleasurable culmination of all that has transpired in his life.

He is also the author of *Let The River Flow*, 1986; *How To Thinks Yourself to Happiness*, published in 1984, and *The Small Businessman and His Problems*.